Scribe Publications
THE AUSTRALIAN BOOK OF ATHEISM

Warren Bonett owns science-based bookshop Embiggen Books on Queensland's Sunshine Coast. He has been working for several years to increase scientific literacy in the community as a public speaker, blogger, and organiser of public science events. He is an active member of the Atheist Foundation of Australia, the Humanist Society of Queensland, the Australian Skeptics, and the Rationalist Society of Australia.

THE AUSTRALIAN BOOK OF ATHEISM

Edited by Warren Bonett

SCRIBE
Melbourne

Scribe Publications Pty Ltd
PO Box 523
Carlton North, Victoria, Australia 3054
Email: info@scribepub.com.au

First published by Scribe 2010

Typeset in 10/14 pt ITC Officina Serif.

Printed and bound in Australia by Griffin Press.
Only wood grown from sustainable regrowth forests is used
in the manufacture of paper found in this book.

National Library of Australia
Cataloguing-in-Publication data

Bonett, Warren (editor).

The Australian Book of Atheism.

9781921640766 (pbk.)

1. Atheism–Australia. 2. Belief and doubt. 3. Secularism–Australia.

211.80994

www.scribepublications.com.au

* CONTENTS

INTRODUCTION

Warren Bonett

IT'S OFTEN PROCLAIMED THAT ATHEISM IS ANOTHER RELIGION, AND that as atheists we are just attempting to replace god-based religions with the worship of materialism and rationality. Such criticisms assume atheists are all of one mind, probably Richard Dawkins'. Some atheists believe we should sit back and let the secularising hand of history slowly take its toll; others, that we should lobby for specific and widespread changes to religious tax exemptions and the preferential treatment religion receives in the media; and still others don't even think there's any problem at all. *The Australian Book of Atheism* is the first attempt to bring to light the range of thought among Australian atheists about these issues.

The idea for this book first germinated when I was living in London, where I saw videos of Sam Harris and Richard Dawkins speaking about how well low-religiosity societies function (in terms of education, crime rates, politics, et cetera) in comparison to America. They named Australia as one of these countries. After many conversations with friends and family, it became obvious to me that most people I knew, and even those I had seen in the media, felt that Australia was largely uninfluenced by religion in most ways that mattered. I had so many factoids bubbling away in my head that I felt refuted this but, other than a little blogging and online forum discussions, there seemed to be no way of bringing them to a wider audience. And who was I to do so, anyway?

1

My thought was, we need more Philip Adameses and more Jane Caros, and perhaps a locally based Christopher Hitchens or two. So after a little researching with my friend Chrys Stevenson in early 2009, I wrote to around 80 Australians who at one time or another had publicly expressed discomfort with the position of religion in Australian society, and we were off. As we reached the 25-contributor mark, the Atheist Foundation of Australia announced that they would be co-hosting the Global Atheist Convention in Melbourne the following year. This prompted a bit more public discussion than usual. One common question was: if atheists don't believe in anything, what do they have to talk about?

In order to fully answer this question, we need first to explain what it is we mean by 'atheism'. Given that atheists are frequently derided as immoral, intolerant, cold-hearted, evil, racist, strident, misguided, and 'just waiting for that last-minute conversion before death', it's probably a good place to do this.

The Atheist Foundation of Australia defines atheism as 'the acceptance that there is no credible scientific or factually reliable evidence for the existence of a god, gods or the supernatural'.[1] While compelling on its own, this definition isn't quite enough to form a strong naturalistic atheist stance because, as Carl Sagan has written, 'absence of evidence is not evidence of absence'.[2]

In all our observation and analysis of the universe, using everything from electron microscopes to radio telescopes, we've never found anything that even vaguely corresponds to a supremely powerful 'thing' of natural or supernatural character. That is a substantial tick in the absence-of-evidence-for-God box on your next census form. For me, the evidence of absence is given strong support by the masses of data described and verified by anthropology, neuroscience, psychology, and sociology that reveal humans to be a pattern-seeking species prone to finding agency in anything from lightning bolts to cheese on toast.

By way of illustration, did you ever notice the instant flash of anger a person displays towards an object after stubbing their toe? An instant reaction that bypasses reason, holding the object responsible for their injury, even if only for a split second. In pre-scientific times, it wasn't just compelling to believe in spirits, demons, and gods imbuing objects and phenomena with causality; it was simply the only thing that made sense.

Today, we've learned that storms and famine don't happen because the gods are angry. Given that such ideas arose from errors of perception combined with cultural tales, it seems to me there's no good reason whatsoever to even entertain the idea of a supernatural causal agent. So without such perceptual mistakes made by our distant ancestors, the stories surrounding them probably wouldn't have arisen, and the notion of a god may have never emerged, so the religions which grew around them would not have formed.

With this knowledge about ourselves on one side and the lack of evidence for a deity on the other, I feel confident enough to call myself a strong atheist — in the same way that I'm strongly of the view that malicious gremlins don't inhabit my dreadful internet connection and Santa Claus isn't coming down my chimney at Christmas time.

Another important point in terms of defining atheism is that even believers are 'non-believers' — toward gods that are not their own. For instance, a Muslim or a Christian doesn't believe that the ancient Greek gods exist, so they can be said to be atheist towards Greek gods. They are probably also non-believers as far as Kali, the Rainbow Serpent, Uzume, Osiris, and Woden are concerned. Full atheists merely go one god further.[3] You'd think this would give us plenty of common ground but, ironically, theists often unite with other believers in their condemnation of atheists, while using their own atheism about other faiths to keep from cooperating to any meaningful degree on almost everything else. It's quite perplexing that they find nonbelief a bigger threat than the political and military power of other faiths that would prefer them either permanently sidelined, dead, or perhaps just tortured for eternity in the lava pits of hell. Unless they convert, of course — which is an option right up to the last minute!

Even armed with the knowledge that our cause-seeking brains are predisposed to jump to supernatural conclusions based on limited information, and that most religions in history are now defunct, many atheists agree with theists that religion and belief in God remains both good and necessary for the human condition — in particular, the idea that religion and belief in something 'more' keeps the bleakness from our lives and helps console the grief-stricken. It's simply accepted by a large segment of society, many atheists included, that religious scriptures and tradition provide meaning.

It's clearly not the biblical tales of divinely inspired genocide, rape, and torture that provide this meaning. It's probably the amorphous idea of a loving god only vaguely present in the books he's described in. It seems to me that this so-called meaning and consolation can only be felt if the follower agrees not to think too hard about their faith, or the situation they need help with. For instance, if you're grieving for a dead loved one, it would be unwise to dwell on the abundance of people that the Christian God, for example, killed or ordered to be killed — often for astonishingly trivial reasons.

Death, we're told, is too bleak to handle and, again and again, I find that the argument for the value of religion arrives here. It's as if it's regarded as the unassailable position from which to defend the faith, whether a believer or not.

Let's assume for a moment that these defenders are right, in this instance, about the consolation and support religion provides. It still does nothing to give these supernatural-belief supporters any reason to access any other part of our lives. I also suspect that religion provides much less consolation than the community does, whether that community comes from a church, sports club, or knitting circle. Even suggesting this, however, causes defenders of faith to claim that such an argument is offensive.

Within these pages, each essay will inevitably say something that many of faith and unfaith will find intolerant or offensive. This fallback position is not secure. To my mind, it is not even tenable: the expression of critical thought towards ideas is the only protection society has against tyranny. But it is far more than even this. Detailed and public analysis of ideas is perhaps the most significant step in producing better ideas. Many of the atheists I know would feel that this is a truism or, to put it another way, 'bloody obvious'. You don't arrive at improvement by hiding behind the supposedly unquestionable beliefs of dead men. 'You can't question my faith' and 'I'm entitled my beliefs' do not provide an all-access pass to get what you want at the discussion table.

People are entitled to express their ideas, and the following pages contain those of a range of Australian writers. Many will be unknown to the average reader. They are bloggers and other denizens of the internet who have been writing on such matters for years. Others, like *Sun-Herald* columnist Dr Leslie Cannold, and host of *The Science Show* Robyn Williams, will be known to many. Their pieces have been corralled together into broad categories to help demonstrate that these ideas run the full gamut of the human experience in Australia, from everyday social experiences to politics to education to death and dying, and from censorship to neuroscience.

Almost inevitably, there are subject areas that I wish I'd been able to fill, in particular the experience of non-Abrahamic faith-based atheism — as seen, for example, in Indigenous communities. Perhaps someone reading this can write that book in the future, for they are certainly ideas worthy of discussion in the public arena. Words that would not be heard if we all subscribed to the notion that religious beliefs and ideas are untouchable.

NOTES

1. See www.atheistfoundation.org.au
2. C. Sagan, *Demon-haunted World: science as a candle in the dark*, Ballantine Books, New York, 1997.
3. I can't remember where I first came across this idea of merely going one god further. I suspect it was either Sam Harris or Richard Dawkins, but it's likely to be an idea much older than this.

* OVERVIEW

FELONS, RATBAGS, COMMIES, AND LEFT-WING LOONIES: ATHEISM IN AUSTRALIA, 1788–2010

Chrys Stevenson
Historian, writer, blogger

HISTORY IS POLITICAL. THE PORTRAYAL OF MINORITY GROUPS IN mainstream histories, or their omission from the national chronicle, resonates through our sense of national identity, political policies, and contemporary attitudes. There is a saying that history is written by the victors, and it has long been recognised that, if the status quo is to be changed, such histories must be challenged. It is no surprise that a key strategy of any social or nationalist movement is to reclaim the past — to seek out actors, events, and influences which have been omitted or downplayed in mainstream histories, and to stake a claim in the nation's future through reference to the contributions of the past.

An early advocate for African American civil rights, Dr Carter G. Woodson, founded the Association for the Study of African American Life and History, arguing forcefully that African American contributions to America's history 'were overlooked, ignored, and even suppressed by the writers of history textbooks and the teachers who use them'. Racial prejudice, Woodson argued, was 'the inevitable outcome of thorough instruction to the effect that the Negro has never contributed anything to the progress of mankind'.[1] (As atheists, our historical contribution has been similarly dismissed.) In an Australian context, Anne Summers' *Damned Whores and God's Police* (1975) added fuel to the feminist movement by exposing the exclusion of women from Australian histories.[2] Likewise, Sally Morgan's *My Place* (1987) tells of her quest for identity through connection with her family's Indigenous history.[3] Morgan, too, has spoken of the importance of providing an alternative voice to mainstream history in order to promote understanding and counter negative stereotypes.

The contemporary domestic political climate adds urgency to the need to reclaim the history of Australian atheism. Marion Maddox's *God Under Howard* (2005) chronicled the increasing intrusion of religion into Australian politics,[4] but it seems John Howard's political demise did nothing to stem the tide. Instead, under the Labor government of Kevin Rudd and, now, the re-elected government of his successor, Julia Gillard, the last remnants of the wall between church and state crumble unabated as both sides of politics work assiduously to establish their 'Christian credentials'. Any protest against this trend is typically countered with rejoinders that 'Australia is a Christian nation', 'the majority of Australians are Christians', that those who object are simply 'a strident minority', and the familiar taunt, 'What have atheists ever done for Australia?' Aborigines, feminists, ethnic groups, socialists, and other minorities have all been similarly dismissed, and all have utilised historical research in their quest for equality and respect. Now, Australia's non-religious — secularists and atheists — must do the same. The secular future of our nation depends on it.

When I first set out to investigate the history of Australian atheism, I wasn't sure if I would find enough information to fill a chapter. As I pursued my research, I was shocked to find my files rapidly expanding with hundreds of pages of data. This information — readily available, but scattered among a host of historical documents, texts, biographies, and online resources — has never been collated into a single, cohesive, and scholarly account of atheism's role in shaping Australian history and culture.[5] That must be rectified, and soon.

Of course, it is impossible to fill this gaping hole in Australia's historical record in the space of a chapter. Nor can I provide a seamless narrative of interconnected events — the development of Australian atheism has been largely unplanned, scattered, and lacking any semblance of national cohesion. My goal here is modest. I wish simply to introduce some of the felons, ratbags, rebels, commies, and left-wing loonies who contributed so much to our Australian sense of 'self' but whose influence as non-theists has been absent or underplayed in Australia's mainstream histories.

The history of Australian atheism begins with the First Fleet. There was no religious agenda underwriting the settlement of Australia. The colony was founded, primarily, to provide a dumping ground for Britain's convicts, and most of the felons transported to Australia between 1788 and 1831 had little interest in religion. In the late eighteenth century, the attitude of Britain's lower classes towards the clergy ranged from apathy to open hostility. Preachers were seen as the corrupt supporters of the status quo, and the evangelists who serviced Britain's jails and prison hulks only entrenched this fervent anti-clericalism. The distribution of religious tracts on transport ships proved pointless: female prisoners tore out the pages and used them to curl their hair; the men used the leaves of their Bibles to make playing cards; Bibles that escaped intact were sold off in Sydney to buy rum.[6]

Despite the presence of a chaplain, there was no divine blessing at the foundation ceremonies of the new colony on 26 January 1788. Indeed, First Fleet chaplain Richard Johnson complained bitterly that he was 'left to stand under the shade of a tree, and was made to feel that neither God nor I was wanted at the foundation of the new nation'.[7] Administering a penal settlement at the furthest end of the earth meant that religion was often at the bottom of the early governors' priorities. When, after six years, the colony still lacked a church, Reverend Johnson begrudgingly paid for the construction of a building out of his own pocket. Built to accommodate 500 people, the church attracted less than 40 to its inaugural Christmas service in 1793. Four years later, in protest at a government crackdown on compulsory church attendance, the convicts burned the building down.[8]

Female convicts resisted religious instruction as avidly as their male counterparts. In Tasmania, female prisoners raised their skirts and slapped their bare bottoms in unison at a chaplain they called 'Holy Willie'.[9] In Brisbane, a group of female prisoners hooted with derision at a sermon on the value of virtue. Shouting bawdy remarks about the sexual prowess of the officers, the women lifted their skirts and invited the chaplain to demonstrate his own abilities.[10]

By the 1830s, an influx of middle-class free settlers saw Sydney's convict population diluted and church attendance rise. But, even two decades later, the Reverend James Mackenzie observed that Sundays in Sydney were mostly spent 'boating, driving, riding, drinking, visiting, etc.', and that 'most of the churches were more than half empty'. Conversely, Melbourne's churches were reported to be 'packed out', but it is notable that those churches were few and small, and it was said that Sunday observance did not extend any distance out of Melbourne, and not at all into the distant bush.[11]

Indeed, as the convict era drew to a close and freed convicts increasingly sought work in the back blocks of the Australian bush, their atheism was widely disseminated across the western pastoral communities. In *The Australian Legend* (1958), Russel Ward describes the western settlements of the mid-nineteenth century as places where men were born, and lived, without ever entering a church or hearing a sermon or prayer.[12]

The stark realism of bush life only served to increase the workers' scepticism about all things supernatural. Anti-clericalism was rife, and travelling parsons were often met with disdain or outright hostility. In his memoirs, the Reverend Charles Matthews recalls a typical rebuke from a cynical outback publican:

'I don't know what you parsons want, comin' round this back country. You only come about once in seven years, and for all the good yer do when yer do come, yer might just as well stop at 'ome ... I know you all; you're all alike, all on the make, the whole [damn] lot of you. You wouldn't be round 'ere now if there wasn't money in it.'[13]

Matthews also describes how the residents of a western Queensland town headed off an unwanted clergyman 'at the pass':

'At the meetin' one of the boys got up and said he reckoned this bloke was comin' for a collection, so we said he could have his collection if he'd stop away. We'd done without religion so long, we could do without it now. So we took up a collection, and it came to ten quid. Then we sent one of the boys to meet the bloke on the track we heard he was comin', and tell him he could take his collection and "clear", or we'd keep the collection and we'd clear ... He took the collection and cleared. And that's all the religion we've had at our township!'[14]

Out of this spiritual void, says Ward, another kind of 'religion' emerged — the religion of mateship. Contrary to the myth that all morality is derived from God, mateship, as a grassroots moral philosophy, sprang from a godless people in a godless environment. Importantly, Ward does not claim that these atheistic pastoral workers were typical of the average Australian of the period. Of course, by the mid-nineteenth century, many Australians lived in cities and many were religious. Rather, Ward argues that the pastoral workers' self-image and, later, the idealisation of that image in the popular press and in journals such as *The Bulletin*, came to define the archetypal Australian. In turn, the promotion of mateship and practical atheism as laudable characteristics of Australian manhood made the Australian working class particularly amenable to socially progressive, largely secular movements such as Chartism, unionism, feminism, women's suffrage, nationalism, socialism, and communism. In time, mateship became the defining value of Australian national identity.

In the cities, and at the other end of the social scale, an emerging educated middle class and intelligentsia was influenced by Enlightenment values and nineteenth-century modernism. Geographically, Australia was far removed from social movements in Britain, Europe, and the United States, but a regular influx of immigrants and visitors kept colonial society up to date with contemporary ideas. The colonials' thirst for knowledge meant that speakers, writers, and pamphleteers of many kinds found large and enthusiastic audiences. As empiricism and science gained popularity among the Western intelligentsia, freethought, rationalism, scepticism, and atheism were increasingly acknowledged as the mark of the modern thinker.

On the Victorian goldfields, Chartism, an early form of unionism, brought members of the freethinking intelligentsia into alliance with the working class. Many of the leaders of the British Chartists were atheists, and expatriate Chartists, such as journalists Henry Nicholls (an atheist) and George Black (a Methodist), negotiated with the government on behalf of Victorian miners in a dispute which culminated in the bloody, but iconic, Eureka Rebellion of 1853. The influence of the Chartists' secular principles is evident in the Eureka oath, in which the miners swore not by God, but on the Southern Cross depicted on the Eureka flag.

The philosophies of the Enlightenment, bolstered by Darwin's 1859 theory of evolution, spawned a plethora of freethought societies, particularly in Melbourne. The Eclectic Society and the Sunday Free Discussion Society were founded, in 1866 and 1870 respectively, by Henry Keylock Rusden, a central figure in the mid-nineteenth-century rationalist movement. These organisations were dedicated to promoting a more scientific approach towards religion, spirituality, and the social and political issues of the time. Key topics of discussion for these groups included political economy, freethought, divorce, family planning, and eugenics.

Rusden's views were strongly atheistic. He believed that Christianity was the root of man's intolerance. Rusden argued in favour of a morality based on science, the decriminalisation of suicide, the benefits of cremation, divorce reform, and the emancipation of women — all causes that atheists would support today. But, if we are to write the history of atheism in Australia, it must not be a sanitised version. We cannot resile from the fact that our heroes, like all heroes, were fallible human beings. Atheists have no need of saints and, indeed, the errors of the past can guide us as surely as the triumphs. Sadly, Rusden's record as an advocate for rationalism and science is tarnished by his belief in Social Darwinism. Writing in 1876, Rusden said:

> Survival of the fittest means that might — wisely used — is right. And we thus invoke and remorselessly fulfil the inexorable law of natural selection (or of demand and supply), when exterminating the inferior Australian and Maori races ... The world is better for it; and would be incalculably better still, were we loyally to ... apply the same principle to our conventional practice; by preserving the varieties most perfect in every way, instead of actually promoting the non-survival of the fittest by protecting the propagation of the imprudent, the diseased, the defective, and the criminal.[15]

It is no excuse to say that Rusden's views were shared by many of his contemporaries, but it is important to note that Social Darwinism has long since been discredited as a bigoted bastardisation of Darwin's theory, and was explicitly rejected by Darwin himself.[16]

Rusden's freethought societies were the product of a maelstrom of progressive social thought which swept through Australian society in the latter half of the nineteenth century. Some sought utopias, others campaigned for an Australian republic. Socialism, anarchism, and atheism were all in vogue, while science and textual criticism of the Bible fostered a climate of spiritual doubt. Following Darwin, there were secularist attacks on every aspect of Christian orthodoxy, and issues once accepted as biblical authority became popular subjects for public debate. Church attendance declined as religious indifference increased among the working class and intellectuals. Freethought became a highly fashionable topic during this period, with debates sometimes drawing audiences of over 3000 in Sydney and Melbourne.

But the status quo fought back, and the records show that many were harassed, fined, jailed, and had their careers ruined following charges of blasphemy or atheism. In 1879, for example, the iconic Australian novelist Marcus Clarke wrote a controversial article in the *Victorian Review* arguing that the advance of science compelled men to put aside their belief in miracles and abandon any creed which taught that the intellect should be distrusted. Calling for the march of popular enlightenment to continue, Clarke dismissed Christianity as moribund as an intellectual and moral force. The article provoked a heated public debate between Clarke and Church of England bishop James Moorhouse, during which Clarke was accused of atheism. The public row aroused enormous public interest in Melbourne and, while Clarke emerged the intellectual victor, his career prospects were destroyed by the scandal and he died in poverty soon after.

Aborigines also suffered discrimination as a result of being branded as 'atheists'. Indeed, the perception that Aborigines had no gods, and therefore no moral sense, may partly account for the lack of respect accorded to Indigenous people throughout the nation's white history. Prior to the 1830s, it was taken for granted that the 'atheism' of Australia's Indigenous people made them ineligible to provide testimony in criminal trials. 'The evidence of Persons not bound by any moral or religious Tye can never be considered or construed as legal evidence,' intoned New South Wales judge advocate Richard Atkins.[17]

Between 1824 and 1838, former New South Wales attorney-general Saxe Bannister argued forcefully that the requirement to testify under a Christian oath unjustly disadvantaged non-Christians. If such people could not testify, said Bannister, they could not seek redress: a clear violation of their rights as British subjects.[18] Bannister's argument ultimately won through, but it was well into the 1840s before Aboriginal testimony was widely accepted in the colonies.

Even though reluctantly conceded, granting judicial equity to Aborigines provides a glimpse of the inexorable development of an uniquely Australian set of ideals and values in which equity and mateship were increasingly held above tradition and the status quo. That is not to say these ideals were perfectly realised. It was, for example, a long time before women, Aborigines, Chinese, and even the Irish were included in the antipodean vision of a 'classless' society. The developing national ethos, however, was pervasively influenced by the anti-clericalism of the early convicts; the practical atheism of the pastoral workers; the secularism of the Chartists, socialists, and early unionists; and the increasing rationalism of a freethinking intelligentsia. Of course, many — perhaps even most — Australians were pious, church-going, city-dwelling Christians, but this was not the image adopted by the growing nationalist movement, which sought to create and promote a unique Australian national identity.

Gleefully feeding the growing undercurrent of Australian anti-clericalism was the wildly popular *Bulletin* magazine. Founded in 1880 by two Sydney journalists, J. F. Archibald and John Haynes, *The Bulletin* commented irreverently on politics, business, and religion, campaigned passionately for an Australian republic, and nurtured some of the country's finest literary talent. Brazenly anti-clerical, if not outright atheistic, Archibald once remarked to the poet Banjo Patterson that 'the ideal man to reform the world would be a bastard atheist born at sea'.[19]

Concurrent with the popular success of *The Bulletin*, the depression of the 1890s bit hard, and the Australian labour movement gained strength. Building on a social history in which mateship often displaced religion, trade unionism emerged as the new hope for the working man. Church leaders were alarmed by socialism's growing popularity among workers and the intelligentsia. Invoking the 'slippery slope' argument much beloved of theists, they feared that socialism would inevitably lead to communism and, worse, atheism. Their fears were well founded. In 1890, Sydney poet, writer, and atheist Henry Lawson wrote:

Trades unionism is a new and grand religion; it recognises no creed, sect, language or nationality; it is a universal religion — it spreads from the centres of European civilisation to the youngest settlements on the most remote portions of the earth; it is open to all and will include all

— the Atheist, the Christian, the Agnostic, the Unitarian, the Socialist, the Conservative, the Royalist, the Republican, the black, and the white, and a time will come when all the 'ists', 'isms', etc., will be merged and lost in one great 'ism' — the unionism of labor.[20]

In keeping with the popular taste for modern ideas, freethought societies continued to flourish in both Sydney and Melbourne in the 1880s and 1890s. In 1882, the Australian Secular Association (ASA) was established in Sydney. The following year, celebrated British freethinker and former lay preacher Joseph Symes was seconded to Australia to lead the organisation at the behest of British MP Charles Bradlaugh, an outspoken atheist and president of the London Secular Society. In Australia, Symes became a controversial figure. In words that will resonate with today's freethinkers, Symes complained that organised religion was in the grip of 'narrow, forceful men' who used their political influence 'to carry into legislation the social tenets of their churches'.[21] Under Symes' leadership, the ASA lobbied for free speech, an uncensored press, and public access to art galleries and libraries on Sundays. Court challenges followed and, although Symes' reason and intellect triumphed, his health and temperament suffered. His increasingly irascible, dictatorial, and strident approach ultimately led to the ASA's dissolution in 1888.

This was a colourful era for freethought and atheism. One of Symes' associates, pioneer unionist and anarchist John William 'Chummy' Fleming, gained notoriety for spruiking alongside other freethought advocates at Sunday meetings on the banks of Melbourne's Yarra River. Fleming's biographer, Bob James, explains that the Yarra meetings were 'constantly under threat from police, bigots and toughs'. During his years of freethought advocacy, Fleming reported many instances of abuse, intimidation, and threats of physical harm, while in Ballarat, his friend, freethought activist William Lee, was punched, kicked, stoned, and chased by a 2000-strong rabble of Bible supporters.[22]

Despite years of opposition, during which he was arrested and jailed, Fleming never gave up on the cause. James recalls:

Every Sunday until his death [in 1950]... [Chummy] took his stand under a tree at the Yarra Bank and summoned a few cronies with a tattered cow-bell. Draped on the branches of the tree above were two faded red flags with 'Anarchy' and 'Freedom' worked on white. The little man with his trousers rolled at the cuffs would preach in a quavering voice at the inequities of government and religion. With his milky eyes fixed beyond his listeners he would tell of the coming reign of earthly happiness and brotherly love.[23]

Monty Miller was another colourful and highly influential atheist of the period. Miller fought as a pikeman at the Eureka Stockade at just 15 years old and, later, headed the Rational Association in Victoria. A committed unionist and anarchist, Miller was twice convicted for his membership of the illegal organisation Industrial Workers of the World. In his heyday, Miller was an exceedingly popular public speaker, and regularly filled some of Victoria's largest halls and theatres. But, like his compatriot Chummy Fleming, he is most fondly remembered for his regular Sunday engagement on the banks of the Yarra, expounding his freethinking views to anyone who would stop to listen.

Freethought, of course, was not confined to the working class — atheist academics have had a huge influence on successive generations of Australians. For example, Australian composer, writer, and painter George William Louis Marshall-Hall, head of the University of Melbourne's conservatory of music, was a towering figure in the cultural life of Melbourne at the end of the nineteenth century. Hall caused a scandal in 1893 with the publication of his book *Hymns, Ancient and Modern*. Far from a religious text, Hall's work mocked religion with deliciously irreverent doggerel such as:

O David was a worthy king
Merrily could he harp and sing.
He became the father of his nation
By dint of prayer and fornication.[24]

An outspoken atheist, Hall became infamous for his public attacks on Christianity. Hall's enemies at the University of Melbourne used the scandal created by his book to force his dismissal. But, as a testament to Hall's popularity and influence, the majority of the conservatorium's staff and students left with him, reconvening to become the nucleus of the independent Melba Conservatorium of Music, which survives to the present day.

Occurring alongside, and often in cooperation with, the Australian freethought movement was the emerging women's rights movement. Many women, both in Australia and abroad, blamed their discrimination on the influence of the Church. This mindset was embodied in an early feminist slogan: 'No gods, no masters'. Henrietta Dugdale, a member of both Rusden's Eclectic Society and Symes' ASA, founded the Victorian Women's Suffrage Society in 1884. Dugdale blamed the misogyny of the Christian Church for the subjugation of women, describing Christianity as a form of despotism designed by men to humiliate women. Similarly defying the Church, Brettena Smith, another member of the Australian Secular Association, staged public talks on contraception to large, female-only audiences, and defiantly sold diaphragms from her Melbourne druggist and drapery store.

Outspoken atheist Louisa Lawson became known as the Australian 'mother of womanhood suffrage'. Louisa, mother of the poet Henry Lawson, was a formidable woman. She rejected religion early in her life, and was a member of the Spiritualist Association of Sydney — at that time closely aligned with freethinkers, rationalists, and atheists. In the late 1880s, Henry and Louisa founded the Association of Women. Later, after editing *The Republican*, a radical monthly journal, Louisa founded Australia's first iconoclastic feminist journal, *Dawn*, which, by 1890, had accrued 2000 subscribers. Also around this time, Louisa helped launch the Womanhood Suffrage League of NSW. 'Why should one half of the world govern the other half?' Lawson railed.[25]

As a result of these women's brave stance against the churches and the status quo, Australia was one of the first nations in the world to grant female suffrage, with universal suffrage for (white) men and women finally being passed in 1908.

The push for Australia to become a commonwealth of federated states developed slowly during the 1890s, and gained momentum as the turn of the century approached. In 1891, Tasmanian Unitarian Attorney-General Andrew Inglis Clark prepared a draft constitution, which was substantially approved by the delegates at Australia's first constitutional convention. Clark's constitution was the first official document to consider what relationship, if any, the Church should have with the new Commonwealth, and Clark favoured a secular government and proposed a strict separation of church and state. Notably, Clark's original preamble made no mention of God.

As Federation drew nearer, religious institutions increasingly campaigned for the insertion of God into the Constitution, and sought to secure a public role for religion. Edmund Barton, who would later become Australia's first prime minister, argued forcefully for a strictly secular constitution, but was opposed at successive constitutional conventions by those who refused to adopt a document that lacked an invocation to God. The compromise position was to include in the preamble the words: 'humbly relying on the blessing of Almighty God' and to include, as Section 116, a clause reading:

> The Commonwealth shall not make any law prohibiting the free exercise
> of any religion, or for the establishment of any religion, or for imposing
> any religious observance, and no religious test shall be required as a
> qualification for any office or public trust under the Commonwealth.

The Australian states federated in 1901, with a constitution that included an invocation to God, and a clause, Section 116, which was clearly intended by those who drafted it to guarantee a separation of church and state.

Australian nationalism was still in its infancy when war broke out in 1914, and the newly federated Australian states committed troops to defend the Empire. The horror of the First World War presented a devastating challenge to religious faith but also strengthened Australians' sense of national identity. For many, the war highlighted the finality of death, making the white-washed condolences of the clergy appear superficial and banal. Insightfully, in his 1915 poem 'Church Parade', Leon Gellert imagines the parenthetical thoughts of a Gallipoli soldier confronted with the platitudinous prattling of the padre:

> He giveth mercy for the taking
> And the blessed Day is due
> With a brighter morning breaking,
> Lovelier than ye ever knew.
> ('Nobby Clarke'll take some wakin',
> So will Toby Mason, too!')[26]

The ANZAC legend was integral to establishing a unique sense of Australian national identity. But, as we have seen, the ANZAC's ethos of mateship, irreverence, and contempt for authority did not arise spontaneously on the beaches and in the trenches of Gallipoli, but was already well established through the idealisation of the nineteenth-century atheistic pastoral workers. Just as the harsh conditions of life in outback Australia led to the naturalistic ethos of the bush, the brutal reality of the diggers' environment beggared the belief that a benevolent, interventionist God would come to their aid. Primarily, it was their faith in each other, not in God, that sustained the ANZACS and, as their legend emerged as the defining moment in the young nation's history, mateship was elevated to almost-religious status in the national psyche.

Following the war, Australia's labour movement began to gain strength, and many of the early socialists were freethinkers and atheists. Atheism and anti-clericalism abounded in the socialist, unionist, and labour movements, because religious institutions were widely believed to be complicit in maintaining the status quo. In fact, the links between atheism, anti-clericalism, and the labour movement are clearly expressed by Ernest H. Barker, once general secretary of the Australian Labor Party. In a paper entitled 'The Church is Weighed and Found Wanting', Barker wrote:

> The attitude of the Labor movement in Australia to the church is one of supreme indifference. There is little or no point of contact between the two ... 'What did the Church do when we sought a living wage, shorter hours of work, safe working conditions, abolition of Sunday work, abolition of child labor?' The answer is an almost entirely negative one. ... In how many of the advanced ideas of our time has the Church taken the lead? Is it not renowned for being a long way in the rear rather than in the vanguard of progressive thought and action? It resents any challenges to its ideas, doctrines, or authority.[27]

During the late 1930s, as communism gained strength worldwide, Pope Pius XI called for the establishment of Catholic action groups to resist the communist threat. In Australia, Archbishop Daniel Mannix and B. A. (Bob) Santamaria, then editor of *The Catholic Worker*, responded to the call.

Since its formation in 1920, membership of the Australian Communist Party had risen to 20,000, and it held control of a number of important trade unions. In 1941, Santamaria founded the Catholic Social Studies Movement, and began setting up Catholic power bases within trade unions to wrest control from the Communist Party and prevent further infiltration by atheistic communists.

Ironically, in the 1940s, the Labor Party was led by atheist and revolutionary socialist John Curtin — a former Catholic. As prime minister, Curtin was prepared to work with communist union leaders to achieve industrial peace — an approach antithetical to the views of Mannix and Santamaria. As the decade progressed, tensions between those who favoured closer ties with the communists and the (mainly Catholic) anti-communist zealots increased, ultimately splitting the Labor party along sectarian lines. After losing the 1954 federal election, Labor leader Dr H. V. Evatt, another committed atheist, bitterly accused Catholics of trying to take over the party and turn it into a European-style Christian Democratic party. This schism led to the formation of the (mainly Catholic) Democratic Labor Party (DLP). The impact on Australian left-wing politics was devastating and long-lasting. With the Labor vote split and the DLP directing its preferences to the Liberal Party, Labor was effectively consigned to opposition for the next two decades.

The Communist Party's heyday in Australia was brief, and it quickly declined in popularity after the war. It maintained some union influence through the sixties and seventies, but was disbanded in the early nineties due to lack of support.

But, even as communism declined, atheism maintained its foothold in the nation's institutes of higher learning. Atheism was pervasive in Australia's universities in the 1950s, especially in Sydney. At Sydney University, Scottish-born freethinker Professor John Anderson exercised 'a potent' influence upon his students, who, in turn, became some of Australia's most influential people.[28] Anderson had lectured in philosophy since the 1930s, and was a leading figure in Sydney's intellectual life for more than two decades. In 1931, he founded the Sydney University Freethought Society but, like many freethought leaders before him, Anderson became increasingly authoritarian in his latter years, leading, in 1951, to a major rift with his followers. As a result, the Freethought

Society folded and was superseded by the breakaway Libertarian Society, which became known, colloquially, as the Sydney Push.

Anderson took a dim view of this group of prodigal disciples and broke off all contact with them. But the members of the Push continued to hold him in great esteem. Clive James, one of Anderson's former students and a key member of the Push, reminds us that Anderson:

> influenced whole generations of students, who in turn, because of Sydney University's central place in the tertiary education system, influenced the teachers' colleges, the schools, the broadcasting networks, the emergent media elite, and eventually the entire culture.[29]

But atheists did not have it all their own way. In 1959, American evangelist Billy Graham visited Australia on a four-month crusade, attracting large crowds and triggering mass conversions in the tens of thousands. Ironically, Graham's visit also prompted the foundation of Australia's humanist movement, its objectives being:

> [t]o encourage a rational approach to human problems, to promote the fullest possible use of science for human welfare, to defend freedom of expression and to provide a constructive alternative to theological and dogmatic creeds.[30]

The 1960s saw the rise of right-wing religious lobby groups, reacting against the juggernaut of that decade's cultural revolution. The Festival of Light and the Right to Life are typical of the religious wowsers who objected to law reform on issues like abortion and censorship, and frowned upon the new social mores of sexual freedom and gender equality.

During the 1960s, Archbishop Mannix exploited the power of the Catholic vote to lobby for taxpayers' support for Catholic schools — something which had been clearly rejected by the Commonwealth's founding fathers and resisted by successive governments. Years before, Liberal prime minister Robert Menzies had dismissed Mannix as 'cunning, sinister and a national menace', but Menzies knew that his party's election prospects depended on Catholic preferences.[31] Pragmatically, just before Mannix died in 1963, Menzies announced his intention to approve limited aid for independent schools.

When Menzies retired in 1966, he was succeeded by Harold Holt. Holt's administration was cut short when he drowned while surfing, and the prime ministership fell to John Gorton, an agnostic. At this time, Arthur Calwell led the Labor Party in opposition. A Catholic, Calwell remained faithful to the Church, but struggled with papal authority — he once said that the early Christians exchanged a good religion with Constantine and accepted a set of imperial garments. A Catholic by birth but a humanist by nature, one of Calwell's associates described him as a devotee of 'the great religion of humanity'.[32] Despite his Catholicism, Calwell was a fierce advocate for the separation of church and state, and opposed Menzies' plan to provide state aid for religious schools.

Perversely, when avowed atheist Gough Whitlam assumed leadership of the Labor Party in 1967, it was with the proviso that the party would agree not only to continue but also to expand state aid for religious schools. In 1972, the Australian Labor Party won office for the first time in 23 years, and the Whitlam government tripled federal funds for all schools, government and non-government.

The election of the Whitlam Labor government was greeted with much jubilation in Australia. It was a time of great social change, and Whitlam's forceful and charismatic leadership fostered hopes for a new, more modern, liberal society. It was during this period of enormous social and political upheaval that the Atheist Foundation of Australia (AFA) was established as a breakaway group from the Rationalist Association. John Campbell guided the foundation through its early years, and was succeeded by Keith Cornish, who held the presidency from 1976 until 2005 — committing a lifetime of service to the atheist cause.

During its three years in power, Whitlam's government introduced no-fault divorce, ended conscription, launched a national health scheme, drafted an Aboriginal Land Rights Bill, returned land to the Gurindji people, amended Australia's racist immigration laws, banned racially selected sporting teams, supported equal pay for women, put contraceptives on the medical-benefits list, and made all university education free.

Making tertiary education free led to an explosion in university attendance and a rapid expansion of the educated middle class. This was pivotal in propagating more liberal, secular values, and hastened a decline in religious affiliation. Indeed, under Whitlam, irreligion became trendy, and Whitlam's cabinet was heavily staffed with atheists — Jim Cairns, Bill Hayden, Lionel Murphy, Doug Everingham, 'Moss' Cass, Tom Uren, and Jim McClelland, to name just a few.

Whitlam's administration was, controversially, cut short after the Opposition blocked supply and the governor-general, Sir John Kerr, agreed to dissolve parliament. Standing on the steps of the Old Parliament House, Whitlam roared, 'Well may we say "God Save the Queen", because nothing will save the governor general!' Following the dismissal, the Whitlam government lost the federal election, returning Australia to conservative rule for another nine years.

While most Australians welcomed Whitlam's many liberal reforms, the funding of religious schools remains a contentious issue to the present day. The Australian Council for the Defence of Government Schools (DOGS) was launched in 1964 in order to mount a legal challenge to Menzies' proposal to provide limited state aid to private schools. Faced with powerful opposition from religious institutions and from both state and federal governments, it took until 1980 for DOGS to finally gain fiat and have their case heard in the High Court of Australia.

Early in 1981, the High Court handed down its decision, ruling, by a majority of six to one, that the provision of funding to religious schools did not, in any way, breach Section 116 of the Australian Constitution. The only dissenting judge was Justice Lionel Murphy, a state-school-educated atheist. As well as opening the floodgates for public funding of private schools, the case established that Section 116 of the Constitution did not guarantee a separation of church and state. This was, as DOGS points out, a 'demonstrably perverse interpretation of what the founding fathers considered to be prohibited by the establishment clause'.[33]

In 1983, former union leader Bob Hawke led the Labor Party to victory in the federal election. Hawke, a minister's son, had been religious in his youth but found the hypocrisy of the church increasingly distasteful. Despite being an outspoken atheist during his union days, he became more circumspect about his views upon entering parliament. Bill Hayden, who was dethroned as leader of the party in favour of Hawke, raised an eyebrow at Hawke's latter-day claims to agnosticism. In an address to the Council of Australian Humanists in 1986, Hayden said:

I recall that a former colleague of mine — Bob Hawke — used to forthrightly declare he was an atheist when he led the ACTU [Australian Council of Trade Unions]. On his way to Parliament I noted that there had been a delicate but undeclared shift. He would murmur, when asked on the topic, that he was an agnostic.[34]

Whether atheist or agnostic, Hawke was never tolerant of religious wowsers. He once boasted: 'Do you know why I have credibility? Because I don't exude morality.'[35]

In 1989, in a move that was widely considered to be compensation for his deference to Hawke's political ambitions, Bill Hayden was appointed as governor-general. Controversially, Hayden became the first governor-general to be sworn in by affirmation, insisting that, as an atheist, he could not in good conscience swear an oath. Hayden's atheism also prevented him from taking up the position of chief scout, a role traditionally held by the governor-general. In his history of Australia's governors-general, Brian Carroll writes:

Only one [governor-general] was enough of an atheist to assume office by affirmation rather than oath, but there were those who were not as church-going as some people might have expected.[36]

Labor survived the 1991 federal election, but Hawke did not. He was toppled from leadership by the brash and ambitious Roman Catholic Paul Keating. While Keating exploited his Irish-Catholic roots for political purposes, he was scathingly critical of the traditional churches, which he viewed as instruments of 'entrenched privilege and moral conservatism'.[37]

The 1990s saw a remarkable increase in the number of Catholics and evangelicals in senior positions in the Liberal/National coalition. In 1992, Christian conservatives within the coalition united to create the Lyons Forum, a faction which sought to influence policy in areas such as censorship, family, marriage, and sexuality. Indeed, the forum's theological agenda became transparently obvious when Kevin Andrews, one of its leading figures, initiated a private member's bill that brought an end to the Northern Territory's 1995 euthanasia legislation. Liberal leader John Howard was not a member of the Lyons Forum, but was sympathetic to its cause. Howard's shameless exploitation of the right-wing Christian vote during his 12 years as prime minister is documented in Marion Maddox's *God Under Howard* (2005).

Labor was well aware of the tactics of the Lyons Forum. MP Anthony Albanese observed:

> The Lyons Forum ... is an organised right-wing religious cell in the Liberal Party — it's old fashioned vanguard politics.[38]

Oddly, as the congregations of the nation's traditional churches dwindled to almost nothing, the increasingly noisy distraction of Australia's Christian Right grabbed the attention of politicians of all stripes. Like children entranced with a bright and shiny bauble, they became distracted by the dazzling potential of blocs of votes from megachurches like Hillsong, in return for conservative, 'family friendly' policies. In 2000, alarmed by this move towards religious pork-barrelling, a group of Labor politicians, led by atheist Dr Carmen Lawrence, formed a crossfactional Humanist Group to counter the growing influence of religion in parliamentary debates and decisions.

Significantly, irreligion continues to grow in Australia. Between 2001 and 2006, the country's non-religious sector rose by more than 27 per cent.[39] In fact, the number of Australians with no religious affiliation is growing faster than any of the country's religious denominations, and twice as fast as the high-profile Pentecostal churches. Meanwhile, the mainstream parties move inexorably towards the Christian right, leaving only the left-wing Greens to defend the tatters of secular Australia.

Indeed, when Julia Gillard assumed the leadership of the Australian Labor Party in June 2010, it soon became clear that her atheism would change nothing. Despite publicly confessing her disbelief, she quickly reassured the Christian constituency that her 'values' derived from her Baptist upbringing,[40] pledged $220 million to extend the National Schools Chaplaincy Program, refused to overturn a massively unpopular plan for compulsory internet censorship, and asserted her opposition to same-sex marriage. After the 2010 federal election, Gillard's government retains only a tenuous hold on power — maintaining government only through the support of the Greens. It remains to be seen whether Labor's near defeat and the greater influence of the Greens in the Parliament and in the Senate will help to reverse the trend against secularism.

Consolingly, there have been some rare, shining moments of non-partisan secular solidarity. In 2006, a private member's bill proposing the legalisation of the 'morning after' abortion pill, RU486, was initiated by a cross-party coalition of female politicians. In response to strident opposition from health minister Tony Abbott (a Catholic and former seminarian), Greens senator Kerry Nettle famously wore a T-shirt emblazoned with the slogan, 'Keep your rosaries off my ovaries'.[41]

Since the terrorist attacks of 11 September 2001, there has been a worldwide resurgence of interest in atheism. The influence of the 'new atheists', particularly Richard Dawkins and Sam Harris, breathed new life into Australia's existing atheist and freethinking communities, and motivated many more to join atheist, humanist, rationalist, and sceptics organisations. Many used the networking power of the internet to form atheist or freethought Meetup groups in their local communities. In fact, the internet has been integral to bringing Australian freethinkers together and in disseminating atheist arguments, humanist ideals, scepticism, and rationalism.

In March 2010, the Atheist Foundation of Australia and the American-based Atheist Alliance International combined to present the Global Atheist Convention in Melbourne — a major gathering of more than 2000 people. Also in 2010, the AFA launched advertising campaigns in Hobart and Melbourne, in which council buses were emblazoned with the message: 'Atheism — Celebrate Reason'.[42] Australian atheism's new high profile, in concert with social and political issues such as the National Schools Chaplaincy Program, the debate over compulsory internet censorship, and the election of conservative Catholic Tony Abbott to the Liberal leadership, have made the increasing intrusion of religion into national politics a dominant and contentious issue in the contemporary national discourse.

History is political. As Australian secularism is increasingly threatened, we must not allow the claim that Australia is a Christian country built on Judeo-Christian values to go unchallenged. It is time for us to bring our atheist heroes — too often dismissed as felons, ratbags, rebels, commies, and left-wing loonies — into the spotlight. As we have seen, Australian national identity, with its ethos of mateship, equality, and justice, derived substantially from these Australian atheists — often fighting against the churches. Atheism has a long and proud history in Australia, and it is time for atheists to claim our place in the national chronicle, and to have our voices heard in the halls of Australian political power.

NOTES

1. H. Aptheker, ed., 'The Correspondence of W. E. B. Du Bois', *Current Biography Yearbook 1944*, University of Massachusetts Press, Massachusetts, 1997, p. 742.
2. See A. Summers, *Damned Whores and God's Police: the colonisation of women in Australia*, Penguin Books, Ringwood, Victoria, 1975.
3. See S. Morgan, *My Place*, Fremantle Arts Centre Press, Fremantle, 1987.
4. See M. Maddox, *God Under Howard: the rise of the religious right in Australian politics*, Allen & Unwin Academic, Sydney, New South Wales, 2005.
5. Two exceptions (although they cover only a limited time period) are Russel Ward's *The Australian Legend*, Oxford University Press, Melbourne, Victoria, 1958, and Allan M. Grocott's *Convicts, Clergymen and Churches: attitudes of convicts and ex-convicts towards the churches and clergy in New South Wales from 1788–1851*, Sydney University Press, Sydney, 1980. I have drawn heavily upon both these texts in this chapter.
6. *Convicts, Clergymen and Churches*, pp. 56, 110, 76.
7. R. Ely, *Unto God and Caesar: religious issues in the emerging Commonwealth 1891–1906*, Melbourne University Press, Clayton, Victoria, 1976, p. 75; also quoted in *Convicts, Clergymen and Churches,* p. 58 (original quote from *Sydney Mail,* 29 November 1896).
8. *The Australian Legend*, p. 91.
9. *Convicts, Clergymen and Churches*, p. 87.
10. ibid., p. 131.
11. ibid., p. 98.
12. ibid., p. 93.
13. *Convicts Clergymen and Churches*, p. 185.
14. ibid., pp. 185–186.
15. D. Hollinsworth, *Race and Racism in Australia*, 2nd edn, Social Science Press, Katoomba, 1998, p. 90.
16. A. Desmond and J. Moore, *Darwin*, Michael Joseph, Penguin Group, London, 1991, p. 598.
17. D. E. Kirkby and C. Coleborne, *Law, History, Colonialism: the reach of empire*, Manchester University Press, Manchester, 2001, p. 141.
18. R. Smandych, 'Contemplating the Testimony of "Others": James Stephen, the Colonial Office, and the fate of Australian Aborigines Evidence Acts circa 1839–1849', *Australian Journal of Legal History* 8 (2), 2004, p. 242.
19. A. B. Paterson, 'JF Archibald: great Australian journalist', in C. Choat (ed.), *Collected Prose*, e-book at http://gutenberg.net.au/ebooks06/0607731.txt
20. G. Partington, 'One Nation's Furphy', *Journal of Australian Studies* 22 (57), pp. 23–30.
21. B. James, *Anarchism and State Violence in Sydney and Melbourne 1886–1896: an argument about Australian labor history*, 1986, Ch. 4.
22. B. James, *Chummy Fleming (1863–1950): a brief biography*, Libertarian Resources, Parkville, Victoria and Monty Miller Press, Broadway, New South Wales, 1986, text at www.takver.com/history/chummy.htm

23. ibid.

24. R. J. W. Selleck, *The Shop: the University of Melbourne, 1850–1935*, Melbourne University Press, Victoria, 2003, p. 410.

25. S. Pearce, 'From Bush Battler to City Editor: Louisa Lawson and "The Dawn" ', *Journal of Australian Studies* 54–55, 1997, pp. 12–21.

26. A. Rennie, 'Australian Spirituality Through a Poetic Lens', *Champagnat: an International Marist Journal of Education and Charism*, May 2008, pp. 48–63.

27. D. M. Brooks, *The Necessity of Atheism*, BiblioBazaar LLC, Charleston, South Carolina, 2008, p. 205.

28. P. Coleman, *The Heart of James McAuley: life and work of the Australian poet*, Connor Court Publishing Pty Ltd, Ballan, Victoria, 2006, pp. iii–iv.

29. C. James, 'Renegade at the Lecturn: Australia's national philosopher — John Anderson', *The Monthly*, July 2005, at www.themonthly.com.au/books-clive-james-renegade-lecturn-australia039s-national-philosopher-john-anderson-67

30. Allan Hancock College, 'Religion and Politics in Australia: organised secular opposition to religion', Lecture 20 (notes), Australian National University, 15 October 2007, text at http://arts.anu.edu.au/polsci/courses/pols2081/2007/L20_POLS2081.pdf

31. S. Holt, 'The Irish legacy', *Eureka Street*, 22 May 2006, at www.eurekastreet.com.au/article.aspx?aeid=842

32. Dr William Moloney, Calwell's predecessor as member for Melbourne, cited in Lindsay Tanner's Arthur Calwell Memorial Lecture, 19 September 2003, text at http://australianpolitics.com/news/2003/09/03-09-19a.shtml

33. 'D.O.G.S. and the High Court Case', Australian Council for the Defence of Government Schools, at www.adogs.info/dogs_high_court_case2.html#006

34. B. Hayden, 'Speech by the Hon. Bill Hayden AC on Receiving the Australian Humanist of the Year Award at the Council of Australian Humanists Societies Convention in Brisbane on 30 March 1996', text at http://home.vicnet.net.au/~humanist/resources/cahs.html#

35. 'Australian Prime Ministers', *Convict Creations (History)* at www.convictcreations.com/history/primemine.htm

36. B. Carroll, *Australia's Governors General: from Hopetoun to Jeffrey*, Rosenberg Publishing, Kenthurst, New South Wales, 2004, p. 7.

37. T. Frame, 'The Labor Party and Christianity: a reflection on the Latham Diaries', *Quadrant*, 1 January 2006, p. 26.

38. *God Under Howard*, p. 68.

39. Australian Bureau of Statistics, '1301.0 — Year Book Australia, 2008: 14.39 Religious Affiliation', at www.abs.gov.au/ausstats/abs@.nsf/7d12b0f6763c78caca257061001cc588/636F496B2B943F12CA2573D200109DA9?opendocument

40. Julia Gillard interview with Jim Wallace, Australian Christian Lobby, 6 August 2010, video at http://australianchristianlobby.org.au/make-it-count

41. 'I'll wear ovaries t-shirt again: Nettle', *Sydney Morning Herald*, 10 February 2006, at www.smh.com.au/news/national/ill-wear-ovaries-tshirt-again-nettle/2006/02/10/1139465826319.html

42. Initially, the AFA's advertisements were rejected by the company responsible for bus advertising, requiring the matter to be mediated by the Anti-Discrimination Commission. See Laura Parker, 'Atheist message misses local bus', *Sydney Morning Herald*, 9 January 2009, at www.smh.com.au/news/national/atheist-message-misses-local-bus/2009/01/08/1231004199169.html

THE CONSTITUTION, BELIEF, AND THE STATE*

Max Wallace
Author of *The Purple Economy*, director of the
Australia New Zealand Secular Association

AUSTRALIA AND NEW ZEALAND ARE CONSTITUTIONAL MONARCHIES: democracies that have as their head of state a royal person whose antecedents' rule was once absolute. Briefly, where kings and queens once ruled, they now are content to reign. Typically, they claimed a divine right to rule, sanctified by a religious authority happy to comply in an arrangement that saw religion share the reaping of taxes from the population, while both monarchy and church remained tax-exempt.

The tax-exempt status of the monarchy and the churches is the foundation of all subsequent political structures. Whether we know it or not, whether we like it or not, a portion of our taxes, possibly as high as 10 per cent, in keeping with the ancient tithes scale, go to enrich the monarch and churches. This approximate figure is calculated by taking religious enterprise subsidies and tax exemptions as a proportion of total government revenue.[1] There are variations according to nation.

Our constitutional monarchies employ the British smokescreen, shared by similar European and other governments, that having a figurehead who is 'above' politics is good for everyone, an enduring symbol of national unity that represents a history of some value.

Beneath the patriotic rhetoric, what this arrangement is really about is maintaining church power and monarchical influence in a democracy through the lubricant of tax-exemption and government grants.

---

* 'Separation of belief and state' will be used here interchangeably with 'separation of church and state' as the latter phrase, long accepted in legal, historical, and political literature, does not adequately express the secular idea that government should disassociate itself from all forms of private belief, religious or otherwise.

In such an arrangement, there is no true constitutional separation of belief and state, as occurs in a republic. Since Australia and New Zealand are not yet republics, but have a common queen as head of state who also happens to be the supreme governor of the Church of England in Britain, it follows there could hardly be such a separation when the head of state is a leader of an enduring religious tradition.

Most Australians and New Zealanders do not know much about constitutional and tax issues. The meaning of the Constitution is not taught in schools. If they go to university, most do not do law degrees. Even if they do, they may not give much thought to whether having a queen who is simultaneously a leader of a long-standing religious tradition as well as head of state is at odds with the idea of constitutional separation of church, other forms of belief, and state. Accountants and other would-be tax-avoidance legal specialists are not encouraged to turn their minds to these matters.[2] Even if they did, the privileged status of the exemption for churches and monarchs is not required reading in tax-law textbooks.

Importantly, there is no separation of religion or belief in England. The Church of England is the national religion of England, thanks to an act of parliament. It achieved this status in 1533, after Henry VIII split with the Vatican, setting up the Church of England so he could divorce his wife and marry another. He controlled both church and state. The Church of England is so entrenched in England that the prime minister appoints its bishops to the House of Lords, where they participate in government.

This was the constitutional arrangement that Australia and New Zealand inherited while they were being colonised in the eighteenth and nineteenth centuries. This was not long after the 4 July 1776 American Declaration of Independence from Britain, following its successful revolution. America would eventually become the Republic of the United States, with a constitutional separation of church and state.

New Zealand remained part of the colony of New South Wales until 1840, when it became a separate dominion of Britain. At that time, the Treaty of Waitangi was established between the Maori people and the British government, setting out the rights of the Maori people in this new nation.

No New Zealand constitution was ever written — as is the case in Britain today, where there is also no written constitution.

In 1901, the colonies of Australia decided to federate, to become one nation with a federal government, while retaining state parliaments. During the nineteenth century, each of the Australian colonies wrote their own constitutions, setting out the rules for government. The dates of these constitutions were: New South Wales, 1840; Tasmania, 1854; Victoria, 1855; South Australia, 1856; Queensland, 1859; Western Australia, 1859. These constitutions are still in force today. None of them has a clause separating church and state.

The relationship between religion and the state was a hot issue in New Zealand and the Australian colonies in the nineteenth century. Central to the debate was who was going to run schools. Churches believed that what children needed most was religious instruction. They fought tooth and nail the alternative idea that education should be free, secular, and compulsory.

The fight over access to children's minds, via what they were taught through the curriculum, was one of the routes to political power, for, if you could educate the future nation's leaders in the one true belief, you could ensure your religion's prominence in government, and thus promote your particular Christian cause.

Access to the minds of the Indigenous, who were considered 'pagan', was granted to missionaries as a matter of course. The will to proselytise and impose the Christian truth, as they saw it, on the unwilling or unconverted is at the heart of the Christian project, if you take it at face value.

There were conventions in the 1890s to discuss what would be in the Constitution for the new federal Australia. The churches believed religion should be emphasised to make it plain that Australia was a Christian nation.

In short — best summarised in Richard Ely's *Unto God and Caesar* (1976) — the founding fathers were earnest in their collective belief that Australia should be a secular nation with a separation of church and state.[3]

Partly to placate the religious lobbying, they agreed to include the words 'humbly relying on the blessing of Almighty God' in the preamble to the Constitution. That is the only mention of religion in the Constitution, except for Section 116, which reads:

> The Commonwealth shall not make any law for establishing any religion, or for imposing any religious observance, or for prohibiting

the free exercise of religion, and no religious test shall be required as a qualification for any office or public trust under the Commonwealth.

[Note: this section does not say there is a separation of church and state in Australia.]

Meanwhile in New Zealand, in 1877, the Education Act made education free, secular, and compulsory. The state did not fund religious schools — that is, those schools where parents insisted their children be taught with Christian emphasis.

Almost immediately after secular schools were set up in Australia and New Zealand, the churches began lobbying to have religious education or instruction (pick your word) for at least one hour a week in the state schools, in addition to running their own schools. They succeeded.

Christian lobbying also succeeded in having referenda asking Her Majesty's Subjects (as we were then) the question of whether the word 'secular' should be dropped from the education acts of Queensland and Victoria. They failed in Victoria, but succeeded in Queensland on 13 April 1910.[4] To this day, officially, Queensland education is not secular, at least in principle — and, to a significant extent, in practice. A campaign is being spearheaded by the Humanist Society of Queensland to have 'secular' put back into the act, timed to coincide with the centenary of its removal.

So, given the Constitution did not say that there was separation of church and state in Australia, and there was not even a Constitution in New Zealand to consider the matter, this all-important question slipped off the radar and completely out of the consciousness of both nations, where it had barely registered, in any case.

Matters stirred in the 1950s when Australian prime minister Robert Menzies decided he would break with the long-standing principle of no state aid to religious schools by introducing federal payment of interest on loans by church schools in the ACT, tax deductibility for school fees up to 50 pounds as a tax deduction, and tax deductibility for school building donations.[5]

Immediately, there was alarm. To understand the nature of that alarm it is important to know about the very significant constitutional law case, the Everson case, in the United States in 1947. That case decided there was a separation of church and state in the US and, as a consequence, the minimisation of funding of religious schools was confirmed.

This is still the case. In the United States, 90 per cent of all students go to state schools. The remaining 10 per cent go to mainly private religious schools that are largely church-funded. In 1961, the first Catholic president, John Kennedy, said: 'I believe in an America where the separation of church and state is absolute ... where no church or school is granted any public funds or political preference.'[6]

In Australia now, about 65 per cent of students go to state schools, 20 per cent to less-endowed but still adequately resourced Catholic systemic schools, and about 15 per cent to the wealthy religious and non-denominational private schools. Forty-three per cent of Catholic children attend state schools, as their parents cannot afford the minimum fees for the systemic schools.[7]

In New Zealand, about 86 per cent go to state schools, 10 per cent to Catholic schools, and about 4 per cent to private schools. The Catholic schools were 'integrated' by law and stealth into the state educational system in 1975.[8] What this means is that the government decided to pay for religious schools in order to lock in the religious vote.

And so it was for Australia. When Whitlam was elected in 1972, he dramatically increased funding for religious, mainly Catholic, schools. He sacrificed public-school funding to get elected. So, the question became, was it unconstitutional, as in the United States, for the state to fund religious schools in this way? It took 25 years for a case to test the constitutionality of religious schools funding to reach the High Court as the plaintiffs, the Defence of Government Schools organisation, did not have legal standing. Logs were thrown in their way at every turn. Eventually, the Victorian attorney-general agreed to support the case.

In rejecting the Defence of Government Schools case, the High Court explicitly denied separation in Australia. The chief justice, Sir Garfield Barwick, endorsed Justice Wilson's view, which was that Section 116 'cannot be viewed as the repository of some broad principle concerning separation of church and state, from which may be distilled the detailed consequences of such separation'. Justice Stephen said of Section 116: 'the provision ... cannot answer the description of a law which guarantees within Australia the separation of church and state'.[9]

The High Court also distinguished Australia from England with its established church, as described above. Certainly, the lack of an established church is an element of separation of church and state but, while it is a necessary condition, it is not a sufficient one. For Australia and New Zealand to have a separation of belief and the state, both nations would need to become republics. Separation would need to be written into that new arrangement. That is what should be put to our peoples in future referenda for republics. But in the 1999 referendum for a republic in Australia, there was no mention of separation. Why?

Partly because of the possibility that separation could open the question of religious-school funding again, and also possibly lead to questions about the tax-exempt status of religion in our two countries, as described above. Church figures were actively involved in the republican movement, and they keep separation of belief and the state off the agenda. That does not apply to the small Republican Party of Australia. At its 2009 convention, it came out in total support of separation.[10] The New Zealand Republican movement has openly addressed the question of secularism.[11]

Nevertheless, the problem with all this is that billions are flowing to churches, mainly through tax exemptions and government grants. While it can be argued that their relief-of-poverty charities have a role to play, it is absurd that Australia and New Zealand fund the already-very-wealthy religious to be religious — because they are themselves legally charities — while science needs all the dollars it can get to help us preserve the planet.[12] That is, taxation is foregone to 'advance religion', which is a private matter, while science, which has public application, finds it a struggle to get all the funding it needs — even in the face of global warming.

Unfortunately, little of the above finds its way into university politics, education, history, and sociology textbooks, or constitutional law courses. This is partly because of straight-out academic indifference and incompetence, and partly because of religionist influence across many departments in our universities, where religion is endlessly privileged.

It is a truism of sociology that an informal reality usually proceeds behind the public face of social action. In this case, the informal reality is one of power, money, and status. This, of course, is what religion is all about. But occasionally, some Christians have reflected on their lot.

On 11 November 1975, the very day Gough Whitlam was sacked as prime minister, there was an item in *The Age* detailing an Anglican Church report entitled 'The Politics of Living'. The report seems to have disappeared without trace, but *The Age* cited its main findings. It concluded:

> In a truly democratic society no group may claim exclusive privileges as a right ... the church is yet to come to terms with the fact that Australia is — and has been for a long time — a pluralist society, and not a Christian society ... An attempt to argue that the church, because it is the church, has some inherent, superior right to privilege is bound to backfire as it becomes clearer that Australia is and must be a secular society.[13]

Amen to that.

NOTES

1. For calculations of the cost of religion to the Australian economy see J. Perkins and F. Gomez, 'Taxes and Subsidies, The Cost of "Advancing Religion" ', *Australian Humanist* 93, Autumn 2009, pp. 6–8.
2. But see N. Renton, 'Taxpayers' Sacrifice to the Churches', *The Age*, 6 May 2008, at www.theage.com.au/business/taxpayers-sacrifice-to-the-churches-20080505-2b50.html
3. R. Ely, *Unto God and Caesar*, University of Melbourne Press, Melbourne, 1976.
4. I am indebted to Hugh Wilson for this point. See information at www.thefourthr.info
5. 'Howard Re-writes the State Aid Blackmail Story', Media Release, Defence of Government Schools, 10 February 2009, at www.adogs.info
6. 'Should You Pay Taxes To Support Religious Schools?', Americans United For Separation of Church and State, Washington, 2008, at www.au.org
7. S. Price, 'Catholic Schools Too Expensive, Says Bishop', *Sun-Herald*, 19 August 2007.
8. J. Dakin, *The Secular Trend in New Zealand*, New Zealand Association of Rationalists and Humanists, Auckland, 2007.
9. *Attorney-General (Vic) (ex rel Black) v. The Commonwealth* (1981) 146 CLR 559.
10. See 'About Us', at www.therepublicans.com.au
11. L. Holden, *The New Zealand Republic Handbook*, Republican Movement of Aotearoa New Zealand, Auckland, 2009.
12. Legally, to 'advance religion' is a form of charity in itself. See M. Wallace, *The Purple Economy: supernatural charities, tax and the state*, Australian National Secular Association, Melbourne, 2007, and 'Taxes and Subsidies, The Cost of "Advancing Religion" '.
13. M. Baker, 'Church Hit over its Privileges', *The Age*, 11 November 1975.

RELIGION AND THE LAW IN AUSTRALIA

Clarence Wright
Lawyer

WHEN CONSIDERING THE 'LAW', COMMENTATORS AND LAY PEOPLE sometimes tend to treat it as a concrete 'thing'. Oliver Wendell Holmes described this tendency as ascribing the law the characteristic of a 'brooding omnipotence in the sky'.[1] In an article about religion and the law, it is apt to note that jurisprudential scholars have moved away from the notion of the law being an omnipotent (and occasionally malevolent) entity within our world. However, we ought to be mindful that at the time of Australian colonisation by white settlers, European jurisprudence had few tools to deal with novel disputes in the law other than to appeal to the 'natural law' described by Thomas Aquinas. This natural law was to be interpreted or 'found' from the eternal law, described in Aquinas' *Summa Theologica* in the following manner:

> It is clear, however, supposing the world to be governed by divine providence ... that the whole community of the Universe is governed by the divine reason. Thus the rational guidance of created things on the part of God, as Prince of the universe, has the quality of law ... This we can call the eternal law.[2]

Accordingly, the natural law was immutable and thus 'if a human law [a law made by man] is at variance in any particular with the natural law, it is no longer legal, but rather a corruption of law'.[3]

This religious and unsophisticated ideal of just law resulting solely from 'God's' direction, through his Holy Text, the Bible, no longer forms a significant influence on jurisprudence. Commentators, such as Jack Balkin, now recognise that it is a misdescription of the law to ignore its human connections and that human subjectivity requires treatment of 'the sociology of knowledge as a full partner in the jurisprudential exercise'.[4] In this way, the study of the history of law provides us with documentation of social morays of the time; or, as Oliver Wendell Holmes writes: it is 'perfectly proper to regard and study the law simply as a great anthropological document'.[5] I intend here to examine the record of legal development in Australia to better understand how religion has influenced our society.

THE FIRST LAWS OF AUSTRALIA

The first laws of Australia were developed by the first Australians, who arrived on this continent more than 40,000 years ago (some 34,000 years before 'God' created the universe).[6]

It is unknown whether the first Australians had a legal system on their arrival; however, as Fred Wolf discusses in *The Dreaming Universe* (1994), a legal system was present in Aboriginal society prior to white settlement and strongly connected with the religious or spiritual belief of the Dreamtime, '[A]n infinite spiritual cycle ... more real than reality itself. Whatever happens in the Dreamtime establishes the values, symbols, and laws of Aboriginal society.'[7] These laws governed much of Aboriginal life, including trade, as documented with foreign peoples such as the moccasins, exclusive partnership between a woman and a man (though not always between a man and a woman), coming-of-age ceremonies, and uses of land and treaties such as those made between John Batman and various Aboriginal elders.[8]

The possession of Australia by Captain Cook on 22 August 1770, and subsequent arrival of the First Fleet and establishment of a settlement at Sydney Cove on 26 January 1788, would lead to a direct clash between the laws of Aboriginal Australians and the laws of the British Empire. The British had developed various laws to deal with colonisation of other people in the process of building their empire. Blackstone's *Commentaries on the Laws of England* refer to the cases of *Blankard v Galdy* and *Case No 15 — Anonymous*, in which it is established that colonisers would carry their laws into a 'new and uninhabited land' but that the laws of a conquered land would carry on until the king imposed new laws.[9] It is argued that this was 'obviously based, though without acknowledgement, upon principles' in the Christian mindset. Further, that 'Church and court scholars had constructed justification for this; the Europeans were, after all, bringing Christianity and civilization and if the native peoples resisted they were breaching natural law'.[10]

Even though the religiosity of the early white settlers is sometimes doubtful, the legal precedents resulting from the Christian mindset were treated as Gospel. It was on the basis of these legal principles that Governor Bourke, through the Colonial Office of New South Wales, declared that the colony was 'terra nullius' on 10 October 1835; that is, a declaration that no one owned the land in the colony of New South Wales prior to the British Crown. This fiction remained the law of Australia and was confirmed at various times for 153 years, until High Court's decision in *Mabo v the State of Queensland (No 2)*, when native title was recognised.[11]

RELIGION AND THE CONSTITUTION

Through the nineteenth century, the various colonies began to develop an identity that was separate from the many homelands of its people. Nonetheless, the legal model imposed on the people of Australia was a slight variant on the eigtheenth-century British models, which incorporated a raft of values in English law at the time of possession.[12] In developing a new identity, the nineteenth-century colonists sought to 'struggle to shake off Imperial supervision and interference'.[13] It was in this light that the colonies would choose to federate into the single country of Australia. However, rather than strike towards an imaginative new framework for this country, the founding fathers in Australia would look across the Pacific to their brothers in America for inspiration.

As pointed out by Sam Harris, the Constitution of the United States of America 'does not contain a single mention of God, and was widely decried at the time of its composition as an irreligious document'.[14] Although the religious motivations, if any, of the writers of the US Constitution are often debated, it was clear that on the issue of religion, they held to a separation of church and state. Thomas Jefferson's views on the subject could be considered zealous from his writings, such as:

History, I believe, furnishes no example of a priest-ridden people maintaining a free civil government. This marks the lowest grade of ignorance, of which their political as well as religious leaders will always avail themselves for their own purpose.[15]

It was from the fire of reason above religiosity that the US founding fathers ensured that the government of the United States would never be able to insist on certain religious belief on persons entering the government in Article VI, Section 3 of the US Constitution, which states: 'no religious Test shall ever be required as a Qualification to any Office or public Trust under the United States'. The First Amendment to the Constitution went further to prohibit imposition of religion on its people, stating: 'Congress shall make no law respecting an establishment of religion, or prohibiting the free exercise thereof ...' These clauses were taken almost word for word by the Australian founding fathers when they drafted Section 116 of the Commonwealth of Australia Constitution Act:

The Commonwealth shall not make any law for establishing any religion, or for imposing any religious observance, or for prohibiting the free exercise of any religion, and no religious test shall be required as a qualification for any office or public trust under the Commonwealth.

This wording was first produced at the Constitutional Convention of 1891. There was some concern raised by the founding father Henry Higgins at the Constitutional Convention of 1898 that this clause did not go far enough and should have also restricted the legislative powers of the states. Hanks points out that this was in part pragmatic politics, as 'such a clause could persuade "free thinkers", concerned at the preamble's recognition of "Almighty God" to support the Constitution at the forthcoming referenda'.[16] Despite Higgins' concerns, both Section 116 and the preamble remained.

Any concerns about a conflict between the preamble and Section 116 would be thoroughly quashed by the comments of High Court Chief Justice Latham in *Adelaide Company of Jehovah's Witnesses vs the Commonwealth*, wherein His Honour decided that 'no law can escape the application of s. 116 simply because it is a law which can be justified under ss. 51 or

52, or under some other legislative power'.[17] His Honour went further, at paragraph three, to state:

> The prohibition in s. 116 operates not only to protect the freedom of religion, but also **to protect the right of a man to have no religion**. No Federal law can impose any religious observance. *[my emphasis]*

As a legal and anthropological document, it is arguable this decision shows the recognition of atheism and agnosticism within Australian society at the time, together with the will to accept and protect people holding those beliefs.

There are, however, boundaries on this equal protection, as shown in the Jehovah's Witnesses case, which reveals that the High Court was more concerned with the protection of the Australian State than religious freedom. The case concerned attempts by the Commonwealth to seize the assets of the Jehovah's Witnesses on the basis that the organisation was prejudicial to the Commonwealth's wartime efforts, pursuant to National Security (Subversive Associations) regulations. Chief Justice Latham held that: 'The Constitution protects religion within a community organised under a Constitution so that the continuance of such protection necessarily assumes the continuance of the community so organised'.[18] Thus, although Atheists, Christians, Muslims, Jews, and Jehovah's Witnesses receive equal protection under the law to believe, there is little protection of an act or omission (such as avoidance of military conscription) carried out in accordance with that belief which contradicts the needs of the state and community at large.[19]

Protecting the rights to religious (and non-religious) observance does not, however, mean that religion does not impact on our society and, consequently, our legal system. Legal issues surrounding religious belief have been raised at various times since the Jehovah's Witnesses Case, both before the courts and in the legislative process. However, the High Court has never taken the sweeping approach of the Supreme Court in the United States with respect to their similar constitutional clauses, such as in *Everson v Board of Education*. In that case, Justice Black provided a raft of prohibitions on the state and federal governments, including, among others: passing 'laws which aid one religion, aid all religions or prefer one religion over another'; 'No person can be punished for entertaining or professing religious beliefs or disbeliefs, for church attendance or non-attendance'; and 'No tax in any amount, large or small, can be levied to support any religious activities or institutions, whatever they may be called, or whatever form they may adopt to teach or practice religion'.[20]

The Everson case was concerned with the use of public monies to fund transport to schools, which mainly benefited religious schools. It was claimed unsuccessfully that this was indirect support for such religious schools and, accordingly, unconstitutional. In Australia, the High Court examined similar claims with respect to funding religious schools in *Attorney-General (Vic) (ex rel Black) v Commonwealth*, otherwise known as the DOGS case, in which a claim was made that financial assistance to private religious schools would amount to contravention of Section 116 of the Constitution.[21] The court generally found that an Act of Parliament for appropriation of funds to be provided to a religious school would not in itself be a law establishing a religion. As Chief Justice Barwick pointed out: 'A law which in operation may indirectly enable a church to further the practice of religion is a long way away from a law to establish religion as that language properly understood would require it to be if the law were to be in breach of s.116.'[22] Justice Stephen decided that the provision of funding to religious schools in equal proportions to the funding given to government schools or the schools of other religious groups would not offend Section 116:

> It follows that even if the framers of our Constitution had seen fit to adopt verbatim the terms of the First Amendment, they would have been doing no more than writing into our Constitution what was then believed to be a prohibition against two things, the setting up of a national church and the favouring of one church over another. **They would not have been denying power to grant non-discriminatory financial aid to churches or church schools.**[23] *[my emphasis]*

Thus, the Commonwealth continues to provide funding to the states, which eventually migrates to the religious education of children throughout Australia. Though this may seem counterintuitive, the application of Section 116 of the Constitution provides that all faith schools and schools with no religious ties are treated equally and without discrimination.

As a side note on religion in Australian law generally, the High Court has also lent itself to defining what is a 'religion' in *Church of the New Faith v Commissioner of Payroll Tax (Victoria)*, wherein Acting Chief Justice Mason and Justice Brennan formulated a two-step test for religion, requiring that 'first, belief in a supernatural Being, Thing or Principle; and second, the acceptance of canons of conduct in order to give effect to that belief'.[24]

Thus, on a legal and anthropological basis, atheism could not be considered a religion, as it openly discards the supernatural and does not follow any conduct accordingly. This would be fine, except for the arguably discriminatory relief from taxes which religious organisations enjoy. That is, however, a matter best dealt with another time. I would prefer to turn the focus now to areas of remaining inequity in our legal system that relate to religious organisations.

RELIGIOUS ORGANISATIONS COMING BEFORE THE COURTS

While we could surmise that the courts of Australia have sought to treat Australians equally without discriminating on the basis of a litigant's religious beliefs, there remain wider issues involved in the administration of justice than the decision-making processes of judges. In the common law adversarial system, which was inherited from the English colonisers, the role of the advocate in shaping the issues which a judge considers cannot be underestimated. It is a well-known source of injustice within the legal system that powerful organisations can obtain superior legal representation and thereby influence the course of justice, or as Chester Porter QC states in *The Conviction of the Innocent*, 'The adversarial seesaw may well tilt the wrong way because the Crown or the defence cases have been over-weighted, or underweighted'.[25]

Anyone who has had serious dealings in the law will be cognisant that lawyers will only ever have two of the three characteristics of being excellent, timely, or cheap. Thus it is that in litigation, the financial resources to retain high-quality legal representation that quickly deals with legal issues are highly preferable, if not necessary, for success.

Religious organisations have significant resources, and have been described as the 'hidden giant of the Australian economy'.[26] The Catholic Church in Australia alone had revenue of 16.2 billion dollars in 2005, which would make it one of the five largest organisations in Australia by order of income. This degree of wealth and power of religious organisations is often applied for the purpose of retaining top legal teams to appear in courts on matters which are important to their faith. I will examine two such examples (from a very long list) that show a contrast in how courts react to such powerful influences.

Peter & Elspeth

In the case of *Peter & Elspeth*, the Family Court of Australia re-examined a child-custody dispute in which the role of the Exclusive Brethren was a significant factor.[27] The Exclusive Brethren are a closed evangelical religious movement that has been active since 1848 in Australia, New Zealand, the UK, and North America. Exclusive Brethren adhere to a strict avoidance of persons outside their church, with whom they do not socialise or even share a meal. Their connection is supported by biblical authority such as Matthew 23:8, 'but be not ye called Rabbi: for one is your Master, even Christ; and all ye are brethren'. The Exclusive Brethren have actively sought to influence legal affairs, including obtaining an exemption from voting and workplace laws, together with meeting and allegedly donating funds to political parties.[28]

The litigation was between Elspeth, who was a devout member of the Exclusive Brethren, and her ex-husband, Peter, who had left that organisation. It was acknowledged that, 'the father's decision to leave the faith precipitated the parties' separation in 2003 and ultimate divorce'.[29] In December 2006, Justice Benjamin ordered both parents to have custody rights of the three remaining children under the age of majority, with Peter to have limited custody over weekends.[30] When Peter attended Elspeth's house to collect the children, they were not made available. It is reported that the children indicated that they would not go with their father. On the basis of this, Peter made an application that Elspeth and two associates had contravened the court's orders. Justice Benjamin granted orders on the basis of that application, which included imprisonment of Elspeth and her two associates.[31]

Elspeth did not go to prison; rather, she was admitted to a psychiatrist with acute stress, which would eventually also lead to a diagnosis of breast cancer (the Full Court would later quash those convictions).

Several applications were filed by both litigants that would eventually lead to the matter coming before Justice Brown. It is interesting to note, at this point, that the Exclusive Brethren had retained a firm of solicitors and junior counsel that was led by Ackman QC, a distinguished senior member of the Victorian Bar. In the meantime, Peter was unrepresented and appeared for himself.

Justice Brown considered the 'twin pillars' of the law with respect to child custody, being the need for a meaningful relationship between the children and both parents and the need to protect the children from psychological and physical harm. These two legal principals fall within the overriding concerns of a court to act in 'the best interests of the child'. However, the evidence led before Justice Brown brought her to a conclusion that, given the exclusive nature of the children's life with their mother, granting any custody rights to the father would psychologically damage the children and, accordingly, such rights were not granted. This in spite of the argument made by Peter that it would be important to build a relationship with the children before the, supposedly, imminent death of Elspeth. The court, however, gave weight to evidence suggesting that the children's 'emotional needs for support by their extended family [within the Exclusive Brethren] during these traumatic years must take priority over any needs they may have for a long-term relationship with the father and any questions about the Exclusive Brethren's compliance with court orders for contact'.[32]

While we should be careful not to be critical of an unrepresented father's efforts against a seasoned and experienced legal team, it must be noted that much of the evidence presented would have been more rigorously dealt with had Peter been financially able to retain such counsel himself, including concessions made by Peter in cross-examination that he did not have a relationship with the children, or that the practices of the Exclusive Brethren were not damaging to those children. However, it is significant that the narrative of the case was allowed to drift away from the original litigation before Justice Benjamin, where evidence was accepted that:

the behaviour of family members and other members of the Exclusive Brethren in discouraging the children from spending time with their father and counselling them to 'put up with' such time, **amounted to**

psychologically cruel, unacceptable and abusive behaviour towards these children.[33] *[my emphasis]*

There is no reason to suspect that that behaviour changed, even in light of the illness of the mother. As a result of the orders made by Justice Brown, Peter shall have no contact with the children. His communication with them will be by collecting their school reports from his children's school, so long as the children are not present at the school at the time.

While it would be tempting to criticise Justice Brown's decision, that decision is a correct application of the relevant law. Rather, criticism should be targeted towards the inequity of the adversarial process in adducing evidence before the court.

Re: McBain

We ought to be aware that a religious organisation's access to financial and legal resources will not always result in success before the law, as was shown in the case of *Re McBain; Ex parte Australian Catholic Bishops Conference.*[34] The Re: McBain litigation related to reproductive technology of In-Vitro Fertilisation (IVF). Such technology represents a threat to traditional morality as devised by religious groups — in particular, where such technology is used outside of the traditional arrangement of heterosexual marriage.

In the case of Re: McBain, the Australian Catholic Bishops Conference sought to intervene against what was considered to be a fairly simple legal question. The facts of the case were that Lisa Meldrum approached Dr McBain with a request for IVF treatment. Dr McBain found that as Ms Meldrum was not married, in accordance with Section 8 of the Infertility Treatment Act, he could not treat her. Dr McBain then commenced proceedings against the State of Victoria in the Federal Court for orders that the law was invalid. Justice Sundberg of the Federal Court found that provisions in the Victorian Infertility Treatment Act which restricted provision of IVF services to married couples were inconsistent with the Commonwealth Sex Discrimination Act, and thus invalid pursuant to Section 109 of the Commonwealth Constitution.

This legal point was uncontroversial in itself, and the State of Victoria declined to appeal the decision any further. However, such a ruling represents a transition from sole acceptance of a nuclear family, and the traditions of the Church. These attitudes were made clear in the later submissions to the Victorian Law Reform Commission when seeking to amend the infertility legislation. Dempsey discusses various submissions regarding this position, including the following:

> My fundamental argument comes from natural law. In the natural world (where there is no advanced medical technology and where healthy men and women are fertile) a baby is produced only when a fertile man has sex with a fertile woman. Nature discriminates. It produces no babies from same-sex couplings. It is not discriminatory for society to replicate in law a pattern that occurs naturally by the discrimination of nature itself.

Dempsey would disagree, in that '[b]iological explanations for the family based on God-given decree would seem to demand that the heterosexual nuclear family has existed in unchanging form throughout history when this simply cannot be substantiated in the historical record'.[35] Personally, I find the argument made by the religious for natural law to discriminate against non-heterosexual couples from using IVF technology internally inconsistent, as that same natural law would also rule out use of the technology between heterosexual couples that had been, otherwise, unable to procreate.

Despite the high-powered legal team assembled by the Bishops Conference, and numerous submissions that the Bishops ought be allowed to intervene, the High Court was not prepared to accept the submissions of a party, even one as eminent as the Bishop's Conference, simply to adjudicate on a point of law. As Chief Justice Gleeson puts it:

> [b]ut for one citizen to say that a judge wrongly decided a case in favour of another citizen does not give rise to a matter. Nor does a complaint by the Attorney-General of the Commonwealth that a law of the State of Victoria has been held invalid, by a decision which is accepted by, and binds, the State of Victoria, in circumstances such as the present, give rise to a matter.[36]

On this basis, the appeal made by the Bishop's conference was dismissed. Thus, the role of social conscience of a nation as it relates to an individual's dispute does not fall upon the Church.

CONCLUSION

There have been significant advances in the sophistication of legal analysis since the proclamation of *Summa Theologica* by Thomas Aquinas. The law, as practiced in this country, has revealed itself to be open to the religious (and non-religious) views of its people, rather than imposing axioms of religious belief as a foundation for giving justice. Thus, it would not be realistic for an atheist or agnostic to fear the law as though it were some 'brooding omnipotence in the sky'. Rather, the development of the law of Australia documents a society that is increasingly prepared to tolerate and protect not just those of faith but those who lack faith.

Nonetheless, we should be aware that the mere existence of active atheists and agnostics in our society represents a threat to religious organisations, whose financial and legal resources leave those organisations in a position to use the law as a tool. We should be prepared to criticise religious groups exercising the law in this manner, whether that is democratically — through our electoral rights and contact with elected representatives — or through public support or criticism of judgements made through our courts. If we, as atheists, are prepared to exert such pressure, then we shall reap the benefits of a society and legal system that continues to evolve towards greater equality for all.

NOTES

1. M. de W. Howe (ed.), *The Holmes-Laski Letters*, Oxford University Press, London, 1953, p. 822.
2. T. Aquinas, Summa Theological, Question 91, Article 2, in *Selected Political Writings* (trans. J. G. Dawson), Macmillan, New York, 1948.
3. 'natural law immutable': *Quotient* 94, Article 5; 'if human law ...': *Quotient* 95, Article 2.
4. M. Freeman, *Jurisprudence*, 7th revised edn, Sweet & Maxwell, London, 2001, p. 1257; J. M. Balkin, 'Understanding Legal Understanding: the legal subject and the problem of legal coherence', *103 Yale Law Journal* 105, 1993, p. 110.
5. O. W. Holmes Jr, 'Law in Science and Science in Law', *Harvard Law Review* 12, 1889, p. 443. (Note: While I am not a realist in Holmes's fashion, I consider his reasoning remains a foundational underpinning for the move away from traditional positivism, and thus is relevant to the modern lawyer.)

6. J. Diamond, *Guns, Germs and Steel*, W. W. Norton & Company, Inc, New York, 1997, p. 297.

7. F. Wolf, *The Dreaming Universe: a mind-expanding journey into the realm where psyche and physics meet*, Simon & Schuster, New York, 1994.

8. The treaty made by John Batman and eight Aboriginal elders for the land around Botany Bay is available from the National Archives of Australia at www.foundingdocs.gov.au

9. *Blankard v Galdy* (1693) 90 ER 1089; *Anonymous* (1722) 2 P Wms 75; 24 ER 646.

10. A. MacAdam and J. Pyke, *Judicial Reasoning and the Doctrine of Precedent*, Butterworths, Sydney, 1998, p. 336.

11. *Cooper v Stuart* (1889) 14 App Cas 286; *Milirrpum v Nabalco Pty Ltd* (1971) 17 FLR 141; *Mabo v the State of Queensland no. 2*, (1988) 166 CLR 186.

12. R. Moffat, 'Philosophical Foundations of the Australian Constitutional Tradition', *Sydney Law Review* 59, 1965, pp. 77–9.

13. P. Hanks, *Constitutional Law in Australia*, Butterworths, Sydney, 1996, p. 4.

14. S. Harris, *Letter to a Christian Nation*, Bantam Press, London, 2007, p. 19.

15. T. Jefferson in a letter to Baron von Humboldt, 1813.

16. The preamble text: 'Whereas the people of New South Wales, Victoria, South Australia, Queensland, and Tasmania, humbly relying on the blessing of Almighty God, have agreed to unite in one indissoluble Federal Commonwealth under the Crown of the United Kingdom of Great Britain and Ireland, and under the Constitution hereby established', in *Constitutional Law in Australia*, p. 537.

17. *Adelaide Company of Jehovah's Witnesses v Commonwealth* (1943) 67 CLR 116 at paragraph two.

18. ibid at paragraphs 131–2.

19. *Krygger v Williams* (1912) 15 CLR 366.

20. *Everson v. Board. of Education*, (1947) 330 U.S. 1.

21. *Attorney-General (Vic) (ex rel Black) v. The Commonwealth* (1981) 146 CLR 559.

22. ibid at paragraph 583.

23. ibid at paragraph 610.

24. *Church of the New Faith v Commissioner of Payroll Tax (Victoria)*, (1983) 154 CLR 120 at paragraph 136.

25. C. Porter, *The Conviction of the Innocent*, Random House Australia, Sydney, 2007, p. 245.

26. A. Ferguson, 'God's Business', 29 June – 5 July, *BRW*, 2006, pp. 42–46.

27. *Peter & Elspeth*, (2009) FamCA 551.

28. Q. McDermott, 'The Brethren Express', first broadcast on the Australian Broadcasting Corporation Channel on 15 October 2007. Available for download at www.abc.net.au/4corners/special_eds/20071015/brethren/default.htm

29. *Peter & Elspeth*, paragraph 4.

30. ibid at paragraph 45.

31. ibid at paragraph 50.

32. ibid at paragraph 155.

33. ibid at paragraph 93.

34. *Re McBain; Ex parte Australian Catholic Bishops Conference*, (2002) HCA 16.

35. D. Dempsey, 'Active Fathers, Natural Families and Children's Origins: dominant themes in the Australian political debate over eligibility for assisted reproductive technology', *Australian Journal of Emerging Technologies and Society* 4 (1), 2006, pp. 28–44.

36. *Re McBain* (2002) at paragraph 26.

* PERSONAL

ON BEING A PART-TIME ATHEIST

Robyn Williams
Broadcaster, science journalist, author

THIS MAY BE DIFFICULT. HOW DO I DESCRIBE NOT THINKING ABOUT something? I don't think about golf. Or ballroom dancing. Or shopping for laxatives.

And I hardly ever think about God.

This is not meant to be a smug assertion. I am, sometimes, forced to give God a thought, like today, writing this piece. But not normally, preparing for work, riding on the bus, making radio programs, reporting science. God doesn't arise. Not with me.

Why do I labour this point? For two reasons. Firstly, atheists such as I am don't organise their lives to harass believers, or to plot their downfall or the global elimination of their faith. We are largely tolerant — and realistic. Could we ever hope to wipe out the Catholic Church, turn St Peter's Square into a rock arena, and convert every basilica into an art gallery? Not really. Do we respect the right of others to believe what they want? If it's harmless, yes indeed. Note: harmless!

Secondly, I could be wrong. I don't imagine this to be likely, given the range of mostly weird beliefs to which the conventionally religious subscribe. However, I'm not omniscient, and most vaguely God-bothering folk I know personally (not many, come to think of it) are benign and unevangelical. So the topic hardly comes up. But absolute proof is unobtainable, so I'd be as arrogant as the Inquisition if I were to demand that believers must recant. Yet, these days, newspapers are full of casual references to 'militant atheism' and 'fundamentalist' unbelievers campaigning for ascendance. Yes, some of the Brit godless did find a few quid to put signs on buses saying that God may have left the building. So what? I saw it as a bit of a giggle: two fingers to the sky, making a change from all the pious posturing of the other side(s).

When you examine other 'stories' in newspapers, about Richard Dawkins, for instance, establishing summer camps for atheistic youths, a bit like madrassars for the Anti-Christ, it turns out (and I asked him) that the newspapers simply made it up. Richard had given a bit of money to the scheme — it wasn't his at all.

What has actually happened in the last few years is that atheists have become thoroughly browned off with all that's done 'in the name of God' — from the annoying, such as the banning of stem-cell research, a field of science which could alleviate untold suffering, to the utterly unspeakable, such as the wanton rampage in Mumbai in early 2009, when young Muslim thugs killed people for God as casually as Martin Bryant killed the picnickers at Port Arthur.

So much vociferous evil. So much rabid destruction. No wonder Richard Dawkins turns up with *The God Delusion* (2006) and Christopher Hitchens with *God is Not Great* (2007). Long overdue!

Do they want to assassinate all vicars and raze the mosques? Hardly. We spend many a day conversing with people of the cloth, accepting invitations from archbishops and, in my case, having as much pleasant discourse with my friends in the ABC (Australian Broadcasting Commission) Religious Department as we do with anyone else. We enjoy the company of well-meaning human beings whose views differ from our own, without feverishly seeking to 'convert' them. And we all loathe assassins.

It is a convenient smear to dismiss most of us (and we are not a job lot, not even much of a 'movement') as if we're after world domination. We are, however, sick of the hypocrisy. We watch the faithful in office in Downing Street, the Oval Office, or the governor's mansion in Texas, declare war or unhesitatingly impose the death sentence, and we are appalled. What does their God of love and forgiveness mean to them if an electric chair or a Trident missile is part of the deal?

What about the science of God? That has been worked over quite a lot in recent times. Oxford anthropologist Robin Dunbar has found that our brains are organised to conjure (I use the word without blush) several layers of awareness, including the highest: the spiritual.[1] It is of benefit, apparently, and I would concur: such a mental versatility is of tremendous use in giving us a lofty commitment to our natural surroundings and our tribe. Not just a bunch of trees, lakes, and hillsides — but a land to which we are bound at a higher level. Not just a collection of families and individuals forming a mob — but a 'chosen' people with a greater purpose than mere survival. It is easy to see this mental agility taking the extra leap to the godly.

Consolations of religion are obvious. Hope, triumph over death, ultimate forgiveness, and atonement are all on offer. The utility of gods in an evolutionary sense is also obvious. God is good politics once the population has risen in numbers and, especially, once they have settled to form villages, towns, and cities. You can unify the rabble with a totem or a church. Control!

What puzzles the atheist, even about full-square mainstream religions, is how many odd, or even mad, shibboleths they insist upon. Virgin birth, transubstantiation, healing with hands, past-lives therapy, celibacy (!), walking on water, astral travel ... I don't mind turning water into wine, in principal, but I can never get the hang of it.

How do you manage to get sensible grown-ups to sign up to such tosh? How can half (or even a third) of America be so credulous? Richard Dawkins says that it comes from our willingness, wired until the teenage years, to be obedient to parents' or elders' instructions. If we did not accept adult advice in a hostile world, we'd soon be eaten by tigers or fall off the cliff. Being malleable to the cult leader, or bishop, is part of the same evolutionary psychology.

Some scientists see a tendency to depression as but a manifestation of the mechanism to yield to the strong leader. Maybe we were allowed to recover from this mental genuflection when in the wild, surrounded by family and tribe. Maybe it wilts into depression only when we are isolated in the modern world with its crowded distances.

Control. Obedience. A built-in mechanism for the rise of human civilisation. So, what about moral codes? Much has been made of the Bible, the Qu'ran, the holy books of instruction, as sources for our better conduct — ultimately, our kindnesses and better values. There is no doubt this may have codified them, with Egyptian ideas of altruism being transferred and reinterpreted as Christian expressions of love and self-sacrifice.

Is this directly inspired by God? Hardly! Or, as Richard Dawkins has repeated so often, which bit? The stoning of unbelievers, the crushing of women, or the emancipation of the poor? You can select an almost-infinite and endlessly contradictory range of options. Maybe that's the idea. Consistent it is not; more a running record of what any gang of bearded despots happened to hand down to the masses at any one time.

Is the secular source any better? It depends on which one you have in mind. Lots of cultures have produced dystopias even without the help of priests. You know the list. Christopher Hitchens has a good one, and points out the ex-seminarians (Stalin) or god-like emperors (Mao) — but I won't bother to recite it again.[2] It is significant, however, to see how well tyrants who present themselves as deities have emulated those theocracies.

I prefer to look at societies in general. Some allow people to decide via the democratic mechanisms that have flourished since the Enlightenment; some crush any variety of voices. The point is that you can do either 'in the name of God' as well as without Him. It is unhelpful simply to divide cultures according to how well they are churched and to try to discern any strength of an effective moral code accordingly. France and Italy are supposed to be Catholic. It's hard to tell these days. Their public ethics seem laudable. Cambodia and Iran are inescapably pious. Look at them!

We have a moral code because we must. Sarah Hrdy has written about our 'cooperative parenting', necessitated because our children are so vulnerable for so long, and looking after them is beyond one mother.[3] From the beginning, we must be altruistic — or die. We are also capable of the most horrendous acts. Just glance at this excerpt from a 2009 interview with a woman named Kamate, who survived an attack by rapists in a now-defunct militia in Congo:

> Their main purpose was to kill my husband. They took everything. They cut up his body like you would cut up meat, with knives. He was alive. They began cutting off his fingers. They cut off his sex. They opened his stomach and took out his intestines. When they poked his heart, he died. They were holding a gun to my head ... They ordered me to collect

all his body parts and lie on top of them and there they raped me —
twelve soldiers. I lost consciousness. Then I heard someone cry out in
the next room and I realised they were raping my daughters.[4]

I could offer unlimited examples of such ghastliness. So could you.
There is no end to our cruelty, our willingness to extend its agonising
capriciousness or sheer abundance. As I've said before, quoting Sartre
(who was in turn quoting Stendahl), 'God's only excuse is he doesn't exist'.
No god could oversee such horror. No sensible believer in God could, in
good conscience, sign off on such a deity.

We are cruel in defined circumstances. It is predictable. In the end, as
in Golding's fable *Lord of the Flies* (1954), the community will break down.
Our survival depends on cooperative assent to rules for the greater good.
The coming environmental turbulence will be the ultimate test of this.
Cormac McCarthy's novel *The Road* (2006) is a possible apotheosis.

It is not surprising to see various manifestations of ethical codes
preserved in everything from holy books to songlines, nor to note that
many should have similarities. We could not live without them. It is
more likely that they, like us, have gradually evolved and been refined
in different circumstances. Saying that they are in the name of God is an
interesting metaphor, but not much more. A more apt metaphor might be
that of a blind watchmaker, as used by Richard Dawkins in the book of the
same name (*The Blind Watchmaker*, 1986). It's a concept he uses to describe
the blind processes of natural selection.

It is indeed stunning to confront complexity, whether it be a brain cell, an
eye, a slime mould, a galaxy, or a baby, let alone a watch. We can account for the
evolution of each of these, and don't need God as an engineer of the
cosmos, of bodies, or of watches. But we could agree that evolution
through natural selection was God's chosen mechanism. We can also agree
that he was in no hurry to set up his chosen sons and daughters — us
— in our Earthly parish, and was inclined to wait eight billion years, for
some reason, before even getting around to the solar system. He could be
incredibly lazy — or distracted! We can also fudge around his profligacy
in creating a galaxy 100 million light years across, let alone the rest of
the universe, when he needed only a speck of planet — but that's His
eccentricity, perhaps.

The argument can recede forever. He wanted nearly seven billion souls; he needed four billion earthly years to make them; he chose classical physics, quantum mechanics, and Darwinian techniques to 'create' what's here. If you insist on this, I can only shrug and leave you to it. It seems, at least, incredibly messy. God, surely, could have managed something more elegant.

Believers will tell you only that this is 'His' way. It passes all understanding. Sure does. Some frolic. The elegance comes when you subtract God from all this natural confusion. You can then see millions of different experiments in being, some yielding towering grace and intricacy, some tragic failure. Broken watches everywhere, and such brilliant timekeeping as well. Each of my cells has a 24-hour cycle. So do yours. Without our thinking about it. In 2009, we celebrated both the bicentenary of Darwin's birth and the sesquicentenary of his explosive work *On the Origin of Species* (1859). Darwin knew little of circadian rhythms, or of genes or DNA. Yet, he saw how biological complexity could arise over massive amounts of time.

Again and again, modern science has added further proof to this original great idea. I shall offer only one example. Apes have one more chromosome than humans; yet, we are supposed to be related. This is a highly significant difference that would crush our kinship unless an explanation could be found. Molecular biologists looked closer. Then they found the answer. Our chromosome number two is a double, fused in the middle. There is the missing element, after all. The story holds.

Multiply this coherence millions of times and you get consistent and wonderfully convincing proof. Say God did it, and you add nothing. You diminish the wonder by adding fairy dust. What about the abiding mysteries, some of which may defeat us forever? The purpose of evolution, the contradictions in physics, the fate of the universe — the meaning of life?

The first lot, the mysteries, will gradually fade. But not entirely. Modern science has been around for, say, 400 years, since Galileo opened up the heavens with that first adapted telescope — maybe for less than 200 years, since Coleridge asked at the BA meeting in Cambridge in 1833 what natural philosophers should be called now that they got their hands dirty. Dr Whewell, Master of Trinity, offered 'scientist'. Someone objected that it sounded too much like 'atheist', but the name stuck. Given the brevity of science as a tool of investigation (rather than as a 'pure' conjecture à la Aristotle) it is stunning that we have discovered so much, not that there remain a few great unanswered questions.

What about the meaning of life? Douglas Adams was fond of twisting this to 'The Meaning of Liff'. The question does rather sound like the title of a Monty Python movie. The meaning is what we make it. I do not need an ever-observing deity or the promise of an after-existence to make every day full of meaning and relish. Nor do millions of others. Every second counts. Not necessarily in a transcendent way (breakfast is merely fun — rarely a route to nirvana), but in ways that we enjoy and value beyond their prosaic place in the immensity of time and space.

Is this absurd? Insufficient? Not to most of us. No more than the contortions of theologians about how old we shall be when enjoying eternal existence in some afterlife. Will I be 65 forever? Or 15 again? Will we have hormones still, appetites, any of the rewards of our physical senses? If not, how can we still be ourselves? Why should Muslim males have access to scores of virgins but not us, and what happens to those virgins (in heaven?!) when they have been used? Is eternity without bodily functions? Is it an endless church service and obeisance to a demanding God?

I much prefer this Earthly limit. My own experience of near extinction, during a cardiac arrest in 1988 when I flatlined for nearly a minute, was instructive. Nothing. Blank. Extinction. So I awoke once more, here on Earth.

Give me The Meaning of Liff any day.

NOTES

1. R. Dunbar, *The Human Story*, Faber and Faber, London, 2004.
2. C. Hitchens, *God is Not Great: how religion poisons everything*, Twelve Books, 2007.
3. S. Hrdy, *Mothers and Others: the evolutionary origins of mutual understanding*, Harvard University Press, Massachusetts, 2009.
4. From A. Hochschild, 'Rape of the Congo', *New York Review of Books*, August 2009, at www.nybooks.com/articles/archives/2009/aug/13/rape-of-the-congo

ATHEISM: AN EXPLANATION FOR THE BELIEVER

Dr Colette Livermore
Medical doctor, author of *Hope Endures*

In my soul I feel just that terrible pain of loss ... of God not being
God — of God not really existing.
Mother Teresa

OUR BELIEFS ARE NOT IMMUTABLE. THERE IS A FINE LINE BETWEEN FAITH
and disbelief, and much two-way traffic between the opposing camps. I was
a believer and member of Mother Teresa's order for 11 years. In 2004, after a
long struggle, I finally had to admit my faith had left me. It is not an easy
thing to leave the convictions of a lifetime, and it can put some friendships
under strain, with hostile questions and disparaging remarks, but there
was nowhere else to stand, nothing else to say. Wars are fought, and torture
and psychological duress are still used to make converts, even though our
humanity is defined more by our actions than our beliefs. Atheists and
theists sometimes hurl insults at each other across the trenches, but heroes
of the human spirit are found on both sides of the faith divide, as is the
love for beauty, truth, and for experiencing the sheer delight of being alive.

Religion deals with issues of meaning surrounding birth, the way to
live a good life, death, and suffering. It gives us a community. It provides
ceremonies to accompany life's milestones, and teaches a moral code,
fostering compassion and truthfulness. However, some forms of belief have
a mistaken view of the self, which they believe is sinful and perfected by
humiliation, correction, and submission. Some groups demand its followers

yield their intellect and will to a religious authority that is held to be the sole conduit of the divine will.

For 11 years, I was a sister within the order of Mother Teresa. I joined as an idealistic but naive 18-year-old wanting to help even up life's lottery in response to the footage I saw of starving children in Africa. The path I was taught by Mother Teresa, a Nobel laureate and considered a 'living saint', involved total surrender through vowed obedience. The self was to be suspected and renounced; it was not to be trusted, and was considered prey to self-deception. Mother Teresa asserted that 'she, who has herself for a guide, has a fool for a guide'. However, if the inner core of one's being is surrendered, what protection does the individual have against tyranny? Of being compelled to do what the self, if it survived, would consider unjust or unwise? The self prevents us from being automatons. If one's executive control is abdicated, it is impossible to act wisely. As Isaiah Berlin asserted: 'dogmatically believed-in schemes are almost always the road to inhumanity'.[1] I experienced this first hand when obedience and the rigid structures of the religious timetable obstructed my response to suffering people because it was the wrong time of day or not our type of work, even though I was constantly taught the poor are Christ in a distressing disguise.

Many of us have heard Richard Dawkins citing the quote from the US physicist Steven Weinberg: 'With or without religion good people can behave well and bad people can do evil; but for good people to do evil — that takes religion.'

Why can this happen? It is because believers submit to religious obedience, which is equated by their organisations with goodness. This is accompanied by the restriction of access to knowledge. Blockades are erected to prevent members attaining information and making their own decisions. It is another form of control. Disobedience is considered conceited and willful, and is punished by humiliation, censure, condemnation, and possible excommunication. If a church representative says: 'Send that dying child away; it's not the right time or day to help them,' or, 'You are not to be trained for your work,' they end up harming those they are trying to help, through neglect or incompetence. If a person in this situation keeps silent when they should speak, then perhaps evil will be done in the name of God by a good person out of cowardice, ignorance, or the mistaken conviction that this is how God wishes them to act. The Church has for too long equated holiness with obedience as it seeks to gain control and induce conformity in its 'flock'. The simile says it all. Obedience may be an expression of stupidity, mindlessness, or cowardice.

Some religions consider truth to be something immutable and absolute that cannot change or be understood anew. Believers are not encouraged to explore the stirrings of doubt within them, and are counselled that their misgivings and questions are a God-given, purifying trial or dark night of the soul. Wide reading, listening to diverse opinions, and debating the conflicting ideas could clarify the situation, but that response is often not permitted and the person is left to struggle alone. Mother Teresa may have evolved in her form of belief, or have even become a non-believer, if she had not practised thought-blocking, confession, pretence, and penance in response to the many questions that plagued her. Perhaps she was trapped by her own public image and her role as a 'living saint' and head of a large religious order. She may have felt she could not admit her uncertainties. She projected absolute certainty, and told me she had no doubt.

'So many unanswered questions live within me — I am afraid to uncover them — because of the blasphemy — If there be God — please forgive me.'

...

'The whole time smiling ... Could they but know — how my cheerfulness is the cloak by which I cover the emptiness and misery.'[2]

She goes on to say that in the darkness she longs for God — for an answer, for something to help make sense of the raw suffering that she has encountered. Trying to reconcile these opposing forces she felt would unbalance her, and so she stuck unswervingly to the old rules and ways of doing things, and equated them with fidelity to God. As Professor Max Kamien observed: '... such people crave certainty and security, and obtain it by going back to their simple roots. Their existential doubts are answered through placing their trust in the arms of their god. And this can make them serenely impervious to new information.'[3]

Reinforcing mental barricades and denying the contradictions within us is not the way to deal with this inner anguish we sometimes face. My personal answer is to make peace with the doubt, to follow the threads of thought, even if they lead me to conclude that I AM is not. Truth and love are sacred to all traditions. If we are intellectually honest and don't deny our inner stirrings, if we try to live a life of love, then in this way, as Flannery O'Connor said, we have enough certainty to make our way but it is in the darkness. We keep ourselves open to the questions and sit with them in a 'cloud of unknowing'.

Within some groups, information is censored: even in secular education, youth are barred by home schooling, and in some religious schools from free access to accepted scientific thought and knowledge. The young person matures unaware of the diverse opinions and scientific evidence that exist beyond their religious cocoon, and mistake what they know for all there is to know. A person should not be constrained in an intellectual and spiritual straightjacket by the dogmas and strictures of their faith. Suppression of thought drowns the intellect and leads to immaturity and stunting of the personality. An individual must be allowed the freedom to explore, to float and let their ideas find equilibrium; to fashion for themselves a set of principles that helps them respond to the world with intelligence.

At the heart of many people's scepticism about organised religion is the contradiction between belief and behaviour. The history of the Catholic Church certainly gives us cause for concern about the interpretation of Jesus' command to love each other, even our enemies. Its record has been marred by hundreds of thousands of deaths, burnings at the stake, paedophilia, and the consequences of the prohibition against condoms; yet, this is not what has shaken my belief.

Christian theology is underpinned by the story of Salvation history: the fall, the promise of the Messiah, foretold in the prophet Isaiah's Suffering Servant, the crucifixion, and the cornerstone of the whole theological edifice — the resurrection. Sin, we were taught, brought suffering and death into a previously idyllic world. But we know from the fossil record that there was suffering, disease, death, and species extinction even before humankind evolved and were able to sin. The suffering of humankind is just a continuum of the struggle for survival integral to the natural order.

The suffering of Christ was thought to be necessary to satisfy the demands of God's justice; however, I think of Christ as a radically truthful man who met a similar fate as many other people of courage.

In my own life, I have asked and not received, and sought and not found. My God lived in a cloud too thick for prayer to bring peace. Of course, I was rebuked for even expecting God to act. This was not faith but superstition; a childish belief in a magician God. 'Ask and it will be given to you; search and you will find ...' was not a clear promise to the poor in spirit, but something that needs much Biblical scholarship to understand. In my ignorance, I prayed for those with cancer that the unremitting pain might end; I prayed for a child racked with tuberculosis that his life's promise might be fulfilled; I prayed to be able to help a mother in an obstructed birth — and 'The sky and the earth were silent as always'.[4] God, we are taught, is powerfully present in the world, but silent and not detectable. The beauty of nature is an expression of God but not so its fury. I came to the conclusion that the universe was insensible to the plight of humans as they struggled to survive.

The Catholic Church continues to encourage the practice of intercessory prayer, and includes the Prayers of the Faithful in her liturgies. Miracles are used as official proof that people such as Mother Teresa are saints in heaven. The learned disparage such understanding as 'poor theology'; however, the Church continues these practices and no learned clarification is proffered. I was told, 'The God you disbelieve in is not God at all', and so the circular arguments go on. Christ worked many miracles of healing and compassion, but how are these to be understood? Did they happen? Are we ignorant to believe they did? How do we know what is true? It is my opinion that we cannot know.

I no longer believed in an interventionist God, but for a few years hung on to a belief in the incarnate, servant-God who emptied Himself and suffered with humanity. Christ, who endured evil but was not conquered by it, and responded with goodness to viciousness. I told myself that somehow God could not stem the tide of suffering and evil in the world — that it was an insoluble mystery, and it was not my place to question. In the end, God's plan will be revealed: 'He will wipe away every tear ...there will be no more death and no more mourning or sadness or pain', as it says in Revelation 21:4. As the British mystic Julian of Norwich asserted in the fourteenth century as England tried to come to grips with the Bubonic

Plague: 'All shall be well, and all shall be well and all manner of things shall be well'.

So we come to the last and most important miracle, the Resurrection — if hope is lost on Earth, is there life after life? I cannot believe there is; that all the people that ever lived are somehow held in being. There is no reason to suppose this is so. We fall to the ground like the sparrows and return to the earth. That is all — *carpe diem*.

So after many years of searching and reading, 'something shifts, giving in to the pressures that have built for decades in the tectonic plates that support our poor notions of reality, then, suddenly, a whip crack splits the air about us and we are no longer able to judge our world by the means with which we have habitually judged it.'[5] My faith was no longer tenable.

Belief is a deeply held personal conviction that is little affected by words and arguments, and evolves, if it is allowed to, by confronting life's realities and trying to make sense of personal experience as we deal with our human vulnerability to suffering and death. Hostile arguments breed defensiveness and reinforce mental barricades. It is best to lay aside the polemics and work together to relieve the suffering in the world, rather than adding to it through ideological conflicts. At the core of the great religions is a simple rule: treat others as you would wish to be treated, a principle that can be practised by believer and non-believer alike. All of us are able to recognise hypocrisy and know that the test of any conviction is the life it sustains. A well-lived life is a masterpiece, not an accident. We can glean from the world's religions, from the humanities and science, the way to live a beautiful life. A life of compassion is one in which we are always learning and trying to make connections between peoples with energy and vigour.

NOTES

1. I. Berlin, 'The pursuit of the ideal', in *The Proper Study of Mankind: an anthology of essays*, (ed. H. Hardy and R. Hausheer), London, 1997, p. 16.
2. B. Kolodiejchuk (ed.), *Mother Teresa: come be my light — the private writings of the "Saint of Calcutta"*, Doubleday, 2007.
3. Quote from Professor Max Kamien, source unknown.
4. C. Milosz, 'Prayer', at http://themote.info/archive/archive_poetry_pt4.htm
5. A. Miller, *Landscape of Farewell*, Allen & Unwin, 2008, p. 11.

FAR ABOVE RUBIES

Tanya Levin
Social worker in women's health, author of *People in Glass Houses*

SARA IS A GIRL IN MY SON'S PUBLIC PRIMARY-SCHOOL CLASS. SHE HAS thick, long hair and bright, shiny eyes. She is pretty, but that's not what makes her so engaging. She is prone to bursting into hysterics for no reason at all, and she won't always tell you why. She likes to pull faces when the teacher's not looking. And she'll do all this on School Pancake Day, when parents are everywhere.

When I pull out my camera during the half hour in which the parents are allowed into the sanctity of the classroom, Sara grabs her friends and they twist their mouths up with their fingers and roll their eyes back, posing for a shot I can never send her parents. After the flash, they giggle into each other and run off back to their desks.

Sara is bright. She reads a lot, Sam tells me, because she's not allowed to watch television at home or play on the computer. He is too young to understand that her parents are more than strict. No one at her house is allowed to do such things.

Sara's not even allowed to watch the videos — educational or otherwise — that the school has on hand for rainy days or tired teachers. But she won't feel different for very long. After this year, she will transfer permanently to her religious school, where the rules of education will match the ones at home and temple. She will be taught the curriculum of her birthright religion's history, ethics, spirituality, facts, and fiction. She will learn that femaleness is weakness and submission, that the impulses and pleasures of the flesh exist to be suppressed, and that laughter is seen as taking the fear of the All-powerful way too lightly. This Sara will be extinguished.

My heart cries, Goodbye, Sara. I want to slip her my phone number and say, call me if you ever need to get out; but she is way too young and it is not my place. Goodbye, happy, bouncy, spontaneous Sara. Goodbye to your humanity, your liberties, your rights. They are taking you into the fold seriously now, so it is time to say farewell.

Sara's mother took three years to make eye contact with me. I knew she wasn't supposed to anyway, and when she eventually smiled and said 'hi', once, quietly, in passing, I nearly fell over.

There was another woman from their community who would often say hello, quite blatantly, and smile, and make eye contact, almost as a sign of defiance. I wondered how her escape would unfold from the room with no doors. I wondered if, once, she had started out as Sara.

Will Sara be trapped in social isolation if she does ever get out? When the child grows up and steps out of the religious wheelchair they've been pushed around in, it's not so easy to walk. It takes time to learn to use the muscles that have atrophied. To be able to think with reason and not fear. To see beauty in the world, in other people, and even in yourself without the guide dog they say you'll always need. To sleep at night without the sedation of prayer or reindoctrination. Will Sara know another way?

The children's teacher tells me she'll be fine. I shake my head. 'No, she won't,' I say. 'She won't be fine at all.' She's a girl-child being raised in fundamentalism. Fundamentalism prepares girl-children to be grateful female servants. I was raised by them. And I used to be a very grateful servant myself.

Becoming an atheist for me was not a choice as much as an inevitable end. A process of elimination. After all, my teenage weekends were spent in the Hills Christian Life Centre, a small, vibrant Pentecostal church in a Sydney suburb. Its annual music conference, Hillsong, brought it the most publicity and evolved over the years into its name, logo, branding, and music style. The little church of 300 people that I joined at age 14 now has branches in Capetown, Paris, London, Kiev, and Stockholm, and boasts over 50,000 members worldwide.

I was a happy Jewish born-again Christian, particularly because my parents had told me I was, and so did my church. My mother joyfully pointed out the verses in the New Testament that offered rewards, first for the Jew and then for the Gentile. We were doubly blessed, she would remind me, often in the presence of my goy father. I lived a fulfilled, saved life, doing my best not to sin, and being all that I could be for Jesus. Still, there were all of these nagging thoughts. Otherwise known as doubts. Otherwise known as sin.

Being a born-again, spirit-filled fundamentalist on fire for Jesus Christ gives you the opportunity to saunter through life as if you were on a safari, getting up close to the heathen sometimes, but not so close that they can bite. I came from a church that preached predestination: the concept that, since God is omniscient, He already knows who's hell-bound, and a lot of pastors can tell just by meeting someone. Not only was I one of the chosen people, but I was also one of the Chosen People, and doing the best a Jew could do, given most Jews' refusal to recognise the Messiah, then and now. It definitely looked like I was on some winning teams.

Good for me. Except for the gross injustices I saw in the world and in the Church and in the Bible. I emigrated from South Africa two years after the White Australia Policy had been repealed, and knew, again because of my mother's gasps, that this country was not racist, because white men did manual labour. Nelson Mandela was still in jail, and there were no homeless people I could see, in my suburb, anyway. But even then it was pretty clear how daunting the future was for Hillsong girls.

Now, I already had a lot of questions, or doubts, or sins, to be precise, in my teenage years that I wasn't supposed to have, and certainly not in the presence of God's congregation. The pastors had never taken to me, maybe for this reason, and while their response — 'You're going to love Bible College' — was promising, it did nothing to ease my logical and increasingly bothered mind.

After all, it wasn't for me to demand an answer to world hunger. 'My ways are not your ways, says the Lord, my thoughts are not your thoughts', says the Lord in Isaiah. Lucifer's conception, and his ultimate metamorphosis to Satan, the Enemy and, moreover, Sadistic Torturer in Charge of You Forever If You Screw Up, troubled me, but I knew that this was the true gift of free will. We could accept everlasting life or be eternally punished in every facet of our existence. This riddle alone nearly pushed me right off the edge.

Still, Job did a whole lot of questioning, and all he ended up with was boils and dead children. I know God gave him twice the children back, but I always wondered if he maybe hadn't been attached to the first ones, and didn't just want new ones to sit in the dead ones' chairs at dinner. Besides, these were all men, and women should be silent and not ask questions. They should be submissive. That's what we knew. We heard about Eve, the helper and companion.

We never heard about Queen Esther or Deborah or Jael or Ruth. Only Moses the stuttering outcast, David the gigolo, Paul the ultimate nagging Jewish mother. There I was going again. Swimming upstream, going against the grain, making trouble. And this was only in my own head.

Feminism was for me a natural progression, because at Hillsong women must love being treated like doormats. All in the name of a good marriage, of course, for this is the essence of femaleness. Women's roles revolve exclusively around being a good wife and mother. If, for some reason, a female is unmarried, it should be because she is under the age of 16, over the age of 90, or going through a very recent separation, as it is known, the D-word still being considered rather unattractive. Whisper it, please, if it comes to mind. Failing these categories, the unbetrothed are constantly encouraged to prepare for marriage and motherhood, like a virgin waiting eagerly to be sacrificed. They must live as if they were about to meet the kind of husband God would want them to marry. Which could be any moment now.

We had been taught according to Proverbs 31. Not the first nine verses, which deal with justice and the distribution of alcohol. We never heard about those. Instead, we were schooled as women to be as the Proverbs 31 woman. Stepping one step up from the 'Submissive Wife' movement so popular in the States, the Proverbs 31 woman is all of those things without actually being human. She is Mrs America and the Bride of Christ. Even if this is not what the original passage was about.

There is no mention of context at Hillsong, though, unless it suits a pastor's purpose. That the Proverbs 31 woman lived in the Middle East some thousands of years back is neither here nor there. What's deemed exciting is how relevant it is to today's woman. Hillsong thrives on preaching the Bible's relevance, an oxymoron to some.

The evidence was clear that I was a Proverbs 31 FAIL from early on. While the pastor's wife would guide us gaily through our destiny according to the

Old Testament (the hard one, the serious one, the one that was back when God was meaner than he is these days), I was getting a different message.

With increasing frequency, it occurred to me that there were three different readings of the Bible: the words on the page, the understanding of everybody else — aka Hillsong (HS) — and me, with my perverse and unholy views. Proverbs 31 seemed no exception.

v.10 Who can find a virtuous woman? For her price is far above rubies.
HS: It is a wonderful thing to be virtuous and people will value you.
Me: Israel must be full of sluts. How much are the rubies compared to camels or shekels, since it only costs 50 shekels to rape a virgin and keep her?[1]

But Chastity was just the beginning.

v.11 The heart of her husband doth safely trust in her so that he shall have no need of spoil.
HS: She is trustworthy and pampers her man.
Me: He's watching her closely, so she's overcompensating out of fear.

v.12 She will do him good and not evil all the days of her life.
HS: This woman has unfaltering femininity, which is to be kind, loyal, supportive, loving, and perfectly so. So much to aspire to.
Me: The Proverbs 31 woman is a Stepford Wife.

v.14 She is like the merchants' ships, she bringeth her food from afar.
HS: She goes to a lot of trouble to make her husband's dinner the way he likes it.
Me: How else is she like these merchants' ships? Why won't she shop locally?

v.15 She riseth also while it is yet night, and giveth meat to her household, and a portion to her maidens.
HS: She's not lazy and she provides for everyone, unceasingly.
Me: Why can't she sleep? Why is everyone else eating and not her? She's eating-disordered.

Besides this, what about the maidens, or maidservants, as they are sometimes translated? If they're busy helping her, how the hell are they going to be Proverbs 31 women? No one ever mentioned the maidservants. I always wanted to know more about the maidservants.

v.16 She considereth a field, and buyeth it. With the fruit of her hands she planteth a vineyard.

HS: She is a very clever businesswoman who can make decisions like men do — almost.

Me: Hang on, let's back up here just a minute. Why does she get her food from afar and plant a vineyard at home? Is she the alcoholic or is it the husband? Is that why she gets up so early, to knock back a few before the day starts?

v.18 She perceiveth that her merchandise is good; her candle goeth not out by night.

HS: She works hard and knows what she's doing. She works late into the night.

Me: She loves staying up late trying on the stuff she got shopping. Another universal assumption about women. She is a selfish energy-waster. Maybe she's into the hard stuff. Maybe that's why she can't sleep.

v.23 Her husband is known in the gates, where he sitteth among the elders of the land.

HS: She married very well because she's so virtuous and helpful.

Me: Another liquid lunch. Bernie Madoff used to sit among the elders of the land.

v.26 She openeth her mouth with wisdom and in her tongue is the law of kindness.

HS: She is beyond human.

Me: She is a tedious robot who never gets PMT.

v.27. She looketh well to the ways of her household and eateth not the bread of idleness.

HS: She revolves her life around her home and family. How fantastic.

Me: She's obsessive compulsive. Must be a nightmare to live with.

v.28. Her children arise up and call her blessed, her husband also and he praiseth her.
HS: She is a success because her children and her husband said so.
Me: Her kids know she's OCD and so does her husband, so they all sleep in.

v.29 Many daughters have done virtuously, but thou excellest them all.
HS: She is the best female in the pack.
Me: Why is her husband speaking to her as a father? Will the competition go on forever between her and the other daughters? Am I the only one who finds these things gross?

v.30 Favour is deceitful and beauty is passing, but a woman who fears the Lord is to be praised.
HS: God doesn't care if you're beautiful, only that you're a good Christian woman.
Me: So the winner is the girl who's the most scared of God. Great.

Perhaps if we girls had been offered something else besides marriage to make us worthwhile and childbearing to save us, the story would have had more appeal. Not that there's anything wrong with either. But, while the girls at youth group were designing their dream wedding dresses, and the excitement was exclusively about engagements, weddings, and babies, specifically in that order, thank you, I just wanted to know, what else?

Our role models were pastors' wives, and sometimes at a stretch, pastors themselves; still, it didn't matter how many books they had written or smells from alcoholics they had borne with a smile, nothing they accomplished was as wonderful, as fulfilling, and as important as being a good wife and mother. For, according to the natural order of things, God is like the CEO, and Jesus is his managing director. The human husband is the head of the household. Then the wife, then the kids. The way it's supposed to be.

I was spending my time preparing for university, and the girls around me were getting ready to get married. Was there really nothing else?

After finishing high school without going technically insane from these doubts and sinful thoughts about the ridiculousness of the Bible, I went to university and started an Arts degree. I enrolled in Biblical

Studies, ready to learn the answers to my questions from an academic point of view.

Shockingly, the lecturer taught on the assumption that the Bible was contradictory in multiple ways that I had not yet even imagined, and he had evidence to boot. The conflict within branched out unexpectedly, and I found it impossible to complete the course. Could these people not see that there was an ultimate logic to the Bible that just hadn't quite explained itself yet? And then a pagan pressed a feminist text into my hand. It was very difficult to understand at first, because it talked about women as if they were something other than virgins, wives, or mothers. The more I went on, though, the more sense it seemed to make, heretical or not.

Feminism mentioned that there might be more to life than flax, wool, and scarlet. And, hesitantly, I listened to this strange articulation of so many of the questions in my mind. I was sold. Yes, people, feminism is a gateway ideology to atheism. The fundamentalists know it, and I know it. You light that fire and there may be no going back.

After getting my head around feminism, I began to understand sociology. I conceded, after a prolonged time, that there were many people living out there happily without Jesus. But, while I no longer attended Hillsong after I was about 20, I spent years convinced I was hell-bound. Old emotional beliefs die hardest.

It wasn't until 2002, about 12 years after I stopped attending Hillsong, that, having heard rumour of a scandal, I went back. Even then, I still wished things could be different, but I knew that I was more than a little unsaved. At this meeting, Brian Houston, the senior pastor of Hillsong, made an announcement after the service concerning his father, Frank, by this time old and in retirement. Frank, the pilgrim from New Zealand who had founded Hillsong's mother church, Sydney Christian Life Centre, had been accused of a 'serious moral failure', according to Brian. That he had been accused of numerous sex offences against young people was never specifically named. Brian's plea was for prayers and support for his family. No mention of the Church's zero tolerance for child abuse, or compensation for the alleged victims. And, while the congregation gave a standing ovation, I realised that if anyone was hell-bound, it wasn't me.

Three years after that disturbing and liberating Sunday morning, I was doing research for my book on Hillsong, *People in Glass Houses* (2007). I came into contact with a successful young man whose brother had converted to Pentecostalism as a university student and had never left the Church. This man told me that he had investigated the entire movement thoroughly, first hand, in order to reach out to his brother. All he found was fraud and nonsense, and the chasm between him and his brother was growing wider.

One evening, we sat down to discuss his findings. I took the opportunity to ask him all those nagging questions that were still plaguing me years later. What made this meeting different was that my acquaintance, an atheist, was not afraid of questions. He answered each one with the logic, science, and scepticism I had been craving. My biblical world view had been long thinned out, but that night it shattered.

Suddenly, my state of mind went from black and white to colour. All of the restrictions of fundamentalism seemed to vanish as I considered philosophy, art, anthropology, science, literature, and culture in a whole new light. The greys weren't grey at all. They were human. Love, fear, anger, joy, lust, sloth, hatred, and jealousy were human experiences, not just categories on the Do and Don't lists. People were people, not walking mistakes to be corrected.

The Bible didn't make sense because it doesn't make sense. How revolutionary. The Bible seems like a collage of psychotic episodes, archaic laws, and drunken poetry — because it is. This was very exciting, and exponentially liberating.

From then, I was an atheist. Another religion had never been an option, nor had a softer, more inviting and inclusive form of Christianity. I'm too easily distracted to meditate, and had no desire to do this life the first time, much less be reincarnated to start over. Besides, spending over a decade tormented by the ridiculousness and immorality of Christianity versus the destruction of my everlasting soul had been plenty for me.

The next day, I asked my neighbours and lots of other people, 'Are you an atheist?' Surprisingly, a lot of them said yes. I giggled like I'd found a secret club of renegades. I'd never even thought to ask. Since then, it's been hard to see life through mystical glasses at all. Logic is liberation.

Not all atheists are feminists, and not all feminists are atheists. I am both because I believe they have so much to offer each other. And it sure beats being a Proverbs 31 girl. There's nothing I like more than a hot loaf of the bread of idleness, fresh out of the oven with a stick of butter.

I can't sew, I'm hopeless at farming, and don't wear a whole lot of purple. But I have freedom of thought, which is worth way more than rubies. And maybe, if we keep working at it, Sara will some day, too.

NOTES

1. Deuteronomy 28: 'If a man happens to meet a virgin who is not pledged to be married and rapes her and they are discovered'; 29: 'he shall pay the girl's father 50 shekels of silver. He must marry the girl, for he has violated her. He can never divorce her as long as he lives'.

GROWING UP ATHEIST

Hon. Lee Rhiannon
Green Member for the Senate

WHEN I WAS LITTLE, BEDTIME WAS A HAPPY TIME. MY FATHER, A WONDERFUL storyteller, would weave words into magical worlds for me. My favourite character that he created was Sammy the Sea-elf, a wee person who lived in a cave under the rock platform at North Bondi. From quite a young age, my father also started regaling me with tales from history, science, and politics.

Some may reel back in horror and interpret this as indoctrination of the young. For me, these stories were ventures into the world of ideas, and they stimulated my quest for knowledge. I grew up with what our family called 'dell' and 'bell' stories — 'dell' came from 'fairy-dell', and was short for make-believe stories. 'Bell' was a corruption of 'sensible', and short for factual stories. By the time I was about ten or 11, Dad was still offering me the choice of a 'dell' or a 'bell' story. I favoured the latter.

These days, as a Greens Party MP I spend much of my time talking with people — in parliament, at briefings and community meetings, and in many informal discussions and chats. At a recent event, I addressed a group of Christians. At the break, a young woman approached me to pleasantly explain how much God meant to her, and asked if I could answer some of her questions.

In summary, her questions boiled down to: what do I believe in? She said she had not met an atheist before, and was concerned for me, as she did not understand how I could have a belief system without God being part of my life. I tried to convey to her that I have a strong set of values and aim to live each day by my principles. I also explained to her that I am very happy with my life. We had what I thought was an interesting discussion, but I think she went away still troubled that I did not have God in my life. To be fair, she was not arguing that everyone should believe in a Christian God, but she clearly thought my life would improve if I connected with some god.

For me, the conversation triggered thoughts of my life, growing up as an atheist. My parents were atheists and all the significant adults in my younger years were atheists. It is too simplistic, however, to say I was raised an atheist. I was raised to analyse, criticise, and evaluate the world around me. It was not so much that I was taught there was no God, but that I was educated about what was known about our world, the importance of values and principles, and respect for those with different views. God as an all-powerful, all-knowing force did not figure in my upbringing. God could not explain the world around me. While I certainly missed out on gaining some knowledge of the workings of different religions, I would in no way change what I gained.

When I was young, my parents were members of the Communist Party of Australia. We often had people visiting, and discussions and debates would ensue about the latest ban-the-bomb activities, campaigns to raise living standards, and various union-based actions.

For me, the political struggles of the 1960s were experienced with Australia becoming increasingly involved in the Vietnam War, and the Askin and Menzies governments' attacks on unions and workers. With my two uncles active members of the Waterside Workers Federation (today the Maritime Union of Australia) and many of our visitors active unionists, I was hearing about these struggles firsthand. I was picking up that life was not just about analysing the world, but also about having a say and working with others to right wrongs. My school days expanded the wide horizons that home life offered.

Even when my parents decided that I should go to religious instruction classes in primary school, my own outlook did not shift. In making this decision, my parents had not had a change of heart about their beliefs. I can remember that they discussed their decision with me. They strongly believed students should not be obliged to go to scripture, but they did not want me singled out because of their views. Their main concern was that they did not want me isolated from my local and school community. My father also talked to me about respecting other viewpoints.

So, off I went to Church of England scripture classes. As my only foray into formal religious classes, I was left no wiser about the workings of the Church. The minister for our weekly classes was very elderly, and the primary-school boys figured he was fair game and peppered his attempts to convey his favourite Bible passages with the constant question, 'Who made God?' The old minister had not learnt the art of handling the curly questions, so the message I took away was that the Church is short on answers.

After a time, I decided I no longer wanted to attend these classes. As the only child who did not go to scripture, I was offered the wholesome option of cleaning the school toilets. Fortunately, this arrangement did not last long after my parents went to the school to complain.

At high school, it turned out that I was among three or four students who had the all-important note from their parents that they could skip scripture. We were left to our own devices to do some schoolwork or run messages for the teachers. I was certainly not on the outer at high school because of my views or those of my parents. My public education was what I would hope all children of all nations have access to, as we had excellent teachers that educated and challenged us. My high-school years were in the 1960s, and the shakedown of years of conformity had already touched our all-girls school. The principal tolerated, and in her own way encouraged, our political actions — opposition to the Vietnam War was a strong commitment of many fellow students and myself. My science and English teachers expanded my horizons, so each day was a delight.

My passion was science. Although, at the time, I was in no way on a mission to find my own proof of the origins of the world to combat the narrow, simplistic view that God made everything, I can remember being delighted by classes on evolution and how life first appeared on our planet.

Growing up in the 1960s, I barely had a thought for religion. It really did not figure in my life. But for some of the students I went to school with, it did. There were a few devout Christians, and they started off each day with a prayer-group event. I remember at times reflecting on what I thought would be the contradictions they would grapple with, as they undertook studies that, for me, in terms of a logical, rational approach to the world, exposed their religion as just a set of stories with no factual basis. But there lay another lesson for me. For most of these young women, there was no anguish. Their beliefs sat comfortably with their education, which for me exposed and undermined the very basis of God-centred beliefs.

Around this time, I joined the Young Humanists. While we organised a few events on politics, philosophy, and ideologies, this largely served as an excellent social network. Some came to the Young Humanists through friends. For others, our parents encouraged us to join. This was a time of great transition, where the dominance of religion in so many aspects of life was starting to fall away, and I think our parents were looking for ways for us to socialise outside church-based activities.

My passions at this time were biology and politics. My science teacher was brilliant, and I loved my lessons and studies. I can still remember being taught about photosynthesis. I was amazed. To my mind, that one lesson explained so much about the world — sunlight, food production, atmospheric gases. It opened up an understanding of the astonishing interconnectedness of our natural world.

It was around this time that someone gave me a copy of Irving Stone's *Clarence Darrow for the Defence* (1941). I think this was the first book that I could not put down. I was already aware of the attempts of creationists to discredit the work of Darwin and the theory of evolution. Stone's book covers the famous US case that became known as the Scopes-Monkey Trial. I was shocked to read that a teacher, John Scopes, was charged under an Act that prohibited the teaching of evolution. In Tennessee schools at that time, it was illegal for public-school teachers to teach that human beings evolved from other organisms.

The way Mr Darrow built up his case and cross-examined the witnesses was thrilling. I can remember being deeply moved by this book, thinking of my own teachers, and wondering how this terrible case had impacted on Mr Scopes. I realised that I had not considered that people who did not adhere to a strict religious outlook could still be persecuted.

Stone's book was an exciting read, with some powerful lessons for me in regard to the damage that conservative forces can exert, through legal process, on freedom of expression and the right to an evidence-based education. The excitement of this trial lived on for our family through the Hollywood movie *Inherit the Wind* (1960). My father was keen on most movies, and we saw this film, with Spencer Tracy playing a fictionalised version of Clarence Darrow, on a number of occasions. He was a fan of Spencer Tracy, but I am sure the theme of this movie was also something that he delighted in.

My atheism also gave me a framework for raising my own children. When they started at school, attending non-scripture was no longer an issue. Lots of parents chose this option for their children.

In the ensuing years, I have watched how the debate around non-scripture time has developed. I see it as an enormous advance that, in the space of a few decades, there has been a shift from an expectation that all students will attend school-based scripture to consideration of studies on ethics and philosophy being offered to students who do not attend the weekly religious instruction classes.

The long-standing New South Wales education policy actually prohibits children from undertaking any formal education during the periods allocated for scripture. The pressure is mounting for this to change. I understand that seven Parent and Citizen associations in this state have nominated their school to be part of a pilot for the teaching of ethics while other students attend religious instruction. For the public-education system, I think in time we will come to question if there should be any religious instruction in schools at all. There is a clear argument that the family, and not our public schools, should handle religious matters.

As a parliamentarian, one of the few times I have actively engaged in the issue of religion was in my early years as an MP, when I unsuccessfully attempted to replace the Christian prayer recited at the beginning of sittings with a non-denominational statement. My thinking was that this would be step towards creating a more inclusive and tolerant state, as parliament was home to MPs of many faiths and beliefs, representing a similarly diverse community.

The curious thing is that, as Australian society has become increasingly secular, religion has more than ever begun to creep back into political life. The musings of former prime ministers Kevin Rudd and John Howard, and, most recently, Joe Hockey, on religion are a case in point.

As I reflect back on my years as an atheist, I am conscious of how rarely I have used that word to describe myself. There is definitely no shame in using the term. Apart from filling out forms, it was not the starting point for how I have defined myself. These days, I like to weave into conversations my atheist outlook.

One thing that got me thinking about how we present as atheists was a recent Gay and Lesbian Mardi Gras. There was a huge contingent of the Sydney Atheists, and I took great pleasure in seeing such a public display from those with a non-god-centred view of the world. It was the first time I had seen a group of atheists come together in such a public way.

So, after a lifetime of what I had thought was as an open and proud atheist existence, I have decided that it is time to out myself even more.

AGNOSTICS ARE NOWHERE MEN

David Horton
Author, retired zoologist and archaeologist

PEOPLE OFTEN CLAIM TO BE AGNOSTICS IN RELATION TO RELIGION IN MUCH the same way as every politician, no matter how far right their ideology, will claim to be a centrist. It seems to be seen as a kind of cosy position to occupy, not frightening the horses of atheist or theist, and at the same time presenting oneself as being oh-so-reasonable — a person who is prepared to listen to the evidence from all sides before making up their mind. Not for them the certainties of denying or affirming the existence of a god; no, the eternal sunshine of the agnostic mind is always waiting for one more piece of evidence before finally making a decision.

And to the outside world, that is, the media, agnostics are also seen as being part of the reasonable centre, not one of the happy-clappy-evangelicals, or those stern, grey atheists (no better than communists, really), but just good, honest, make-up-your-mind-when-the-evidence-is-all-in, average citizens. Agnostics tend to be seen by theists as ripe for the plucking: people willing to suspend disbelief when tempted by the odd miracle, or good music, or splendid robes. They tend to be seen by atheists as people on the right side of the barricades, needing only a bit more of an injection of rationality to come out of the closet and pull on the 'I fundamentally believe in atheism' T-shirt.

Agnostics see themselves as jolly, reasonable people, and as realists who acknowledge the inconvenient truth that it appears to be equally true that if the religious can't prove the existence of God nor can atheists prove the non-existence of God. 'Why can't an atheist be more like an agnostic?' they sing. 'Agnostics are so honest, so thoroughly square; eternally noble, historically fair ... so pleasant, so easy to please. Whenever you're with them, you're always at ease.' The world would be a much better place, they think, if we could just get rid of all this unseemly squabbling between atheist and theist and settle down to the mellow world of the agnostic where everyone gets along.

So all-pervasive has this mythology become that atheists are constantly criticised these days for being nasty to the religious believers. If only they could play nice like the agnostics, so the story goes, then we could all get along, and the religious believers, with their noses no longer out of joint as a result of the ceaseless atheist attacks, might themselves gradually see the light and convert to agnosticism, and then the world would be a paradise, with virgins for all.

A similar kind of dialogue has emerged as the creationists try to extend their intelligently designed tentacles further and further into schools everywhere. And once again, the opposition to this move is framed as those nasty Darwinists being totally unreasonable when just a little give and take would see everyone happy. There are, sadly, just so many stubborn people obstructing the oh-so-reasonable demands of the world of religion.

That standard bearer of American twenty-first-century enlightenment, ex-Governor of Alaska and Republican candidate for Vice President of the United States in 2008, Sarah Palin last year, during the election campaign, expressed her belief that creationism should be taught in schools:

'Teach both. You know, don't be afraid of information ... Healthy debate is so important and it's so valuable in our schools. I am a proponent of teaching both ... My dad did talk a lot about his theories of evolution,' she said. 'He would show us fossils and say, "How old do you think these are?"'

Asked for her personal views on evolution, Palin said, 'I believe we have a creator'.[1] In her response, of course, Palin is just parroting the various pastors she's come into contact with, and is also following the Republican Party of Alaska platform on education:

We support teaching various models and theories for the origins of life and our universe, including Creation Science or Intelligent Design. If evolution outside a species (macro-evolution) is taught, evidence disputing the theory should also be presented.[2]

American writer Debi Smith, in an otherwise refreshing attack on Palin (for example, on how she reconciled her religious beliefs with the invasion of Iraq), says:

Maybe there is such a thing as intelligent design AND evolution. And I might agree (though I haven't given it a ton of deliberation) that both evolution and creation could be taught. Why not? Why can't we show all sides, anyway? What exactly are we afraid of? A revolution of learning and ideas? Do we really need to compartmentalise learning, and our youth, by denying them the ability to debate the issue fully and openly (without undue influence or coercion from either camp)? And who knows, maybe by opening it all up, we'd evolve more quickly towards comprehending the grand theory of everything scientists are searching for (and which just might prove the existence of intelligent design and evolution).[3]

So this is, apparently, a more thoughtful version of Palin, and an appeal to reason and logic and fairness that has been the modus operandi of those evangelicals wanting to teach creationism under the guise of 'intelligent design'. Who could argue, eh? Let the two 'theories' contend, and let children make up their own minds ('without undo influence or coercion from either camp').

What nonsense, and based on a complete misunderstanding of how science works. Are Debi and Sarah proposing that we teach the geocentric theory of the solar system (or the universe) alongside the heliocentric one ('without undue influence or coercion from either camp')? Do medical students get taught about the humours as well as bacteria and viruses? Is witchcraft back on the agenda? Um, well, yes, apparently. Does spontaneous generation hold its own? Phlogiston? How about teaching psychology students about demonic possession? Oh, hang on — Sarah would certainly want that one, too. Do genetic students learn about the role of blood in transmitting inheritance as well as DNA? Is there a place for crystal spheres, the homunculus in the sperm, the constant manufacture of blood by the liver, the inheritance of acquired characteristics, the music of the spheres, and unicorns? Does alchemy reappear in the chemistry class? Do Earth, Air, Fire, and Water get equal time with the periodic table of elements? Do stones fall at different rates depending on their weight?

And the answer, of course, is an emphatic 'NO'. All of these topics (as well as creationism, aka 'intelligent design') are important in understanding the history of science. And that is all. They are dealt with early in a science course, as a means of understanding how we got from there to here; but the proposition that all of these once-held, but now long-discarded, beliefs should remain in any scheme of teaching ('without undo influence or coercion from either camp') is laughable. 'Intelligent design' isn't an equally tenable theory with evolution; it is the theory that was discarded by scientists as the reality of evolution was demonstrated over 100 years ago. It is no different to any of the other discarded theories in the other sciences. Old theories don't run in some parallel universe where they remain equally valid: they are replaced, superseded, left behind.

And furthermore, while university students can happily deal with the idea that over the last few hundred years science has developed its understanding, we don't ask school children ('without undo influence or coercion from either camp') to decide for themselves whether alchemy is a valid approach to chemistry, or whether the Earth goes around the sun, or vice versa; we simply teach them the facts. And if this is coercion from one side, then so be it. Reality does have a coercive bias.

So next time you hear this innocent-sounding, ever-so-reasonable, 'teach both sides' proposition, ask yourself where you would draw the line — at what point do you decide that something doesn't have 'two sides'? But you don't have to make that decision — science makes it for you. All you have to do is teach the latest scientific findings (with or without some historical background, where needed, to provide context) — science is the mechanism that human beings have developed to investigate the real world. Once you start presenting ancient mythologies as having equal weight with the latest scientific knowledge, you are well on the way back to medieval times, where monks were the teachers and the Bible was the textbook. Ultimately, we would turn all schools into madrassas, differing only in the brand of religion with which the chanting students are being indoctrinated. And then we would need a whole new scientific revolution to repeat history and get us back to where we were before this religious insanity re-emerged in the late-twentieth century.

'Religious insanity' provides a neat segue into the topic of this essay. If you understand that there is no evidence, absolutely no evidence, no evidence of any kind, not even a scintilla of a suggestion that there might be some evidence — if we only knew where to look — for the existence of anything you might call God (or indeed anything of any supernatural kind), then you are an atheist, not an agnostic. And if you think there is such evidence, then you are a theist, not an agnostic. Let's see, that means the place for agnostics is ... nowhere. Or at least in a surreal queue waiting for evidence that there isn't even a suggestion of. A bit like waiting at a blank wall in the vain hope someone will build an ATM in front of you ... at some point, maybe.

Being agnostic is a bit like voting for the Iraq war and then saying later that you only did so because of the dodgy intelligence, knowing all along that there wasn't dodgy intelligence; there was in fact no intelligence — the war was going to happen because of neoconservative ideology. Or like pretending that there was no difference between Gore and Bush. Or like being a little bit pregnant. Either you believe that something supernatural called 'God' exists or you don't. There isn't any halfway house in this element of human culture. There is no spectrum of proof for the existence of a supernatural being ranging from no proof, through to sort of more-or-less-suggestive proofs, through to strong, hard evidence. If there was such a spectrum then an atheist would be one who believed that none of the proofs were any good, a theist that all the proofs were really believable, and an agnostic that there was no hard evidence, but that some of the suggested proofs had some merit. But there isn't such a spectrum. Accepting any of the so-called proofs for the existence of God makes someone theist, not agnostic, and accepting none of them makes someone atheist, not agnostic.

So, no room for agnostics, and it's time they declared themselves — are you with us or against us? (Now, who said that before?) If you are not on the side of the atheist angels then you are on the side of the evangelical devils. And there is a battle coming for the soul of the Enlightenment, for rationalism, and humanism, and a return to secular societies. If you are not on the side of the humanists, then you are on the side of the people who strap explosives to their bodies and explode them in a crowded market place. Or on the side of the evangelicals holding up placards saying, 'Death to Faggots'.

So come on, you 'agnostics', which way are you going to jump from the fence, and which side of the barricades are you going to land on? There are only two sides, not three, to the question of religion, and if you aren't part of the solution you are part of the problem. Come on down! Or as seventeenth-century English dramatist Thomas Otway said in 1683, 'These are rogues that pretend to be of religion now! Well, all I say is, honest atheism for my money.'[4]

There are many things in life about which we can be absolutely certain — gravity comes to mind, and the evolution of the Galápagos finches, and the circulation of blood, and the importance of gun control. An agnostic about gravity could quickly become a believer in it by stepping out of their apartment window. Which perhaps indicates that an agnostic requires a visceral slap in the face to recognise something as true or false in any practical sense of the words. The question then becomes: how much evidence or lack of it is required to give the agnostic that slap?

On the other hand, there are many things that no one could believe in: George Bush as a great president; or a 6000-year-old Earth balanced on the back of a tortoise; or Fox News as a fair and balanced place for political debate. So, no room for agnosticism about any of those, or you might start thinking there were weapons of mass destruction in Iraq, or find yourself up to your eyebrows in turtle poo.

But there are many things one could be agnostic about. Here is an example from the political history of which Sarah Palin was a part. It was often asked in 2008 whether Barack Obama would be a progressive or a conservative (with a small c) president of the United States. There were people who passionately believed that Barack was JFK re-incarnated, and would govern in the same enlightened and liberal way as that great man. There are others who believed with equal passion that Obama only differed from Hilary Clinton in being black and male, and would be just as much a creature of the corporations and the Democratic Leadership Council as she would. Both beliefs were passionately held, both could draw on much evidence for either conclusion, and both were argued vigorously. But neither proposition could be proved, and the third belief one could hold (which I hold), is an agnostic one — that we don't have enough evidence either way to be sure, and that we won't really know until he is well into his first term as president, or even long after he is gone, from the vantage point of history.

Agnosticism is also possible in relation to whether there is life elsewhere in the universe. And this is interesting, but is the reverse of the situation with religion. There is no direct evidence that life exists elsewhere in the universe. You could then simply deny that there is any other life, or you could believe there is and that the evidence will be found sooner or later. Or you could say: we know life arose once on this remarkably unremarkable planet. We now know that other stars do indeed have planets. And we even know that there are stars with planets that are potentially Earth-like in both size and position, relative to their own star. Since we can observe very few planets, we can logically deduce that there would be many billions more of such potential Earth-like planets. An agnostic might say, 'Well, chances are, that means there is highly likely to be life on other planets.'

'On the other hand,' our astronomical agnostic might say, 'it could be that the chances of life evolving on Earth were very small, and therefore by chance it may never have arisen elsewhere.' So you could certainly be genuinely agnostic about the chances of life elsewhere in the universe.

But there is simply no comparable position in relation to a 'god'. No equally balanced sets of data, no probabilities to be evaluated. There is, simply, no evidence of any kind for a 'god'. Indeed, the total lack of evidence is seen by religions as a plus, because the less evidence there is, the more faith (which is a virtue after all) is required. And faith, they think, trumps rational thought. Only in sheep, say I. That is, to be an agnostic about anything requires evidence both for and against a proposition, with the agnostic balanced equally between the two. This doesn't mean a balance between 'there might be; prove there isn't' and 'there isn't; you prove there is'— those are mutually exclusive ways of looking at the world. This whole debate about agnosticism is interesting not because of agnostics themselves, but because of the insights it can give into how we know about things, and why we believe in things.

The scientist starts with the strongest belief of those things for which there is the most data, gained from experiment or observation, and as they move down through subjects with less and less data or poor quality data, so they proceed with greater and greater caution. The religious follower, on the other hand, has the strongest belief for things for which there is no evidence, strong belief in things for which there is little evidence, and, as often as not, rejects propositions fully supported with data if they conflict with religious ideology. Those who say they are agnostic about religion need to think about which of those scales they belong on. So keep your 'agnosticism' for politics where it is healthy (I don't think a passionate faith in any politician is good for democracy). But in relation to religion? Either come into the church or stay out, but don't stand in the doorway or block up the halls.

It is worth noting that the 'atheism as a religion' misunderstanding is alive and well. I have been accused of demanding that people believe exactly what I believe, and therefore I am no better than a religious leader. I want to respond to this not in order, as it were, to clear my good name, but to make a more general point. While in many countries in the world, I would be killed for being an atheist, and in others I would be ostracised, and in many more I would either legally or practically be prevented from running for political office, the reverse — being persecuted for being a theist — is not true. I don't care what personal beliefs people have, and I have friends with a spectrum of beliefs on which we agree to disagree. Now, it is true that I think the world would be a better place if all six billion of us were atheists, but it is clear that I can't make that happen anytime in this millennium. Note that I don't think that the world would then be a perfect place, or even a good place. Human beings would still fight as a result of economics, or culture, or history, or skin colour, or psychology, or nationalism, but at least taking religion out of the mix removes one particularly tenacious reason for mutual distrust and hatred. Listen to fundamentalists of any religion and you will find yourself listening to psychotic thought processes that would get them put into a Cuckoo's nest. Trouble is, they have a get-out-of-the-asylum-free card — and that is religion.

In the second place, I am not suggesting that science knows everything. Even making such a suggestion reveals a misunderstanding of science, which can never know everything, by its very nature. But to say something like, 'Well, science has only just discovered dark matter, so how do you know God isn't out there, too, beyond the reach, either temporarily or permanently, of Earth-bound science?' is to misunderstand again the nature of science and, indeed, the nature of religion. It is commonplace that early societies on every continent, while understanding much about the natural world around them, nevertheless were completely mystified by phenomena such as thunder and lightning, the seasons, earthquakes, tides, madness, comets, life, and death. In addition, because they knew (and knew they knew) so little of the world, the dark corners of their knowledge became populated with dragons and demons. Out of all these known unknowns came religion, and I don't think we have to look any further at religion as an evolutionary product, or as being hardwired into human psychology (though some aspects of it for individuals are certainly genetic).

Now, what science has done in the last few hundred years (following on from much older work by the Greek and Arab cultures) is to work out, sometimes in broad terms, often in very fine detail, how our world (in the widest sense) functions. The whole framework is in place, through the work of scientists in all of the disciplines of astronomy, physics, biology, chemistry, geology, and so on. It is certainly the case that new discoveries are being made all the time, and in the case of astronomy and physics, big discoveries. Big questions are being asked, such as: is string theory the explanation of the structure of matter? How did matter come into being during the Big Bang? And is the universe infinite? We are also asking smaller questions, about the exact nature of particular stars and galaxies, or the history of Mars and Venus. But that doesn't mean that if we manage to make an even bigger and better telescope we will suddenly discover God lurking behind some dark matter, or sitting on a quasar just beyond the reach of current telescopes. I thought we had gone well beyond the concept of heaven being 'up there' beyond the stars, but it seems not when you read some comments from religious people. Science could have discovered 'God' but not by building bigger telescopes. I'll come back to that, but first a bit of a digression.

It has been said that there is no such thing as medicine and 'alternative medicine', there is simply medicine that works. That is, if there is anything among all the crazy beliefs about homeopathy, and naturopathy, and iridology, and Chinese herbs, and reflexology, and crystals, then it will, when demonstrated to be effective, be adopted by mainstream medicine. This stuff isn't rejected because of stubbornness, but because in order to know whether a treatment is effective it has to be scientifically tested. Mere belief doesn't cut it when it comes to cures for cancer, or making the lame walk. Similarly, one of my respondents noted that there is really no such thing as the supernatural. There is the natural world, and then if something appeared from beyond the natural world, as it were, it would be incorporated into an enlargement of our understanding of the limits of the natural world (this is essentially the case with dark matter, for example).

Now we can return to the question of scientists finding God (so to speak — I don't, by the way, believe that you can be both religious and a scientist, but that's just one of my many prejudices). What 300 or so years of science has given us is not just an understanding of how individual parts of our world work — how the brain functions, how the solar system was formed, the history of the Grand Canyon, the chemistry of our bodies, gravitational forces, and so on — but how all of these individual studies fit together. When science began, it began as a single subject; that is, natural philosophy (as distinct from religion). Over time, it was split into more and more subjects as the amount of knowledge became far too much for any one brain to handle, and people became more and more specialised. But these different subjects — astronomy, biology, physics, and the rest — don't operate in isolation from one other. Nor do they contradict one other. They are, quite clearly, all reporting back on the same universe. Nothing uncovered by the geologist contradicts what the biologist is working on; the chemist is unsurprised by theories on the composition and function of distant stars; the physicist has no quarrel with the climatologist; the psychologist and physiologist are comfortable dinner companions; the botanist and archeologist can lie down together in an excavation.

In a god-driven universe, none of that could be true. By now, cracks would be appearing as tens of thousands of scientists work away at finer and finer details. At some point, someone would have said: 'Just a minute, this experiment isn't working, there is some unknown factor coming into play.' At some point, a biologist would find a species with no evolutionary history; a doctor would find a miraculous recovery; a geologist would find that the Earth was only 6000 years old; a chemist would find a mixture of chemicals that behaved in some inexplicable way. In short the supernatural would begin to appear, as the whole natural structure described by science was revealed as being affected by some outside agency. And then the religious leaders could say, 'I told you so,' and the scientists would eagerly set about trying to uncover the nature of this mysterious outside agency that had previously only revealed itself to the Pope and his brother Infallibles.

This hasn't happened, of course, and we are at least 100 years beyond it happening. It ain't going to happen now. The last gasp of an attempt to find it is the phoney science of 'intelligent design', and the craziness of the young Grand Canyon and the humans with dinosaurs on Noah's Ark. These are people who are pretending to be scientists who have found evidence of Christianity, processes that don't fit within the mainstream scientific body of knowledge. Just like homeopaths, who pretend to have found cures that are beyond mainstream medicine. But there is no such thing as 'alternative medicine', and no such thing as 'alternative science', only science that can be tested and proved.

To come back to the main point — there is no alternative body of learning which points to a god of any kind — there really is just the natural world. So there is no room for agnosticism as a general philosophy in relation to religion.

This is not to say that you couldn't be agnostic about the historicity of some parts of the Bible. I think that most of it is mythology, or poorly recorded distant folk memories, or wishful thinking. For example, was Jesus Christ a real person? Not much evidence (indeed, arguably none) for such a person, but I think this proposition is one you could be reasonably agnostic about.

But whether or not there was a real person who corresponded in some way to some of the events, described in such contradictory ways in some of the manuscripts that got included in the random collection of ancient bits and pieces we now call the Bible, is irrelevant when it comes to the 2000 years of failure to demonstrate the presence of any kind of supernatural element beyond the world of science, described so well after 200 years of success. Agnosticism about some events and causes in the passing parade of history is a valid intellectual position. Agnosticism about alternative medicine, or climate change, or evolution, or imaginary friends, is not.

NOTES

1. T. Kizzia, 'Creation Science Enters the Race', *Anchorage Daily News*, 27 October 2006, at www.adn.com/sarah-palin/background/story/217111.html

2. Republican Party of Alaska, at www.alaskarepublicans.com/partyplatform.aspx [link no longer active]

3. D. Smith, 'My Lunch with Sarah', 1 October 2008, at www.commondreams.org/view/2008/10/01

4. T. Otway, *The Atheist*, Act III, 1.31, 1684.

STORM

Tim Minchin
Comedian, musician

Inner North London, top-floor flat,
All white walls, white carpet, white cat,
Rice paper partitions,
Modern art and ambition.
The host's a physician,
Bright bloke, has his own practice,
His girlfriend's an actress —
An old mate of ours from home —
And they're always great fun
So to dinner we've come.

The fifth guest is an unknown,
The hosts have just thrown
Us together as a favour
Cos this girl's just arrived from Australia
And she's moved to North London
And she's the sister of someone
Or has some connection.

As we make introductions
I'm struck by her beauty —

She's irrefutably fair
With dark eyes and dark hair,
But as she sits,
I admit I'm a little bit wary,
Cos I notice the tip of the wing of a fairy
Tattooed on that popular area
Just above the derriere,
And when she says 'I'm Sagittarian'
I confess a pigeonhole starts to form ...
And is immediately filled with pigeon
When she says her name is Storm.

Chatter is initially bright and light-hearted,
But it's not long before Storm gets started:
'You can't know anything,
Knowledge is merely opinion,'
She opines, over her Cabernet Sauvignon
Vis-a-vis
Some unhippily
Empirical comment made by me.

'Not a good start,' I think.
We're only on pre-dinner drinks
And across the room
My wife widens her eyes,
Silently begs me, 'Be Nice' —
A matrimonial warning
Not worth ignoring,
So I resist the urge to ask Storm
Whether knowledge is so loose-weave
Of a morning
When deciding whether to leave
Her apartment by the front door
Or the window on the second floor.

The food is delicious and Storm,
Whilst avoiding all meat,
Happily sits and eats
As the good doctor, slightly pissedly,
Holds court on some anachronistic
Aspect of medical history
When Storm suddenly insists,
'But the human body is a mystery!
Science just falls in a hole
When it tries to explain the nature of the soul.'

My hostess throws me a glance —
She, like my wife, knows there's a chance
I'll be off on one of my rare but fun rants,
But I shan't.
But my lips are sealed.
I just want to enjoy the meal.
And although Storm is starting to get my goat,
I have no intention of rocking the boat ...
Although it's becoming a bit of a wrestle
Because, like her meteorological namesake,
Storm has no such concerns for our vessel:

'Pharmaceutical companies are the enemy
They promote drug dependency
At the cost of the natural remedies
That are all our bodies need.
They are immoral and driven by greed.
Why take drugs when herbs can solve it?
Why use chemicals
When homeopathic solvents can resolve it?
I think it's time we all returned to live
With natural medical alternatives.'

And try as hard as I like,
A small crack appears

In my diplomacy dyke.
'By definition,' I begin
'Alternative medicine,' I continue
'Has either not been proved to work,
Or been proved not to work.
Do you know what they call alternative medicine
That's been proved to work?
Medicine.'

'So you don't believe
In any natural remedies?'

'On the contrary, actually —
Before we came to tea
I took a natural remedy
Derived from the bark of a Willow tree,
A painkiller that's virtually side-effect free.
It's got a weird name ...
Darling, what was it again?
Maspirin? Baspirin?
Ah, Aspirin!
Which I paid about a buck for
Down at my local drugstore.'

The debate briefly abates
As our hosts collects plates,
But as they return with desserts
Storm pertly asserts,

'Shakespeare said it first:
There are more things in heaven and earth
Than exist in your philosophy.
Science is just how we're trained to look at reality.
It doesn't explain love or spirituality.
How does science explain psychics?
Auras? The afterlife? The power of prayer?'

I'm becoming aware
That I'm staring,
I'm like a rabbit suddenly trapped
In the blinding headlights of vacuous crap.
Maybe it's the Hamlet she just misquothed
Or the sixth glass of wine I just quaffed
But my diplomacy dyke groans
And the arsehole held back by its stones
Can be held back no more.

'Look, Storm, I don't mean to bore ya
But there's no such thing as an aura.
Reading auras is like reading minds
Or tea leaves or star signs or meridian lines.
These people aren't plying a skill,
They're either lying or mentally ill.
Same goes for those who claim to hear God's demands
And spiritual healers who think they have magic hands.

By the way,
Why do we think it's okay
For people to pretend they can talk to the dead?
Is it not totally fucked in the head
Lying to some crying woman whose child has died
And telling her you're in touch with the other side?
I reckon that's fundamentally sick.
Do we need to clarify here
That there's no such thing as a psychic?
What, are we fucking two?
Do we actually think that Horton Heard a Who?
Do we still believe that Santa brings us gifts?
That Michael Jackson didn't have facelifts?
Are we still so stunned by circus tricks
That we think that the dead would
Wanna talk to pricks
Like John Edward?'

Storm, to her credit, despite my derision,
Keeps firing off clichés with startling precision,
Like a sniper using bollocks for ammunition.

'You're so sure of your position
But you're just closed-minded.
I think you'll find
That your faith in science and tests
Is just as blind
As the faith of any fundamentalist.'

'Hm, that's a good point, let me think for a bit ...
Oh wait, my mistake,
That's absolute bullshit.
Science adjusts its beliefs
Based on what's observed.
Faith is the denial of observation
So that belief can be preserved.
If you show me that, say, homeopathy works,
Then I will change my mind,
I'll spin on a fucking dime;
I'll be embarrassed as hell,
But I will run through the streets yelling,
"It's a miracle! Take physics and bin it!
Water has memory!
And while its memory
Of a long-lost drop of onion juice seems infinite,
It somehow forgets all the poo it's had in it!"

You show me that it works and how it works
And when I've recovered from the shock,
I will take a compass and carve "fancy that"
On the side of my cock.'

Everyone's just staring now,
But I'm pretty pissed and I've dug this far down,

So I figure, in for penny, in for a pound ...
'Life is full of mysteries, yeah,
But there are answers out there.
And they won't be found
By people sitting around
Looking serious
And saying, "Isn't life mysterious?
Let's sit here and hope!
Let's call up the fucking Pope!
Let's go watch Oprah
Interview Deepak Chopra!"

If you're going to watch telly,
You should watch *Scooby Doo*.
That show was so cool,
Cos every time there was a church with a ghoul
Or a ghost in a school,
They looked beneath the mask, and what was inside?
The fucking janitor or the dude who ran the waterslide!
Because throughout history
Every mystery
Ever solved has turned out to be
Not magic.

Does the idea that there might be knowledge
Frighten you?
Does the idea that one afternoon
On Wiki-fucking-pedia might enlighten you
Frighten you?
Does the notion that there may not be a supernatural
So blow your hippy noodle
That you would rather just stand in the fog
Of your inability to Google?

Isn't this enough?
Just this world?

Just this beautiful, complex,
Wonderfully unfathomable
Natural world?
How does it so fail to hold our attention
That we have to diminish it with the invention
Of cheap, man-made myths and monsters?
If you're so into Shakespeare,
Lend me your ear:
"To gild refined gold, to paint the lily,
To throw perfume on the violet" ... is just fucking silly.
Or something like that.
Or what about Satchmo?
"I see trees of green,
Red roses too ..."
And fine, if you wish to
Glorify Krishna and Vishnu
In a post-colonial, condescending,
Bottled-up and labelled kind of way,
Then whatever, that's okay.
But here's what gives me a hard-on:
I am a tiny, insignificant, ignorant bit of carbon.
I have one life, and it is short
And unimportant ...
But thanks to recent scientific advances,
I get to live twice as long
As my great great great great uncleses and auntses.
Twice as long to live this life of mine.
Twice as long to love this wife of mine.
Twice as many years of friends and wine,
Of sharing curries and getting shitty
At good-looking hippies
With fairies on their spines
And butterflies on their titties.

And if perchance I have offended,
Think but this and all is mended:

We'd as well be ten minutes back in time,
For all the chance you'll change your mind.'

* EDUCATION

PUBLIC EDUCATION IN QUEENSLAND: SMART STATE OR EVANGELICAL PLAYGROUND?

Hugh Wilson MA
PhD candidate, member of the Australian Secular Lobby, Secular Public Education Lobby, The Fourth R, and the Back in the Act campaign

I maintain that State Schools are and must be the source of immense evil ... From the vilest of habitations, from the lowest of public houses, from the wretched tenements that crowd by-streets reeking with immorality of every description, the polluted children, who have never seen anything but vice, are gathered in and placed in daily intercourse with the children of the decent poor ...
— *Article in* The Register, *1884* [1]

MANY INTERNATIONAL-RELATIONS PRACTITIONERS LIKE TO BELIEVE THAT religion in the West played no significant part in the running of our notionally secular democratic nation-states from the Treaty of Westphalia in 1648 until the ill-fated date of 11 September 2001, which initiated the Bush-Blair-Howard triumphal 'crusade against evil'. Here in Queensland, the spectre of religion, more specifically Christianity, has haunted, stalked, and plagued our public education system since 1859, when Queensland was born.

Only briefly, from 1875 to 1910, was Queensland's public education system secular. Today, 100 years after the word 'secular' was expunged from the public education record and practice, the current education minister, and committed Christian, according to his electorate website, the Honourable Mr Geoff Wilson MLA, wrote to the Australian Secular Lobby (ASL) advising us that '... the government currently has no plans to re-introduce the word "secular" into legislation'.[2]

The ASL arose by accident, formed by concerned parents to tackle the increasingly prevalent evangelical religiosity of Queensland state schools.[3] This short account seeks to tell something of the nature of the problem first uncovered in 2006, at a primary school in Toowoomba. The initial problem, largely concerning the wrong application of religious instruction (RI) as a default position rather than the legislated-for option for parents and students, then exploded with the introduction of the Howard–Bishop National Schools Chaplaincy Program (NSCP). This was, and remains, a massive Howard 'Australian values' political-confidence trick, costing Australian taxpayers $165 million directly, and threatening to cost billions more if the Australian Christian Lobby (ACL) and its supporters from the many Christian sects get their.[4] The ACL hopes to see in place one fully-funded school chaplain in every school in Australia. Scripture Union (SU), the dominant Queensland employing authority for school chaplains in Education Queensland (EQ) state schools, refers to this taxpayer largesse as a 'downpour' and praise God, not Howard or we taxpayers, for it.[5]

Following close on the heels of school chaplains came hordes of evangelical church volunteers: Hillsong Church designed and implemented gendered programs and, more recently, Christian 'mentors' have been allowed to work alone with 'at risk' students. These have included Baptists and other religious believers, organised by the Baptist-centred organisation World Vision. Almost as a mild side distraction, the Queensland Studies Authority, the peak body that decides what school students learn, declines to 'design out' the allowed and practised teaching of creationism and intelligent design in Queensland state-school science classes, or in any other class an individual classroom teacher might feel inclined to inject a little 'religion' into.

All of this has been accepted without question by successive education ministers and premiers, all of whom now promote Queensland as 'the Smart State', presumably with our education system forming the rock on which Queensland's future stands.

For our part, the ASL believes that Queensland needs to put its 100 years of nonsecular public education behind us, dropping it into the sectarian dustbin of history from whence it first sprang. Queensland needs to fill the currently vacuous phrase 'the Smart State' with genuine meaning, embarking on a real 'education revolution' by first putting 'secular' back in the Act (the Queensland Education Act). Following that action, Queensland then has a chance to progress and develop into a multicultural, multi-faith, and non-faith state that is reflective of, and accepting of, the new cultural and religious realities of Queensland, of Australia, and of the so-called globalised world we all inhabit in the twenty-first century.

PROBLEMS EMERGE

In 2005, I was the Darling Downs Branch, Toowoomba District, elected representative of the peak Parents & Citizens' state body, the Queensland Council of Parents and Citizens' Association (QCPCA).

It was in this capacity that I dealt with a parent from a Toowoomba primary school. His daughter had been told in the RI class that, because she was a girl, she was a lesser person than a boy and, for good measure, she was informed that all sinners will burn forever in Hell. The parent was aghast, and took the school to task over the RI volunteer's attitudes. This sort of experience, so we have learned subsequently from dozens of parents across Queensland, is not unusual among today's evangelical RI volunteers.

I met the parent as he struggled against a wall of EQ obfuscation and directed him along the official path of complaint, into the district office, the regional office, and on to the director general's office. On the way, I managed to find a flow chart outlining how RI was supposed to work in schools in the *Religious Instruction in School Hours* (RISH) book, known within the hallowed halls of EQ in Mary Street as the Blue Book. This flow chart was so useful in the ensuing discussions that EQ subsequently 'disappeared' it, although they claimed it was 'being reviewed'.[6]

Actually, the Blue Book appears to have been held up by the Religious Education Advisory Committee (REAC), a little-known or publicised group of religious leaders and educators who meet with EQ quarterly. This group appears to have ready access to the inner ear of whichever minister sits in judgement of our education processes, and seems, to our supporters at least, to operate as theocratic fifth columnists, undermining any and all rational approaches to the proper role of public education. The REAC minutes are now freely available from EQ, and are well worth asking for to see just how complicit EQ has become in preventing the proper functioning of the Education Act requirements concerning RI, and to see how EQ employees fail, as far as the minutes show, to correct any wrong-headedness from the no doubt well-meaning but sadly ill-informed REAC members.

Toowoomba's *Chronicle* ran a story featuring our angry parent and his, by then, quite strident views on EQ's capacity to run our schools. An enquiry was established by EQ, but only following the punishing public exposé, and the school RI processes were examined.[7] From this experience, we uncovered many interesting insights into how EQ ignores the Education Act, how it uses RI as a default position to cram students into RI rather than allow access to the legislated-for 'alternative program', how it whitewashes parents, how staff coerce students and parents into RI against their wishes, and how the nexus between evangelical extremists from outside the school works with the more fervent evangelical staff from inside schools, and within senior management ranks.[8]

We also learned that 80 per cent of students at this school should never have been placed in the RI program, because their parents had not nominated a religion on the enrolment form.[9] From these abuses of trust, never mind the law, was born a localised web page called 'The Fourth R', designed to highlight these local issues before we knew how widespread the disregard for the Education Act was. From this group sprang the ASL, as we realised the full state-wide extent, and danger, of not having a secular public education system in Queensland.

EQ's level of contempt for the Education Act was stated in another *Toowoomba Chronicle* article later, in a quote from the Darling Downs QCPCA president. On being challenged by the then Education Minister, Rod Welford, EQ discovered our 80 per cent figure was quite conservative when taken across the state.[10] This is a significant finding that shows a widespread disregard for the intention of the Education Act of 1910 and the current one, right across EQ. This disregard of law and policy is the source of many of our 'religious' problems today in Queensland schools. Of chaplains, we shall learn more shortly.

1859–1875

When Queensland came into being, splitting from New South Wales into the new Australian colony in 1859, there was much debate over the future of education. Schools, all 13 of them, were split between 'national', with three at North Brisbane, Warwick, and Drayton, and ten 'denominational' church-run schools elsewhere. Governor Sir George Bowen undertook to keep all funded unless the new Queensland Parliament decided otherwise. The Board of National Education was established in 1860, but Bowen held back from establishing a denominational board because there were then no bishops from the Church of England, or Rome, in Queensland.

As the election to the first Queensland Legislative Assembly unfolded, one of the major issues of debate and division concerned state aid to religion, including the funding of denominational schools and the provision of secular teaching within them. High farce followed, and Queensland ended up with the requirement to have five hours of secular instruction five days a week in denominational schools removed altogether, and a sectarian form of state-funded education came about. Years of sectarian bickering ensued, and attempts were made to halt denominational teaching in state-aided schools while calls for a purely secular (meaning at that time a non-sectarian) education system arose. This ultimately led to a Royal Commission in 1874, chaired by Justice Lilley, an opponent of church schools, assisted by Samuel Walker Griffith, the attorney-general, also not a church-school supporter. The findings include this comment:

> ... dogmatic religious instruction is the business not of the State, but of the several churches; and that the State is neither entitled nor required to undertake the teaching of the distinctive doctrines of any sect or to contribute funds for that purpose.[11]

They could, however, see merit in allowing, before or after school, religious teachers to instruct members strictly of their own faith, who attended state schools, in special religious instruction. Not any hint of the term 'religious education' can be found — always 'religious instruction', and always strictly restricted to members of particular faith groups, or sects. And, of course, the only religion on offer was Christianity. The Royal Commission findings led to the Education Act of 1875.

An understanding of the 1875 Education Act is vital to appreciating the situation Queensland is in now. This Act produced a genuine 'education revolution', and one that someone like Prime Minister Rudd would not have the courage to repeat, never mind Premier Bligh. From 1875 to 1910, Queensland state schools were secular havens of rational thinking and teaching. There was no RI in school time, no Bible lessons, and no school chaplains recruiting for Jesus would have ever been allowed to set foot on the school grounds. It was a golden age for some, and, naturally enough, a time of despair and gnashing of teeth for the religious busybodies, zealots, and fearful faith-filled.

Sectarianism was, predictably enough, rife as Christian fought Christian to protect their flock from the perceived untruths of others. The Bible became an issue, with moral turpitude being seen as something that only the Good Book could resolve. One is reminded of the Governor of Virginia, Sir William Berkeley, who said, 'Thank God there are no free schools or printing ... for learning has brought disobedience and heresy into the world, and printing has divulged them ... God keep us from both'.[12]

The battle to get the Bible into schools resulted in the hand-wringing Bible League undertaking a referendum of its own membership, which saw a vote of 21,101 in favour and 1427 against. This was enough to convince Premier Robert Philp to change the Education Act regulations in 1902 to allow the first half-hour each day for clergy to give RI to those students whose parents gave permission. This was then withdrawn once the government realised it was in conflict with its own 1875 Act. This led, ultimately, to the whole state referendum of 1910, which introduced RI and Bible lessons in school hours.

The imposition by religious leaders on public school education has been going on since Queensland began. Not content with their own faith schools, funded these days by the long-suffering taxpayers, religionists continue to seek to impose their beliefs on everyone. The rise of secular schooling in 1875, though, must not be seen as a period of 'secular enlightenment'; rather, it was a reaction to too many Christian sects each wanting their own school system, which was finally understood to be as wasteful then as it is now. The move to secular public schooling in Queensland was also seen to be going further than many had intended it to. Apparently, so keen were the religionists to protect their own turf, none had actually understood the ramifications of their actions, and the pendulum of progress was clawed back a notch or two.

However, 1875 and 1910 were both a long time ago. The colony of Queensland was far more homogeneous then than it is now. Christianity was less of an issue than which sect of that same religion people belonged to.

The Queensland of today is very different and needs a different approach to how religion is discussed and taught in our public schools.

While it is impossible to state the precise numbers of EQ schools not complying with the Education Act as it relates to RI, we know from contact with parents who volunteer information, and from our own research of school web pages, that it is very high indeed. Schools frequently design their own documents, ignoring the EQ templates altogether, or altering them to deceive parents into thinking they must answer the optional 'what is your religion?' question. The forms dealing with RI, RIS Form C1 and RIS Form C2, are frequently not mentioned on the web page, or are unknown altogether in the school.[13] RIS Form C2 is misapplied in many schools and used as a second grab at filling the RI classes. Many school principals totally ignore the Education Act requirements to remove non-RI students from the RI class, leaving them sitting at the back of the class, despite the law. The NSCP funding requires parents to give informed consent via a 'chaplaincy consent form'; this all too often is unknown or not distributed by schools or, as we find on many school web pages, is the subject of another non-conforming redesign of the EQ template.

All this has been pointed out, numerous times, to EQ, the Department of Education, Employment and Workplace Relations (DEEWR), and the NSCP guardians, and generally it is ignored. Sometimes, as in Toowoomba, EQ compels 'this' principal to get everything in order but not 'that' principal, depending on whether the ASL has lodged a complaint with the EQ senior managers. But the minister and his directors general ignore all advice from us that EQ schools are not being run as the legislation and policy require them to be.

Since first Peter Beattie and then John Howard undertook to fund school-based religion more directly with our tax dollars, giving some $10 million of Queensland taxes and $165 million of Commonwealth taxes to provide frequently untrained and educationally unqualified school chaplains to state schools, the rate of religious intrusion into our non-secular public schools has multiplied. The figures from Gillard's department show that Queensland scored about one third of the $165 million, a telling statement on the mindset of Queenslanders themselves. Initially, Scripture Union (SU) was the sole provider of chaplains to EQ, and of the (about) 506 school chaplains in Queensland, one is now employed by the Buddhist employing authority, one or possibly two by independent Christian bodies, and the remainder by SU. Although the funding documents require the denomination of the chaplain to be discussed and agreed at the school level, and entered by the principal onto the DEEWR paperwork, DEEWR advises us that it has no idea what denomination at least 405 chaplains belong to, and neither is it the least bit concerned that this information is missing. The ASL has a fair idea that these 405 'missing in action' denominations can be listed under the generic rubric 'evangelical'.

The ASL has numerous reports from parents indicating that little or no public discussion and consultation was held within schools prior to the decision to take up the NSCP funding offer. When such matters have been raised with DEEWR, its response has been to ring the school principal and ask if the report is correct. When the inevitable negative response is received, DEEWR then considers its 'enquiries' are at an end and its task complete. The parents, however, have made it patently clear to us, that DEEWR has, all too frequently, simply handed cash out with little or no checking at the school level, and with little or no desire to conduct a total audit commensurate with reasonable expectations for the spending of public monies.

One of the outcomes of the NSCP funding has been to embolden evangelical/Pentecostal/fundamentalist/Baptist groups to push even deeper into the school grounds using Hillsong-designed and -owned programs, particularly 'Shine' for girls and 'Strength' for boys. These are gendered programs, ostensibly secular but clearly pro-religious, which means, of course, pro-Christian. One high school we have found does list 'Shine' as having 'religious content' on the chaplaincy section of the school web page, but such honesty is a rare find.

While EQ prohibits 'evangelising' and 'proselytising' within the school grounds, and DEEWR prohibit 'proselytising' at all on our tax dollars, there is little doubt from the reports the ASL receives that both occur when chaplains are about. One only has to read the chaplaincy plans that schools are required to post — but few do — on their websites to see this. Not only that but it is clear from the outset of SU involvement in state schools — funded, it must be noted, with an initial donation of $42,000 from the Assembly of God (AOG) sect in 1989 — that it was in this to recruit souls for Jesus. One only has to read the 'SU Queensland Strategic Objectives' contract, signed between SU and EQ school principals, to see just how closely EQ is working with SU to facilitate evangelising and proselytising in state schools. Judith Salecich quotes Richard Jessup, who said of the initial plan for school chaplains, 'It was Keith's vision ... His vision was to take the gospel to every secondary student in Queensland', which is not quite the same as John Howard's 'friend in the playground' offer.[14]

EQ approved the first AOG-inspired chaplain in 1990, five years after it had first acknowledged the intrusion of these evangelists into state schools with the 1985 'Policy Statement 2A — Religious Education in Schools'. In 1992, ALP education minister Pat Comben gave the green light for SU to become an employing authority. In 1994, the Queensland Teachers Union (QTU) complained that:

> The great increase in participation [of church communities in public schools] has been facilitated by officers of the Queensland Department of Education who have encouraged the promotion of and provided practical and financial support for, what is in essence the institutionalisation of church influence in state schools.[15]

The usual sectarianism that dogs Christianity continued throughout the 1990s, as Archbishop Hollingworth warned against the 'theological emphases' that might arise when allowing evangelical chaplains open access to state schools. Later, Hollingworth emphasised his concerns by saying that 'the work on the ground is being increasingly dominated by fundamentalist groups teaching a narrowed theology unacceptable to most mainstream churches'.[16] Hollingworth was right to hold those fears, as Salecich points out to her readers in a discussion on the 'official' and 'unofficial' aims of chaplains in state schools. Here we learn that:

> Unofficially, LCC personnel, school administrators (those who are Christians), SU Queensland staff and Chaplains, regard chaplaincy in Queensland state schools as a Christian ministry. Avis (1999) asserts that ministry is a means of fulfilling the task or purpose (i.e., mission) of the church.[17]

Naturally, SU CEO Tim Mander agrees with this view of chaplaincy as a path through the schoolyard directly into the soul of students and their families, as he expands on the great benefits to be gained from SU religious camps, when camps and school chaplaincy combine to recruit. Below, he is commenting on the drowning death of a girl on Easter Monday in 2009. First brought to an SU religious camp by her school chaplain during her primary school years, the girl was a high-school student when she drowned. As the church filled with SU chaplains, and her family and friends, to celebrate her life, Mander seems to be saying that she died in order to bring her community together in a demonstration of the value of SU and chaplaincy, in a sacrifice seemingly on a par with that of Jesus:

> For the majority, this was the first time they had been inside a church. This experience demonstrates that school chaplaincy and SU Qld camps mobilise whole communities. SU Qld's vision to engage children and young people with Jesus, the Bible and the local church has led to a whole community in the Caboolture area now experiencing connections to God and his Church.[18]

Mander and SU refer, in a rather patronising manner, to the role of state school chaplains as being to bring 'hope' to students, which is reminiscent of the Howard–Bishop view that state schools were values-free zones. It is hard to imagine that EQ can hear these statements about its/our 'hope-free' schools without ever flinching just a little at the sharpened stick being thrust into its eyes; but, evidently minister and director general after minister and director general are happy to admit, through their total silence, that state schools are indeed the empty shells with no 'hope' that Mander, SU, Howard, and Bishop have implied they are.

Perhaps the final indignity our public education system suffers from these days is provided here by a parent of six state school children. What follows is an account of just how the chaplain-inspired Shine program works in state schools. And here it must be understood that EQ has no 'official' idea what happens during these sessions (even though it seems many of its staff are involved in running them), no interest in 'officially' finding out, and has told the ASL that Shine is not endorsed by EQ, even though schools offer it as an alternative to compulsory sport. The ASL knows the identity of the author below and the school involved, but publishes this account here with all names withheld to protect both the parents and the students from EQ. The parent has said that should any suitably senior EQ manager determine that 'enough is enough', he will happily cooperate in the undoing of Hillsong's grip on state schools and on the minds of our children. His call for a return to a secular status echoes the call from the ASL to 'get secular back in the Act' and free our Queensland public education system from its current virtual theocratic status:

The following account is of my and my eldest child's experience so far with the 'Shine' programme as it is facilitated through my children's state school. I have six children and the experience I recount below was that only of my eldest. With five more children negotiating, or yet to negotiate, Queensland's public school system, which until recently I had supposed to be secular, I have a manifest duty to them to air my concerns wherever I can find a willing audience or platform.

I will state at the outset that I do not impose any belief systems on my children; rather, anything and everything is open for debate around our crowded dining table. Enquiring and sceptical thinking is encouraged in our house; indeed, this is how my concerns about Shine first emerged. Four of my six children lost their mother to cancer at an early age, and yet I doubt a better combination of well-adjusted, happy and intelligent children exists. This, for my new wife and I, is practical evidence that our parenting approach is on the right track. Indeed, such an approach, teaching young people to think, not what to believe, should be the only mission of our Queensland state school system.

This was indeed the view of government back in 1875, when the Education Act insisted that only secular education be taught in public schools. But the Act was amended via a referendum in 1910, and all references to the word 'secular' were expunged. Students today are thus fair game for the evangelisers and proselytisers who are allowed to enter our schools under the auspices of Religious Instruction, the NSCP chaplaincy scheme, and the new activity of Christian mentors organised by groups such as World Vision and assorted local evangelical churches — all too frequently aided and abetted by like-minded principals and staff.

This epistle then is fired by outrage that we are forced to contend with and mediate state-sanctioned religious infiltration. As is the case with Shine, where ideological content is not disclosed to parents and students either when the permission slip to attend comes home, or when I have sought to gain further knowledge of the programme.

Similarly, ideological content in the Chaplaincy programme, organised by Scripture Union, a self-confessed evangelical organisation designed specifically to recruit school children to Jesus, is officially denied. Opting-out of these programmes is thus, in the first instance, inhibited by their apparently disinterested motives, and in the second instance by dearth of a suitable option for those stragglers who are not taken in. Like religious instruction in primary schools, and unlike programmes such as instrumental music, Shine is not properly extra-curricular or optional; it takes the place of educational routines and in many schools is offered by Education Queensland as an option to compulsory sport, thereby undermining all attempts to introduce young people, and their parents, to the need for regular exercise.

This is both a letter of outrage, then, and a desperate plea that we reprise the enlightened thinking of 1875, and make Queensland State Schools genuinely secular, as the real 'education revolution' of the late nineteenth century provided Queensland with at the outset of our public education system. Our multi-cultural and multi-faith, and increasingly non-faith, society demands this if we are to be motivated by reason and represented by impartial government.

An innocuous enough looking form came home some months ago for parents to sign, offering a programme for girls designed to build confidence and self-esteem — 'Shine'. There was no mention of any specific religious or ideological content, so we signed our daughter on, though I was dubious about the apparent emphasis on the body that the programme seemed intent on. Body image is probably the most important issue for young girls (and boys) to come to terms with in a culture obsessed with it and there is a wealth of information pointing out the damage caused when girls are directed down the path of 'looking beautiful' to comply with the more distorted images our economic system requires to keep it motoring along.

My daughter talked all about 'Shine' after the first session. Each one of us is unique, special and here for a reason, she was told. An assortment of other special things were also discussed, amongst which were time, mobile phones (because they keep us in touch with friends. But my children do not have phones, so this upset my daughter) and wedding rings. Several married women present elaborated in turn on just how special the latter item was. 'Time' was special because no one knew how much they had; 'only God knows that', the girls were told.

The girls were also entertained with the song, and lyrics, of 'Mirror', my daughter told me. My wife and I eyed each other knowingly across the table; the song is a Christian fundamentalist dirge available via various impassioned performances on the internet.

After this, each Monday 'Shine' became the topic of discussion as we were forced, according to our lights [ideas], to help our children deconstruct, understand and then question the messages received at school. There is not room here for a verbatim account, of course, suffice it to say that over the next few weeks it became clear that the girls were being urged to adopt the kind of passive/conservative Christian stereotypes that we are all long familiar with: they were being groomed for domestic and spiritual bliss as demure brides of Man and Christ.

This went against the spirit of self-reliance, curiosity, empowerment and equality that we encourage in our house for girls as well as boys (we have three of each). On Monday evenings, now, we regularly find ourselves openly contradicting what was being taught at school. Exasperated, I phoned the school and politely asked for a copy of the form I'd originally signed, to see what it said about content. The receptionist asked if I wanted to discuss the matter with the 'Shine' presenter. I said 'no' and that I just wanted the form for now. Within half an hour I was phoned first at home then at work (by two different teachers it later transpired) by the 'Shine' presenter, who, somewhat alarmingly, is also my daughter's teacher, and was rudely questioned about the nature of my enquiry. I responded that I'd merely asked for the form, but under persistent questioning I confessed that I was indeed very concerned from my daughter's accounts about the nonsecular nature of the programme. I asked again for the form, as well as any other documentation on the programme. I have subsequently received the form but nothing else.

That evening, it emerged that my daughter had also been questioned as to my motives, and invited to withdraw from the 'Shine' programme. She said 'no', as she didn't want to be separated from the entire female contingent of the class. It is curious how the content seems calculated to seduce any and all young girls. It also transpired that my daughter had been privy to the commotion my private phone call had caused. Both grade seven classes, interconnected, were left in limbo as the matter was frantically discussed, phone calls were made and my daughter and I were questioned. One wonders at the eagerness to eject my daughter, an extremely quiet and sensitive child, when the agenda is disinterested benevolence?

This outrageous invasion of my privacy was also a source of embarrassment, bordering on harassment, for my daughter. As for myself, I now visit the school knowing that my whole family is probably the subject of gossip amongst at least some of the patently evangelical school staff, public servants all, who should be able to divorce their personal beliefs and values from their role as educators, in what clearly needs to be a secular school system. The obvious question is, if the 'Shine' presenters are doing nothing untoward, why are they so secretive and ludicrously, and offensively, defensive?

To my great relief, my daughter opted not to go to the 'Fluoro' night recently, where the little princesses get to really shine, but the next day her gobsmacked best friend exclaimed to my daughter that she was right and that 'they're all Christians'. It seems the entertainment there included spirited accounts of how various attendees had found God and been saved. And all this in a State School in the modern West, where centuries ago leading lights, in much more Christian cultures than our own, wisely decided on strict separation of church and state, and on secular education.

Queensland in particular, so I've learned, dispensed with secular schooling one hundred years ago. Before a 1910 referendum, Queensland State Schools were unambiguously secular, and at a time when religion was comparatively monolithic and moderate in nature. Modern Australian society bares no comparison in its diversity of cultures, faiths and non-faiths, and yet our schools are allowing extremist Christians in at the back door.

It is patently obvious, to me, that the 'Shine' programme is an insidious and concerted, but thinly veiled, attempt by evangelical fundamentalists to 'get at' our children. Indeed, since my interest was fired, I have found various damning evidence that makes this an incontestable and indefensible conclusion. Via the ostensibly disinterested NSCP Chaplaincy and 'Shine' programmes, and who knows what else, Australia's state schools are prey to the covert proselytising and machination's of zealots. This is a sober assessment and an accurate account of my family's experience — indeed, there is much more I might say on the subject.

On my family's behalf, I demand that my children's education be secular. My wife and I should not have to monitor and contradict Christian ideology foisted on our children at school. Wiser heads, prior to 1910, insisted explicitly that secular education only be taught in state schools; this is on the public record. With many years of overseeing my children's education still to come, am I to expect plenty more of this kind of opportunistic exploitation of a breach that the Shine programme exemplifies? I fear so, and worse, since I now understand that Education Queensland and the Queensland Studies Authority both condone, at least by not condemning it, the practice of individual teachers using the unscientific intelligent design (ID) and creationism models as an integral part of science teaching across Queensland.

There must be serious and concerted effort to restore secular education to our public system of education. Whatever people's private religious beliefs, or non-beliefs, may be, they should be left at the school gate, where the sign should read 'Beware of the Dogma'. The susceptible innocence of children should be protected from all vested interests at school, and education rehabilitated, once again, to the strict pursuit of education and learning.

NOTES

1. 'Evil Companionship in State Schools', *The Register*, 20 May 1884, p. 7.
2. See 'About Geoff', Geoff Wilson MP, at http://geoffwilsonmp.com/about.php; G. Wilson in a letter to the Australian Secular Lobby, 15 June 2009.
3. See the Australian Secular Lobby website at www.australiansecularlobby.com
4. In Queensland, the correct phrase, in use since the 1910 referendum, is 'religious instruction' or 'RI', notwithstanding that many people mistakenly refer to RI as RE, meaning 'religious education'. There is no RE offered in Queensland state schools. There are QSA courses for OP inclusion available to all Queensland schools that offer comparative religious education, but only a minority of faith schools access these, and no state schools.
5. See 'Downpour: The Chaplaincy Challenge', SU QLD, at www.suqld.org.au/downpour
6. This was in a range of telephone calls between myself and Ron Williams and the Mary Street offices of Education Queensland, and also in an email from EQ in Mary Street to me. The 'review' is now complete, and a new policy document is on their website at http://education.qld.gov.au/strategic/eppr/schools/scmpr021. There is no flow chart. We have a copy of the draft flow chart that was to go up, sent by EQ to Ron in August/September 2009.
7. M. Miller, 'RE Teaching Puts Girls Down a Rung From Boys, Claims Parent', 23 May 2006, p. 5; K. McIntosh, 'Debate Over RE Class in State School', 8 June 2006, p. 8; M. Miller, 'RE Teaching Report "Backs Father's Stand"' 20 November 2006, p. 5, all in *The Chronicle*.

8. This was discovered by Ron Williams when he attended the meetings called by EQ to resolve the issues. Both 'The Fourth R' and the ASL have received unsolicited emails from parents all around Queensland that show the same behaviour.

9. This came from a meeting at Middle Ridge State School, attended by Ron Williams, who was told by the school administrator that 80 per cent of the enrolment forms had no religion listed in the voluntary question. See also H. Wilson, 'Pulped Forms a Lesson in Public Bungling', *The Courier Mail*, 12 January 2007, p.29; M. Miller, 'RE Teaching Report "Backs Father's Stand" ', *The Chronicle*, 20 Nov 2006, p.5, and G. Berghoffer, 'Form C Spells Confusion', *The Chronicle*, 8 January 2007, p.8.

10. ' "Our evidence is that as many as 80% of parents never indicate which religious group they belong to, leaving the space blank, which has meant that principals should have checked to see where to put the student – in the RI class or the required alternative program," Ms. Allison said.' Cited in 'Form C spells confusion'.

11. Cited in B. Upham, *God and Caesar in Australia: aspects of church and state from 1788*, Zeus Publications, Burleigh, 2009.

12. Cited in G. L. Paine (ed.), *Southern Prose Writers: representative selections, with introduction, bibliography, and notes*, Litton Educational Publishing, 1947.

13. RIS Form C1 goes to parents who sign their child up to RI by filling out the optional religion question with some form of faith. RIS Form C2 goes to parents who leave that question blank, advising them, as with C1, what is on offer. This form is redundant since the Education Act is clear: no religion nominated, no RI class and straight to the 'alternative' class.

14. Keith Drinkall and Jim Rawson represented Scripture Union in the initial discussions with Ed Qld and a range of church leaders, starting in May 1989. See J. Salecich, 'Chaplaincy in Queensland State Schools: an investigation', PhD thesis, University of Queensland, 2001, p. 29.

15. ibid., p. 41.

16. ibid, p. 42.

17. ibid, p. 113.

18. 'Brandi Met God at an SU Qld Camp', *Pacific News*, July–September 2009, p. 5, and at www.scriptureunion.org.au/documents/PacificNewsJUL-SEPecopy.pdf

THEOLOGY IS NOT PHILOSOPHY

Peter Ellerton
Winner of the 2008 Australian Skeptics Critical Thinking Award, teacher of secondary school philosophy

IT'S CONCEIVABLE THAT THIS TYPE OF DISCUSSION COULD DEGENERATE INTO an argument about definitions. I could, given the plethora of literature out there about theology, philosophy, and the nature of knowledge, find a handy set of statements that would define away the issue and show clearly that theology is not philosophy, simply as a matter of fact. But this would be somewhat disingenuous. It would also be unsatisfactory as an intellectual exercise to merely dismiss theology as a poor cousin of philosophy, or to brand it as nothing more than an argument in which the premises assume the conclusion. Rather, I would like to approach theology by considering its effectiveness as a tool for the development and deployment of the critical thinking and reasoning skills normally developed in true philosophical training. We can then explore how readily one can tease apart the two arenas of rationality and faith without destroying the substrate of theological discourse. This will provide, in my view, the ultimate test against which theology can be said to stand or fall as a valid branch of philosophy.

Before we move too far along this track, I need to explain what philosophy is, and just as importantly what it is not. Popular conceptions of philosophy tend to centre around its role as a tool for pondering the meaning of life with vague, hand-waving discussions about esoteric and largely irrelevant points. As a teacher of philosophy, and of mathematics and the sciences, I take a completely contrary view. Philosophy in the

Western tradition is a coolly analytical, precise tool for the construction and dissection of ideas. Those skills with which we might imagine a critical-thinking education is most closely associated, such as the ability to analyse an argument, to recognise flaws in logical constructs, to determine the nature and reliability of claims about the world, and to communicate sophisticated ideas in written and verbal form, are most elegantly assembled together within a philosophical education. Contrary to popular belief, it is rare for philosophers to discuss aspects of meaning insofar as we relate it to greater purpose, but I will address this later.

I teach teenagers philosophy in their final years of secondary school. This is both challenging and rewarding, for pretty much the same reasons, the most significant of these being that students are asked to confront not only their beliefs and ideologies but also the process by which they were created. At the core of this is an understanding of epistemology, the branch of philosophy that inquires into how it is that we know something to be true. While children of this age are certainly known for having strong opinions, one finds more often than not that these are bootstrapped from popular opinion or built from the inherited beliefs of their elders, all bound together with an unhealthy amount of confirmation bias and overuse of proof by volume. This might seem problematic to a teacher of philosophy, but in fact it is a rather desirable situation. Teenagers usually combine the ability to stretch ideas to universal conclusions, using a minimal amount of thought or evidence, with an almost spooky capacity to adapt and change to new paradigms. They have not yet concreted-in their opinions as part of their identity. In short, they are engaged, imaginative, and malleable — ideal philosophical fodder. It is in this environment of engagement, openness, and willingness to explore that we can plant the seeds of ideas and provide a methodology for testing and nurturing them as they grow. This last point is critically important: it implies that different ideas will flourish in different environments, and in turn leads to a kind of meta-analysis of which environments promote the best ideas. This is also the point upon which I will conclude, so let me continue to build some context.

As well as teaching philosophy, I chair a panel that moderates philosophy assessment across the state of Queensland, and in this capacity I often get inquiries from schools about how we might help them set up courses or help resource existing ones. All well and good, but several teachers have regretfully pulled out of discussions as a result of their school claiming that students' needs in developing critical-thinking and reasoning skills are catered for by current theology-based programmes. While all too often such courses are naught but studies in comparative religion, some do attempt to move onto the playing field of critical analysis, and it is these that I will be addressing. Now, if you have been engaged in education for any length of time, even if you've just been loitering in the hallways, you will be aware of the trend for offering courses in higher-order thinking skills. It has become well accepted that there is a bounty to be had in producing good thinkers, and that perhaps the usual suite of subjects would benefit from some targeted instruction outside the normal scope. No argument there, but this leads to the pointy end of my claim: theology is not capable of delivering these skills. Rather, theology promotes an acceptance of avoiding, minimising, or otherwise refashioning philosophical analysis, inductive reasoning, and deductive logic, while dishonestly brandishing them as the legitimate tools of its trade. It cannot therefore claim the status of a working field of philosophy. This is a reasonably feather-ruffling statement, so let's explore the workings of theology and see how they may appear to a student learning the basics of thinking skills.

I am aware of the very broad brush with which I apply my treatment, and it is an easy assertion that this will lack even a veneer of sophistication, but recall that I am focusing here on the lessons a student would learn, explicitly and implicitly, from a general introduction to theology. While all faiths claim a theology of sorts, in the main I will be using examples from Christian theology, as it will be most familiar to the majority of readers, and also most representative of school-based educational experiences in Australia at the moment. This does not necessarily exempt other theologies from these criticisms.

THEOLOGY, TELEOLOGY, AND CIRCULAR REASONING

I wrote in my opening paragraph that I could dismiss theology in its entirety as an argument whose premises assume its conclusions. If true, this is a lethal charge. To do such a thing is to engage in circular reasoning, the most common example of which would go something along the lines of: 'You can trust me because I always tell the truth'. The conclusion is that you can trust me, and the premise is that I always tell the truth.

How do I know the premise is true? Because I assume the conclusion; around we go. The most unsubtle example in a theological context would be: 'We can believe the Bible because it is the word of God, and we know it is the word of God because the Bible says so'. No theologian of any training would use such an obviously hopeless argument, but keep this one handy. I have certainly heard creationists say that only God knows what happened in the beginning, since the Bible tells us that he was the only one there.[1] This is but one shade removed from our example.

The term 'premises' refers to the building blocks of an argument. They are the things we take to be true, or given, for the purposes of the argument. No premises means no argument, so it is vital that we have something solid upon which to begin the reasoning process. Premises are also the things upon which those engaged in argument must agree for there to be any progress towards a conclusion. Consider that a foetus has a heartbeat at around three weeks after conception. Those who take as a premise that a heartbeat implies humanity will not be able to argue the moral issues around abortion with those who do not use the same premise. There will always remain unresolved conflict between groups who do not accept each other's premises. We will see this simple point, that we need to agree on some premises before we can begin to argue, has serious consequences for the acceptance of theologians into the community of philosophers.[2]

So is theology circular — that is, does it assume the conclusion — and if so, how? Well, it may not be directly obvious, but it does — and it is embedded deeply enough to cause some serious logical suppuration.

I need to bring in another concept to properly explain my point. Theology has the disadvantage of being a teleological field.[3] This means that it assumes that an end point exists for the world; more specifically, that the events in the physical universe all work towards a predetermined outcome. This is not just a physical wind-down of the universe according to thermodynamic principles, but rather a designed outcome which all present goings-on in some sense strive to fulfil. All activity indeed may be explained by reference to this ultimate purpose. An analogy would be the behaviour of a team of builders and engineers on a building site; their behaviour only makes sense in light of what the end product will be — a building. As a collection of activities and events, their collective and individual behaviour would be inexplicable otherwise. Careful readers may now glimpse where

I am going. One of the major fault lines that runs through theology as a discipline, at least in any attempt to present it as philosophy, is how difficult it is to avoid circular reasoning within a teleological framework. In such an environment, human behaviour can only be explained by reference to the ultimate goal. Why do we do X? Because we need to move towards Y. How do we know? Because Y is designed so that we must do X. Why do we quest for meaning? Because we all unconsciously yearn to know God. How do we know? Because God designed us so. Any way you'd like to phrase it, it comes out chasing its own tail.

Let's return to my previous point, regarding the necessity of agreeing on the premises before we can meaningfully engage in argument. When your reasoning is in any way circular, no one can agree on your premises unless they accept the conclusion beforehand. I cannot argue rationally with someone who wishes to explore the role of God's purpose for humanity if I do not believe there is a God. All that is available to me is an insistence on more evidence. Hence, no argument is possible. It is this inescapable aspect that neatly cleaves off theology from the rest of philosophy, for which rational argument is indispensable.

A (blessedly) brief visit to a website that makes available an encyclopaedia of Catholic doctrine provides some of the other logical fallacies that lie only a scratch beneath the surface of theology.[4] Just staying with the Ts, under 'The Blessed Trinity' we find 'proof of doctrine from scripture' and 'proof of doctrine from tradition'. First-year philosophy students will be baying. Under 'Transubstantiation' sits 'before proving dogmatically ...' Philosophy students will now require sedation. These are classic examples of fallacious reasoning from any entry-level critical-thinking text. 'Proof' is a definable term that cannot be realised by using justifications from scripture, tradition, or dogma. Indeed, the idea is contradictory and counterexamples abound.

THE MEANING OF MEANING

All this creates a certain finality; but it gets even worse. When you assume a teleological perspective, certain questions become not only permissible but necessary. For example, a theologian must accept the validity of questions such as 'What is the purpose or meaning of life?' or 'Why did God create the world?' Just because a question may be expressed through language does not imply that it has a meaningful answer. 'Why are mermaids orange?' is a good example (and your unconscious response that they're not orange goes to show how powerful the temptation to leap from the hypothetical to the actual really is when meaning and language lock horns). It is logically possible that human life has no meaning beyond that which we choose to give it, and outside the biological desire and need to procreate.

Not only do such questions block our way, but hitherto unneeded concepts extrude from the landscape. Consider the necessary acceptance of a soul. While philosophers have spent considerable effort attempting to understand how a physical system such as the brain can give rise to a mind, if indeed there exists such a thing, it is far from a done deal. The infamous mind–body problem deals with how the corporeal could interact with the mental, and while there are several possible solutions to this, none in a philosophical sense have any relationship to such a creature as the human soul.[5] The quagmire created by an acceptance of propositions such as the existence of the soul is apparent in attempts to reconcile theology with modern philosophy and science. Consider the Catholic Church's deliberations of when and how the human soul entered the evolutionary machinery — all in all, an unhappy spectacle.[6]

Unfortunately, these additional notions are accompanied by truncations or outright negations of other philosophical concepts, as though some conservation law was in operation in which old ideas need to be discarded to make room for others. One of several that come to mind is the free will versus determinism debate, having implications in philosophy of mind, consciousness, and ethics, to name but a few. Theology must of course reject any questioning of free will, since to do so would allow humans to remove choice from their interaction with the world, and hence personal responsibility and therefore sin would become redundant. Thus appears, by the way, one of the stickier points of theology. If God is indeed all-knowing, then what you will be doing in five years' time and where you will be doing it cannot be an open question; indeed, it is fixed. How then can we choose to be elsewhere doing something else?[7] I'll place this point in context shortly as we discuss one of the genuine overlaps between theology and philosophy.

It is important here to distinguish between valid philosophical inquiry phrased in a manner such as 'What is a good life?' or 'How should we live?'

from questions of greater meaning or purpose that are not necessarily in themselves meaningful. The previous two questions might seem just as arbitrary as those of meaning and purpose, but they are distinctly different. Simplistically speaking, 'what' or 'how' questions are qualitatively different to 'why' questions, and do not require a teleological perspective.[8] In fact, this moves us nicely to another of theology's faultlines, the derivation and justification of morality.

THE QUESTIONABLE ETHICAL ROOTS OF THEOLOGY

Consider how philosophy approaches the question of ethics, which is a reasonable example of how philosophy approaches most things. Ethics is defined in the *Oxford Dictionary of Philosophy* (1996) — in which there is no entry for theology, by the way — as: 'The study of the concepts involved in practical reasoning: good, right, duty, obligation, virtue, freedom, rationality, choices ...' and as the '... scepticism that may attend claims made in these terms'. Notice here that we have both specific terms that require some effort to define and a means by which subsequent, sceptical claims based upon these meanings can be assessed. Put more simply, ethics is about what we do in a moral context and why we decide to do it.[9] Philosophically, this requires a deep questioning of the premises of any given ethical position, and a system of reasoning that will lead to prescriptive behaviour, at least for basic modes of human operation. Being able to explain why we hold an ethical viewpoint is as essential as carrying out the implied behaviour — ethics does not merely equate to a code of conduct; it is the active engagement with significant aspects of human behaviour from a moral perspective using a rigorous framework of reasoning. One cannot be moral just by being rigid.

What then of theology? Does it start and progress the same way? Clearly not. Theology must of needs base its morality (duty, obligation, et cetera) on the text of its holy books. This is non-negotiable and, at least when the text is clear, directly translatable into a system of behaviour. The resulting codes of conduct may indeed be admirable and worthy of emulation, but this is apparent from a discussion of the outcome after the fact, not as an act of its development. Moreover, much of what might be justified as morally correct could have been done in a secular philosophical system. A clear example is that of the 'golden rule', wherein we are encouraged to behave towards others as we would wish them to behave towards us. All major religions embrace this — it notably pre-dates Christianity and Islam — and it has been independently derived on a number of occasions.[10]

One might at this juncture be comfortable with enacting the commandments of holy text while giving a nod to any supporting philosophical analysis; however, in practice this is untenable. All too often, moral commandments appear which seem to have little in the way of philosophically viable justification. Many religions reject homosexuality, place women in a submissive role, condone extreme acts of violence against those who blaspheme, and generally throw their authority around beyond the constraints of philosophically defensible positions. In such cases, one of three outcomes is possible: either the text is ignored (the directive against eating shellfish is generally overlooked by Christians), a reasoned position is seen as irrelevant in light of the imperative to follow scripture, or the reasoning process is conscripted to produce the outcome required.[11] None of these can pass muster as a valid ethical approach.

Much is made of placing these things in historical contexts, invoking the power of metaphor, or even questioning the accuracy of translations (exploding, by the way, any claim that the book is the literal word of God); but what we have, regardless, is a serious epistemological flaw. Theology must ignore information from the same source as that from which it draws its epistemological credibility, using criteria that cannot be referenced to any internally coherent process. This cannot resonate with a divinely gifted morality.[12] It is also telling that many Catholic institutions do not teach applied ethics; that is, the philosophical examination of private and public issues, generally topical, which involve a moral perspective. One can only assume a reliance on centrally distributed dogma in such cases. What is particularly biting is the insistence by some that without organised religion there can be no moral compass. All in all, this does not bode well for claiming parity with the methods and rigour of philosophical inquiry.

Given the above ethical paucity, I turn now to an aspect of theology which, while not appearing to the layperson as an obvious contrast with philosophy, nonetheless displays a certain self-centredness that seems unbecoming of a supposedly academic discipline.

THE CULT OF OBFUSCATION

Religion, and therefore theology, has long had a monopoly on the numinous. The sense of wonder we all share about our existence, and the myriad possibilities that existence entails, is a fundamental part of our character, and constitutes what for many people are the most meaningful moments of their lives. It is unfortunate that the word 'numinous' is not more frequently used, as we seem to be left with terms like 'religious', 'spiritual', or 'heavenly' to describe such emotional experiences.[13] In truth, these can be intensely intellectual experiences — as Einstein himself was so clearly able to articulate on many occasions — as well as transcendent. The deference too readily shown to theologians when science reaches the present limits of its explanatory powers shows the currency of this paradigm. But what binds these experiences and institutions together, apart from tradition? The only argument theology can make for the exclusivity of its hold is that they are states only explicable by reference to God. Conclusions which are again bound tightly in the premises. I would suggest that if this central thread was to be pulled, the entire fabric of theology would unravel, and its academic frailty lie naked, but perhaps I should resume a more mundane analysis for the moment.

One of the most bothersome dimensions of theology, and a direct consequence of this hijacking of the transcendent, is its celebration of the mysterious. Don't get me wrong, there is nothing negative about enjoying having a mystery to solve, but it's really not enough to rest at that point; you have to get on with some serious analysis if you are playing the game for real. One need only attempt to understand the nature of the trinity, and to read some of the material written about this, to see how far removed from explanatory power, and indeed logical coherency, the language of theology has become. It's a common enough trait for humans that we feel we understand something better if we name it, but the names should carry us a little further up river, and not just leave us flopping about in the same muddy waters.

There is an animated Youtube clip that shows an epiphany occurring for a young man, wherein he suddenly realises that questions such as 'Who made the world?' can now be answered.[14] His conclusion is that it must be 'the thing that made the things for which there is no known maker!' This is encircling a gap in knowledge, or even a perceived gap, and defining it by what it doesn't say, a good example of which might be calling a gap in space a 'black hole', and hence claiming to bring it into the territory of the known. Once we allow this, all manner of 'explanations' are possible. God becomes 'that which is', 'He who must be obeyed', 'the source of all things', 'meaning beyond meaning' or 'that which surpasses all understanding'. I hear the mermaids calling. I am reminded of the random-quote generators found on the web that produce meaningless drivel in management speak by randomly combining a collection of otherwise unconnected stock phrases — 'maximise potentiality through leveraged buyback' and the like. Philosophers are mind-bogglingly pedantic about the meaning of terms, and might excuse an occasional vagueness of terminology, but it seems theology is powered by them. I suggest that you do not research an explanation of transubstantiation (the changing of crackers and wine into the body and blood of Christ respectively, and defined in the same site quoted earlier as 'conversio substantialis', which really helps) without an industrial strength tolerance for vagaries. It's one thing to be unclear about your subject matter, but it is quite another to be seeing obfuscation as an end point. This smearing, or dilution, of meaning is a dangerous educational message for students, and one that teachers of all disciplines strive to dispel.

FAITH AND REASON

I will sharpen my view here and speak of how this tendency to match a vagueness of vision with a vagueness of language has a more sinister side, and one that I think nails the cognitive colours to the mast of theology. I speak of the central role of faith. Since St Anselm, theologians have considered their work to be that of 'faith seeking understanding'. In fact, I see this much-lauded phrase as a rather good example of my point.

Kierkegaard famously claimed that full acceptance of the Christian doctrine, while not independent of reason, required, at the last, a 'leap of faith'. I won't go too far into his particular meaning, but you can clearly see this idea upheld as a fundamental aspect of most religious acceptance. At one point, you simply need to 'give yourself over', 'surrender to a higher power', 'submit to the grace of the Lord' or some such act of willful negation of your autonomy. People often speak of the sense of freedom, the giving up of earthly priorities, that these moments bestow upon them. I would not like to say that this of itself excludes any perspective of philosophical standing, as if such things are outside rational discourse. As a human experience, it has meaning and relevance and needs to be integrated into any sensible philosophy, but the aforementioned enclosing of transcendental experiences in an exclusively religious framework removes the experience from analysis, and is decidedly unphilosophical. I shall go further and suggest that since faith, by definition, is the acceptance of things without a rational reason to do so, what we really enjoy about the 'leap of faith' is the jettisoning of any requirement that our belief system can or should be represented by any philosophically argued position. It is the sense of freedom from having to explain why you hold a certain view or act in a certain way.

Interestingly, one of the most powerful moments in a philosophy classroom is when students come to the realisation that if they cannot explain why they hold a particular view then they have little reason to continue to do so. This is at the core of our notion of critical thinking, and should be one of the most highly valued outcomes of education. I cannot argue that this abdication of reason is not in a sense freedom, but it is not a freedom I would like to see as an integral part of any educational philosophy. Faith seeking understanding has an inescapably oxymoronic feel. There is no sense in which we can reasonably articulate why we choose not to be reasonable; no way we can understand why we should forsake understanding. Faith is belief without reason. No matter what arguments are drafted to the cause of theology, there is no escaping this ultimate truth. It is a central lesson in any theological educational setting.

PHILOSOPHY OF RELIGION

Is the sort of epistemological vagueness that I have outlined so far what most people assume when they think of theology? In my own experience, I would say not. There is far less distance between theology and philosophy in the common view than most philosophers would like to imagine, but possibly one area has a genuine claim from both, and in this area alone theology may be said to be operating in true philosophical mode. It is called philosophy of religion.

As I have mentioned earlier, philosophy of religion is often understood to be some sort of comparative analysis of the world's religious beliefs, or perhaps some kind of vague, theological morass. Both views are quite wrong, as in fact it is one of the most clearly logical and refreshingly unambiguous areas of philosophy; so much so that it often serves as an introductory unit to philosophy in general. It is in this area that we find statements and logical examinations of all the proofs for and against the existence of God.

The cosmological argument, an example of the sort of thing I mean, is an oft-touted 'proof' of the existence of God, and has the following logic:

Premise 1: All things (effects) have a cause, so all things which physically exist must be caused.
Premise 2: The universe exists.
Conclusion: The universe must have had a cause (sometimes called the prime mover), and this is God.

While this has some initial interest as an argument, a moment's thought shows the infinite regression that must follow. What caused God? Some do argue of course that the first cause must be supernatural and hence exempt, but this negates the first premise that all things have a cause. Similarly, they may argue that God is outside the natural chain of cause and effect, being a supernatural agent, and so may claim prime-mover status. But either way as soon as the term supernatural is invoked, this ceases to be a logical argument. Really, we are back into 'the thing which needs no maker' mode, which has no place in philosophy. The other thorn in the side of this argument is that there is no connection between the prime mover and any particular deity (Christian, Hindu, Muslim, et cetera), but we'll let that slide.

The 'argument from design' (reborn as 'intelligent design', and just as soundly thrashed by the arguments of the eighteenth-century philosopher David Hume then as it is today), the 'problem of evil' (why does suffering exist if God is all-powerful and all-merciful?), and a range of other affirmations and negations of God's existence are subject to cool, logical analysis. The problem of free will and the all-knowing God alluded to earlier sits neatly in this investigative framework, and is one of the ways in which the logical consequences of the nature of God is explored. What is the outcome? In each case, whether a proof of or a proof against the existence of God, the argument cannot stand.

To date, philosophers of religion have neither proved nor disproved anything, but have simply shown that the arguments so far offered do not stand up to close critical scrutiny. Philosophy of religion in its purest form is simply an exercise in argumentation using the claims of God's reality or otherwise as grist for the cognitive mill. If theology draws any other conclusion, it has moved outside philosophy and falls prey to the criticisms I have outlined above.

CONCLUSION

There are many other examples, both specific and general, that I could use as illustrations of the shortcomings of theology as a tool for building critical-thinking skills, but space and time are limited (another interesting philosophy of religion topic) and enough has been said to comfortably rest my case. I have suggested that reason has a discoverable, discernible, and readily articulated architecture that can easily be brought into service in constructing critical-thinking programs. Those with authentic philosophical training are well versed in this, and are essential to their effective design and delivery. Theologians, on the other hand, wave a toy sword of reason while undermining much of the etiquette and protocol of philosophical thinking, all the while claiming to toil under the banner of true philosophy. To be fair, there is no usurping going on, no claim of supremacy outside the obvious one of holding absolute truths, but any perceived camaraderie between the two disciplines is a false one.[15]

What conclusion can we draw about theology in the classroom as a substitute for proper philosophical inquiry? Consider the relationship between science and creation science, that strident attempt to justify scientifically a literal interpretation of the Bible. In which environment would a student best learn the nature and practice of science? Is it one in which ideas are freely formed, rigorously tested, and develop along a path laid down by evidence, or is it one in which evidence is either ignored as flawed or interpreted only within a pre-established and non-negotiable theory? The answer is clearly the former. Similarly, we cannot view the theological environment as fertile for the seeding and nurturing of ideas, given the stark contrasts with philosophy that I have outlined here.

The arguments of theology that attempt to justify belief in God are both insufficient and poorly constructed, and do not serve as good educational examples of clear thinking. As with so much of philosophy, and most particularly with educational philosophy, it is the process that counts.

Conclusions only have merit insofar as they can be strongly argued. I often say to my students that I do not really care what it is they think, but I am passionate about why they think it. This is the opposite of indoctrination. It is the challenge to think as you will so long as your opinion can be justified; the challenge to make that justification robust enough to survive the testing ground of rational inquiry — a challenge which theology fails utterly to meet. It has no place in the critical-thinking classroom.

NOTES

1. Ken Ham of the infamous Creation Museum in Kentucky is on film saying this to schoolchildren.
2. I pause to acknowledge that while premises may be agreed upon for the purpose of argument, they need not be wholly accepted. A quote, dubiously attributed to Aristotle, suggests it is the mark of an educated mind that one is able to entertain ideas without accepting them.
3. Theologians and philosophers can use 'teleological' in ways that may include human nature as the end point of our striving — for example, our goal is happiness, which we seek because of our nature — but I speak here of a more clearly articulated vision of that towards which we strive.
4. See the New Advent website at www.newadvent.org
5. I direct the reader to the works of John Searle, who has put much of this in a satisfying perspective.
6. One could begin with Pope Pius XII's encyclical of 1950, 'Humani Generis', and follow with several official pronouncements from popes John Paul II and Benedict XVI.
7. While there are answers to this, for example 'compatabilism', it remains a lively area of argument.
8. Note that 'what is the meaning of life?' essentially means 'why are we here?' The syntax is clearly not exact, and indeed sloppy, but serves the purpose of making this qualitative distinction. A better distinction might be between questions of meaning and function, though ask a philosopher what she means by 'mean' and you will be there all week.
9. Morality may sometimes be separated from ethics when focus is on the terms 'duty' and 'obligation', while ethics relates more to practical reasoning and is inclusive of morality.
10. It appears in the writings of Confucius, for example.
11. The directive against eating shellfish is in Leviticus 11:10.
12. The secular explanation is that we use our extant sense of morality to determine which bits of religious texts are those we should follow and which bits are those we should ignore.
13. Numinous: surpassing comprehension and understanding.
14. See 'The Thing That Made the Things for Which There is no Known Maker', at www.youtube.com/watch?v=IVbnciQYMiM, posted by NonStampCollector.
15. In fact, there are theologians well versed in logic and philosophy (even writers of logic texts), but they keep separate books, arguing in different modes when doing theology or philosophy.

EVOLUTION VS CREATIONISM IN AUSTRALIAN SCHOOLS

Professor Graham Oppy
Professor of Philosophy, Head of the School of Philosophical,
Historical, and International Studies at Monash University

ON 25 FEBRUARY 2008, IN AN ARTICLE ENTITLED 'FAITH SCHOOL BOOM "Creates Division" ', Michael Bachelard of *The Age* reported:

> The principal of Chairo Christian School in Drouin, Rob Bray, said that both evolution and creationism were taught in his school's science class. 'We don't hide the fact that there is a theory of evolution, and that's how we'd present it, as a theory,' Mr Bray said. 'We teach it, explain what it is, and at the same time we present clearly and fairly, and we believe convincingly, the fact that our position as a school is that God created the heaven and earth ... There wouldn't be any point of being a faith-based school if we didn't think that God was the creator.'

The article noted that there are now more than 200,000 children — almost 40 per cent of non-government school students — attending a religious school outside the main Catholic, Anglican, and Uniting systems. Further, it expressed the concerns of Professor Barry McGaw, head of the Australian Curriculum, Assessment and Reporting Authority (ACARA) Board, and the deputy prime minister, Julia Gillard, that the rapid growth of faith-based schools threatens the social cohesion of the nation. 'These people often form a narrowly focused school that is aimed at cementing the faith it's based on ... If we continue as we are, I think we'll just become more and more isolated sub-groups in our community,' said Professor McGaw.

Not so long ago, most people would have found it unthinkable that 'creation science' could come to occupy such an important place in public debate, that it could be taught so widely in science classes in our schools, and that it could be accepted by such a large part of the population. In what follows, I will provide a short history of this development, and then consider how we ought to respond to the current state of play.

CREATIONISM IN AUSTRALIA

In 1947, Victorian journalist John McKellar established the Australian Evolution Protest Movement (AEPM), a branch of a similar organisation in Britain. Under the leadership of McKellar and, later, Christadelphian John Byrt, the AEPM endured until 1979, with very little public attention. Throughout most of its history, the organisation had around 100 members, though it grew to as many as 350 in the mid-1970s.

In the 1970s, the AEPM sponsored visits to Australia by the US creationists Duane Gish (1975) and Harold Slusher (1978). These visits, and surrounding events, prompted the formation of the Christian Science Association (CSA) in South Australia in 1977 — led by medical doctor and young-earth creationist Carl Wieland. In 1980, after the CSA merged with a like-minded group in Queensland, it was renamed the Christian Science Foundation (CSF).[1]

By the mid-1980s, CSF had a staff of fourteen, led by Carl Wieland, paediatrician John Rendle-Short, and science teachers Ken Ham and John Mackay. Within a few years, Ham relocated to Kentucky, where he established Answers in Genesis (a name that CSF itself adopted in 1997). Under Ham's direction, the CSF later opened a $32 million 'Creation Museum' in Petersburg, Kentucky. In 2006, the Australian branch of Answers in Genesis, headed by Wieland, changed its name to Creation Ministries (International). By then, Mackay was heading up an independent organisation, Creation Research, which, like Creation Ministries, has its Australian headquarters in Brisbane.[2]

Groups like CSF, Answers in Genesis, Creation Ministries, and Creation Research have pursued a range of strategies to try to influence public opinion. On their own account, the most important and successful strategy is direct ministry in church services. But these groups also run public meetings, family camps, live-in conferences, and so forth, and produce a mountain of materials — magazines, journals, DVDs, and so on —

that are disseminated through these various activities. Moreover, these groups work hard to get their materials into schools and taken up for consideration in the old media — newspapers, radio, television. And they also have a large presence in new media — especially on the internet. It seems hard to deny that all of this activity has had a considerable impact on Australian opinions about the origins of life.

In 2005, an opinion poll conducted by UMR Research showed that 43 per cent of Australians accepted a scientific account of the origins of life, 28 per cent took the Bible to offer the most plausible account of the origins of life, 12 per cent held a view that harmonised biblical and scientific accounts, and 17 per cent were undecided. Among Christian denominations, 51 per cent were creationists (including 83 per cent of those belonging to Assemblies of God, 60 per cent of Baptists, and 31 per cent of members of the Uniting Church).[3]

OPPOSITION TO CREATIONISM IN AUSTRALIA

The Australian Skeptics was formed in 1980 in the aftermath of a visit to Australia by James Randi. Randi, an American magician, had become famous for publicly debunking and exposing paranormal claims from spoon-benders to faith healers. From the mid-1980s, members of the Australian Skeptics (including, in particular, palaeontologist Dr Alex Ritchie) became increasingly vociferous in their attacks on creationism. However, the most spectacular opponent of creationism in Australia was undoubtedly geologist Professor Ian Plimer.

In 1997, following several years of bitter public debate, Plimer took creationist minister Allen Roberts to court, alleging Allen's claims that natural geological formations in eastern Turkey were really Noah's Ark breached the Australian *Trade Practices Act 1974*. (Plimer details his arguments against Roberts in his 1994 book *Telling Lies for God*). Although Plimer lost the case on a technicality, the judge acknowledged that Allen had, indeed, made false and misleading claims. It should have been a pyrrhic victory for Allen. But it has been plausibly argued that Plimer's often belligerent and abrasive outbursts against Allen resulted in a considerable surge of public sympathy for creationism.[4]

The Australian scientific community was generally slow to respond to the growth of creationism in Australia. It was not until the mid-1980s that the Australian Academy of Science and the Geological Society of Australia began official campaigns to halt the teaching of creationism in science classes in Australian public schools. Before then, there were few scientists, other than Plimer, who supposed that creationism posed a serious threat to Australian science. However, by the mid-2000s there was seriously organised opposition to creationism in the scientific academy — as witnessed, for example, by No Answers in Genesis and its huge number of links to other Australasian anti-creationist websites.[5]

Of course, it is not only the Australian scientific community that opposed the growth of creationism in Australia: many religious organisations outside the evangelical Protestant wing were happy to join the resistance. In 1986, the Catholic Education Office in Sydney instructed parish schools not to teach creationism; and one of its staff, Barry Price, wrote *The Creation Science Controversy* (1990) a full-dress expansion of his blistering 1987 booklet 'The Bumbling, Stumbling, Crumbling Theory of Creation Science'.[6] Since then, the Catholic Education Office appears to have softened its line on teaching intelligent design in schools. Catholic Archbishop George Pell recently claimed that he is 'agnostic' on the question, saying he welcomed discussion of alternative theories in cases where evolution is taught in an 'anti-God' way.[7] Thankfully, there have been many other religious figures who have been prepared to say that creationism and the intelligent design movement are manifestations of 'bad religion'.

CREATIONISM IN AUSTRALIAN SCHOOLS, 1980–2000

In the early 1980s, the Queensland minister for education, Lin Powell, took the view that 'teaching the Theory of Evolution without drawing attention to counter-theories is in fact to present to boys and girls dogma disguised as science'.[8] Around this time, creationism was on the syllabus in Queensland secondary schools, but after 1983 it ceased to be required teaching.[9]

In the mid-1980s, a CSF survey showed that Western Australia, the Northern Territory, and New South Wales taught evolution and did not recognise creationism as science; South Australia had no policy on the teaching of evolution and creationism; Victoria had recently deleted evolution from the curriculum, and left the choice of what to teach to schools; Tasmania did not have widespread teaching of evolution; and

Queensland taught evolution 'only as a theory', and not in a way that would 'challenge religious beliefs'.

In 1986, a Sydney television station conducted a telephone poll of 30,000 Sydneysiders. Asked whether schools should teach that God created the world in six days, 65 per cent of respondents to the poll said 'yes'. In 1991, a poll by the Australian Institute of Biology suggested that 12.6 per cent of first-year biology students in Australian universities believed in 'special creation', and a further 41.4 per cent of these students believed in 'theistic evolution', otherwise known as intelligent design.[10]

A significant factor in the spread of creationism in the Australian community has been the rise in the number of small Christian schools in the outer suburbs of our capital cities. According to the Australian Association of Christian Schools, there were more than 30,000 students attending 151 Christian schools in 1991; but, in 2003, there were over 75,000 students attending 253 Christian schools.[11] From 1986, the Labor government's policy to reduce competition to public schools limited the development of new private schools. In 1996, the policy was abolished by the Howard government, and this may account for the growth spurt since then.[12]

CREATIONISM IN AUSTRALIAN SCHOOLS SINCE 2000

Since 2000, as the teaching of creationism in science classes has become more prevalent in Australian schools, there have been some interesting new developments. I shall give just three examples here.

On 10 August 2005, Brendan Nelson, then federal minister for education, science and training, gave an address to the National Press Club in Canberra. On the day prior to his address, Nelson had met with delegates from Campus Crusade for Christ (CCC), having earlier watched their DVD *Unlocking the Mystery of Life: intelligent design*, which CCC was then in the process of distributing gratis to all Australian secondary schools. Nelson said:

> Do I think the parents in schools should have the opportunity, if they wish to, for students also to be exposed to [intelligent design] and to be taught about it? Yes, I think that's fine. I mean, as far as I'm concerned students can be taught and should be taught the basic science in terms

of the evolution of man, but if schools also want to present students with intelligent design, I don't have any difficulty with that.[13]

On 20 October 2005, the Australian Academy of Science released an open letter representing more than 70,000 Australian scientists and science teachers. This letter, including the following text, was published in all major Australian newspapers:

> The Academy sees no objection to the teaching of creationism in schools as part of a course in dogmatic or comparative religion, or in some non-scientific context. There are no grounds, however, for requiring that creationism and intelligent design be taught as part of a science course. The creationist account of the origin of life is not ... appropriate to a course in the science of biology, and the claim that it is a viable scientific explanation of the diversity of life does not warrant support.[14]

From September 2005, reports began to emerge that the Pacific Hills Christian School at Dural planned to include the theory of intelligent design in its science classes.[15] An SBS television report on these classes provoked a complaint from Chris Bonner, former president of the Secondary Principals Council. An investigation by Christian Schools Australia and the Board of Studies NSW followed, but reached the conclusion that the school had met its requirements for teaching the science syllabus at years 7 to 10. In December 2008, the school was cleared of breaching state-curriculum requirements for the teaching of evolution. Commenting prior to the handing down of the verdict, Greens MP John Kaye observed that it was unsurprising that no private school in New South Wales had been disciplined for pushing creationist propaganda in science classes because, with the board handing over its only investigation to Christian Schools Australia, 'the fox had been put in charge of the hen house'.[16] After the verdict was handed down, Kaye further observed that the board's ruling set a dangerous precedent that failed to protect the integrity of the science curriculum and 'opened the floodgates to [its] religious invasion'.[17]

There are similar developments that might be mentioned here, but the above examples should suffice for the purpose of our subsequent evaluation.

WHAT SHOULD WE THINK?

There is a spectrum of views about evolutionary theory that can be taken by theists whose religions regard the Old Testament as Holy Scripture. At one end of the spectrum, there are theists who regard the claim that God created the universe as myth or metaphor; at the other end, there are theists who think, on the basis of their reading of Genesis, that the universe is about 10,000 years old. For the purposes of our discussion, the key distinction is between (i) those theists who suppose either that the standard scientific account (according to which the observable universe is about 13.8 billion years old) is massively mistaken, or else that God has made particular interventions in order to bring about life and, in particular, human life, on the Earth, and (ii) those theists who suppose that the standard scientific account of the history of the observable universe is at least roughly correct, and that there have been no divine interventions in the course of that roughly 13.8-billion-year history (except, perhaps, for the bringing about of some miracles — incarnation, resurrection, et cetera — of very recent provenance).

Young-earth creationists (those who suppose that the universe is about 10,000 years old or less) deny the teachings of a large range of well-established sciences: biology, geology, palaeontology, archaeology, and so forth. More moderate creationists (for example, those who suppose that God has made just a few particular interventions since creating the Earth), find rather less to deny in the teachings of established sciences. However, as a minimum requirement, most of those who want to see 'creationism' taught in Australia's science classes want to insist that human beings do not have 'naturally' shared common ancestry with other animals — and that brings their beliefs into direct conflict with the teachings of evolutionary theory.

It is worth observing that theists who are happy to accept that human beings do have a 'naturally' shared common ancestry with other animals will be hard pressed to find anything in current secondary school science curricula to which they can object. For example, there is nothing in the key knowledge required in the Victorian secondary biology curriculum that conflicts with the view that God created the universe, but does not intervene in the unfolding of the course of nature according to the dictates of natural law — except, perhaps, in order to allow human beings to witness miracles, or to receive communications from God, and so forth.[18]

Recent controversies about the teaching of intelligent design in our schools have missed the main point. While evolution is taught, quite rightly, as scientific fact, no speculation is made about whether the origins of life emanated from natural or supernatural causes. The curriculum, as it stands, indicates no commitment to scientific naturalism (the view that reality is exhausted by the natural universe), or to any other competing metaphysical view about the ultimate origins of the universe. So, the proper answer to those who seek 'equal treatment of the hypothesis of intelligent design' in science classes is that this hypothesis already gets equal treatment, since none of the many competing theories about the origin of the universe are taught in Australian schools. The topic simply has no place in the curriculum. In short, as naturalism is not currently taught in relation to the origin of the universe, then to add the hypothesis of intelligent design would unduly privilege that unproven thesis.

Setting aside the irrelevant considerations introduced by proponents of intelligent design, we return to consideration of those who want to introduce to science classrooms views that contradict well-established theories in biology, geography, palaeontology, archaeology, and so forth. Someone who asserts that human beings and chimpanzees do not have a common ancestry, or who asserts that the observable universe is about 10,000 years old, plainly makes assertions that are relevant to the standard biology curriculum. If giving 'creationism' equal treatment in science classes means that these kinds of claims should be given equal treatment, then the scientific community needs to explain vociferously to our politicians and educators why these claims should not be given that equal treatment.

The most obvious point to make is that there is an overwhelming scientific consensus against the claims in question. It is not scientifically controversial that the universe is about 13.8 billion years old; it is not scientifically controversial that human beings and chimpanzees have a common ancestry. The Australian Academy of Science statement on creationism and intelligent design says that 'the explanatory power of the theory of evolution has been recognised ... by all biologists, and their work has expanded and developed it'.[19] Given that the Australian Academy of Science is the obvious choice to be the final arbiter of a national science curriculum — and hence, in particular, of a national biology curriculum — one would need to have very compelling competing reasons to justify the inclusion of creation science in the Australian secondary school science curriculum. The simple fact is that creation science has no acceptance whatsoever in the mainstream scientific community, and should, therefore, have no place in our children's science classes.

There is no scientific reason to include creation science in the school curriculum. Despite this, it might be argued that parents should be allowed to determine key elements of the education of their children. While the teachings of evolutionary theory are no threat to the beliefs of many religious believers, those teachings clearly are a threat to the teachings of some strands of evangelical Christianity (and Islam, and other major faiths). If we suppose that parents have a right to raise their children in the religious faiths that those parents espouse, then we might be tempted to think that parents have an implied right not to have their children exposed to teachings that are likely to undermine those religious faiths. Following this line of thought, it might be argued that parents have a right not to have evolutionary theory taught in secondary schools as part of the science curriculum.

There are at least three major flaws in this argument. First, of course, it is not an argument for 'equal time' for evolutionary theory and creation science; rather, at its heart, it is an argument for the removal of evolutionary theory from the secondary school science curriculum. Second, if this line of thought works here, then it must apply universally. It would mean that nothing could be on the school curriculum that would give offence to some religious believers. As a corollary of this policy, no religious instruction could be allowed in schools (except in those schools whose student bodies were carefully selected on sectarian lines). Third, if this argument were accepted and applied universally, it would have serious consequences elsewhere. For instance, there would need to be very extensive censorship to ensure that nothing was published or broadcast that might be accessed by children whose parents' religious sensibilities were susceptible to offense by the material in question. In short, it would require the kind of repressive, theocratic rule that exists in some other parts of the world.

The idea that parents might have a right not to have their children exposed to teachings that may undermine their religious faith is at least, prima facie, opposed to other ideas that have an important place in our national conscience. Our Australian ethos includes a very strong general commitment to freedom of speech and freedom of expression. By extension, we are committed to ensuring that our scientific community enjoys these same freedoms. Freedom of speech must be severely compromised in a society in which parents claim an untrammelled and unlimited right not to have their children exposed to teachings that are likely to undermine their religious faith. Moreover, even if we suppose that parents should have a right to protect their children from certain kinds of teachings, it seems overwhelmingly plausible to suppose that there are at least two kinds of teachings that must be exempt from this right: scientific teachings, and teachings about basic civic rights and responsibilities. If creation science was to become good, established science, then there would be no problem including it in the secondary science curriculum, and non-theistic parents would have no right to argue that their children were being religiously indoctrinated. But, as we have already noted, there is simply no likelihood that that will happen.

There are broader issues in the background here. It seems right to think that we ought to recognise freedom of religious belief and religious expression. Granted this recognition, perhaps we might say that each person's right to religious freedom should be proportional to their willingness to grant that same right to those who do not share their particular beliefs. In other words, in order to maintain social cohesion, people who demand rights must be prepared to grant those same rights to others. Those who would claim more for their own religious beliefs than they would be prepared to give to the beliefs of others should, quite properly, have their claims refused. Similarly, those whose claims would tend to undermine the social order that underpins our religious freedoms should also be denied.

I have argued, above, that proponents of creationism and intelligent design are not arguing for equal time in Australian science classrooms, but rather to have their position privileged above, or even to replace, the mainstream scientific consensus. I have argued that, if applied universally, protecting children from views contrary to those of their parents would require extreme prohibitions upon freedom of speech and expression, and the imposition of the kind of censorship that one sees in the world's most restrictive theocratic regimes. Further, I have argued that to grant these 'rights' to a particular section of the religious community would, inequitably, restrict the rights of others who do not share their particular views. In effect, the proponents of creation science and intelligent design are claiming rights for themselves that they are not prepared to extend to others.

Given this, (and building upon Barry McGaw's and Julia Gillard's concerns about the effect that faith-based schools might have on social cohesion), it seems to me that it is possible to defend the claim that the push for creation science is a potential threat to 'the social cohesion of the nation'.

WHAT SHOULD WE DO?

There are two current developments that may have significant implications for the debate about the inclusion of creation science in the science curriculum in Australian secondary schools. On the one hand, there is presently a concerted push for a national school curriculum. On the other hand, there is also careful consideration being given to a Religious Freedom Act.

The Australian Curriculum, Assessment and Reporting Authority (ACARA) is currently in the process of developing a national curriculum that spans education from kindergarten to the end of secondary schooling.[20] In its present incarnation, the 'Shape of the Australian Curriculum: science' proposal includes the teaching of both evolutionary theory and geological history in years 7 to 10 and, perhaps unsurprisingly, makes no mention of creation science.[21] Of course, we can expect to see vigorous lobbying from creationists for the inclusion of creation science in the mooted national science curriculum — lobbying that should be met with even more vigorous opposition by friends of science.

The Education and Partnerships section of the Race Discrimination Unit of the Australian Human Rights and Equal Opportunity Commission (HREOC) is currently conducting an inquiry into freedom of religion and belief in the twenty-first century.[22] This inquiry is, in part, a follow-up to the 1998 HREOC report 'Article 18: freedom of religion and belief in the

21st century'.[23] Included among the recommendations of the Article 18 report is the enactment of a Commonwealth Religious Freedoms Act. This would include sections on discrimination and incitement to hatred on the grounds of religion and belief. It is currently being suggested that, in relation to employment, the Act should permit some exceptions to anti-discrimination laws for religious institutions.[24] It is also anticipated that the section concerning incitement to religious hatred would allow exceptions relating to genuine academic, artistic, scientific, or media-related statements or expressions.[25]

One possible — perhaps even likely — consequence of the recommendations described above is the further entrenchment of the teaching of creation science in Australian faith-based secondary schools. It is, at best, unclear whether the clause which provides some unspecified exemptions for scientific expression will be sufficient to protect the teaching of evolutionary theory against the charge of incitement to hatred on the grounds of religion and belief. It is also unclear whether faith-based schools will be permitted to employ only creationists as science teachers, via the clause that allows discrimination in order to avoid injury to the religious sensibilities of adherents of particular religious beliefs.

It seems to me that there are reasonably strong grounds to support the proposals of ACARA, and that there are very strong grounds to be worried about the likely outcome of the inquiry into freedom of religion and belief in the twenty-first century. Proponents of creation science are very well resourced, and they represent a sizeable part of the Australian population — around 42 per cent, according to the UMR research cited earlier. Consequently, there is simultaneous lobbying on many different fronts, and it is difficult for those who would keep creation science out of our secondary schools to defend against the many different attacks that are being made. Nonetheless, I think that we should be doing all that we can to resist: there are many different, quite fundamental reasons why creation science should not be taught in science classes in secondary schools, and those reasons can be put publicly in simple and easily understood arguments.

When Rob Bray, principal of Chairo Christian School, says: 'we present clearly and fairly, and we believe convincingly, the fact that our position as a school is that God created the heaven and earth ... There wouldn't be any point of being a faith-based school if we didn't think that God was the creator', he says nothing that engages with the content of current science curricula in Australian secondary schools. It is vital that we demand much more detail on proposals to teach creationism and intelligent design in science classes than has currently been provided. Perhaps then the real agenda will be revealed. The fact is, no one, and certainly not the creationists, seriously thinks that competing religious accounts of the ultimate origins of the universe ought to be taught in science classes. If that is what creationists ask for, then they are engaged in special pleading on behalf of their religion because, currently, none of the many unproven speculations are taught as part of our secondary syllabus. On this basis, then, their pleas should simply be ignored. However, if creationists want to their objections to well-established scientific claims (for example, that human beings and chimpanzees have a common ancestry) taught in science classes, then, while it is true that these claims do engage with the content of current science curricula in Australian secondary schools, the proper response is that there are simply are no good scientific objections to these claims.

What of the prospect that creationism might be taught in our secondary schools, but in some other part of the curriculum? We saw above that the Australian Academy of Science 'sees no objection to the teaching of creationism in schools as part of a course in dogmatic or comparative religion'. It is not entirely clear that we should agree with this judgement, either. True enough, creationism is part of the contemporary religious landscape, and it should be taught in any comprehensive course on comparative religion. However, the thought that creationism might be taught as part of a course in dogmatic religion in schools that are also genuinely teaching evolutionary science is plainly problematic. At the very least, conveying such mixed messages to students is likely to hamper genuine learning in science classes. If a student is taught in a religion class that human beings and chimpanzees do not have a common ancestry, is it plausible to suppose that it won't affect their learning when confronted with the parts of evolutionary theory that teach just the opposite?

Perhaps it might be replied that many students will be taught these things in Church and Sunday school. But then, I think, what ought to be said is that we are committed (a) to private freedom of religious belief and religious expression, and (b) to public education in science and basic civic rights and responsibilities. And then we should say that, in Australia in the twenty-first century, this is just how the chips fall.

NOTES

1. Information in the preceding two paragraphs is taken from R. Numbers, 'Creationists and Their Critics in Australia: an autonomous culture or "the USA with kangaroos"?' *Historical Records of Australian Science* 12 (1–12), 2002, pp. 109–120.
2. Information in this paragraph is from 'Creation Research UK', British Centre for Science Education, at www.bcseweb.org.uk/index.php/Main/CreationResearch
3. 'Museum Breathes Life into Creation Fossil', Insights (Uniting Church of Australia website), at www.insights.uca.org.au/2005/march/creation-theology.htm
4. For Dr Alex Ritchie's take on the 'Great Australian Evolution Trial', see 'Creation Science and Free Speech' at www.noanswersingenesis.org.au/creation_science_and_free_speech2. htm. For further interesting material on this episode, see J. Lippard, 'How Not to Argue With Creationists', at www.discord.org/~lippard/hnta.html
5. See 'No Answers in Genesis', at www.noanswersingenesis.org.au/index.htm
6. See B. Price, *The Creation Science Controversy*, Millenium Books, Sydney, 1990.
7. E. Orr, 'Intelligent Design to Enter School Classrooms in Australia', *Christian Today*, at www.christiantoday.com/article/intelligent.design.to.enter.school.classrooms. in.australia/3887.htm
8. J. Knight, 'Original Arguments: Queensland's fundamentalists push for "creation science" in schools', *Australian Society*, 1 July 1984, pp. 18–19.
9. Martin Bridgstock and Dr Ken Smith were both prominent in the fight to have creationism removed from the science syllabus in Queensland secondary schools. See for example www.skeptics.com.au/articles/australianperspective.pdf and www.embiggenbooks.com/ skeptics.html#bridgstock
10. Information in the last two paragraphs is taken from 'Creation in Schools', *Bible Science Newsletter*, August 1987, available for download at www.cai.org/bible-studies/creation-schools. This information is also in 'Creationists and Their Critics in Australia'.
11. A. Morrow, 'The Public Purposes of Education and the Teaching of Creationism-as-Science', *Australian Options* 41, 2006, pp. 27–89.
12. See R. Martin, 'New Federal Funding Policies — An Attack on Public Education', *Australian Education Union*, available for download at www.aeufederal.org.au/Publications/ NewFedFundingattack.pdf
13. See D. Sutherland, 'Intelligent Design Hits Australia' at The Committee for Skeptical Inquiry, at www.csicop.org/intelligentdesignwatch/oz.html
14. The full text of the letter is available on the Australian Academy of Science website at www.science.org.au/policy/creation.htm. The release of the letter coincided with the airing of an episode of *Catalyst* that considered the debate about intelligent design in Australia, including an interview with Dr Ted Boyce, the principal of Pacific Hills Christian School. After the show, an online poll attracted 9357 votes on the question of whether intelligent design should be taught in science classrooms, with 66 per cent voting 'no' and 34 per cent voting 'yes'. The transcript for the *Catalyst* episode is available at www.abc.

net.au/catalyst/stories/s1486827.htm

15. 'Intelligent Design to Enter School Classrooms in Australia'.

16. A. Patty, 'Creationism v Science: school on report', *Sydney Morning Herald*, 25 November 2008, at www.smh.com.au/news/national/creationism-v-science-school-on-report/2008/11/24/1227491462490.html

17. A. Patty, 'School in Clear Over Teaching Creation', *Sydney Morning Herald*, 8 December 2008, at www.smh.com.au/news/national/school-in-clear-over-teaching-creation/2008/12/08/1228584743350.html

18. See 'Biology: Victorian Certificate of Education study design', Victorian Curriculum and Assessment Authority, at www.vcaa.vic.edu.au/vce/studies/biology/biologystd.pdf

19. See the Australian Academy of Science website at www.science.org.au. I think that the Academy exaggerates slightly when it says that all biologists recognise the explanatory power of the theory of evolution. However, it is not in question that almost all biologists do this: the number of creationists who belong to the Academy is very small — less than 0.1 per cent — and the number of biologists among those creationists is also very small.

20. For more information, see the Australian Curriculum, Assessment and Reporting Authority website at www.acara.edu.au/default.asp

21. 'Shape of the Australian Curriculum: science', Australian Curriculum, Assessment and Reporting Authority, at www.ncb.org.au/verve/_resources/Australian_Curriculum_-_Science.pdf

22. '2008 Freedom of Religion and Belief in the 21st Century' discussion paper, Human Rights and Equal Opportunity Commission, at www.humanrights.gov.au/frb/frb_2008.pdf

23. 'Article 18: freedom of religion and belief', Human Rights and Equal Opportunity Commission, at www.humanrights.gov.au/pdf/human_rights/religion/article_18_religious_freedom.pdf

24. Recommendation R4.1 in ibid.

25. Recommendation R5.3 in ibid.

INTELLIGENT DESIGN AS A SCIENTIFIC THEORY

Graeme Lindenmayer
Retired engineer, author, member of the Rationalist Society of Australia

INTELLIGENT DESIGN (ID) HAS BEEN PROPOSED AS AN ALTERNATIVE OR A modification to the theory of evolution. Evolution is a scientific explanation of how there came to be so many different forms of life on Earth. It also explains how there came to be similarities between different types of life form, and differences between individuals of a particular type. Evolution attributes all these differences and similarities to natural processes. It supports and is supported by, but should be distinguished from, those sciences that describe details and processes of known life forms, relationships between life forms, and the time sequences of living and extinct forms.

ID proposes that an intentional process of design is, or was, necessary to produce some or all forms of life. Its proponents claim that many features of organisms could not have arisen as described by evolutionary theory or, in their words, are too complex to have happened by chance. Commonly quoted examples of such complexity are human beings and such organs as the eye. Many scientists have criticised the idea of ID. They claim that it is unscientific, and just another form of creationism proposed in opposition to evolution for religious reasons.

While this may be true, it doesn't always need a belief in a particular religion for someone to be persuaded that ID is more likely than evolution. A feeling that there must be a reason behind everything combined with wonderment at some aspect of nature may be enough. But many committed Christians accept evolution and reject ID.

Some proponents of ID accuse supporters of evolution of being constrained in their thinking and guilty of scientism; that is, of having a blind faith in the truth of science. While the usual view is that science is always subject to correction, however well it fits all that has been discovered about the world, some scientists and others do have blind faith in its truth, including the theory of evolution. But scientific theories should be judged on their own merits, irrespective of the behaviour, beliefs, or motives of their proponents.

SCIENTIFIC THEORY

Because it has been raised as an alternative to or, perhaps, a component of evolution, ID deserves impartial examination as to whether it is a credible scientific theory. Theory is one of the two components of science, the other being observation — that is, observation of any and all aspects of the world. To be accepted, observations (which often include measurements) should be continually and rigorously confirmed by independent observers, using, where possible, independent methods of observation. We usually then think of them as facts.

Theory is the explanation that logically links all observed facts. There have always been observations for which no completely consistent logical explanation could be found, and theoretical scientists continually think outside the box in search of new explanations, which must then be tested. Proponents of ID say they are doing just that. I propose to look at ID as a theory, including implications of its basic concept and what it might explain better than evolution can. To do this, I will first sketch out some aspects of evolutionary theory.

EVOLUTIONARY EXPLANATION OF THE DEVELOPMENT OF SPECIES

The basic concept in evolution is that when organisms reproduce, the offspring are similar to but often slightly different from their parents. Occasionally, the differences give the offspring some survival and reproductive advantage, which may lead to gradual predominance of the new form. If, over many generations, advantageous changes accumulate, significantly different life forms develop. This is a continuing tentative natural process that enables species to selectively adapt to their environments, making the most of opportunities in the presence of competitors, predators, and parasites, which also have developed in the same process. Evolution is not at all like a whirlwind in a junkyard assembling a Boeing 747, as the eminent physicist Fred Hoyle once described it.

The (inheritable) differences between parent and offspring are explained by observed processes, mainly changes (mutations to their genetic material; that is, their DNA. All living organisms are structured and operate in accordance with recipes coded into their DNA. Mutations continually occur in DNA because of irregularities in the workings of the cells, caused by exposure to unusual chemical conditions, extraneous DNA, or radiation. In most cases, the internal controls within the cell correct the change. In most other cases, the effect of the change is trivial or harmful. In a few cases, the change gives some advantage, at least for the environment that the organism finds itself in.

Evolution can be illustrated using the development of a complex organ, such as the eye. A long series of tiny steps starts with a mutation that produces a blob of tissue that happens to cause a reaction affecting the organism when light falls on it. Each successive step provides additional advantage, such as registering the direction of the light, improving focus, and distinguishing detail, colour, and movement, producing the many different types of eyes observed among a wide range of species. For each change to be viable, other parts of the organism need to be able, perhaps initially not very well, to take advantage of it.

We see evolution operating in some of the species that we have unsuccessfully tried to exterminate. We see it in the fossil record where, despite remaining undiscovered steps (the missing links), scientists can now comprehensively join the dots. They continually find further fossil evidence, and are able to confirm or correct the fossil picture using analysis of DNA. Richard Dawkins has described evolutionary processes so persuasively in his books, such as *The Blind Watchmaker* and *Climbing Mount Improbable*, that they seem to be self-evidently true. But Newtonian mechanics also seems self-evidently true. So might there be a successor to evolution — the biological equivalent of relativity? Such a theory need not discredit evolution, but might refine or reorientate it. Could ID be such a theory?

A new scientific theory should be able to predict future discoveries. So, what predictions were made by the theory of evolution? When it was first formally proposed, there was little evidence of sequential development of the various species, but it was predicted that new fossils would be found that, together with known fossils, would demonstrate chains of development, and that evidence of the ages of various fossils would support the associated developmental sequence. New fossil finds did indeed do just that. And as new sciences developed — for example, molecular biology and the various methods of establishing the age of fossils — the genetic relationships and time sequences discovered continued to confirm the predictions and to correct some assumptions about earlier discoveries.

This should not stop any alternative explanation from being considered. But, if an alternative is proposed, it should also propose a process that does not contradict observed fact. A competing theory should also show how it overcomes any failings of evolution. So, what are the failings?

Critics point to evolutionary explanations of such things as why in human beings the life span is much longer than the period of reproductive ability (in contrast to other species) or how various social characteristics arose. These are speculative stories that often sound plausible and might be shown to have parallels in computer models. But they are generally incapable of being tested, or of leading to testable predictions. Often they are countered by alternative speculations that also invoke evolution. Sometimes they may be useful in investigation or therapy. Similarly, there are arguments among biologists and palaeontologists about how evolutionary processes best fit specific observations.

Another perceived failing is the purposeless, or apparent mechanistic, feel of evolution. This offends the intuitive expectations of many people who consider that life has some spiritual aspect. This is not a scientific objection, and would be hard to defend in any scientific argument. But the evolution of consciousness from inanimate matter is something that scientists and philosophers still debate.

These arguments are about biology, palaeontology, et cetera, and have no bearing on the credibility of evolution as a theory. Similar arguments abound in most sciences.

Biologists have as yet produced no satisfactory theoretical series of possible steps by which inanimate matter might have developed into living organisms. This is neither a concern nor a refutation of evolution, which is about differentiation of species, not the origin of life. But if ID proposed a feasible observable process, it would indeed be a new breakthrough.

However, the key argument is that the type of incremental changes proposed by evolution could not possibly produce such complex forms. Biologists, palaeontologists, and geologists consider that there is ample evidence to refute this objection, which will be examined in detail later.

Prevailing theories, including superseded ones, have always had plausible defenses against objections. New theories often have a hard time — well-known examples are that continents drift and that *Helicobacter pylori* is the main cause of stomach ulcers. But if they can convincingly address the evidence and solve niggling problems, they will prevail. So, what about ID?

IMPLICATIONS OF A DESIGNER:
INTELLIGENT DESIGN AS A SCIENTIFIC PROCESS

ID proposes that desired new forms of life have been intentionally brought into being. No observed natural process supports this, so additional ones would be required. None seem to have been proposed or predicted — at least in the peer-reviewed scientific journals — so I will suggest what a serious theory would need to propose.

It seems reasonable to expect a theory of ID to include conceptualisation, detailed design, and assembly. The design might be expressed into the genetic code (which would require comprehensive and precise knowledge of the function and activation of the code). The designed organism would then be assembled using materials in a construction factory — perhaps by inserting the associated codes into a cell as is now done in genetic engineering or cloning. But what type of cell, and how would it be nurtured to adulthood? Alternatively, entire adult organisms might be assembled; but, if so, how?

And what, specifically, is designed: each species separately, or just some key beginnings and processes? If the latter, it seems very close to evolution, as some ID proponents think. In all cases, the theory needs to propose processes (showing how each design becomes a living organism), how separate species emerge, why there are differences between individual members of each species, how successive generations of a species develop adaptations to environmental conditions, and how some members of a species are born with DNA-related diseases. This might imply separate, and sometimes faulty, design of each member of each species, including, perhaps, micro-organisms.

Alternatively, the designer might have produced the mutations that evolution attributes to natural causes. But how? And what prompts trivial or harmful mutations? And what about the natural causes of mutations that have already been identified?

Clarifications and proposed processes for these and any other issues would need to be compatible with the consistently observed biological and physical processes and/or predict the discovery of new processes.

There is a pseudo-scientific claim in support of ID that if an organism has a greater information content than that of the sum of its individual parts, then it must be the product of design. No justification is supplied for this, and there is no reason to suppose it may be true. No evidence has been reported about any measurements of information content of an organ or organism, compared with that of the parts.

THE DESIGNER

A theory of ID would not be complete or sufficient without proposing relevant attributes of the designer. It would need to describe what prompts or compels the designer to make and implement a design, how the designer determines the details of each specific design, and how the designer knows about and interacts with what we call the material world. If new types of forces and/or entities are needed, they should be described in a way that allows independent checking.

If the designer is part of the cause-and-effect natural (that is, material) world, the theory should be able to describe or predict relevant observable processes. If the designer is outside the material world, it might still use observable processes, but an account would be necessary of how such interaction would occur.

If the proposed processes of design and implementation are not observable, even indirectly, the existence of the designer would be purely a matter of faith. For thousands of years, there has been speculation about what might exist beyond the observable world. No unequivocal answer has been found, and there is no apparent way of finding one. No designer that was too mysterious for human beings to describe could be part of a scientific theory. So it is important for a scientific theory of ID to propose characteristics of the designer that are compatible with what is observed about organs and organisms, and also with the processes by which the design might be created and implemented.

With no attributes of the designer yet proposed, what can be learnt or suggested by looking at life forms in general? As an arbitrary preliminary attempt, some salient things we observe are:

* a very large number of different life forms (species)
* all species depending on DNA for their form and function
* some species with organs that are inefficient or damage-prone
* gradations of development of specialised organs in successive similar species
* certain types of organs appearing on different occasions in very different species
* extinctions of large proportions of species, after which quite different forms emerge, and gradually change and adapt
* some species closely adapted to a specific environment and ill-adapted elsewhere
* many species with a relationship of interdependence with other species of very different kinds
* species with several, apparently unlikely, stages in their life cycle
* micro-organisms living in rock deep below Earth's surface
* a cruel food chain, with most species being the prey of other species and/or the host of parasitic species
* one species, *Homo sapiens*, that is apparently intent on destroying or enslaving other species
* species significantly modified by human intervention through selective use of inherited characteristics, both like and unlike those of their parents

This list suggests a designer with different perspectives and values from ours. While we might try to deduce what these may be, it provides neither refutation nor justification of ID. The list suggests apparent flaws in the structure of some species, but we should not assume that an intelligent designer would want perfection if there could be such a thing as a perfect organism. An ecosystem needs each of its member species to have both strengths and weaknesses, and some possibility of adapting to changes in its environment.

From this list and, dubiously, using human criteria, some possible conclusions could be that the designer:

* uses only one foundation (DNA) but is very versatile within it
* is not trying or able to produce trouble-free designs
* is not solicitous of the welfare of designed forms
* may be experimenting
* may have objectives not apparent to us
* or there may be more than one designer, and they are playing
  some competitive game, reminiscent of science-fiction stories
  or computer games

All this is pure speculation, suggesting how something might be gleaned, or postulated, about a designer. But it is hard to find anything in nature that might reveal the attributes mentioned earlier that a designer would need.

To prevail against evolution, ID should propose attributes and processes without contradicting accredited observations, and explain things that evolution cannot. The only serious postulated failing in the theory of evolution is the matter of complexity, claimed by proponents of ID. It will now be examined.

TOO COMPLEX TO HAVE HAPPENED BY CHANCE

The idea that evolution is too complex to have happened by chance raises three questions: What does complex mean? How complex is too complex? What does chance mean?

The word 'complex', like the word 'difficult', implies some relationship to human ability. Puzzles are difficult or complex when you don't know the method of solution, but simple when you do.

Chaos theory has shown that many processes that seemed to behave in a very complex way can be described by a fairly simple equation. Cellular automata — computerised simulations of reproduction — demonstrate that complex forms can arise from simple beginnings, using a few simple rules for the survival of members of the present generation and production of the next. A fishing line can easily get into a very complex-looking tangle that takes a lot of unravelling. Fishing lines and mathematical figures are, of course, much simpler, and contain far fewer components, than living organisms. But they can come together into ever-larger combinations by obeying just a few rules of nature.

Something may look complex when it has a lot of components. But as each one is examined and the interrelationships are understood, the whole may be explained. Many molecules have a very complex shape because the various forces acting within their component atoms push them into tangled contortions. The laws of nature produce complex forms everywhere, in ways that are explicable, even though they might require many steps.

A rough way of comparing complexities would be to compare the number of parts. A refinement would be to compare the number of different kinds of parts, and then the number of relationships and types of relationships between the parts. But when we marvel at living complexity, it is usually not these statistics that impress us but that the particular organ or organism performs so well.

A puzzle may be too complex for a four-year-old child but not for a ten-year-old, because spatial, numerical, and other concepts develop as a child matures. A problem may be too complex to resolve without certain information. Many mathematical problems that were too complex to calculate without a computer have been solved using one.

These concepts of "too complex" relate to circumstances. So, what circumstances make evolution of species impossibly complex?

Proponents of ID say that most organs and organisms could not be functional if certain significant parts were removed. They call this irreducible complexity. They also claim that organs could not function in any form simpler than they currently exist. The structures of biological organs are continually being investigated, categorised, and recorded, and their operations better understood. They generally, and specifically the ones referred to as being irreducibly complex, are found to have simpler counterparts in present or extinct species. And the very first ones? They appear to have come from simple changes that brought new types of capabilities, as in the description, given earlier, of the development of eyes.

A similar claim is that, since all components of complex structures specifically complement each other, they must have been designed together. The evidence shows that biological components develop in step with each other.

An improved model of a designed artefact — for example, a motor vehicle — may incorporate a dramatically new version of any of its parts or a major rearrangement. In an evolutionary process, such types of change are impossible, because no intermediate step will survive if it delivers an overall disadvantage. Therefore many organs with inherently inefficient or damage-prone features persist over long periods of time and across a range of similar species. This shows that they are stuck in an evolutionary rut rather than being the result of design. One example is in the eyes of mammals, including human, where the nerves carrying the signals from the retina to the brain are in front of the retina, partly blocking it from what it is viewing. Some unrelated species, such as cuttlefish, have eyes somewhat similar to mammalian eyes but which developed separately without this flaw — that is, the nerves are behind the retina. There are many other examples of evolutionary ruts.

But, accepting that some adaptations might have occurred through natural processes, could all the modifications required by evolution have really occurred by chance? To answer this, we should examine the concept of chance.

CHANCE

To say something happened by chance means that either it was unexpected or we can't tell precisely what caused it. The history of science and technology is replete with discoveries that occurred because something went wrong — that is, happened by chance. Chance occurrences bring significant people together in all fields of life, and continually affect the course of history.

Many significant things in most people's lives happen by chance: their first meeting with their future life partner, the way they started in their chosen profession, or how they were the unlucky victim of some accident. Almost everyone can remember several trivial coincidences in their lives. Coincidences happen in great profusion, just through sheer probability. For example, if there are 23 people gathered together (for reasons that have nothing to do with birthdays) there is about a 50/50 chance that there will be at least one pair with the same birthday. Make it 30 people it's worth betting on. When you understand a process, you can see how such apparently unlikely coincidences may really be very probable.

Proponents of ID who talk of specified complexity, alleging a very high improbability of evolution, do not understand this. Their improbabilities relate to a process where all the components of a particular organ or organism somehow come together to complete a pre-designed arrangement in one single step. This is the antithesis of evolution, in which, at each of many steps, the actual outcome was just one of many potential alternatives — reminiscent of some of the iterated processes described by chaos theory, but with unknown parameters.

With large numbers of organisms continually taking in and converting food and energy in a changing and chemically reactive environment, very many significant interactions keep occurring, inducing inheritable mutations to very many individuals. Continual mutations to DNA make it very probable that some members of succeeding generations will be able to survive or prosper whenever their environments change.

The same kinds of mutation enable people to breed different strains of plants and animals. In different breeds of dogs, for example, selection of size and structure of the body, structure of the retina, innate inclination, and ability to round up sheep or retrieve game, for example, are driven by the requirement to perform specific tasks, rather than to survive specific environmental conditions.

The great range of environments on Earth, changing from place to place and from time to time, continually provides opportunities for the diversifications to develop into new species. The prolific progeny of most species, each having to struggle to reach maturity, amplifies this process. Chance, therefore, makes evolution eminently feasible.

An analogy might be made between the production of slightly different versions of each organism at each new generation and a very powerful computer examining thousands of possible chess moves and their consequences at each stage of a game. Evolution takes many millions of years and produces the world's ecosystems. The computer, on a vastly simpler scale, defeats a strategically thinking chess grandmaster in the short time of a game or tournament.

This doesn't mean that speciation must have occurred through natural processes, but it discredits the argument that evolution is statistically unlikely. Indeed, to attempt to calculate the probability of anything that happened to have developed in such lengthy, complex, and unknowable circumstances would be futile.

CAN INTELLIGENT DESIGN STAND UP AS A THEORY?

In the public debate about ID, much of the heat is the result of people's hopes that a scientific theory will support their religious, philosophical, or political beliefs. But no scientific theory — evolution, ID, or anything else — should ever be considered as the final word. A theory is merely a tool — for explaining observations, for guiding and assisting further research, and for the development of new technology.

Sometimes evidence supporting a new theory is staring us in the face but is not recognised. Occasionally, a new entity is discovered; for example, the nuclear forces during the twentieth century. Many scientific riddles await solution at this moment. But no new theory will be accepted as correct unless it is useful or reflects the evidence more logically than any other.

There seems to be no existing observation of nature that would put the theory of evolution in need of any replacement or revision; for example, the discovery of organisms that could not have resulted from evolution. Examples might be ones similar to existing species, but with some organs radically different — like cats with non-mammalian eyes — or whose form and processes depended on something very different from DNA. No such evidence has yet been found.

This discussion has put both ID and evolution on trial, but it is an uneven situation. A refutation of ID would merely affirm the standing of evolution, which is supported by extensive evidence. But a refutation or weakening of evolution would not yet mean that ID must be true, because of the weakness of the current claims in its favour.

At this stage, ID is an incompletely developed reaction to the theory of evolution. Its concept introduces an entity and types of processes that are unknown to science. To be a scientific theory, it would need to propose testable processes that logically explain the diversity of species, and characteristics of the designer compatible with those processes. None appear to have been offered.

This is not to say that it would be impossible to develop a successful rigorous theory around the idea of ID, but the difficulties introduced by the concept seem insurmountable.

ATHEIST 2.0: REFLECTIONS ON TEACHING IN FAITH SCHOOLS

Kylie Sturgess
Teacher, researcher, blogger

IT IS 1999 AND I AM TOLD THAT, AS AN EMPLOYEE OF THE NATION OF Islam, one of my duties is to supervise the female students of the college while they participate in Dhuhr. I make sure that my brightly dyed Coke-label red hair (invisible in the course of everyday work) is even more firmly sealed under my hijab, and go to the second floor of the mosque to sit quietly in a corner and observe.

It's my job. I'm an atheist who works for religious schools, and I'm not ashamed of it. It pays about the same, or slightly more, than working in the public system and (as I discovered during a career spanning slightly over ten years), these places are happy to hire me. It's not without Enterprise Bargaining Agreement battles, nor additional hours of work — neither is it exempt from the usual responsibilities and stress that many teachers face. These people hire me to work as an educator. That's what I think I do.

Upon graduating from a Catholic university, I discovered that, whenever I became employed in the secondary school private system, there was an automatic assumption that I must be a member of the faith. However, 'which faith?' was never raised by my employers — particularly when working as an English as a Second Language/Dialect teacher. I suspect that one of the reasons why is because there weren't many teachers who chose to take that speciality in their degree. Maybe it was because many teachers who graduated with those qualifications found jobs more readily in the remote and rural areas of the state, despite the lure of inner-city employment and proximity to friends and family. Tales of how the big-city schools demanded that you 'hit the ground running' was a deterrent among my little class of graduates, and we talked of how, as young people, being a part of a country community held quite an appeal.

I ended up working as a relief teacher for my first year at a little suburban Catholic school, chasing drama students out of the wings, where they hid to snog passionately during rehearsals. At least I could head into Fremantle afterwards and drown my 'what am I really doing with my life?' thoughts in a cappuccino. Mind, I doubted I'd get a good espresso so easily in the remote north-west or rural south, and circumstances led me to stay relatively close to the city ever since.

When I graduated with a Diploma of Education, the college required mandatory theology units, which gave me 'accreditation A'. That meant I was able to be employed in the Catholic system, but not to teach Religious Education (RE). I'm not sure if that really applies anymore, and I suspect that there are further requirements for teachers since I graduated.

When I completed a Masters degree in education several years later, I attended another compulsory class in theology and ethics, and enjoyed discussions with Latin-speaking overseas students about the difficulty of being religious in the modern age ... even though a snarky Josephite nun made disparaging comments throughout my tutorial on pornography and the Catholic marriage. I didn't get along with everybody — let's face it, who does? — but I loved the look of the campus, enjoyed my philosophy classes with a lecturer who specialised in the middle years of Nietzsche, and saw firsthand the contradictions and tensions felt by those trying to live the 'good Christian life'.

Despite my quiet lack of faith, one of my jobs at an Anglican school had me teaching two years of Christian Education along with my English courses. I attribute this to too many required classes scheduled and — as it seemed the trend — too few teachers adequately qualified to do the job. Flipping through the hand-written, smudged, photocopied lesson plans (all of us hailing from a range of faiths, from Catholic to New Age Buddhist to 'I'm not really sure'), the RE teachers met once a month to puzzle over whether the fifth paragraph was really saying 'blessed are the cheese makers', and whose responsibility it was to make a pretty banner for the Year 12 graduation service, in honour of a visiting religious dignitary.

The enthusiasm of my Year 9s turned several kilograms of cellophane and many kilometres of butcher's paper into an ecclesiastic eisteddfod for that particular occasion. They would do anything to get out of drawing yet another Stations of the Cross montage, even if it meant doing all the really fiddly fringed bits on the streamers.

Being an atheist in a religious school doesn't come without a crisis of confidence about, 'What are you doing with your life in these institutions?' or, 'Are you part of the problem?'. I've heard homilies that claimed that Nostradamus was somehow equivalent to Jesus with his prophecies. That overcoming drug addiction was only possible with the grace of God. Even finding the best parking space at the Burswood Casino apparently depends on how many in the car can chorus the 'Hail Mary' in unison. I would help track down absconders from chapel, and tentatively developed a short list of 'meditations you could do during the homily if you really can't handle it' for the more militant, trapped teenager.

Was I part of the problem of religious indoctrination that is claimed to happen at such institutions? I'd openly sympathise, and defend my handful of students who silently fumed during their observance of Ramadan, when faced with end-of-term tutorial parties with snacks like ham-laden pizzas. When school counsellors negotiated and commiserated with the occasional crisis of faith among students, I saw similar crisis points among my colleagues. In the staffroom, we watched a fuzzy broadcast of buildings falling on 11 September 2001, and tried to come to terms with how to handle colleagues who turned to fundamentalist beliefs in times of grief and loss. Religion provided many answers to those in times of crisis, because that's one of the things religion offers to people, whether they're considered the right answers or not. How often was it really damaging to them? How often were the classes about indoctrination rather than being a discussion about differences and cultural education? Were the God-fearing narratives really that convincing, after acknowledging the influences of the outside world upon their modern minds?

I learned at such institutions that the likelihood of removing supernatural beliefs through education was an empirical question that wasn't, and doesn't yet seem to be, resolved. Many of the supernatural beliefs held by friends, students, fellow staff, and community members, during that time and since, just weren't religious-based. Many were entirely personal, and often brought them into direct conflict with the teachings of their church. Individual differences weren't hardwired or merely due to indoctrination — they were so implicitly tied in with personal experiences and the influence of their culture that was a part of their identity. The narratives constructed and the stories told reflected notions that appeared entirely plausible to the masses. Yet, most of the time, we all seemed too bothered by the working week to get into much debate about 'just how plausible'; we'd settle for a middle ground of tolerance rather than face additional stress.

I'd say that many of my coworkers were dedicated to mainstream educational needs first and foremost, and not indoctrination or propaganda. More often than not, my fellow employees would put aside their religious beliefs to discuss vital social needs rather than those religious beliefs — or the lack of them. In fact, most of the time it was due to the guidance of the students, who were unpredictable with their passions and alert to contradictions (especially if they thought they could neatly divert from a lesson-plan set for the day with an in-class debate). There was no end of 'Look what I found', or 'Did you see on the news...?', or 'Did you know what X just said in the class we just had then? They don't understand how the world really works, do they?'

I was once presented with a graph in an abstinence-only religious-education book (sneaked to me by my incredulous, yet giggling, Year 11 class). It claimed that engaging in sexual activity leads to an emotional meltdown — clearly inspired by some bastard-mixture of *Bridget Jones' Diary* and *When Harry Met Sally*. Some parents of my students even wrote parodies of it to the local paper. It's a little difficult to worry about 'indoctrination in the classroom' when the Parents and Teachers meeting had everyone laughing about such a ridiculous book!

Was I just surrounded by moderates wherever I went? Was it the mythical Australian catchphrase 'she'll be right' that diluted the fundamentalism which hypothetically lurked beneath the surface, waiting to pounce and brainwash us all? I started thinking that maybe atheism was the very least of people's concerns about religion being relevant to young people. Especially after a desperate youth counsellor tried to justify at what point his Bible-reflection course transmogrified from the advertised 'journey towards faith' into a hyperglycaemic festival of kids seeing how many marshmallows they could stuff into their mouths while saying 'chubby bunny'. Or seeing a lovely, enthusiastic young teacher reduced to sobs in the corner of the staffroom after 30 students announced en masse that they 'wouldn't be having anything to do with this World Youth Day until the government does something about human rights in this country' — and could they do a petition for visitors to sign on Parents' Visit Day instead?

Perhaps I was lucky with the schools I worked at, in comparison with some — I found the ethos of a school underpinned the sense of collegial interaction, despite the inevitable variations of faith among the community. Expressions of solidarity, subsidiary, participation, and equity were all fine by me, particularly when Enterprise Bargaining Agreement negotiations had staff united 'for the good of all'. I recall one instance of whispering to an RE teacher, in the middle of a parents' information session, about how 'Joanna's father must be helping her out with her RE homework'. The dad in question was bawling out an administration representative for his 'failure to live by a set of values consistent with the Christian faith and deluding them with weasel words — as defined by the investigation task on authenticity, due just last week in this very school!'

Maybe it was the cultural tendency towards 'a fair go' that led us to choose a Halal restaurant for our coworkers at the end of the year; maybe it was because we knew that personality and professionalism trumped feeling too uncomfortable about the paranormal beliefs being touted by representatives, and knowing that 'if things went too far', someone would 'have a quiet word'. We were usually soft with each other rather than strident, placating rather than dictatorial. As educators first and foremost, it just 'didn't do' to be too passionate beyond your subject area or when coaching netball. Even then, you'd be the first to make fun of your failings, just to get a laugh after a typical 60-hour working week.

I learned more about the power of meditation and stress-relief through attending religious ceremonies than at any of the professional development days run by over-enthusiastic, quasi mental-health experts.

For example, doing teacher duty in a mosque is a very meditative experience, particularly when you don't know the language. You find yourself admiring the mosaics and listening to the musical cadence of the ceremony. At least, I thought then it was music that I was hearing, but it wasn't in Arabic. The tempo was wrong — in fact, it sounded more like

African polyrhythms than the Qur'an. Then I realised that the student two rows in front of me was not, in fact, engaged in the thralls of religious fervour, but had sneaked in a Diskman and was engrossed in bopping to Tupac under her burqa.

My familiarity with American rap is rather limited. I was vaguely aware that Mr Shakur had a passing acquaintance with Islamic belief but was not in fact Muslim. However, this didn't really help the student's case when she was asked to explain herself to the imam; in desperation, she informed on half a dozen friends who were doing a brisk business in bootleg Jay-Z and Brandy albums across both campuses. I was reminded of this experience many years later, when I discovered how the choirgirls from another institution were trading gigabytes of hymnals and hallelujah choruses (and a few more Jay-Z, Tim Minchin, and Frank Zappa tunes) in MP3 format, clogging up the shared server space until it crawled to a stop.

I wonder sometimes if this will be the future of the educational institutions that I work at: crawling to a stop in the face of technologically savvy young people who share comedy routines that blatantly challenge the teachings of their school; hamstrung by copies of *The God Delusion* (2006), which is on the syllabus as suggested reading for the philosophy and ethics course, picked up on the bestseller shelves as a 'must read'. Would more relevant narratives than those found in the Bible prevail, like the documentary *Plumpton High Babies* (2003), which explicitly shows that one is not doomed to ignominy, suicide, and/or prolicide if you fall pregnant outside of marriage?

After more of a decade of seeing fundamentalism destroy communities, create wars, and actively target the young people we worked to educate as literate and questioning citizens of the twenty-first century, will the 'quiet word' about 'don't go too far' in promoting one's religion ... be the final nail? Maybe it is more complicated than that — but then, I've always had a different kind of faith about things.

* SOCIAL AND CULTURAL

FUNDAMENTALISM, RELIGION, AND SCIENCE

Dr Martin Bridgstock
Author of *Beyond Belief*, Senior Lecturer in the School of Biomolecular and Physical Sciences at Griffith University

WHAT EXACTLY IS FUNDAMENTALISM? TO WESTERNERS, THE OBVIOUS answer is that fundamentalists are Christian militants who take the Bible literally. They are so called because of an influential set of books — titled *The Fundamentals: a testimony to the truth* — which appeared between 1910 and 1915.[1] *The Fundamentals* had little early impact, but over time a powerful Christian movement developed with the fundamentalist label. If you ask, you will find that fundamentalists regard themselves as being heirs to a long tradition of religious truth, a small group of people keeping the true faith alive through the centuries.

Theologian James Barr spells out some of the Christian fundamentalists' key beliefs, and these are the kind of doctrines we might expect fundamentalists to espouse:

(a) a very strong emphasis on the inerrancy of the Bible, the absence from it of any sort of error;

(b) a strong hostility to modern theology and to the methods, results, and implications of modern critical study of the Bible;

(c) an assurance that those who do not share their religious viewpoint are not really 'true Christians' at all.[2]

Historian George Marsden views fundamentalism as being more like a social movement:

... a loose, diverse and changing federation of co-belligerents united by their fierce opposition to modernist attempts to bring Christianity into line with modern thought.[3]

However, one of the most noticeable features of the modern world is that there is more than just one kind of fundamentalism. Christian fundamentalists often differ from each other on many points of dogma, and it has become clear that similar movements exist in other religions.[4] As we shall see, we can substitute the name of some other religions in Marsden's formulation and it still tells us a great deal. The key issue is opposition to any compromise with modernisation.

What is it about the modern world that so appalls fundamentalists? In the modern intellectual world, there is a great deal. Starting in the last century, scholars insisted upon treating holy scripture simply as texts to be analysed, rather than as holy wisdom.[5] Recently, for example, they have concluded that over 80 per cent of the sayings attributed to Jesus were not actually uttered by him.[6] Scientists tell us that the Earth is astonishingly old, and that we emerged from 'lower' creatures through natural evolutionary processes rather than those described in the Bible.[7] Archaeologists report that many key events described in scripture — such as the Jews' escape from Egypt and their conquest of Canaan — never happened.[8]

These intellectual threats are not the only problem for devout Christians. Social changes also seem profoundly godless — gay marriage, public displays of sexuality, decline in religious observance — and so the reaction of conventionally religious people may be close to panic. In the light of this, a fierce counter-movement, stressing the unchangeable nature of the basic faith, seems quite understandable.

We should note two other important points. First, fundamentalism is a fairly recent movement. It is little more than a century old. Fundamentalists regard themselves as heirs to an ancient tradition of correct faith, but they usually know little of their own history.[9]

Second, fundamentalism is always at war on at least two fronts, and sometimes more. Since fundamentalists regard themselves as being the possessors of the one true faith, it is clear that they will always be opposed to those of other faiths and to those with no faith. In addition, fundamentalism is often in conflict with other people of the same faith. For example, Christian fundamentalist literature is full of attacks on 'liberal Christians', whom they doubt are really Christians at all. In short, fundamentalists are people with strong religious beliefs who see their basic ideas as under attack by massive changes in the modern world.

We are all familiar with the concerns of Christian fundamentalism. It puts great stress upon conversion and being 'saved'. Allied to this are a set of conservative moral positions, including opposition to abortion, sexual laxity, gay rights, and scientific findings that appear to contradict the Bible.

On the other hand, there is no particular reason why fundamentalism should be confined to Christianity. Adherents of other religions may also be anguished by modern developments. The key difference, as we shall see, is that context and history causes different fundamentalists to focus upon different divine truths, and to oppose different enemies.

NON-CHRISTIAN FUNDAMENTALISMS

In this section, we will look at Jewish and Islamic fundamentalists, who are perhaps the most important from an Australian perspective.[10] Jewish fundamentalists fall into two broad groupings. One, the Haredim, or God-fearing Jews, begin with the assumption that they are God's chosen people and, further, that God has laid upon his people a mass of rules to live by. Many fundamentalist Jews seek to observe these rules, in the belief that God will eventually come and exalt them for their faithfulness.

Samuel Heilman and Menachem Friedman stress that only a small minority — less than 5 per cent — of all Jews fall into this category.[11] These Jews are much influenced by the lifestyles in the Jewish ghettoes and villages of central and eastern Europe a couple of centuries ago. As Enlightenment thought burst upon Europe, people inside and outside the Jewish communities began to question whether Jews should be segregated in this way: weren't Jews people like anyone else? The possibility of leaving the Jewish way of life and becoming part of a larger community appeared.

Jews reacted to this change in different ways. Some opted for assimilation, leaving the ghettoes and the restrictions of Jewish community life. Others fiercely rejected any compromise, and opted to follow, as closely as they could, the way of life God had prescribed for his chosen people. These formed the modern Haredim, now very prominent in Israel and also in other major Western cities such as New York.

What do the Haredim want? Above all, they want to be left alone to study and to pray, and to observe God's rules. They become angry if outsiders disrupt their efforts, but for the most part they are not belligerent, and do not threaten the rest of us.

The other type of Jewish fundamentalism is quite different, and far more aggressive. In the book of Joshua, we read how God assisted the ancient Israelites to conquer Canaan — and, incidentally, to massacre many non-combatants — and promised that it would always be theirs.[12] Therefore, some modern Jewish fundamentalists — known as the Gush Emunim, or Bloc of the Faithful — feel impelled to reoccupy the ancient land of Israel.[13]

The catch here is that the modern State of Israel does not occupy all of the land that, these people believe, God promised to the Jews. Many fundamentalist Jews believe the West Bank territories, Gaza, and other areas belong to them. Of course, since God's authority far exceeds that of any earthly regime, this means that this type of fundamentalist Jew does not hesitate to occupy lands which they regard as theirs.[14] Opinions vary, but some members of the Gush Emunim (or GE) regard the territory of Greater Israel as extending all the way from the River Nile in Egypt to the River Euphrates in Iraq.[15] Relentlessly, the GE supporters have set up colonies on the West Bank, occupied buildings, and sought to strengthen their hold upon the land.

The influence of GE settlers in this sensitive part of the world has been to inflame worldwide religious tensions. Perhaps the most dangerous event was in 1984, when a plot to blow up the Muslim mosque upon the Temple Mount was foiled by Israeli intelligence. Some observers judged that, if the plot had succeeded, a world war might have resulted.[16] It seems clear that this variant of fundamentalism is profoundly dangerous to the rest of the human race.

This brings us logically to the most terrifying brand of fundamentalism: Islamic. On the face of it, though, there can be no fundamentalism of this type. How can we apply the term 'fundamentalism' to a religion which, by definition, regards its sacred writings as the word of God? The answer lies in the history of Islam.[17]

By the time that the Prophet Muhammed died, in 632 CE, the Arabian Peninsula was Muslim. What happened next is one of the most astonishing events in history. Islam conquered a large section of the world, creating an enormous empire. Islam was spread by the sword, and many died. Jews, Christians, and some others were tolerated, but the supremacy of Islam was not to be questioned.[18] Out of this empire, Muslims created a glorious civilisation. However, fearsome assaults from the outside — such as the Mongol conquests and the expulsion of Muslims from Spain — severely disrupted the Islamic empire.[19] Worse, in later centuries, the Christian countries of Europe and America outstripped the Muslim ones in military power, economic power, and science and technology.

In these circumstances, it is logical that many Muslims — unlike most Christians or Jews — will equate religious correctness with success. They will argue that modern-day Islam has lost its early religious commitment, and will also note the early military successes of their faith, compared to its recent savage defeats.[20] We might expect, therefore, that modern Islamic fundamentalists will stress a pure, unsullied faith, and also the importance of being prepared to fight ferociously in defence of what they believe.

Muslim fundamentalists believe that Westerners must be repelled, pure Islam recovered, and the Muslim faith enshrined in law, and that this is essential to restore the glories of the golden age. In consequence, Islamic fundamentalists face at least four major enemies. We have already met two of them.

All fundamentalists are profoundly hostile to the sinful, secular, modernising Western world. In addition, they are hostile to less-rigorous practitioners of their own faith, whom they regard as little better than atheists. However, fundamentalist Muslims face at least two more enemies. One is the State of Israel. The success of this small Jewish state — at the expense of Muslims — is seen as an outrage and a humiliation. In addition, fundamentalist Muslims are equally hostile to Westernisers in their own countries. Leaders of predominantly Muslim states often attempt to imitate governmental structures from Europe or North America. For Muslim fundamentalists this is to be opposed, as Western structures often displace the focus upon Islam.[21]

HOW DO FUNDAMENTALISTS SEE THE WORLD?

As we have seen, different types of fundamentalist have different priorities. In all cases, fundamentalists portray themselves as maintaining the original sacred insights of their religion, whereas they are actually selecting and interpreting doctrines that suit them.

Fundamentalists are completely prepared to make use of modern technology to accomplish their goals. Ayatollah Khomeini travelled by aircraft, and spread his message through tape-recorded speeches. Osama Bin Laden used videotapes, and appropriated jet aircraft to use as weapons. Modern Christian fundamentalists use television programs to spread their message, and have sophisticated databases to help them focus their message onto the right audiences.[22]

At the same time, fundamentalists often see the world in very different ways to the rest of us. Sociologist Steve Bruce spells out some of the key differences. If we can grasp these, we have some insight into the fundamentalist way of thought. One difference is that fundamentalists believe strongly in active, intentional agency. If something undesirable is happening, somebody is causing it. The idea of unexpected consequences is not congenial to fundamentalists. So if church attendances are down, women are moving out of the home, and gay marriage is becoming common, this is not a consequence of unplanned social trends: somebody is causing it, and behind that somebody is probably the Devil.[23] In this way, many complex issues are reduced to matters of personal morality, and are simplified to the point where discussion is nearly impossible.

Another difference is that fundamentalists tend to lump all their opponents together.[24] This is fairly common: most of us do not see the fine differences between viewpoints we disagree with. Fundamentalists, though, carry this to the extreme. Muslims lump together the State of Israel and other Western nations, although often the latter disagree strongly with what Israel is doing. Christian fundamentalists lump together atheists, liberal Christians, evolutionists, pornographers, feminists, and many other groups, as being those responsible for bad developments in the world today.

Finally, fundamentalists live in a world of signs and secret symbols. They often regard God — and Satan — as constantly at work in the world around them. Given sufficient attention, they believe, these messages can often be decoded. The Devil's face can be seen in the smoke from the World

Trade Center; the number of the Beast, 666, can often be decoded from assorted texts.[25] As Bruce points out, this set of mental blinkers radically changes the way that fundamentalists look at the world:

> It grossly over-simplifies, imputes an underlying moral order to everything, readily demonises its opponents and finds reds (or whoever the conspirators are) under every bed.[26]

In short, fundamentalism creates a readily accessible bunch of people to hate, blames them for everything that is seen to be wrong, and tells the fundamentalists what to do about it. The difficult and painful process of trying to understand the complex modern world is completely avoided.

WHAT DO FUNDAMENTALISTS WANT?

So far, we have looked at the nature of fundamentalism and some of its characteristics. But what do fundamentalists want? To find this out, it is best not to take their public pronouncements at face value. Fundamentalists are quite shrewd at tailoring their statements to fit a broad audience.

Ultimately, what fundamentalists want is a godly society. They want religion restored to its primary place, and for it to permeate all aspects of our daily lives. Fundamentalists are not primitives, but they do want 'sacred' beliefs and practices from the past to be given weight in the future. To non-believers, of course, this looks uncomfortably like a theocracy, and indeed many fundamentalists favour this.

As we have already seen, exactly what these key doctrines are varies from time to time and group to group. Among Jews, for example, the Haredim and the Gush Emunim have quite different views on what their religious duties are. In the same way, Western Christian fundamentalism is an uneasy alliance of disparate groups whose disagreements often erupt into outright feuding. The issues vary; it is the attitude and the approach that remain the same. So far, Christian and Jewish fundamentalists have not succeeded in taking over a state, so we do not know how they would behave.

In the Muslim world, on the other hand, two fundamentalist regimes have taken power, and their conduct is most revealing. In Afghanistan, after the 1996 collapse of the Russian-backed regime, a fundamentalist

Islamic regime, the Taliban, took power. There was never any pretence of democracy, and indeed the Taliban appear to have had the support of units of the Pakistani army. Once in power, this regime proceeded to remove many civil rights, slaughter its opponents, and downgrade the possibility of girls being educated.[27] It also destroyed historic statues because they were not Islamic, and provided a base for Osama Bin Laden's al-Qaeda network. This led to the Taliban's downfall, as the network made terrorist attacks upon the US and invited an inevitable — and ferocious — retaliation.

The other case where fundamentalists took power was in Iran. Here, they were led by the astute Ayatollah Khomeini, and undoubtedly had much initial support. In the late-1970s, after a prolonged and savage insurrection, the unpopular Shah was deposed, and the Islamic Republic took its place. In hindsight, it is pretty clear that most Iranians had little or no idea what the new regime could be like.[28] It has now been in power for 30 years, and looks more and more like an ugly, repressive religious dictatorship. There is still some support for the fundamentalists, but democracy seems to matter less and less: what holds the regime in place is force and terror.

It seems most unlikely that a fundamentalist regime of any description could sustain itself in power for a long period with democratic support. This is because the goal of fundamentalism is, at base, profoundly inimical to most human aspirations. Steve Bruce aptly captures the deep, underlying goal of fundamentalism in this revealing comment: 'The goal of resistance is to recreate the excitement and commitment of the original believing community'.[29]

This is an important insight, and it contains within it the key to why, in the long run, fundamentalism cannot succeed. Most of us could not live our lives in a continuous religious frenzy, even if we wanted to. Some people can achieve this excitement for a limited period, but most of us inevitably lapse into the ordinary world. Indeed, as Gellner shrewdly remarks, most of us need a profane, routinised area in our lives.[30] Therefore, a state formed amid religious excitement, and embodying that excitement, is likely to find itself with profound problems. Most people will lapse from the ideals they espouse, and so the state will find itself having to enforce its will upon a less and less supportive public. In the long run, it appears, a fundamentalist state cannot survive, and is likely to be overturned, or to lapse into dictatorship. This appears to be happening in Iran, though whether the Islamic state will fail or simply become a dictatorship is not yet entirely clear.

FUNDAMENTALISM, TECHNOLOGY, AND SCIENCE

Fundamentalism has a profoundly ambiguous attitude to technology. On the one hand, as we have already seen, fundamentalists make copious use of the latest science-based technologies to spread their message. However, fundamentalist enthusiasm for technology wanes sharply when they consider the biomedical area. Often, Protestant fundamentalists join with Catholics in their fierce opposition to abortion, cloning, and other reproductive technologies.[31] This sharp disjunction in their thinking probably has at least two causes. First, since God created man in his own image, it seems clear that tinkering with God's biological plan constitutes an attempt to topple God from his supreme position — something that is naturally anathema. Second, many of these technologies threaten the traditional position of the family, and of the male and female roles within that family. Therefore, since fundamentalists believe strongly in the traditional household, with the man at its head, they are opposed to any developments that threaten this.

The fundamentalist view of science is even stranger. On the one hand, they do recognise that the material benefits that surround us are, to some extent, the product of science. For Christian fundamentalists, since God gave human beings the right and duty to control everything on Earth, science-based technology looks very much like a divine tool for achieving this goal.[32]

On the other hand, science — some science, at least — makes fundamentalists uncomfortable. The historical sciences — notably cosmology, geology, and evolutionary biology — paint a picture of the past radically at variance with that portrayed in the book of Genesis. In particular, fundamentalists find it outrageous that, according to biologists, we are descended from the same ancestors as the modern apes, and that, in the more distant past, we are related to all living things on Earth.[33] Less noticed, but just as important, is the range of scientific findings which indicate that the Earth and universe are extremely old, and that they originated in a primeval explosion.

What are fundamentalists to do? A popular strategy is to seek to mould science into something compatible with the Biblical views. After all, if the Bible is completely correct, then eventually science must yield findings that verify its statements. This has led to the development of creation science, and intelligent design — attempts by fundamentalists to remake science into an enterprise compatible with their view of the Bible.[34]

However, at the most profound level, science's lack of dogmatism makes it profoundly different from the immovable assumptions of fundamentalists. In addition, because fundamentalists wed themselves to a particular set of dogmas, it seems inevitable that at some stage they will find themselves unable to accept the findings of science. There is simply no way of reconciling scientific open-mindedness and rigour with fundamentalist dogmatism.

SOME KEY POINTS ABOUT FUNDAMENTALISM

This survey of fundamentalism has shown us some rather surprising features of these movements. First, fundamentalism is not a literal resurgence of ancient religion. It is a selective retrieval of older beliefs, repackaged in an attempt to recreate the original religious frenzy and to defend believers against the perceived threatening world.

Second, fundamentalists are usually at odds with other religious people, including those of their own religion. They regard non-fundamentalists as little better than atheists. If they cannot convert them to their viewpoint, they will struggle against them bitterly.

Third, fundamentalists are at odds with the entire legacy of the Enlightenment, which acknowledged the fallibility of human ideas and made clear that by accumulating and critically evaluating evidence we can better our understanding of the universe.[35] Fundamentalists believe that they know better than this. They believe that they have the truth, and it only requires a moral effort to accept it. Those who do not make that effort are to be condemned.

Fourth, fundamentalists live in a world which is often profoundly different from ours. They love their children, for example, but believe that they must protect them from hellfire by indoctrinating them with fundamentalist precepts. They read signs and symbols into events around them, and believe that evil happens because evil people — and demons —

desire it, rather than because of unforeseen events. Reasoning from this, they look for people to blame.

Fifth, fundamentalists are often unethical. This may seem strange, because their entire ideology is based around moral concepts. However, their stress upon certain beliefs means that most of the ethical rules that we live by are secondary, and may even be disregarded by fundamentalists. For example, years ago, I was staggered to find that creation scientists' references to science were often blatantly falsified: as far as I could tell, fundamentalist zeal completely overrode the elementary duty to tell the truth.[36]

A far more dramatic case involves Muslim fundamentalists. Any Muslim scholar will tell you that Muslims have a religious duty to fight in defence of their religion. However, they are enjoined to spare the lives of civilians and non-combatants.[37] Clearly, this is completely incompatible with flying aircraft (loaded with civilians) into buildings (packed with civilians), or exploding bombs in crowded trains and markets.

SOME WEAKNESSES OF FUNDAMENTALISM

Steve Bruce makes a number of points about the weaknesses of fundamentalism. These are all important, as the fanatical, triumphalist nature of the movement can often create the impression that it is stronger than it really is. One point is that fundamentalists are usually not a majority. In the West, Christian fundamentalists are strongest in the US, but even there they do not constitute anything like a majority of the population. What is more, non-fundamentalist groups can, when the necessity arises, often out-campaign — and indeed out-spend — the fundamentalists in political battles.[38]

Another point Bruce makes is that by focusing upon personal morality — and often abusing their opponents for their lack of it — fundamentalists inevitably draw attention to their own conduct. The list of fundamentalists caught in immoral activities — often sexual or financial — is startlingly long.[39]

Bruce also points out that fundamentalism's habit of dividing the world into 'them and us' means that they find it difficult to form alliances. After all, it is hard to form working coalitions with people whom you regard as at best faithless and at worst motivated by the Devil. And, of course, people who have once been denounced by fundamentalists are unlikely to forget this and become allies in the future. Bruce makes the point that fundamentalists find it hard to work with people from other religious groupings, and then goes on to make two important points:

> They are also not good at tolerating differences even within the camp of the faithful. There is also a problem with sustaining commitment. Zealots become quickly disillusioned. ... Religio-political mobilization thus tends to come in waves that are as short as they are intense.[40]

This all suggests that fundamentalist movements can create a great stir, can win local victories, but will find it hard to mount the kind of sustained, broad-based campaigns that will ensure they gain full political power. In the one case where they have managed this — Iran — their regime seems to be increasingly repressive and unpopular.

WHAT TO DO ABOUT FUNDAMENTALISM

In that context, what can we do about fundamentalism? We face the problem of being committed to democracy and freedom, yet having to deal with a powerful movement which believes in neither. In Western societies, we are most likely to come up against Christian fundamentalism, so this is probably the one we need to know most about. Most fundamentalists are badly educated, so some points can be made which might shake them a little, or at least persuade them not to parade their ignorance quite so aggressively.[41]

A first requirement, then, would be to acquaint oneself with the basic ideas of fundamentalism, and some of the major objections. I find James Barr's book *Escaping from Fundamentalism* (1984) to be of especial value, and there are many others.[42] This does not mean that everyone must become a theologian. It does mean that we should all have some idea as to why fundamentalism is wrong, and perhaps know where we can gain more information if we need it. An insight into the nature of fundamentalism is also useful, and Steve Bruce's book is an excellent point from which to start in this direction.[43] For a detailed understanding of fundamentalism, the results of the Fundamentalism Project — five volumes and 3400 pages — are superb, but perhaps more than most of us can absorb.[44] From these tomes the paper by Ammerman on North American Protestant fundamentalism is a gentle and informative beginning.[45]

In addition, we should be aware of what the fundamentalists are doing, and also should be aware that within the movements there is a profound anti-democratic impulse. Therefore we should be alert to fundamentalism's latest machinations, and be ready to counter those that undercut any of our precious institutions, such as democracy and science.

What about other fundamentalisms? Since 9/11, it is clear that Islamic fundamentalism is generally more violent than its Christian counterparts. Although there is nothing in Islam which opposes democracy — rather the reverse — Muslim countries have little in the way of democratic traditions, and so Islamic fundamentalists are far less restrained by ideas like tolerance and constitutional action. Islamic fundamentalists are very aware of the history of humiliation and the high-handed interventions that Western nations have forced upon their peoples, and this accounts in part for the savagery of the backlash.

How should we handle Islamic fundamentalism? As Gellner argues, most Muslims, like the rest of us, do need stable day-to-day lives, and the savagery of fundamentalism is as alien to them as it is to us.[46] Because of the West's tradition of high-handed action, therefore, we must not intervene where it is not necessary. In addition, we can strengthen the hands of non-fundamentalists within Islamic nations, and this necessarily means making life better for their inhabitants. For example, the prosperous Muslim nations of South-East Asia appear to be winning the battle against fundamentalist terrorism, while those elsewhere are doing far less well. Regardless of our own beliefs, we have a strong stake in a peaceful, prosperous, secure Islamic world.

As for the Gush Emunim, there is a great deal of evidence that the encroachments of that group and its allies are a profound source of rage for many Muslims, and a source of support for Islamic fundamentalists. This is because Palestine looms large in the consciousness of many Muslims. The actions of the Jewish state — which does not restrain the GE — are seen as outrageous, and the Christian states of the West are seen as supporting Israel.

The answer to this is fairly simple, at least in principle. We must make it clear that we support the existence of the State of Israel, and also of a Palestinian state next to it. The only viable goal is for both states to be peaceful and secure. We should therefore oppose the activities of all who seek to undermine this goal — which includes the GE and the Islamic fundamentalists.

My last point is the most general. Most who read this article will be atheists or agnostics. I do not fall easily into either category. If there is religious truth, I would like to know what it is, and so far I have not found it. One thing I can see clearly is this: undogmatic people of any persuasion have an advantage over the fundamentalists. As Bruce has pointed out, fundamentalists find it difficult to work with people of other beliefs.[47] If there are issues where we agree with some people of religious faith, then, in my view, we should be prepared to work with them on those issues. It should be clear from what I have said that not all religious views are the same. Some would destroy anyone who disagrees with them, others are tolerant. Some would undermine and destroy modern science, others would not.

Fundamentalism is not going to go away, and its supporters are numbered in the hundreds of millions. In my view, we should be prepared to cooperate with people whom we may disagree with on other issues. Moderate religious believers of all kinds may be our natural allies. In the grim struggles with fundamentalist bigotry that lie ahead, that may be one of our main advantages.

NOTES

1. A. C. Dixon (ed.), *The Fundamentals: a testimony to the truth* (12 vols), Testimony Publishing Company, Chicago, 1910–1915 (later volumes edited by R. A. Torrey), e-book available at www.archive.org/details/MN40295ucmf_2

2. J. Barr, *Fundamentalism*, SCM Press, London, 1981, p. 1.

3. G. M. Marsden, *Fundamentalism and American Culture*, Oxford University Press, New York and Oxford, 1980, p. 4.

4. See for example S. Hunt (ed.), *Christian Millenarianism from the Early Church to Waco*, Indiana University Press, Bloomington, 2001.

5. R. W. Funk, R. W. Hoover, and the Jesus Seminar, *The Five Gospels: what did Jesus really say?*, Polebridge Press, New York, and Don Mills, Ontario, 1993, pp. 2–3.

6. ibid.

7. D. J. Futuyma, *Science on Trial: the case for evolution*, Pantheon Books, New York, 1983.

8. I. Finkelstein and N. A. Silberman, *The Bible Unearthed*, Touchstone, New York, 2001.

9. Barr, *Fundamentalism*, p. 16.

10. There are fundamentalists in the Sikh religion. However, since these have less impact upon Australians, we will not take their analysis further. See T. N. Madan, 'The Double-edged Sword:

fundamentalism and the Sikh religious tradition', in M. E. Marty and R. Scott Appleby (eds), *Fundamentalisms Observed*, University of Chicago Press, Chicago and London, 1991, pp. 594–627.

11. S. C. Heilman and M. Friedman, 'Religious Fundamentalism and Religious Jews: the case of the Haredim', in M. E. Marty and R. Scott Appleby (eds), *Fundamentalisms Observed*, pp. 197–264.

12. See the book of Joshua 1: 3–4.

13. G. Aran, 'Jewish Zionist Fundamentalism: the Bloc of the Faithful in Israel (Gush Emunim)', in *Fundamentalisms Observed*, pp. 265–344.

14. ibid., pp. 278–79.

15. ibid., p. 278; the book of Joshua 1: 3–4.

16. *Fundamentalisms Observed*, pp. 267–68.

17. J. L. Esposito, *Islam: the straight path,* Oxford University Press, New York and Oxford, 1998, p. 19.

18. ibid., pp. 33–35.

19. ibid., p. 60 and p. 205.

20. A. A. Sachedina, 'Activist Shi'ism in Iran, Iraq and Lebanon', in *Fundamentalisms Observed,* pp. 403–456.

21. ibid., pp. 410–411.

22. S. Bruce, *Fundamentalism,* Polity Press, Cambridge and Malden, 2008, p. 14.

23. ibid., p. 114.

24. ibid., pp. 114–15.

25. ibid., pp. 115–16.

26. ibid., p. 119.

27. B. R. Rubin, 'Afghanistan under the Taliban,' *Current History* 98, February 1999, pp. 79–91.

28. 'Activist Shi'ism in Iran, Iraq and Lebanon', p. 436.

29. Bruce, *Fundamentalism*, p. 13.

30. E. Gellner, 'Fundamentalism as a Comprehensive System: Soviet Marxism and Islamic fundamentalism compared', in *Fundamentalisms Comprehended*, pp. 277–287.

31. See *The American Prospect,* 17 December 2001, for a special issue relating to this topic.

32. See Genesis 1:28.

33. This is discussed in M. Bridgstock and K. Smith (eds), *Creationism: an Australian perspective*, Australian Skeptics, Melbourne, 1986.

34. For example, B. Forrest and P. R. Gross, *Creationism's Trojan Horse,* Oxford University Press, Oxford and New York, 2004.

35. For example, N. Hampson, *The Enlightenment*, Penguin, New York and Harmondsworth, 1976.

36. For example, M. Bridgstock, 'The Reliability of Creationist Claims', in *Creationism: an Australian Perspective*, pp. 63–66.

37. For example, *Islam: the straight path*, p. 59.

38. Bruce, *Fundamentalism*, p. 88.

39. ibid., pp. 88–89.

40. ibid., p. 85.

41. T. Correno, 'Fundamentalism as a Class Culture', *Sociology of Religion* 63 (3), Fall 2002, pp. 335–361.

42. See James Barr, *Escaping from Fundamentalism*, SCM Press, London, 1984; examples of other texts include J.S. Spong, *Rescuing the Bible From Fundamentalism*, Harper, San Francisco, 1992, and anything by the Jesus Seminar.

43. Bruce, *Fundamentalism*.

44. M. E. Marty and R. S. Appleby (eds), *Fundamentalisms Observed*, 1991; *Fundamentalisms and the State*, 1993; *Fundamentalisms and Society*, 1993; *Accounting for Fundamentalisms*, 1994; and *Fundamentalisms Comprehended*, 1995, all published by the University of Chicago Press, Chicago and London.

45. N. T. Ammerman, 'North American Protestant Fundamentalism', in *Fundamentalisms Observed*, pp. 1–65.

46. 'Fundamentalism as a Comprehensive System', in *Fundamentalisms Comprehended*, pp. 277–287.

47. Bruce, *Fundamentalism*, p. 85.

ATHEISM AND EUTHANASIA

Dr Philip Nitschke
Medical doctor, euthanasia activist, author of *The Peaceful Pill*

> The church says the earth is flat, but I know that it is round, for I have
> seen the shadow on the moon, and I have more faith in a shadow than
> in the church.
> — *Ferdinand Magellan*

THAT HOT SEPTEMBER SUNDAY, I WENT OFF TO LUNCH KNOWING THAT BOB
Dent would die. That's what he wanted: a peaceful death, a compassionate
act that would end the suffering caused by the terminal prostate cancer
that wracked his body. Over the past years, I had worked hard to get
legislation through the Northern Territory parliament that would allow
this. A law that would allow Bob the right to die. Or, more correctly, Bob's
right to receive lawful assistance in this quest.

It was difficult driving to the Darwin suburb of Tiwi on that hot
September Sunday to meet the man I would soon kill, and I felt anxious
and apprehensive. My mind kept trying to anticipate all the possible
problems that could develop. Would I keep my nerve? Would I be able to get
the intravenous cannula into a vein? What if the drugs, or the 'Deliverance
Machine' I had built to deliver them, didn't work? What if I had forgotten
something? What if ...? Nowhere, though, among all of the preoccupying,
pressing concerns, did the question arise: Is this the right thing to do?
I already knew the answer to that.

AN UNGODLY LAW?

The idea of enabling a terminally ill person to receive a legal lethal injection is controversial; passing law to this effect was never going to be simple. It took all the skill of the conservative government leader Marshall Perron to accomplish this, and in May 1995, the Rights of the Terminally Ill Act passed by one vote through the Northern Territory parliament. The Northern Territory, the most secular place in Australia, became the first in the world where voluntary euthanasia was legal. For the first time, a compassionate act that would put an end to suffering was supported by legislation.

Opposition from organised religion was strong. Most Territorians agreed with the change, but the (Catholic) Church did not. They claimed it was a violation of the sixth commandment, and that to kill was an act society could never condone. Their argument: all life is sacred and a gift from God; only God is to decide when it is to end. Those who interfere break God's law.

The Territory legislation meant that, on that September afternoon in 1996, for the first time ever, anywhere, I would be able to kill, legally, to break God's law without penalty. I drove on unaware of the fury that carrying out this simple act of compassion and common sense was about to unleash.

THE EXECUTIONER

The Deliverance Machine performed well. Bob looked at the question on the laptop screen. 'If you press this button you will die — do you wish to proceed?' He quickly pressed the button, held his wife Judy, and died a few minutes later in her arms. I packed up the machine and walked out into the sun. All tension was gone: Bob had received the peaceful death he wanted. It felt good to have been part of this, to have made it happen.

Through the rest of 1996 and into 1997, another three of my patients died peacefully, electively — or as the Church liked to say, were put to death using this law. It was hard going, and knowing you were doing the right thing didn't make it any easier. Every time I packed up the machine and headed off for the appointment, I couldn't escape the feeling that I had become some form of de facto executioner. Standing at the motel door with the suitcase, knowing that when I would leave in a few hours' time the person inside would be dead, was very hard. I wondered how long this would need to go on before other doctors followed in the path that had now been laid.

This question was never answered. The Church was mobilising, pulling strings, calling up favours, searching for some weakness in this new and compassionate law that they could exploit.

WHERE'S THE EVIDENCE?

I had been comfortable with my atheism for a long time. A 'God' made no sense to me. Years in the research laboratories of university physics departments, looking for tiny, almost unmeasurable signals had affected me. I wanted proof, demanded proof, and needed to see evidence. No evidence? No proof — so clearly there could be no God. Search if you will, I thought, but accept the results of any evidence you find.

To my surprise, some of the other physicists did manage to keep their faith. They reasoned that God was the controlling hand. Unmeasurable, but present. A variation perhaps on the 'uncertainty principle' of Heisenberg, lifted from quantum mechanics and adapted. The harder you look, the more difficult it is to position what it is you're searching for. This principle had worked well for subatomic particles, explaining the futility of attempting their detection using conventional means, but God? I listened and argued, but got nowhere and soon gave up. How to argue with those who can see ghosts? I put it all down to some mental aberration, or deficit, possibly genetic, and got on with life. Now, 25 years later, in the Northern Territory, I was again to feel the influence of these believers-in-myth on my life.

ATTRACTING THE ATTENTION OF THE BELIEVERS

It started with a trickle of letters and emails, and became a torrent. The most common accusation was that I had broken 'God's law' and killed. Sometimes an explanation was sought, but the usual reason for contact was to tell me of the serious nature of my crime. Forgiveness, it seemed, was possible, but only if I would acknowledge my sin.

I answered some of this correspondence, taking the time to explain in detail that in my opinion a god, any god, who maintains that all life is his creation, and sacred, must be wrong. There were too many anomalies. 'What about animals?' I would write. 'Aren't their lives sacred?'

The argument was then restricted to the sanctity of human life. God, it seems, has drawn a line that humans are fortunately on the right side of. It is human life that is the sacred gift from God. But this still made no sense to me. 'What sort of gift is one that you cannot give away?' It's not a gift that's being described, but an onerous burden we're being told to endure; a burden disguised as a gift from a god who supposedly loves us. And none of the patients I talked to, those desperately seeking release from their suffering, valued this gift at all.

Some who made contact went into the act, the 'killing', in more detail. 'If you believe that what you did was right, why then did you build the Deliverance Machine?' I was asked. 'Why didn't you just go there, put the needle into the veins, and push down on the syringe?' The machine, they claimed, simply gave me something to hide behind, something that would allow me to escape the intolerable responsibility of my actions. Similar, they said, to putting a loaded a gun into a victim's lap, so that I might claim, after the death, that I was not involved.

My explanation was straightforward. Put simply, the Deliverance Machine was developed to make it clear to all that this act, this 'killing', was the decision of the person who was dying. It was not a case of a comatose and unresponsive person being murdered by a doctor under cover of the new legislation. In addition, the machine allowed me to leave free the patient's personal space. I did not need to be alongside, administering the lethal drugs, taking up space that was better occupied by those they loved. It opened up the personal space of the person about to die, allowing in those closest to them. The machine gave me and the patient the space that was needed.

Others even claimed that the machine was simply an attempt to turn the act of 'killing' into the more palatable act of 'suicide' or 'assisted suicide'. But even suicide, they quickly added, was a violation of God's law, simply an extension of the sixth commandment: 'Thou shall not kill [oneself]'.

BLURRING THE BOUNDARIES

Events in the Northern Territory had shown that many saw the Rights of the Terminally Ill Act as legislation incompatible with the law of God. An orchestrated 'Euthanasia No' campaign emerged, led by *The Australian's* Paul Kelly, Sydney businessman Jim Dominguez, Labor's Tony Burke, and then federal Liberal Party backbencher Kevin Andrews.[1] They argued that those believing in God had a duty to rid the nation of such a law.

God-fearing politicians took up the challenge. Supported by their respective leaders, John Howard and Kim Beazley, these faith-driven politicians proudly hatched a plot to exploit the Constitution, taking advantage of an historical loophole of the reduced power of a territory, and used federal powers to remove the legislation their God found so offensive.

In March 1997, they succeeded. The Australian Senate passed the Andrews legislation. No Australian Territory (the Northern Territory, Australian Capital Territory, or Norfolk Island) could now pass legislation giving residents the right to request assistance to die. Territorians had been disenfranchised. And Australia, the nation that had briefly led the world in providing end-of-life rights to the dying, returned back to the dark ages. The Church had flexed its muscles and won.

SUICIDE: OCCASIONALLY, THE BEST OPTION

And that could have been the end of it. But those believing that God's law should prevail felt the Australian political system was ripe for further manipulation, and set out to exploit this eroding boundary between church and state.

Changes were immediate. Scarcely had the ink dried on Kevin Andrews' Euthanasia Laws Repeal Bill than further initiatives to restrict end-of-life choice were announced. The state would follow strategies outlined by the Church, and make it even harder to control the manner and timing of one's death. The option of lawful help for the terminally ill wanting to die had gone. Those keen to extend God's law moved to make it impossible for people to take that step by themselves.

Experience during the time of the Rights of the Terminally Ill Act suggested that the possible answer to the question of providing end-of-life choice lay not in passing restrictive pieces of legislation at all. Indeed, the whole reason that the law (God's or man's) had any place in controlling end-of-life choices was something of a technological accident. The means to a peaceful and reliable death are not readily available, so the law was able to find a place, gaining a role in controlling and restricting access to those means.

It was clear that if you had your personal means of a reliable and peaceful death, you would not waste your time seeking to make use of euthanasia legislation. Bob Dent would not, in those last weeks of his life, have been visiting doctors if he had a bottle of the euthanasia drug Nembutal in his cupboard. At the right time, he simply would have gone to the cupboard. Access to the means of a peaceful and reliable suicide, the right drugs, and information about how to use them, was an answer to those wanting choice at the end of life.

To outlaw suicide, though, presents some difficulties. Attempting suicide has been a crime in the past, but the acceptance of the medicalised view that those who killed themselves were the victims of psychiatric illness meant that punishment came to be seen as inappropriate. Therapy was now considered the best response, and any strategy that sought to blame the (sick) victim was unacceptable. A smarter approach by those wanting to preserve sacred human life at all costs was to move to make it impossible for anyone to learn how to suicide, or to get what they needed for a peaceful and reliable death.

ONWARD CHRISTIAN POLITICIANS

It was never going to be a simple matter of recriminalising suicide. In the intervening years, lobbyists for the Church had not only increased in voice but their denominational face had changed. Whereas once it was the Catholic Church who led the charge, by 2002, the evangelicals had come on board, most notably in the form of the Assemblies of God congregations and the Australian Christian Lobby. Together, their approaches found a receptive Australian federal government. With increasing numbers of federal politicians electing to take the oath over the affirmation at their swearing in, this is perhaps not surprising.

Parliament's first move was to restrict the flow of end-of-life information. The strategy was simple. If you don't know what to do, then you can't do it. Doubt and uncertainty would keep those thinking of ending their lives from even trying. This knee-jerk federal move towards censorship as an immediate reaction to pressure from Church lobbyists was disappointing. Although a slap in the face to the principle of free speech, the premise that 'all suicide was bad' and the knowledge necessary to carry out this act had to be restricted was accepted without question. Australians, it seemed, were only on this planet because we could not learn how to leave, and we had to be protected from ourselves by a caring church and state.

In 2006, then federal attorney-general Philip Ruddock overturned a decision of the Office of Film and Literature Classification and removed the 'how-to' guide book *The Peaceful Pill Handbook* (2007), by Fiona Stewart and myself, from distribution in Australia. When the Australian Christian

Lobby issued a press release congratulating NSW Right to Life on their 'very encouraging win in having … [the] book banned in Australia', it became obvious just how far our secular politics had been infiltrated by God.

A short time later, the same Australian Christian Lobby had another significant win with the passage of the Suicide Related Materials Act through federal parliament. This quaint legislation was unique in the Western world, making it a crime to use an electronic 'carriage service' (phone, email, internet, et cetera) to transmit end-of-life information. Another use of censorship, and a further attack on free speech. All in the name of God.

In December 2007, the federal government changed, but the new Labor government showed no interest in re-establishing a divide between church and state. Prime Minister Rudd's weekly Sunday church-doorstop media pronouncements became regular television news, and the Christian lobby moved in on new targets. Now, they had their sights set on the internet as another source where information on ending one's life was available. Their solution was simple: ban websites deemed by them as unacceptable. Again, the federal government complied, and moved to make this dream of the religious lobby come true. The myth of an internet 'clean feed' became official Labor policy.

The government's scheme of mandatory internet filtering was announced in 2008. Not only would this 'clean feed' remove pornography from the internet but, with such a mechanism in place, other sensitive topics could also be controlled. Complaints by those pointing to the tenuous Australian concept of 'free speech' were denounced in federal parliament by Stephen Conroy, Minister for Broadband, Communications, and the Digital Economy, as coming from people who would allow access to child pornography. No sooner was the plan for a trial of the filtering software announced by the government than the list of proposed websites to be banned was leaked. Included was Exit International's 'Peaceful Pill' euthanasia site: www.peacefulpill.com.

This category of content is currently under review, but the filters that will restrict internet access to Australians may be legislated in late 2011, or in 2012. The fervour of the Labor federal government on this issue does not point to this intrusive strategy being abandoned. A church–state separation of power has never been more illusory.

In the 13 years that have passed since the world's first euthanasia law was overturned by a government, in a clear and articulated response to pressure from the Church, there has been little to celebrate by those seeking access to end-of-life choices. As the presence of end-of-life legislation might attest, other countries have had better success in maintaining the necessary church–state separation needed. There are now five countries in the world where lawful help to die is available. In Australia, though, we continue to wait.

THE BIG PICTURE: A GODLESS FUTURE

The pendulum has to swing back. Society cannot accommodate the notion that all life is a God-given, sacred gift indefinitely, and we can not continually adhere to this principal insisting that all effort is made to prolonge life, any life, while frustrating with the rule of law the plans of those who wish to leave the planet.

At Exit International meetings around the country, this theme is consistent. As our elderly lament their lack of access to end-of-life information and choice, they equally complain about the compulsion of modern medicine to keep them alive against their will. 'Save the money and spend it on those who still have a life to lead,' they tell their peers at question time. 'I've had enough. Let me go in peace and let me go my way.' Applause usually follows.

My advocacy group is full of those who have found their own answers to the God question. At an average age of 75 years old, these (usually) headstrong individuals are in no mind to be dictated to or patronised. What is important to them is that they have control over how they die. Whether it be the passage of civilising euthanasia legislation or simply the ability to get reliable lethal drugs from Mexico, they don't much mind. But they want, and will eventually get, their way. An ageing wave of baby boomers demanding this sensible option will prevail and, in the process, send the Church scurrying off to reword the sixth commandment.

NOTES

1. M. Gordon, 'Holy Alliance: the inside story of euthanasia's demise,' *The Weekend Australian*, 29 March 1997.

PROGRESSIVE CHRISTIANITY: A SECULAR RESPONSE

Alex McCullie
Lecturer at the Council of Adult Education Melbourne,
writer, blogger, and professional speaker

ATHEISTS ARE COMMONLY CRITICISED FOR STEREOTYPING RELIGIOUS believers. Specifically, atheists are regularly accused of falsely characterising all Christian beliefs as simple 'god in the sky' fundamentalism. In light of these criticisms, this paper examines the progressive end of Christian beliefs — Progressive Christianity — within today's secular society.

For over 1500 years, the promise of an afterlife through salvation has dominated traditional Christian thinking. The physical world is merely a transition to a greater future with God. The Roman Catholic Church, in particular, saw its role as shepherd, saving as many souls as possible through the acceptance of correct beliefs and Church doctrine. Protestants emphasised salvation through faith from the acceptance of the scriptures. Progressive Christians, on the other hand, seek personal transformation in this world through religious experiences and Christian practices. For Progressive Christians, faith has moved from belief to trust.

This paper will examine Progressive Christian approaches to four major areas of religious thought and practice: nature of God, significance of Jesus, status of the Christian Bible, and being a Christian.

TRADITIONAL CHRISTIANITY

Traditional Christianity has been the public face of Christianity for the last few hundred years. It is dominant throughout South America, Africa, and southern Asia, as well as Eastern Europe, Russia, and former

Russian republics. Even in Western countries like Australia and New Zealand, traditional Christianity forms a significant part of Christian practice; especially among conservative Christians and evangelists.

John Hick, renowned philosopher of religion, succinctly characterises and criticises this form of Christianity, with its traditional conception of God:

> In the West we most naturally speak of God. But as used within the Western monotheisms this carries with it the strong connotation of a limitless all-powerful divine Person with such attributes as loving, commanding, judging, accepting, condemning, punishing, revealing, who is the creator of everything other than him/herself and who acts purposefully within the history of the universe and the history of some one particular section of humanity, as recorded in their scriptures. This is the anthropomorphic concept of the Ultimate modelled on our own human nature but magnified to infinity and purified of all limitations and defects.[1]

Gerald Bray describes the traditional relationship between humans and God:

> Human beings form a kind of bridge between the spiritual and the material dimensions of creation because we are the only creatures who have a natural link with both of them. In the material dimension we are very much like the animals and our life cycle is similar to theirs. We are born, we reproduce, we eat food in order to survive and in the end we die, just as animals do. But in spite of these similarities, human beings are not animals. Unlike them, we also have a spiritual dimension, which the Bible describes as the 'image and likeness of God' (Genesis 1:26–27).[2]

However, this view is not unchallenged, with liberal-minded Christians wanting change. Most are aware that politically sensitive issues such as women and open homosexuals in church-leadership roles have created well-publicised schisms in the worldwide Anglican movement between conservatives, typically from African and Asian dioceses, and liberals from Europe, the US, and Australia. The ordination of openly gay man Gene Robinson as Bishop of New Hampshire in 2003 highlighted the internal disputes over scriptural interpretation. The media and communications arm of the Anglican Diocese of Sydney, Anglican Media Sydney, in an online article, 'Scripture "Trumped" in US Decision', reported that:

> The debate over Robinson's suitability to be Bishop high-lighted the deep divide between liberals and conservatives. Liberal argument stressed four points: As a matter of theology, Jesus did not condemn homosexuality, the 'sin' of Sodom was inhospitality, and the 'sin' of the Epistles was acting contrary to one's God-given sexual nature; as a matter of biology, homosexuality is a genetically determined aspect of the human body; as a matter of psychology, homosexuality is irreversible; as a matter of sociology, homo-sexuality is normal — a social category akin to gender or race. God, it was argued, made Gene Robinson the way he was, and God loves him as he is.
>
> Conservatives opposed all of these liberal points, saying homosexuality was not innate, but a choice. As a matter of psychology, homo-sexuality was a reversible condition. And as a matter of sociology, homosexuality was not normal, but an illness or perverse choice.
>
> The centre of the conservative argument, however, was an appeal to Scripture and to the traditions of the Church.[3]

PROGRESSIVE CHRISTIANITY

Over the last century, many theologians, scholars, and laypeople have struggled to accept traditional Christianity (with its 'being-out-there' God, an unconvincing divine Jesus, and its 2000- to 3000-year-old texts) as being worthy of worship in the modern world. Dealing with this credibility gap is now seen as a matter of urgency, as mainstream church attendance numbers in Western countries are in rapid decline.

The Progressive Christianity movement is a response to this crisis. My survey comes from the writings, lectures, and sermons of key figures in this broad-based, largely Protestant liberal movement, including academics Marcus Borg and John Dominic Crossan, and retired Bishop John (Jack) Shelby Spong, as well as Australian sources like the Progressive Christian Network, theologian Val Webb, and Reverend Francis Macnab of St Michael's Uniting Church in Melbourne. Furthermore, *The Canberra Affirmation*, written in November 2008 by the Centre for Progressive Religious Thought in Canberra, provides a useful local framework to survey the ideas of Progressive Christians.

Overall, it's fair to say that Progressive Christianity emphasises personal experience over acceptance of doctrine. By rejecting the authority of traditional doctrines and church teachings, Progressive Christians make their understandings of God, Jesus, and the Bible much more personal and less institutional — and somewhat less accessible — to outside critical evaluation.

NATURE OF GOD

Conceptualising God as something outside of, or beyond, our physical world must always be problematic in today's scientific worldview. How does one use language of the finite to talk of the infinite? Despite protests from many past and present Christian thinkers, most Christians still see God as an interventionist, caring being of infinite power. This is the image of God commonly evoked by the question: 'Do you believe in God?' Progressive Christians, on the other hand, portray God as a pervasive essence — more personal, less institutional and, certainly, more ineffable than the traditional view:

> We affirm there is a presentness in the midst of our lives, sensed as both within and beyond ourselves, which can transform our experiences of this earth and each other. Various imaginative ideas have been used to describe this presentness: 'God', 'sacred', 'love', 'Spirit of Life'. We recognise all attempts at understanding and attributing meaning are shaped by prevailing thoughts and culture. Ultimately our response can only be as awe-inspiring mystery beyond the limits of our ability to understand our world and ourselves.[4]

God is portrayed as an all-inclusive, pervasive, conscious essence, undetectable by any physical means, and unable to be cast with human characteristics. Therefore, portraying God in the human roles of king, lord, master, and judge is rejected as inappropriately applying human desires and values onto an essentially non-human essence. To reinforce God's ineffable nature, Progressive Christians often use references like 'the sacred', the 'more', 'is-ness', 'the good spirit', 'Spirit of Life', and

'God-presence'.[5] So, instead of human leadership comparisons, God is often portrayed as a 'lover' — one who gives and receives love — and an 'illuminator' — one who lights up a new view of reality.

However, despite these more ethereal portrayals of God, most Progressive Christians believe God exists independently of our physical world, is made of different 'stuff'. Progressive Christians still need to assign God enough human characteristics to be loved, worshipped, and admired. It is hard to imagine Christians having personal, loving relationships with something totally foreign to humans. As Marcus Borg says:

> I suggest 'Spirit' as a root image for this model of God, and the phrase 'Spirit model' as a designator for the model itself. It leads to an image of the Christian life that stresses relationship, intimacy, and belonging ... At the heart of Christianity is God. Without a robust affirmation of the reality of God, Christianity makes no sense. And just as important, how we 'see' God, God's relationship to the world, and God's character — matters greatly.[6]

The Canberra Affirmation and other progressive writings are admirable in acknowledging that there are limitations in describing anything beyond our everyday experiences. However, their vague descriptions of God seem like a victory for religious inclusiveness over clarity and specificity, and may come at the cost of justifying any specific Christian religious practices.

SIGNIFICANCE OF JESUS

Jesus has always been the raison d'être for Christianity. There are three distinct 'Jesuses' — the historical Jesus, the Christ of faith, and the Jesus of faith.

The historical Jesus comes from secular historical research as a sketchy profile of a Jew, executed around 30 CE by the occupying Romans. Later followers would declare him as the Messiah, the Christ. A popular conception among many scholars is of Jesus as a Jewish prophet, proclaiming to the poor and dispossessed the overthrow of the ruling Roman and Jewish elite with God's kingdom on this Earth. However, this is disputed by many others.

Over time, Jesus became the Christ of faith, as early Christians attempted to understand his death and their post-death engagements with him. This developed into the divine Christ, as worshipped in traditional Christianity today. Progressive Christians, on the other hand, have constructed a very different Jesus — one of faith, an idealised modern portrait of spiritual man drawn from the Gospel stories of the Christian Bible:

> We honour the one called Jesus, a first century Galilean Jewish sage, nurtured by his religious tradition. A visionary and wisdom teacher, he invited others through distinctive oral sayings and parables about integrity, justice, and inclusiveness, and an open table fellowship, to adopt and trust a re-imagined vision of the 'sacred', of one's neighbour, of life. As we too share in this vision, we affirm the significance of his life and teachings, while claiming to be 'followers of Jesus'.[7]

Contrary to traditional teachings, there is no claim here that Jesus is either God or the son of God. He is characterised as a great man and, often, the greatest of all men.

Integrating the traditional centrality of Jesus — essential to any form of Christianity — within a progressive understanding of God seems problematic for worship. Marcus Borg, in books like *Reading the Bible Again for the First Time* (2002) and *The Heart of Christianity* (2003), speaks of a pre-Easter Jesus and a post-Easter Jesus as two separate understandings.[8] The first is essentially an amalgam of the historical Jesus and the one of faith, while the second is the traditional Christ of faith without the historical claims. This enables Progressive Christians to retain all the theological trappings for Christian worship without conflicts over the historicity of the stories.

The post-Easter Jesus is the one of faith, to whom Christians assign theological trappings without necessarily any historical support. Supernatural stories are interpreted metaphorically. Progressive Christian writers stress an almost postmodernist approach, suggesting that myth and metaphor offer greater truths than those of purely historical facts. As Borg says, appealingly, '... metaphors can be profoundly true, even though they are not literally true. Metaphor is poetry plus, not factuality minus'.[9]

STATUS OF THE BIBLE

> We receive the Hebrew and Christian scriptures known as the Bible, as a collection of human documents rich in historical memory and religious interpretation, which describe attempts to address and respond to the 'sacred'. It forms an indispensable part of our tradition and personal journeys. We claim the right and responsibility to question and interpret its texts, empowered by critical biblical scholarship as well as from our own life experiences. We accept that other sources — stories, poems and songs — imaginative pictures of human life both modern and ancient, can nurture us and others, in a celebration of the 'sacred' in life.[10]

Notice that the Bible is not claimed as the word of God, directly or indirectly, but as the product of human authorship. The affirmation acknowledges that other documents are also considered valid sources for Christian spirituality, even though many Progressive Christians still see the Bible as a primary source of faith.

Borg advocates seeing the Bible in three ways: historical — human product of two ancient communities, expressing their witness to God; metaphorical — understanding the meaning behind the literal language, like comparing love to a red rose; and sacramental — acting as a mediator or conduit between a follower and the sacred. A Progressive Christian uses the Bible to connect with the sacred by drawing personal meanings from the stories without accepting them as historical fact. For John Dominic Crossan, this even applies to the resurrection of Jesus, a traditional core belief for most Christians:

> In a nutshell, these are my conclusions: First, the Easter story is not about the events of a single day, but reflects the struggle of Jesus' followers over a period of months and years to make sense of both his death and their continuing experience of empowerment by him. Second, stories of the resurrected Jesus appearing to various people are not really about 'visions' at all, but literary fiction prompted by struggles over leadership in the early church. Third, resurrection is one — but only one — of the metaphors used to express the sense of Jesus' continuing presence with his followers and friends.[11]

Though denying the historicity of the resurrection, Progressive Christians seek to retain its metaphorical message of personal transformation through symbolic death and rebirth. Most would still agree with John Young, Canon Emeritus of York Minster, that: 'The resurrection of Jesus Christ is not just one aspect of Christianity. We cannot remove a portion of the Christian jigsaw labelled "resurrection" and leave anything which is recognizable as Christian faith'.[12] Progressive Christians are then able to retain a story fundamental with much of Christian theology while avoiding credibility problems with our understanding of the world.

So Progressive Christianity emphasises personal experience over believing in doctrine. Writers argue that they are actually returning to the roots of Christianity by emphasising experience, mythic stories as truth, and trusting acceptance. Leading Progressive Christian commentator on religious affairs Karen Armstrong, an ex-nun, is a world-renowned writer and broadcaster, having published more than 15 books. In an interview on Fora TV, she blames modernity and the Enlightenment for the current 'obsession' with facts and evidence as the only sources of truth.[13] She believes Christians should simply ignore the metaphysical arguments and lead lives as Christians. Acceptance of beliefs may come later.

BEING A CHRISTIAN

> We acknowledge that a transformative path of inclusion and integrity involves living responsible and compassionate lives in community with others.[14]

Progressive writers talk of compassion and personal transformation rather than obedience and servitude. Marcus Borg describes his sense of being 'born again' on a daily basis, even alluding to the resurrection:

> The 'dailiness' of the process fits my experience, as it does that of many people I know. In the course of the day, I sometimes realise that I have become burdened, and that the cause is that I have forgotten God. In the act of remembering God, of reminding myself of the reality of God, I sometimes feel a lightness of being — a rising out of my self-

preoccupation and burdensome confinement. We are called again and again from our tombs.[15]

Theologian John Shelby Spong famously called for a 'New Reformation' by posting his challenges to traditional Christianity in the spirit of Luther's 95 Theses. Here are some, to give a flavour of his complaints:

1. Theism, as a way of defining God, is dead. God can no longer be understood with credibility as a Being, supernatural in power, dwelling above the sky and prepared to invade human history periodically to enforce the divine will. So, most theological God-talk today is meaningless unless we find a new way to speak of God.

...

3. The biblical story of the perfect and finished creation from which human beings fell into sin is pre-Darwinian mythology and post-Darwinian nonsense.

...

9. There is no external, objective, revealed standard writ in Scripture or on tablets of stone that will govern our ethical behavior for all time.

...

11. The hope for life after death must be separated forever from the behavior-control mentality of reward and punishment. The church must abandon, therefore, its reliance on guilt as a motivator of behavior.[16]

Reverend Francis Macnab, of St Michael's Uniting Church in Melbourne, declared the old religion as encouraging people to be 'dependent neurotics'. His new faith appears more humanist, with ten suggestions replacing the negative biblical Ten Commandments:

Commandment 1: Believe in a Good Presence in your life. Call that Good Presence: God, G-D [God modified not to offend Jews] — and follow that Good Presence so that you live life fully — tolerantly, collaboratively, generously and with dignity.

...

Commandment 3: Take care of your home, your environments, your planet and its vital resources for the life and health of people in all the world.

...

Commandment 5: Help people develop their potential and become as fully functioning human beings as is possible from birth, through traumas and triumph to the end of their days.[17]

Progressive Christians like Macnab reject the idea that we are living under universal judgement, and promote morality and ethics as a human concern that should be argued on that basis. Progressives often see Jesus in this context as a moral exemplar.

Furthermore, Progressive Christians, unlike their traditional brethren, promote religious tolerance and plurality. Writers like Marcus Borg, Houston Smith, and Karen Armstrong attempt to emphasise the commonality of the inner, esoteric core of belief across all religions, while respecting the differences of the 'exoteric' cultural shell of differing doctrine and practice.

PROBLEMS FOR TRADITIONAL CHRISTIANITY

So what are the problems for traditional Christianity in our twenty-first century secular society? These are the criticisms by Progressive Christians. Mostly the problems are credibility and relevance, especially to young people.

Firstly, people today seek physical explanations and not religious dogmas to understand the world. Morality is seen as a human affair independent of supernatural influences. By promoting supernatural messages, most traditional religions are being ignored by the young. Their explanations are contrary and an affront to their everyday experiences of life.

Secondly, most people reject a hierarchical model of power and reverence, the foundation of all traditional churches. The days of 'father knows best' and 'divine to rule' are long gone. A promise of a blissful after-life is no longer believable as a reward for life-long dedicated servitude. Lives are no longer 'solitary, poor, nasty, brutish, and short' for people in our society.[18]

Thirdly, despite some vague deference to the Christian Bible, people today cannot take the writings as serious historical fact. The books are works of human authors dedicated to proclaiming religious beliefs in ancient Middle Eastern cultures. Even the existence of the Jewish preacher, Jesus, is questioned by many.

Finally, there is the problem of suffering, or evil. How do we reconcile the existence of an all-powerful, all-loving, morally perfect Christian God with extensive human and animal pain and suffering from natural and human causes? The innocent, the good, and the bad all seem to prosper and suffer equally. Despite years of Christian apologetics — evil teaches us a lesson; suffering is needed to appreciate good; we are born with original sin; we are unable to comprehend God's intentions; and the afterlife is the real goal — the problem of suffering presents the greatest challenge to notion of the traditional God.

PROBLEMS FOR PROGRESSIVE CHRISTIANITY

Whether one sees Progressive Christianity as regaining its mystical roots or simply shedding unpalatable doctrine depends on your point of view. Its social aims are laudable: equitable social justice; human-based morality; and responsible environmental management. I could imagine a Progressive Christian and a secular humanist serving equally well on a hospital ethics committee or an environmental panel.

However, Progressive Christians have effectively denuded Christianity of much of its theology and doctrine, and its claims to authority. Perhaps they have jettisoned the raison d'être of Christianity — the Christ of faith. God is now a pervasive goodness; Jesus becomes a first-century Galilean sage; and the sacred biblical texts are ancient attempts to personify God's goodness. The Bible no longer holds a unique position of authority with the Progressive Christians, with literary works providing genuine spiritual alternatives.

Why bother with any form of Christianity? Today's spiritual-seeker can lead a comfortable secular life supplemented by any one of the New Age spiritualities, no need for Jesus or the Bible. It seems that Progressive Christianity would appeal to committed but disaffected Christians only, leaving aside the vast majority of us — the religiously indifferent.

Is there a future for Progressive Christianity? According to theologian Tom Frame, 'left-leaning, cause-driven, liberal Protestant churches that lack doctrinal rigour and are preoccupied with the promotion of social justice and cultural inclusion will be the first to go'.[19] Unfortunately, Frame's remarks seem compelling.

Gary Bouma, in *Australian Soul* (2006), highlights the shift in the Australian religious landscape 'from rationality to experientialism'. He suggests that traditional suburban churches are being replaced by large evangelical mega-churches and popular informal gatherings of worshippers while neighbourhood churches are ever-dwindling.[20] Progressive Christianity seeks to offer a palatable form of Christian worship, a religion-lite, according to Dan Jones, while retaining the formal structures of Christian practice — God, Jesus, Bible, churches, liturgies, hymns, and prayers.[21] It appeals directly to liberal-minded, church-going Christians seeking a more believable theology. However, younger people, who often have had no connection to church-going Christianity, would be unlikely to consult the Christian Bible for spiritual enlightenment. Two-thousand- to 3000-year-old stories would be perceived by them as irrelevant to today's world.

Ultimately, however, our loud, market-driven secular society has moved away from most formal Christian churches by rejecting their God, biblical myths, and unengaging liturgies. Progressive Christianity's quiet substituting of the unpalatable personal God with a god-essence and historical Jesus sage, though attractive, will likely go unnoticed among the public's desire for easily-packaged twenty-first-century spiritualities. This is unfortunate. A diverse secular society would be better served by socially progressive religious movements, rather than by a plethora of evangelicalism and conservative fundamentalism that seeks to disengage science and modernity.

NOTES

1. J. Hick, *The New Frontier of Religion and Science: religious experience, neuroscience, and the transcendent,* Palgrave, Hampshire, 2006.
2. G. Bray, 'God', in A. McGrath (ed.), *The New Lion Handbook Christian Belief,* Lion, Oxford, 2007, p. 67.
3. 'Scripture "Trumped" in US Decision', Anglican Media Sydney, 23 August 2003, at www.sydneyanglicans.net/news/stories/994a
4. R. A. Hunt, 'The Canberra Affirmation', Centre for Progressive Religious Thought, November 2008, at www.rexaehuntprogressive.com/prayer_collection/an_affirmation/the_canberra_affirmation.html
5. W. James, *The Varieties of Religious Experience,* Viking, London, 1982, p. 511.
6. 'I suggest "Spirit" ... belonging', in M. J. Borg, *The God We Never Knew,* HarperCollins, New York, 1998, p. 71; 'At the heart ... greatly', in M. J. Borg, *The Heart of Christianity,* HarperCollins, New York, 2003, p. 61.
7. 'The Canberra Affirmation'.
8. See M. Borg, *Reading the Bible Again for the First Time: taking the Bible seriously but not literally,* HarperCollins, New York, 2002 and M. Borg, *The Heart of Christianity: rediscovering a life of faith,* Harper, San Francisco, 2003.

9. *Reading the Bible Again for the First Time*, p. 41.

10. 'The Canberra Affirmation'.

11. J. D. Crossan and R. G. Watts, *Who is Jesus?: answers to your questions about the historical Jesus*, Westminster John Knox Press, Louisville, 1996. p. 121.

12. J. Young, *Teach Yourself Christianity*, Hodder Headline, London, 2008, p. 38.

13. K. Armstrong, 'Karen Armstrong in Conversation with Alan Jones', 2008, video at http://fora.tv/2008/02/27/Karen_Armstrong_in_Conversation_with_Alan_Jones

14. 'The Canberra Affirmation'.

15. *The Heart of Christianity*, p. 118.

16. J. S. Spong, *Jesus for the Non-religious*, HarperCollins, New York, 2007.

17. Dr F. Macnab, 'Components of the New Faith: Overview', St Michael's on Collins, video at www.stmichaels.org.au/components-of-the-new-faith/overview

18. T. Hobbes, *Leviathan: or, the Matter, Forme and Power of a Commonwealth Ecclesiasticall and Civil* (ed. A. R. Waller), Cambridge University Press, Cambridge, 1904, p. 84.

19. T. Frame, *Losing My Religion: unbelief in Australia*, UNSW Press, Sydney, 2009, p. 299.

20. G. Bouma, *Australian Soul*, Oxford University Press, Cambridge, 2006, pp. 96, 97–98.

21. D. Jones, 'Resolving the Metaphysical Muddle', *The Guardian*, 9 August 2009, at www.guardian.co.uk/commentisfree/belief/2009/aug/09/religion-armstrong-atheism

ABORTION IN AUSTRALIA

Dr Leslie Cannold
Author, *Sun-Herald* columnist, Adjunct Senior Lecturer at the Monash Institute of
Health Services Research, Fellow at the School of Philosophy, Anthropology, and
Social Enquiry at the University of Melbourne

AUSTRALIAN PUBLIC OPINION ON ABORTION RIGHTS IS CLEAR AND
unequivocal. Australians, 81 per cent to be precise, support a woman's right
to choose.[1] Despite the increased public profile of the issue in recent years,
including several high-profile prosecutions of abortion service providers
and women for the crime of abortion, polling reveals that support of
reproductive rights among Australians, regardless of whether they live in
the city or the country, and their income or education levels, has been
growing since the 1980s.[2]

Religion, or lack of it, does determine where Australians stand on the
abortion issue. Among non-believing Australians, a staggering 94 per cent
support a woman's right to choose.[3] But what most people don't realise is
that the majority of religious Australians, 88 per cent — favour choice in
all or some circumstances, too.[4] Indeed, only among members of the most
conservative Christian denominations, Baptists and Pentecostals, does
support for a woman's right to choose fall below 50 per cent.[5]

It is not just attitudes but the reproductive behaviours of conservative
Christians that contravenes official Church positions on the issue. Indeed,
the abortion rate of American Catholics is higher than that of the general
population, despite 96 per cent of those over 18 using modern contraception,
forbidden by the Pope.[6] In the US, one in five American women having
abortions are evangelical Christians.[7] One explanation for such figures is that
women who are members of religious groups that frown on contraception

and abortion struggle to deploy contraception properly and consistently. This may lead to higher rates of unplanned pregnancy, as well a preference for abortion to resolve it, because of the stigma associated with sexual activity, pregnancy, and motherhood outside of marriage in some faith communities.[8] Indeed, while adoption remains the official solution advocated by conservative churches to unplanned pregnancy, one study suggests that both pro-life and pro-choice see it as the most difficult, and the least ethical, choice.[9]

While women of faith have abortions at the same, if not higher, rates than the general population, they may struggle more to make and achieve resolution about their choices. One study of the medical records of American abortion patients found 27 per cent cited religious or spiritual concerns about their abortion. Among the questions religious women asked service providers were, 'Will I go to hell/be punished for [having an abortion]', 'Am I doing the right thing?' and 'Do I have a right [to make this decision]?'[10] The American Psychological Association also found that having a faith-based view that abortion is wrong, or being surrounded by people who believe this to be so, may increase a woman's risk of psychological disturbance after abortion. The reasons for this seem to relate to known risk factors for poor mental health after abortion, including shame, secrecy, and lack of social support.[11] Our knowledge that negative social attitudes about abortion, faith-based or otherwise, may actually contribute to the psychological problems a small group of women experience after abortion (and which are then exploited by the anti-choice movement in campaigns against abortion) also comes from anti-choice research into the issue. In a cross-cultural comparison of aborting women, a team of well-known anti-choice activists found that, while less than 1 per cent of Russian women were 'traumatised' by their abortion, the figure was 14 per cent among the Americans.[12] In Russia, unlike the US, abortion is a commonly used and uncontroversial method of fertility management.

RELIGIOUS VIEWS ON ABORTION

Even if religious leaders were accurately representing the full range of theological positions taken by their faith, or the views of their flock, on abortion — which, I have argued, they are not — Australia is a democratic, pluralist society. Religious leaders have no right to impose their faith-based views about abortion on other Australians. Philosopher A. J. Coady, himself a practicing Catholic, makes this point clearly when he says:

> it is wrong for [religious] leaders to dictate to those who are not members of their flock: what authority they have does not extend to those who give it no recognition.[13]

One means by which religious leaders seek to soften the impropriety of their attempts to impose their faith-based views about abortion on those outside their flock is to imply, or state directly, that every faith tradition deems abortion sinful, and forbids it. This is not true. Judaism, Islam, Hinduism, Sikhism, Quakerism, Anglicanism, and Methodism all define conditions where abortion may be justified. These will be interpreted more or less liberally depending on the orthodoxy of the practitioner. Buddhism has no official position on the procedure.[14] In the US, the Episcopal and Presbyterian churches, the United Church of Christ and the United Methodist Church, the Unitarian Universalist Association, and Reform, Reconstructionist, and Conservative Judaism all have official statements, adopted by their governing bodies, supporting reproductive choice as a matter of conscience.[15]

Sadly, Australia lacks individuals and organisations willing to clearly articulate the disputes that exist across and within faiths about the morality of abortion. In the US, organisations such as Catholics for Choice and the Religious Coalition for Reproductive Choice not only present alternative faith-based approaches to the abortion issue, but ones that emphasise the moral agency, or conscience, of individual women and their right to decide for themselves.

WOMEN'S MORAL AGENCY AND 'STANDING' IN THE ABORTION DEBATE

The emphasis on individual conscience or moral agency is an important step forward in faith-based discussions of abortion. This is because even religious traditions with less-restrictive approaches to abortion tend not to shy from depicting the pregnant woman as a moral agent, with a perfectly functioning conscience, who can decide for herself about abortion. For example, the Jewish framework, one that bears a remarkable similarly to that articulated in the law in many Australian states, permits abortion in cases where the pregnancy endangers the woman's physical or mental state. But it is an authority (the rabbi in Jewish law, the doctor in Australian law) who is presumed to be the appropriate judge of the pregnant woman's reasons, not the pregnant woman herself.[16]

When pro-choice arguments give emphasis to women's moral agency, questions of standing are brought to the fore. Most contemporary arguments against abortion are foetal-centred. That is, they actually proceed without mentioning women, or their experience of pregnancy, at all.[17]

The foetal-centred argument against abortion can be broken down into four main components: the foetus is alive and/or human; the foetus has a right to life; abortion kills the foetus; and abortion is murder. It is frequently summarised in the image that typically sits behind the newsreader when abortion is in the media: a foetus, looking much like a baby cosmonaut, abstracted from its embedded location within the woman's body and her life.[18] The woman's name and story, her reasons for choosing abortion, are left outside the frame.[19]

Foetal-centred arguments against abortion not only 'disappear' women's bodies and lives from the moral analysis of abortion, they also imply that pregnancy is a conflicting relationship between mother and foetus. This depiction stands in sharp contrast to women's descriptions of the pregnant relationship as one of intimacy and interdependence, in which the woman feels care and responsibility for the foetus and the child it could become.[20] But anti-choice insistence on the antagonistic nature of the pregnant relationship is the basis of their claim that the woman in whose body the pregnancy is taking place is not a fit person to make decisions about the pregnancy's future, or her own. She has a conflict of interest, they contend, that both justifies the intrusion of anti-choice and religious leaders into the debate as 'spokesmen' for her foetus, and renders her own decisions unworthy of respect.

As the above makes clear, problems of standing are not abstract, but pose significant issues for those publicly advocating for choice. In my years as an activist, I've found that if the Pope or a lesser official from any of the established churches opens his mouth on the subject of abortion, a page-one story is his likely reward. Sometimes, this story will undermine, or even push aside, one that reflects either a woman's or medical provider's first hand experience of deciding about, accessing, and supporting women, and/or providing them with safe abortion services. I've also seen the Australian media (perhaps because of a questionable assumption about the universal truthfulness of religious leaders) report hyperbolic or baseless statements by religious leaders that would be derided or dismissed if made by lesser mortals. For instance, during the debate about law reform in Victoria in 2008, Melbourne Archbishop Denis Hart claimed that passage of Victoria's abortion law-reform Act would force the closure of Catholic hospital maternity and emergency departments.[21] Despite its improbability, this assertion was widely reported. Though eventually proved false (the bill passed, and Catholic hospital services remained unchanged), a follow-up story has yet to appear.[22]

NEW ANTI-CHOICE APPROACHES TO RESTRICTING ABORTION

While most religious people are pro-choice, nearly all of the approximately 5 per cent of Australians that have told pollsters since 1987 that they are opposed to abortion in all circumstances are religious.[23] However, it is possible to accept both the premises and the conclusion of the foetal-centred argument against abortion without believing in God. Indeed, since the 1970s, when religious authority and affiliation began to wane in the West, the anti-choice movement has increasingly justified its claims by appealing to secular, rather than biblical, authorities. For instance, medical and scientific evidence is now mainly used to support its view that life begins at conception.[24] In fact, while questions about whether the foetus is alive and human are empirical ones that science can answer, what such facts indicate about how we ought to consider and treat the foetus are questions of value about which people can and will disagree.[25]

Further, and much to the consternation of the anti-choice movement, public acceptance of some of the premises of the foetal-centred argument against abortion does not necessarily lead the public to endorse the anti-choice conclusion that abortion should be banned. For instance, while Americans accept the assertion that abortion involves the destruction of human life, they repeatedly tell anti-choice pollsters that they do not endorse more restrictive abortion laws.[26] In 2005, and despite being asked what appeared to be 'push-polling' type questions, Australians expressed similar reservations about altering existing abortion laws because of concerns about 'the physical health of women who desire termination', and a desire to avoid 'stigmatis[ing] women as criminals for choosing abortion'.[27]

By the 1990s, the disconnect between public acceptance of anti-choice premises and acceptance of the movement's goal of restricting women's access to abortion was clear. As well, new data suggested anti-choice discourse was alienating women by calling them, implicitly in foetal-centred arguments and explicitly at clinic protests, 'murderers'. In reply, some advocates abandoned the foetal-centred approach in favour of a new, woman-centred one. Women-centred anti-choice strategy deploys secular authorities like science and medicine to argue abortion is wrong and must be restricted not because it kills foetuses but because it hurts women.[28]

The standard ingredients of the woman-centred argument against abortion are: induced abortion increases a woman's risk of poor physical or mental health; abortion harms women; abortion is wrong; and women's access to abortion should be restricted. As it happens, academically rigorous research has thus far concluded that, when compared to other ways of resolving a problem pregnancy (namely, abortion or parenting), a single induced abortion does not increase a woman's risk of infertility, breast cancer, prolonged grief, or any other physical or mental health problem.[29]

However, even if future studies proved otherwise, this would lend no support to anti-choice claims that any and all health risks associated with induced abortion justify restricting women's access to the procedure. This is so for a number of reasons. Firstly, because all medical procedures have risks. Adding another to the very low-risk profile of induced abortion (the World Health Organization describes it as one of the safest and most clinically common medical procedures) does not render the procedure so dangerous that restrictions or bans should be considered.[30] Secondly, women are not children, as women-centred arguments against abortion paternalistically imply. The founding of additional risks associated with induced abortion suggests only that abortion service providers must revise the disclosures they make to women considering abortion to ensure the consent they give to the procedure is substantially informed.

Women-centred anti-choice strategies do not attempt to achieve their aims by argument alone. As already stated, I object to the standing that anti-choice and religious leaders are granted in the abortion debate, but at least when we hear their views in the media we are clear about their religious affiliations and anti-choice aims. Knowing this allows us to contextualise their arguments, and to make informed decisions about how much weight to give them in forming our own views.[31] For some anti-choice advocates deploying women-centred arguments against abortion, it is precisely this information, about who they are and where they are coming from, that is omitted. As I have argued elsewhere:

> [Anti-choice advices deploying the women-centred strategy] argue that abortion is wrong because it hurts women ... they depict themselves as having an agenda-less desire ... to protect vulnerable women's rights from being trampled by abortion service-providers.[32]

In Australia, examples of such apparently disinterested advocacy by those who are very interested indeed include priests with PhDs who use their religious title for some audiences but not for others, and individuals with impeccable religious and anti-choice credentials (leadership roles in the pro-life movement, employment in institutions founded by Opus Dei) who identify themselves solely as ethicists, lawyers, or feminists when making arguments in the secular press that abortion hurts women.[33] Anti-choice research suggests that the public does not see them as a source of credible, women-centred information. Thus, it can be assumed that, when not recognised as such, anti-choice messages have better penetration, and that they also have expanded their reach. When an anti-choice activist objects to abortion, that's business as usual. But when a 'feminist' does so, that's news.

The problem of misleading and deceptive credentialing is not restricted to abortion politics. The US-based site Sourcewatch, a project of the Centre for Media and Democracy, has close to 50,000 articles profiling individuals who seek to manage and manipulate public perception, opinion, and policy. The existence of the site, which includes few Australian actors and institutions, points to the importance in Western democracies of the fourth estate shining the light not just into the dark corners of what informants say about their issue, but also on to what they claim and conceal about themselves.

CONCLUSION

Most religious people are pro-choice, but nearly all those with anti-choice views are religious. While women of faith have just as many, if not more, abortions than their secular counterparts, the negative views about abortion and aborting women fostered by some religions may increase the risk of poor mental health such women face in the wake of their choice. The anti-choice movement deploys two strategies to stigmatise abortion and aborting women, and to restrict women's access to safe and legal abortions. One is foetal-centred. It fails to mention women at all; but, by implying that pregnancy is a relationship of conflict, grants standing to religious and anti-choice leaders in the abortion debate at the expense of the pregnant woman herself. The newer woman-centred strategy patronises women by claiming they are incapable of rationally evaluating the risks and benefits associated with medical procedures, and of making good choices for themselves.

NOTES

1. This is the wording of the question asked by the Australian Election Study, as reported in K. Betts, 'Attitudes to Abortion in Australia: 1972 to 2003', *People and Place* 12 (4), 2009, p. 24.
2. K. Betts, 'Attitudes to Abortion: Australia and Queensland in the twenty-first century', *People and Place* 17 (3), 2009, pp. 25–39; M. Simons, 'Ties that bind', *Griffith Review* 8, Winter 2005, at www.griffithreview.com/edition8/103-essay/367.html
3. 2007 data as reported in K. Betts, 'Attitudes to Abortion: Australia and Queensland in the twenty-first century', pp. 25–49. Voters are asked for agreement as to whether women should be able to obtain an abortion 'readily' when they 'want one', or whether abortion should only be 'allowed' in special circumstances. The high levels of support for choice given by non-believing Australians are statistically significant.
4. 2007 Australian Election Study voters data provided to me by Katharine Betts, 2009.
5. These figures, provided to me by Katharine Betts in 2009, are in response to the 2005 Australian Survey of Social Attitudes survey statement: 'a woman should have the right to choose whether or not she has an abortion'. Catholic support for this proposition was 68 per cent.
6. 'The Facts Tell the Story: Catholics and choice', Catholics for a Free Choice, Washington, 2006, at www.catholicsforchoice.org/topics/reform/documents/2006catholicsandchoice.pdf
7. The Alan Guttmacher Institute, 1996, at www.guttmacher.org/media/nr/prabort2.html
8. '30% Higher Than Protestants: high Catholic abortion rate reported', *Los Angeles Times*, 7 October 1988, at http://articles.latimes.com/1988-10-07/news/mn-3576_1_abortion-rate
9. L. Cannold, *The Abortion Myth: feminism, morality, and the hard choices women make*, Wesleyan University Press, Middletown, 2001.

10. 2000 and 2001 data reported by the Abortion Conversation Project in 'Abortion and Spirituality: a survey of abortion clinic staff', Abortion and Spirituality ACP Report, 2007.

11. 'APA Task Force Report on Mental Health and Abortion', American Psychological Association, 2008, at www.apa.org/pi/women/programs/abortion/mental-health.pdf

12. V. M. Rue, P. K. Coleman, J. J. Rue, and D. C. Reardon, 'Induced Abortion and Traumatic Stress: preliminary comparison of American and Russian women', *Medical Science Monitor* 10, SR516, 2004, at www.medscimonit.com/medscimonit/modules. php?name=GetPDF&pg=2&idm=4923

13. A. J. Coady, cited by L. Skene, 'On the Relationship of Church, Law and State', Macquarie Bank Lecture given on 15 October 2002 in Sydney.

14. 'Religious Groups' Official Positions on Abortion', The Pew Forum on Religion and Public Life, 30 September 2008, at http://pewforum.org/docs/?DocID=351

15. 'Perspectives: a matter of faith and conscience', Religious Coalition for Reproductive Choice, October 2008, at www.rcrc.org/perspectives/index.cfm

16. B. Gittelsohn, *How Do I Decide?: a contemporary Jewish approach to what's right and what's wrong*, Behrman House, New Jersey., 1989; 'Chapter 5, Commission's Consultations Outcomes', *Law of Abortion: final report*, Victorian Law Reform Commission, Melbourne, 2008, p. 73, at www.lawreform.vic.gov.au/resources/file/eb4e330768c8449/VLRC_Abortion_ Chapter5.pdf

17. Rare mentions of pregnancy by opponents of abortion tend to follow a 'you play, you pay' line — that compulsory pregnancy and motherhood is an appropriate 'punishment' for women facing problem pregnancies. Where men, forced sex, failed contraception, and negative foetal diagnosis fit into this schema is unclear.

18. American bioethicists Barbara Rothman and Rosalind Petchesky coined this imagery of the cosmonaut. See *The Abortion Myth*, p. 37.

19. For a more extensive discussion of this framing of the issue, see *The Abortion Myth*.

20. In *The Abortion Myth*, I present evidence that it is the latter that most accurately describes women's experience of the pregnant relationship.

21. N. Miller, 'Abortion Law Defiance', *The Age*, 28 September 2008, at www.theage.com. au/national/catholic-hospitals-threaten-to-defy-abort-law-20080923-4ml0.html. In an opinion piece in the Melbourne tabloid *Herald Sun*, CEO of Catholic Health Australia Martin Laverty gave credence to the Archbishop's views, sourced at www.heraldsun.com.au/ opinion/conscience-is-law/story-e6frfifo-1111117566510 [page no longer available].

22. To be fair, Nick Miller from *The Age* did interview Catholic Health Australia's CEO Martin Laverty after the law passed. Despite suggesting that the Archbishop was right to raise concerns about the future operation of Catholic hospital services during the debate, Laverty told Miller there were no immediate plans to alter maternity or emergency services now that the bill was law. However, Miller was unable to get this admission, and the questions it presumably raised about the Archbishop's and Laverty's credibility, into print.

23. Katharine Betts' analysis of 2007 polling figures found that just 1.2 per cent of Australians of no faith oppose abortion in all circumstances, compared to 6 per cent of those who are religious.

24. Petchesky, as cited in *The Abortion Myth*, p. 20.

25. *The Abortion Myth*, p.22.

26. Reardon as quoted in L. Cannold, 'Understanding and Responding to Anti-choice Women-centred Strategies', *Reproductive Health Matters* 10 (19), 2002, p. 172, text available at www.cannold.com/academic-work/RHM-2002/RHMarticle.pdf

27. J. Fleming, 'Australians on Abortion: common ground', *Bioethics Research Notes* 17 (2), June 2005, p. 3.; E. Cox, 'The Politics of Research', *Online Opinion*, 2005, at

www.onlineopinion.com.au/view.asp?article=3469; J. Fleming and S. Ewing, 'Australians on Abortion: common ground', *Bioethics Research Notes* 17 (2), June 2005, at www.bioethics. org.au/Resources/Online%20Articles/Other%20Articles/1702%20Australians%20on%20 abortion.pdf

28. In what I believe is the first journal article on the subject, I try to set out the workings and weaknesses of this strategy. See 'Understanding and Responding to Anti-choice Women-centred Strategies', pp. 171–178.

29. 'APA Task Force Report on Mental Health and Abortion', the Royal Australian and New Zealand College of Obstetricians and Gynaecologists; 'Termination of Pregnancy: a resource for health professionals', 2005, at www.ranzcog.edu.au/womenshealth/pdfs/Termination-of-pregnancy.pdf

30. *Safe abortions: technical and policy guidance for healthcare systems*, World Health Organization, Geneva, 2003; *Essential Medicines*, World Health Organization, Geneva, 2006. The United Nations Millennium Development Goals are eight goals that all 191 UN member states have agreed to try to achieve by the year 2015. They can be viewed at www.who. int/topics/millennium_development_goals/en/index.html.

31. L. Cannold, 'Women's Forum Australia is "Faking It",' *Sunday Sun-Herald,* 28 December 2008, at www.cannold.com/media/2008-12-28-womens-forum-australia-is-faking-it; B. Baxter, Women's Forum Australia — policies and people, at http://unbelief.org/main/wp-content/uploads/2008/01/womens_forum_australia.pdf

32. 'Understanding and Responding to Anti-choice Women-centred Strategies,' p. 172.

33. High-profile offenders in Australia include Father John Fleming, Nicholas Tonti-Fillipini, Melinda Tankard-Reist, and Katrina George, as well as organisations such as the Southern Cross Bioethics Institute and Women's Forum Australia.

WHY GODS ARE MAN-MADE: ATHEISM AND WOMEN[1]

Jane Caro
Author, broadcaster, social commentator, lecturer in the School of Communication Arts at the University of Western Sydney

I AM (AT THE VERY LEAST) A THIRD-GENERATION ATHEIST. I HAVE NOT lapsed from any religious tradition; I was brought up without one. My parents were secular humanists: my father's family were probably Jewish once upon a time, and my mother is such a lapsed Methodist she could probably be called an anti-Methodist.

Clearly, I am rather slow on the uptake, because it only dawned on me very gradually that, even today, this non-religious background is unusual. Most of the atheists I know are in rebellion against something, often a religious tradition that has existed in their family for generations. I have one atheist friend who finally confessed to her devout mother that she was no longer a Catholic. Somewhat to my friend's surprise, her mother was not the least bit bothered by her revelation. Instead, she merely smiled sagely, shook her head, and said, 'Oh, darling, you have no choice'. As my friend is now sending her daughters to a Catholic school, it seems her mother may have had a point.

For me, however, there is no conflict. I regard religions rather the way non-Americans regard gridiron football. I am well aware that it raises enormous excitement and passion among believers, but for the life of me I can't see what the fuss is about. No doubt, those who believe in a God will pity my ignorance and see me as missing out on something; however, for me, it feels not just normal, but right.

There is a liberation that comes from not having to fight my way through the emotional maelstrom and sticky expectations that generations of religious tradition seem to wrap around their followers. I am not battling feelings of guilt or shame. I do not worry about being a sinner, or even just a disappointment to my parents. I do not yearn for old certainties, or even just the mysticism and theatre of religious ceremony. I do not feel like an outcast, a rebel, or even a lucky escapee. Even better, because I am not a lapsed Christian, Muslim, Hindu, or Jew, I have no greater baggage attached to one tradition over another. Nevertheless, as I was born and educated in the West, a society steeped in the Judeo–Christian tradition, it is on that religion that I will be concentrating. Rest assured, however, my feelings about religion are truly ecumenical: I don't like any of them.

Perhaps it is my unusual position of relatively dispassionate observer that gives me such a sense of certainty about religions being man-made. For me, the evidence for this is entirely obvious. Why else would all these Gods have such uniformly misogynistic and defensive attitudes towards women? The religious believe that man was formed in God's image. To me, it appears self-evident that God was formed in man's — complete with womb envy. Indeed, the Genesis story from the Christian and Jewish traditions seems particularly revealing about the unconscious unease men feel in the face of female reproductive power. Talk about re-writing history, not to mention basic biology:

> So the LORD God caused a deep sleep to fall upon the man, and while he slept took one of his ribs and closed up its place with flesh; and the rib which the LORD God had taken from the man he made into a woman and brought her to the man. Then the man said, 'This at last is bone of my bones and flesh of my flesh; she shall be called Woman, because she was taken out of Man.[2]

Yeah … right. Guys, I think your deepest insecurity is showing.

It wouldn't have been so bad, perhaps, if the men trying to explain the mysteries of life and the world to frightened, ignorant, and superstitious people had merely stuck to inflating their own part in the process of creating life. But they had to compound the felony by blaming the other (woman) for their fate, condemned to live in the cruel and brutal reality of the world, rather than in the fantasy paradise of their imaginings.

Seen from a non-religious perspective, even the curse that the Christian God is supposed to have inflicted upon woman because she dared to eat from the Tree of Knowledge — say what? To the non-believer, that this could be a sin is just weird — is extremely convenient for the men relating the story. If you love a woman and enjoy having sex with her, it must be a fearful thing to see the danger and suffering that your ecstasy and desire can so directly cause. Pregnancy, labour, and birth are uniquely difficult and dangerous for human females, thanks to the size of the human infant's head. For millennia, it was common for women to die in agony giving birth, one reason why there are so many stepmothers in fairy tales. In fourteenth-century Europe, for example, men had a life expectancy of 50, women just thirty.[3] Women have only had longer life expectancy than men for about a century — progress that, in my view, is directly attributable to advances in the understanding and treatment of pregnancy, childbirth and, most importantly, contraception. Knowledge, incidentally, that male religious leaders were particularly keen to keep hidden, but more about that later.

It is entirely understandable that loving and decent men found it difficult to reconcile the often-fatal consequences of an activity they needed and enjoyed so much — impregnating women — with their own sense of themselves as good and honourable. Creating a God that openly declared that he had condemned women to suffer in childbirth as punishment for their 'original sin' is an extremely neat way for men to let themselves off the hook. In modern psychology, I believe such a convenient sleight of hand is called 'projection'.

Even the Holy Trinity seems to me to be further evidence of the deep unease with which men experience their own sexuality. Consisting famously of the Father (God), the Son (Jesus Christ), and the — sorry, can you run that past me again — Holy Ghost, the logical third member of such a fundamental trinity, the Mother, is conspicuous by her absence. A chimera — a spirit, a ghost with no physical reality at all — has filled the natural place for woman in the famous trio. Interestingly, it may not only be the unease men feel about their own sexuality that has caused the Mother to take on the shifting shape of a miasma. It may also be the way human infants actually experience the Mother.

As anyone who has cared for small children is aware, human infants only gradually come to understand that their mother is a separate and independent entity who can, and often does, leave them so she can pursue her own agenda. Visit any childcare centre at morning-drop-off time and you will see the pain that is the result of this essential developmental realisation. 'Never mind,' says the childcare worker, holding the struggling and screaming toddler in his/her arms, 'it's only separation anxiety.'

In the comforting fantasy of the Christian heaven, separation anxiety has been banished forever. The Mother no longer has any physical reality or independent agency. She is once again merely a spirit, a feeling, a source of eternal nurture and safety.

The elevation, in some forms of Christianity at least, of the Virgin Mary is also revealing. The miracle of Mary, once again, is that she is sexually pure, and that she gave birth to Jesus without experiencing the touch or lust of any man. Indeed, her creation of the Messiah is clearly the exact inverse of Adam's creation of Eve. The super-human aspect of both Jesus and Mary, their purity and absence of any gritty, messy, human sexuality, has also been a powerful weapon to beat the rest of us with. Christianity has set up unreachable ideals for both men and women, and created endless, useless guilt and misery among its followers when they inevitably fail to live up to such inhuman standards.

Given what we now know about what is commonly referred to as 'grooming behaviour' (a term that usually refers to the methods paedophiles use to reduce resistance and increase compliance in vulnerable children), it is hard for a female atheist like me to see such Christian stories as anything other than a series of psychological blows designed to reduce the possibility of women resisting male emotional and sexual domination. Like the damaged child who often both loves and protects her abuser — particularly if he occupies a position society designates as protective (father, grandfather, stepfather, teacher, scoutmaster, priest), women have reacted to this grooming by trying, as best they can, to accept their secondary status. They have been undeniably, passionately religious, and have sought to live up to the impossible and often contradictory demands placed on them by their religion. The price they have paid in terms of life expectancy, self-hatred, mental health, poverty, and stunted and deformed talents and potentials has been terrifyingly high. But, until relatively recently, what choice did they realistically have? Like oppressed people everywhere, because earthly life seemed so dreadful and yet so inescapable, they put their faith in heaven.

The idea that women are fully as human as men is something that man-made religions seem to constantly struggle over. I love the paradise that is offered to Islamic Jihad warriors and suicide bombers. Apparently, as martyrs for Allah, they will receive their reward in heaven by disporting themselves with 72 virgins. Imagine all those obedient, God-fearing Muslim women who keep themselves pure behind all-encompassing clothing out of their devout worship of their God, only to find that, when they die, their reward for all that virginal vigilance is to end up as a whore for terrorists. Humorist, actor, and broadcaster Stephen Fry had a different take on the tricks such a capricious God could play on his most fanatical followers; they might end up with 70-year-old nuns, he suggested.[4] My own response, when I heard about this extraordinarily male-centric view of the eternal reward, was to wonder what appalling sin those poor virgins must have committed to require such punishment. In other words, the terrorist's heaven was clearly the virgin's hell.

Honestly, if it weren't so terrifying, such infantile and entirely one-eyed visions of the afterlife would be simply hilarious. Of course, apart from what they reveal about the religious fantasists, they are irrelevant, given that no living person can actually know what the afterlife (in the remote possibility that there even is such a thing) might be like. But such is human egotism (I hesitate to say male egotism) that apparently some of us have made it up to reflect entirely our own deepest and most forbidden desires. Female heaven, in my imaginings, would involve silent, well-hung blokes who gave tireless massages and whose greatest pleasure was to do the housework — a bit like life on Earth actually is for many men, when you come to think of it.

The stories that ancient people told themselves to explain what must have seemed a vast, hostile, and unknowable universe understandably reflected the power structures and hierarchies of the time, hence the blithe acceptance of slaves and slavery by everyone in the Bible, including Jesus. Equally unsurprisingly, they also enabled those in power to not only justify their privileged position but also to enhance and increase it by claiming it was divinely ordained. If there really is a God, it just seems far too convenient to me that such a divinity would enable the powerful — virtually all of whom were men — to so comfortably exorcise their psychological demons via religious stories and rules. It is also no coincidence that the controls gods placed on women also served some of the innate biological vulnerabilities of men so well.

The knowledge that one has passed on one's DNA is problematic for males. Not just human males, either. Throughout the animal kingdom, males fight, sometimes to the death, for the right to mate and pass on their genes. In primates, if a previously dominant male is defeated and chased off, the young of the group, his genetic offspring, are at great risk from the new leader. Indeed, a recent report links the size of a primate's testicles to the relative promiscuity of the female of the species.[5] Male chimpanzees have huge testicles, and female chimpanzees are very free with their favours. Gorillas have tiny testicles and tightly controlled harems. Human testicles are somewhere in between. The size of testicles and amount of sperm produced is nature's way of giving the male its best chance of passing on his genes.

This problem simply does not exist for female animals. A woman who gives birth knows she has succeeded in bequeathing 50 per cent of her genetic material to the future. She has fulfilled her biological task. A man, on the other hand, cannot be so sure. DNA testing in recent years has in fact confirmed what many suspected: that some men have been unwittingly putting their energy and resources into children who are not their own. This uncertainty, it seems to me, led directly to supposedly God-ordained traditions, like displaying bloodied bed sheets after the consummation of a marriage, female circumcision, purdah, foot-binding, burqas, chastity belts, eunuchs guarding harems, honour killings, and the 1001 other devices designed to keep a woman from conceiving another man's child.

To be fair, there is a biological logic behind these religious taboos. Men who spread their seed far and wide maximise their chance of passing on their genes. A woman who is promiscuous is terrifying. Who knows which man's child she could end up foisting on her partner? Society attempts to control such women using overt disapproval, insults, the law and, of course, religion. In many religions, sexually independent women are not just disobedient; they are sinners damned to suffer for all eternity. Without this innate biological imperative to pass on DNA to the future, how do we explain the fact that virtually all religious traditions reserve their harshest punishments for promiscuity or infidelity for women, while turning at the very least a blind eye to the much more frequent transgressions of men?

Which leads us directly, of course, to the long, slow battle women have fought to gain not just agency over their own sexual and reproductive lives, but also basic information about their own bodies and how they work. Their enemy in this battle has predominantly been men and their conveniently male-centric religions.

If you believe religions, gods of all kinds are entirely happy to see one half of humanity held in subjection to the other half. According to many of their earthly messengers, they have approved of and even commanded that women be beaten for disobedience, stoned for adultery, raped — at least in marriage — killed to preserve a male family member's honour, and sold as property, either to husbands or masters. Gods have stated that a woman's testimony and word is worth less than that of a man, that she is not to be permitted to speak in public, take part in public life, take 'headship' over a man or, in extreme cases, even appear in public. It was divine intention, apparently, that a woman should have no rights to her children, no right to her own money or an education or, later, any right to vote. It was religious belief that drove what may be the longest and bloodiest pogrom in recorded human history; the persecution and execution of (in the vast majority of cases) vulnerable women accused of witchcraft across Europe between the fourteenth and seventeenth centuries. So blind are we still to the persecution of women that this event is almost never referred to at all, and certainly never called what it was: systematic persecution of one group of humans by another.

To a feminist like me, it is fascinating that witch-hunting reached fever pitch in the reign of James I. James was the king who succeeded the world's second-most-famous virgin, Elizabeth I, and was the only son of Mary Queen of Scots. Elizabeth of England and Mary of Scotland, along with Queen Regent Catherine de Medici of France, made up John Knox's famous 'monstrous regiment of women'. John Knox was a fire-and-brimstone Scottish Protestant who, predictably, loathed women. Is it mere coincidence that God and religion were so conveniently invoked once the 'monstrous regiment' had, ahem, met their maker? Surely it directly served the restoration of the male gender's stranglehold on power to brutally remind women of their God-given second place? We see echoes of this fear of female power today when some religious figures fulminate against witches and the dangers of witchcraft in response to the powerful popularity of phenomena like J. K. Rowling's *Harry Potter* franchise and Dan Brown's *Da Vinci Code*.[6]

In some parts of the world, we still watch women and girls being denied the right to go to school, to work, to get access to healthcare, to drive a car, to vote, to walk the streets unaccompanied, or to even escape deathly peril in the name of a God. In 2002, religious police in Mecca, Saudi Arabia, prevented rescuers from helping girls escape a burning school because the girls were not 'properly' covered. Fourteen of the schoolgirls perished in the flames.

But it is not just in underprivileged and underdeveloped countries where the oppression of women continues. Recently I attended the wedding of two sad young people who had fallen under the sway of what sounded to this atheist like an extremist Christian cult. I later found out they were Baptists. Their vows made me physically wince. The poor deluded young woman promised her husband to 'submit to you as the Church submits to Christ, to respect and support your leadership, and to joyfully serve you in our home'. Boy, has she got a steep learning curve ahead of her. Back in the seventies, even though it was already out of fashion, I still attended some religious wedding ceremonies where the women promised to obey. Without exception, all of those unions have ended in divorce.

Women's lives only began to improve when feminism emerged, thanks to the secular revolution of the Enlightenment. Mary Wollstonecraft, author of *Vindication of the Rights of Women* (1792), could not provide a greater contrast to that first Mary, the so-called mother of God. No virgin, she was a vulnerable and suffering human being, badly used and abused by many of the men in her life. Blessed (if you will excuse the term) with a shining intellect and the clear-eyed courage it took to see through millennia of male hypocrisy, she was despised and vilified in her own time — often by the righteous and the religious — and died tragically, as so many did, in childbirth.

But her words took hold, and in the 300 years since she first put pen to paper, the lives of women and girls, at least in the developed world, have changed beyond anything she could have imagined, and changed unarguably for the better. By almost any objective measure, women in the secular West are better off than they ever have been before. In terms of longevity, economic independence, mental, physical, reproductive, and emotional health, and human rights, today's woman leaves her female ancestors for dead. Unfortunately, however, at almost every step along the way, representatives of God have resisted women's progress.

Even as women's march towards equal rights has gathered pace, at least in the West, the religious have variously continued to oppose higher education for women, higher status employment for women, their right to vote, their right to enter parliament, their right to their own earnings and property, their right to their own children after divorce or separation, their right to resist domestic violence, their right to learn about their own bodies, their right to refuse sexual intercourse in marriage or agree to it before marriage, their right to divorce, contraception, abortion, and sexual information. Less than a century or so ago, if a woman was so badly damaged by successive child-bearing that doctors advised against further pregnancy, the Church resisted her right to use (or even to know about) contraception, and she had to rely on the good will and restraint of her husband to avoid further catastrophic damage or even death. When Marie Stopes, one of the first women to qualify as a doctor in Britain, published her famous book *Married Love* (1918), which aimed to educate and help women and men understand and control their sexual and reproductive lives in marriage, she was condemned from pulpits everywhere. Yet the letters Dr Stopes received from ordinary British men and women in response to her book are both pitiful and eye-opening.[7] Without any doubt, Marie Stopes saved many, many lives — almost all of them female.

When chloroform was invented in the nineteenth century, doctors immediately heralded it as a boon for birthing women. Church leaders, true to form, condemned it out of hand because they believed women's suffering in labour was ordained by God as punishment for poor old Eve's original sin. Fortunately for labouring women everywhere, the then head of the Church of England was herself a birthing mother. Queen Victoria ignored her spiritual advisors as she gave birth to her nine children, and grabbed chloroform with both hands, immediately making pain relief in childbirth acceptable.

Queen Victoria is a great example of why it is so important to have women in positions of power and influence, and why it has been so destructive of gods and their representatives to do whatever they can to keep them out.

To be fair, as women have made gains in the secular and developed world, many religious believers and leaders have changed their opinions and been persuaded about the universal benefit of female equality and opportunity. Many religious feminists argue passionately that there is nothing necessarily godly about the oppression of women; but if, as the Bible says, by their fruits shall ye judge them, even today they are on shaky ground.

In many developing societies, for example, it is virtually impossible for women to refuse sex, particularly inside marriage. Given that conjugal rights were only legally abolished a few decades ago in our own society, due in part to the stubborn resistance of religious leaders, it is hardly surprising that women in the Third World are still battling for such basic human rights.

Indeed, there is something chillingly familiar about the attitude to women revealed by the conversation the late Pope John Paul II had with Dr Nafis Sadik, the director of the UN Population Fund from 1987 to 2000. As she related it, the pontiff revealed a frightening view of male and female relationships:

> I was telling him ... many women became pregnant not because they wanted to but because their ... you know ... spouses imposed themselves on them. He said: 'Don't you think that the irresponsible behaviour of men is caused by women?'[8]

These remarks by a religious leader are reminiscent of the attitude revealed by the former governor-general Archbishop Peter Hollingworth (ex-Anglican Archbishop of Brisbane) in his defence of the priest accused of seducing one of his female students, aged 14, on the ABC's *Australian Story*. 'My information is that it was rather the other way around,' he said of the seduction.[9] This attitude to the duty of care owed by an adult priest and teacher towards a 14-year-old student boggles the mind. Consider for a moment what Archbishop Hollingworth's response might have been if the student in question had been a boy. It is inconceivable that he would have attempted the same defence.

According to many religious frameworks, if women are temptresses they are then to blame for whatever men do to them. The demonisation of women as vessels of potential corruption and temptation is a pillar of many religious traditions. This came to a head in 2006, during the trial of a family of Muslim brothers accused of the brutal rape of some young non-Muslim girls in Sydney. One of the accused used his religious belief and its view of acceptable behaviour by women as part of his defence. Predictably, this caused a storm of controversy at the time, including these comments by Muslim cleric Sheik Hilali:

> If you take out uncovered meat and place it outside on the street, or in the garden or in the park, or in the backyard without a cover, and the cats come and eat it … whose fault is it, the cats' or the uncovered meat? The uncovered meat is the problem.

The sheik then said: 'If she was in her room, in her home, in her hijab, no problem would have occurred'. He said women were 'weapons' used by 'Satan' to control men. 'It is said in the state of zina (adultery), the responsibility falls 90 per cent of the time on the woman. Why? Because she possesses the weapon of enticement (igraa).'[10]

But attitudes like this don't require a dramatic rape to be brought into the open. A year earlier, in 2005, we heard much the same from another Muslim cleric, as reported in *The Age*:

> 'Every minute in the world a woman is raped, and she has no one to blame but herself, for she has displayed her beauty to the whole world,' Sheikh Feiz Muhammad told a packed public meeting in the Bankstown Town Hall last month. 'Strapless, backless, sleeveless — they are nothing but satanical. Mini-skirts, tight jeans — all this to tease men and to appeal to (their) carnal nature.'
>
> There was pressure on Muslim women to unveil,' the sheikh said, and this was because 'they want you to be available for their gross, disgusting, filthy abomination! They want you to be a sex symbol!' The woman who wore the hijab was hiding her beauty from the eyes of 'lustful, hungry wolves', he said.[11]

Once more, it seems to me, men are projecting their own unacceptable feelings and emotions; thus, women are held responsible for male bad behaviour and self-serving reactions. Sheikh Feiz Muhammad's controversial comments, for example, blame a woman's appearance for making a man rape her. There's a breathtaking lack of logic here. Does the sheikh believe the rich make poorer men steal just by being rich, and that this an acceptable defence? Of course he doesn't, and nor does his (or any other) religion. In Islam, according to Sharia law, it is acceptable to cut off the hand of a thief, no matter how flagrantly the person who has been robbed was flaunting their wealth.

It has become commonplace to see fundamentalist Christian preachers fall spectacularly from grace when some sexual peccadillo of their own is brought to light, to the point that whenever I hear someone fulminating about sex and morality I automatically suspect them of being in denial about their own kinky sexual behaviour. Naughty of me, I know, but just like the men who cannot help but respond to the incitement of Western dress, I can't help myself.

In the West, we are slowly beginning to realise that by raising the status of women and girls you improve society for everyone. It is no coincidence that societies where women enjoy high levels of personal freedom are the richest and most stable in the world. We now understand that when you educate women and girls, the benefits accrue to the entire family, rather than simply to the individual. There is even research to indicate that in societies with more women in positions of power and influence, men have a longer life expectancy. Can it also be a coincidence that these societies are also among the most secular and, apart from the US, are often cited as those where belief in a God is dying most rapidly? Looked at from that perspective, it is almost as if God and women's rights are diametrically opposed to one another. As one rises, it seems, the other falls.

No wonder fundamentalist religion appears to fear women's rights more than almost anything else, and no wonder even more liberal religious traditions have so doggedly fought any rise in the status of women. This fear by the religious of women's equality also goes a long way towards explaining the violent and fanatical war against abortion rights currently being waged in the last truly God-fearing democracy: the US. The fact that God and women appear to be so firmly in opposite corners is yet another indication to me that gods are all about men: not just their privilege, their power, and their control, but their insecurities, their fears, and their vulnerabilities. Gods are richly human — there is nothing divine about them at all.

It is impossible in one chapter to do justice to the price women have paid as a result of man-made religion. I have not had room here, for example, to explore the fearful decimation of women by HIV in Africa, helped along by the wicked and paranoid misinformation about the permeability of condoms, promoted by the Catholic Church. Suffice to say, four out of ten girls in Kenya are now HIV-positive, many of them good and virginal God-fearing girls, no doubt encouraged by their religious leaders to 'submit' to their husbands, like my deluded Baptist friend. Their reward for their virginity and submissive femininity is to be infected with a fatal disease on their wedding night.

For me, however, it is not just the gross history of religion's treatment of women that informs my atheism. It is the simple fact of the one-eyed nature of all the world's religions that finally convinces me that all gods are man-made. Even Buddhism, that last refuge of the fashionable Western mystic, has a different attitude to the female of the species. After all, why hasn't the Dalai Lama ever been reincarnated as a girl?

NOTES

1. Some of this chapter has been adapted from Chapter 10 of J. Caro and C. Fox, *The F Word: how we learned to swear by feminism*, UNSW Press, 2008.
2. Genesis 2: 21–23.
3. A. Weir, *Lancaster and York: the Wars of the Roses*, Vintage, 2009, p. 5.
4. *Stephen Fry in America*, BBC, broadcast 12 October 2008.
5. 'Intrasexual Selection and Testis Size in Strepsirhine Primates', P. M. Kappeler, *Behavioural Ecology* 8 (1), 1997.
6. K. Mahoney, 'Should Christians be Reading *Harry Potter*?', About.com, at www. religionandpluralism.org/KarenKing_DaVinciCodeQuestionsObjections_ AJC021504.pdf
7. You can find them in R. Hall, *Dear Dr Stopes: sex in the 1920s*, Penguin, 1982.
8. 'Sex and The Holy City', *Panorama*, BBC, broadcast 12 October 2003.
9. 'The Gilded Cage', *Australian Story*, ABC, aired 18 February 2002.
10. R. Kerbaj, 'Muslim Leader Blames Women for Sex Attacks', *The Australian*, 26 October 2006, at www.theaustralian.com.au/news/nation/muslim-leader-blames-women-for-sex-attacks/story-e6frg6nf-1111112419114
11. P. Bone, 'Religious Extremists an Insult to our Values', The Age, 14 April 2005, at www.theagec.com.au/news/Pamela-Bone/Religious-extremists-an-insult-to-our-values/2005/04/13/1113251680541.html

A ROSE BY ANY OTHER NAME?
SPIRITUALISM AND PSEUDOSCIENCE

Dr Karen Stollznow
Writer, linguist, researcher at the University of California,
host of *Point of Inquiry* radio show

SPIRITUALISM INITIALLY CONJURES UP IMAGES OF A NINETEENTH-CENTURY séance: a round table of people holding hands in a dimmed parlour; a medium in a trance, channelling an ancient mystic, manifesting spirits, and emitting ectoplasm to the sounds of trumpets and disembodied voices. These were the beginnings of modern spiritualist beliefs and practices.

The modern movement was born in 1848, when sisters Katherine and Margaret Fox reported hearing strange 'rapping' noises in their bedroom.[1] These were allegedly the sounds of spirits, and the girls claimed to be conduits through which the dead could contact the living. The girls and their sister Leah introduced the world to mediums and séances during a sensationalist public exhibition in Rochester, New York. Spiritualism became an international craze.

Today, we might also associate 'spiritualism' with smoke and mirrors, magic, and other themes that imply deception. Indeed, spiritualism was founded in fraud. Magician and sceptic Harry Houdini had already debunked specific mediums and séances,[2] but in 1888, after four decades of deception,the Fox sisters confessed publically that their performances were pranks. These 'mediums' had created the 'rappings' and other not-so-paranormal phenomena by cracking their toe joints, bouncing an apple on a string, and acting. Yet, these simple tricks fooled the public, including several scientists. But the confession was ignored, and spiritualism grew.

Spiritualism gradually evolved and expanded to become a fusion of religion, philosophy, and the supernatural. Today, spiritualism and spirituality encompass a diverse range of beliefs and practices, plucked from established religions, philosophy, mainstream knowledge, pseudoscience, and the paranormal.

Spiritualism is difficult to define comprehensively. It is synonymous with the 'New Age' but, for ease of understanding, is often conceptualised as a religion. Similarly, atheism is often framed as religion. Belief systems are not a clear-cut continuum of extreme religious belief through to atheism. We could draw endless analogies between religion, spiritualism, and atheism because there is some overlapping. The concept of religion is a stereotype that functions as our reference point and comparative cognitive model. Spiritualism certainly has parallels with religion.

This essay compares and contrasts aspects of modern religion with spiritualism, and examines a range of popular spiritual beliefs and practices.

Whether spiritualism is just another religion or not is in the eye of the beholder. In fact, this reveals a crucial characteristic of spiritualist beliefs: it does not have any universally defining characteristics. Spiritualism is more disorganised than organised religion. It is eclectic, unstructured, dynamic, and personalised. Like the 'personal God' of Christianity, spiritualism is personal belief based in personal experience. It is the individual's idiosyncratic and selective set of beliefs. Spiritualism is a do-it-yourself belief system, but not one single belief system.

Spiritualism in and of itself might not be religion, but it can include religion. Spiritualist beliefs are a theologian's nightmare. Like voodoo, they often incorporate elements of established religions, blended with pseudoscience and the paranormal. Spiritualist beliefs integrate assorted facets of philosophy, culture, jargon, and rituals from historical religions, whether the believer is aware of the original source or not. Spiritualism draws mainly from Christianity, Judaism, Islam, Buddhism, Hinduism, but also Paganism, Sikhism, Jainism, Zoroastrianism, and indigenous faiths.

Merging religion into spiritualism is at the individual level. One person's unique brand of spiritualism might be theistic, or even atheist. Atheism and spiritualism are not mutually exclusive. Atheism is consistent with many spiritualist outlooks where the individual lacks belief in a deity, and perceives himself or herself as a non-theist but 'spiritual' person.

The theistic spiritualist belief system can be monotheistic or polytheistic. The single deity might be a God, Lord, or Father that is also known by 99 other names, or by a name forbidden to be spoken. There might be a plethora of gods and goddesses. The deity might be a demigod, a god on Earth, an animal, or the actual believer might be a god or goddess. The theistic higher being could be a creator, supreme being, or omnipotent presence. The non-theistic higher power could be the cosmos, Mother Nature, Chi, Prana, Energy, Life Force, Love, Light, or some other capitalised entity.

Unlike the denominations of Christianity and the sects of Jainism, spiritualism is composed of loose, shifting communities that often evade structure and classification. Alternatively, there can be in-group categorisation or methods, such as the theory of homeopathy, the lineages of reiki, or the various schools of yoga. But there are no unifying tenets of belief. Because of this broadness and fragmentation, spiritualism often gives rise to the emergence of new beliefs, generating numerous cults, sects, theories, and religions. For example, Breatharianism (Inedia) is a group of people with the alleged ability to live on light rather than food, while Sylvia Browne founded the 'religion' the Society of Novus Spiritus, a Gnostic Christian Church that incorporates elements of Buddhism, Judaism, Islam, and Hinduism.

Spiritualism is a belief system with no single unifying name. People who practise some form of spiritual belief might describe themselves as spiritual people, but they wouldn't necessarily employ 'spiritualism' as a title for their beliefs, or 'spiritualist' as a label of self-identification. Many proponents value spiritual beliefs for this lack of labelling and lack of rigid rules.

Spiritualism is belief without religious bureaucracy. It is a 'religion' without a rule book. Spiritualist beliefs have no single doctrine, no unitary theory, and no cogent, collective history. They have no ancient divine text, like the Bible, the Torah, or the Qur'an. The truth is God hasn't come out with any good books of late, and it's not cool to read Leviticus over a latte in a cafe — everyone will keep their distance, thinking you're about to proselytise — but you'll look intellectual if you're reading a book by Dr Bruce Lipton or Dr Deepak Chopra. The holy book of spiritualism is whatever self-help book is currently on the New York Times Best Seller List.

For spiritualism, there is no unified hierarchical theological system, no figureheads or earthly representations of a deity. The proponents of spiritualist beliefs might display statues of Buddha, Tibetan flags, and other fashions of their many faiths, but there are no standardised saints, angels, icons, or martyrs to worship. There are no priests, bishops, or popes, but there are venerated leaders of spiritualism. They are more demagogues than demigods; they are authors, academics, psychics, celebrities, and counsellors.

These spokespeople of spiritualism are motivational mentors, such as Eckhart Tolle, Dale Carnegie, and the fire-walking Tony Robbins. There are psychic mediums who claim to talk to the dead, including Allison DuBois, James Van Praag, and John Edward. Psychic Sylvia Browne channels her spirit guide, Francine, while J. Z. Knight channels the 35,000-year-old spirit Ramtha (at least this disproves creationism!). There are godmen and gurus, such as the Dalai Lama, Sai Baba, and the Maharishi Mahesh Yogi. Dr John Gray, Dr Wayne Dyer, and Dr Phil are prophets with PhDs.

There is a Church of Spiritualism dedicated to mediumship, but spiritualist beliefs do not have a unitary church, synagogue, or mosque. The temporary spiritual house of worship is the yoga class, the sweat lodge, and the wellness retreat (clothing optional). There is no holy day, or holiday. There is no formalised liturgical service of vespers or mass; but there are rituals of hot-stone massage and dry brushing. There are no hymns and psalms, only chants and mantras. The transubstantiation wine is replaced by yerba maté. The confessional becomes Primal Scream Therapy. You won't be forgiven your trespasses, but your chakras will be balanced.

Religion and spiritualism often intersect via magic and mysticism. Some customs of the Pentecostal and Charismatic churches, such as mediumship, automatic writing, speaking in tongues, divination, and healing through the Holy Spirit, are also spiritualist practices. Advocates of spiritualism enact their beliefs and petition the powers with not only prayer but other forms of intercession, including meditation, positive affirmations, pilates, yoga, and the use of expensive exercise equipment.

Spiritualism ministers to more than the spirit: it is concerned with mind, body, and spirit. More than salvation for the soul, spiritualism offers chicken soup for the soul (the title of the popular, ever-growing series of inspirational books).[3] Spiritualism claims to be a religion of common sense, with a pragmatic function to treat our more mortal worries. It is a religion of self-help that preaches to its parishioners about health, alternative medicine, ageing, activism, diet, environmentalism, relationships, art, music, career, peace, politics, psychology, science, sexuality, quality of life, and the afterlife.

A myriad of spiritualist books can be found in the self-improvement, New Age, and miscellaneous sections of the bookstore. In these books, the road to Damascus becomes the road to wealth, health, and happiness. Spiritualist authors promise personal gain and benefits, and guarantee healing, luck, love, success, wisdom, and mental health. Rather than discovering God, spiritualist beliefs have an emphasis on self-discovery. A third eye will cure your blind faith.

Religion is about teaching and learning, and offers a framework for morals, ethics, and values. God tells us to 'do unto others as we would have them do unto ourselves'; but He can't help you lose weight. Spiritualist beliefs additionally teach us tools for life issues. Spiritualism claims to be comprehensive, and to have all the answers to our mortal problems and immortal questions. These cover a bizarre gamut of concerns: how to develop confidence, read body language, interpret your dreams, boost brain power, hypnotise yourself, cope with a demanding boss, develop ESP, overcome stress, navigate gender differences, enjoy better sex, cure impotence naturally, balance your yin and yang, look ten years younger, and win friends and influence people. Spiritualism is more holistic than holy.

Instead of entry to Heaven or banishment to Hell, spiritualist beliefs offer more esoteric promises of enlightenment, consciousness, awareness, oneness, wholeness, mindfulness, connectedness, and abundance. Belief will reward you eternally with a sense of bliss, gratitude, and joy. Depending on your cultural preference, it is an individualist spiritual quest to find your true self, or it is collectivist; you become part of the Overmind, or the Greater Whole.

God will help those who help themselves, but religion is often about fate, providence, and acceptance of one's lot in life. This is God's plan. In contrast, spiritualism doesn't wait for God to reveal your life's mission and purpose; a seer or psychic can supposedly tell you instead. Nostradamus, Mother Shipton, and the Bible Code provide us with predictions, prophecies, and warnings (that are interpreted subjectively). Intuitives, sensitives, mediums, astrologers, and tarot readers offer us glimpses into a future (using cold-reading techniques). Why pray and wait for God to respond when you can carry a crystal, burn a candle, or cast a spell, producing immediate results?

Spiritualism is instant karma! There are no ten-week Alpha courses of Christianity, or lengthy rites of confirmation. Your life will improve in the time it takes to read a book and utter 'Om' — or even less, if you read *Enjoy Life and Be Happy in 30 Seconds* (2009).[4] New Age books are replete with two-bit philosophy, inspirational quotes, and quick fixes to transform your life (until the drudgery sets in again and a new book is sought). These are spiritual get-rich-quick schemes.

Religion often seems to be about the power over us, but spiritualism promises to empower us, instead. Spiritualism is proactive, and offers more of a sense of control over our own lives. In spiritualist beliefs, the power of prayer becomes the power of positive thinking. Advocates promise that reading their books and attending their lectures will be a life-changing experience ... for a price. In the business of religion, the spiritualist congregation comprises consumers. There is much more money to be made out of spiritualism than the collection basket.

From Mormon elders to Jehovah's Witnesses, their faith is 'good news' to be disseminated, be it door-to-door or from the pulpit. Bibles are mostly free, and you will find one in your hotel room, should you forget to pack your copy. Spiritualism isn't always free. It is marketed in lecture theatres and infomercials. The promoters have a we-know-something-you-don't-know manner, but they are prepared to sell you this knowledge. The spiritualists have this information, but paradoxically, they claim there is a government cover-up or Big Pharma conspiracy. Like Kevin Trudeau's series of books, this is information '*they* don't want you to know about'.[5] The keepers of the secret have been silenced — until now. Their book and lectures will unlock this secret. They will provide you with the answers you seek. Their products reveal enigmas, lost mysteries, and hidden knowledge. For example, the maker of the 'Magnetic Qi Gong' reports that a 'Tennessee mountain man discovers missing link to eternal youth, previously known only to China's Yellow Emperor and an anonymous Tibetan sage!'[6]

Spiritualist beliefs and practices can be trendy. Celebrities are often spokespeople for their causes and, in effect, they become missionaries for their beliefs. If you loved their movies and music, now try their religion. Madonna promotes the Kabbalah, Richard Gere promotes Buddhism, and Tom Cruise promotes Scientology. Egotistical Hollywood loves spiritualism, because you can be your own god.

Many spiritual beliefs are passing fads. New products, techniques, and theories are hailed as miracles, until it becomes obvious they don't work. The only ambiguous qualifications need be that it is immune-boosting and promotes a sense of wellbeing. In the buzzwords of spiritualism, it must rejuvenate, re-energise, recharge, or rebalance. Like a spiritualist treadmill, new concepts quickly replace old ones. In juice bars, shots of spirulina give way to wheatgrass. Believers go from wearing copper bracelets to magnetic necklaces. Fashionable diets disappear when the founder dies of heart disease.

There is no purgatory or indulgences in spiritualism. Some religions advocate fasting for purity or clarity, but in spiritualese this is 'detox'. Hair shirts and self-flagellation are penance for sin, but in spiritualism the punishments are treatments. The silence retreats, 11-hour sessions of yoga, colloidal silver, ear candling, cupping, oleation, purgation, colonic irrigation, and nasal irrigation with a Neti Pot are so bad they must be good for you.

Your body is still a temple. Diet is an important part of spiritualist beliefs. Jews eschew pork and Hindus avoid beef, but proponents of spiritualism are on the latest restrictive diet, be it vegan, fruitarian, macrobiotic, food combining, low carb, Superfoods, or clean eating. The modern snake oils Acai juice, Tahitian Noni juice, and Himalayan Goji berries are the elixirs of youth, and eternal life.

Like lavender essential oil and a cup of chamomile tea, spiritualism is soothing. It tells us what we want to hear. We don't die; our souls are merely in transition. Sylvia Browne says, 'There's no such thing as death'.[7] Deepak Chopra tells us that we can cure death with reincarnation.[8] We are told that we have all had many past lives that have taught us lessons to prepare us for this current life. Or, if you prefer, there's a spirit afterlife for us where our guardian angels and totem animals watch over us and protect us. Having passed on and crossed over to this Other Side, our loved ones await us there. Psychic mediums claim they can provide us with messages from our deceased family and friends, if you're satisfied with stock messages like, 'Your grandfather said he's sorry', and, 'Your mother loves you'.

Spiritual beliefs can be a coping mechanism for misfortune, and provide the believer with false hope. This is the saddest side of spirituality. Alternative therapists claim to be able to cure the incurable. For thousands of dollars, a clinic in Tijuana guarantees to cure patients of AIDS. Injections of Laetrile (containing cyanide) supposedly cure cancer. For thousands of dollars, a curious zapper device will supposedly heal your dysfunctional liver, purify your blood, balance your emotions, and cure you of illnesses you didn't know you had. Iridologists, chiropractors, aura readers, and acupuncturists promise to treat your chronic pain. Spiritual healers say they can cure terminal diseases with their bare hands, without surgical instruments or anesthesia (or success). For a substantial donation, evangelists like Benny Hinn will perform Jesus-style miracles where the blind will see and those in wheelchairs will walk (because they are only plants in the audience).

Proponents of spiritualism rationalise what they don't like. A spoilt brat is just an Indigo Child who needs to be able to express himself. And if you don't like it, just don't believe in it. With no fixed ideology, believers can afford to go spiritual-shopping for beliefs that suit their individual wants and needs. This cherry-picking gives rise to the ad hoc adoption (and abandonment) of beliefs. People try a bit of everything, and discard what doesn't work, or doesn't suit their biases.

If you are a traditional Christian, you are Christian. If you are spiritualist, you can be lots of different things. Without conflict, a follower of spiritualist beliefs can be a Christian, and a vegan Wiccan reiki master who practises tantric sex and believes in UFOs. You can pick and choose your beliefs. Psychic Sylvia Browne's motto seems to encapsulate the spiritualist ethos, 'Take what you want and leave the rest behind'.

Although there are no strict rules, spiritualist beliefs offer various sets of guidelines for your life. Many authors create their own systems, steps, methods, and programs. The Ten Commandments become Deepak Chopra's Seven Spiritual Laws, or Wayne Dyer's Seven Principles.[9] (Clearly, seven is luckier than ten.) Lust and greed aren't deadly sins anymore; the spiritual sins are not eating organic food and not recycling. Thou shalt not use sulfates, pesticides, and phosphates, or test on animals. It is an imagined war against science.

Spiritualist beliefs are pseudoreligious, and often pseudoscientific. Advocates of spiritualism often harbour irrational and illogical beliefs. They prefer anecdotes to evidence. The evidence demonstrates that crop circles are human-made, that photographic 'orbs' are dust or water particles, and that echinacea doesn't prevent, cure, or decrease the duration and severity of colds. But this evidence is ignored, and crop circles are believed to be created by aliens, orbs are believed to be spirits, and echinacea is one of the world's most popular herbal supplements to 'cure' colds and flu.

Believers know that science is behind their car, the internet, and those lifesaving vaccines (but bear in mind they 'cause' autism!). But when science explains that the near-death experience is a hallucination, or that electronic-voice phenomena is cross-modulation rather than recordings of spirits, it is often dismissed. The counter-argument is that personal experiences are real, and therefore you can't understand or replicate them. As we will see, spiritualism places a great emphasis on the interpretation of personal experiences.

But science still has credibility, and spiritualism is often framed as science. Proponents talk of evidence and proof, and claim that they too were once sceptical. Anecdotal evidence is still evidence, right? Surely numerology is as valid as urology; they are both 'ologies'. Isn't reflexology a subset of podiatry? On the pharmacy shelves those homeopathic preparations are right beside the aspirin. The workplace offers aromatherapy innoculation instead of those painful flu vaccines. Forget the dimethicone; the face cream contains aloe vera, so it's safe, and natural. The beautician wears a lab coat and calls the skin the 'epidermis'. Traditional Chinese medicine has been around for thousands of years. The naturopath has a better bedside manner than the medical doctor. The only thing that supersedes science is the exotic; if it is foreign (and preferably Eastern), it appears to be imbued with authority and wisdom.

Spiritualism also cashes in on the integrity of mainstream fields by appearing to be integrative. Feng Shui is adapted for business, there are reiki tax guides, and psychic financial advisors. Recognisable, trusted terms are used to peddle spiritual concepts persuasively. Spiritual practitioners label themselves with professional titles; there are psychic surgeons, psychic detectives, angel therapists, spiritual advisers, intuitive counsellors, and psychic forensics. Unorthodox practices are portrayed as orthodox methods, such as Ayurvedic medicine and homeopathic vaccines. Dr Bruce Lipton claims to 'bridg[e] science and spirit'.[10]

Fringe studies such as parapsychology and postmodernism have the facade of science. Groups like the 'New Thought' movement sound like think tanks or types of cognitive behavioural therapy. Science is name-dropped in *The Science of Success* (2007) and *The Science of Getting Rich* (2007).[11] There is *The Science of Happiness* (2006) and *The Happiness Hypothesis* (2005). Movements appear to be scientific, with names like Religious Science, Christian Science, the Church of Divine Science, and the Church of Scientology (which also appeals to the social respect for religion). Scientologists and Raëlians blend science fiction, fringe science, and pseudoscience into their theories.

Homeopathic doses of psychology are blended with memory regression theory, physics with hyperdimensional physics, and linguistics with neuro-linguistic programming. Astrology aligns itself to astronomy — and benefits from the homophonic similarities. Birth-chart declinations, graphs, and diagrams give the semblance of science. Electromagnetic readers, digital thermometers, and infrared cameras are scientific tools, used irrelevantly for ghost-hunting. But spiritualism knows not the scientific method, and its approaches are metaphysical, not empirical.

Often, the beliefs and practices are not only unscientific, but the proponents are also anti-science. Science is often perceived as reductionist and materialist. Scientists are seen as cold, clinical, bunny-murdering monsters only interested in making money. Scientists might have a high Intelligence Quotient, but they clearly have a low Emotional Quotient.

Some proponents of spiritualist beliefs actively promulgate wrong and often dangerous ideas. Anti-vaccination organisations engage in fear-mongering campaigns, leaving communities susceptible to contagious diseases. Moon-landing conspiracy theorists jeopardise the public's understanding of science. Historical revisionists threaten to rewrite history erroneously. Al Mcdowell's *Uncommon Knowledge* claims include that: 'the Theory of Relativity is not valid', 'the Sphinx and Great Pyramid were built in 62,000 BC', and 'the universe is not expanding from a Big Bang'.[12] Even if the theory is wrong, it's reinterpreted as 'right'. The end of the world is always nigh, but it suddenly becomes a metaphor for any current global problems. But the next scheduled Armageddon is the real one!

It is useful for spiritualism to endeavour to explain the unknown, but harmful when it actively undermines what is known. Scientists turned pseudoscientists are guilty of this charge. This is academic irresponsibility. These people disregard science, discard what they were taught, yet flaunt their credentials and invoke the lexicon of science with convincing authority. The metalanguage of physics, maths, and neuroscience is adopted to appeal to the intellect of consumers. Fringe scientists try to persuade the public with conventional yet fuzzy labels like 'quantum', 'energy', and 'consciousness'.

'Gut feelings', 'intuition', and 'knowing' are employed to defend extraordinary claims for which there is no extraordinary evidence. Some pseudoscientists couch their claims in ambiguous yet grandiose terms. For example, the book *The Art of Shen Ku* (2001) is 'the first intergalactic artform of the entire universe'. The knowledge contained within it is allegedly 'simple enough for a child, too complex for a genius', 'devastatingly personally applicable in perpetuity', 'governing all conscious progress in any species anywhere', and 'transcending the ultimate barriers of time and space'.[13] Instead of addressing the burden of proof and providing evidence, claimants often expect the sceptics to disprove their outrageous claims.

For its followers, spiritualism fills the void left by the loss of power of religions. Spiritualist beliefs and practices try to fill the shortfalls of religion and the gaps of knowledge. Spiritualism supposedly explains the unexplained, and offers a modern alternative to the historical religions. Self-identifying as a 'spiritual person' conveniently addresses the question, 'Everyone believes in something. What do you believe in?' Otherwise, you're just a soulless, immoral atheist.

Spiritualism fills the spiritual space created by secularisation. This is especially true in a country like Australia, where there is no homogenous religious identity. There is no 'Bible Belt', no enclaves of persecuted parties, or socio-religious groups like the 'Cultural Jews' of the US. There are indigenous beliefs, but no homegrown religion, such as the Church of England. Rather than the famed 'Christian heritage', Australia has a secular heritage. There is no state religion, and no sectarianism.

Australia is nominally perceived as a 'Christian country', due to a history of adopting the religion of our European colonisers. However, perception and practice are not the same thing. Australia is as multi-religious as it is multicultural. All of the major religions have a presence in Australia, but all are on the decline in terms of popularity. Those who have 'No Religion' are part of the fastest growing group in the country, suggesting that we are evolving to become a non-religious nation. To many Australians, religion is a cultural relic.

Personally, I was raised in a secular household. My mother is an intermittent Catholic. My father was not baptised, without any resulting social stigma. I received limited exposure to religion, through Wednesday-morning Scripture and primary-school Christmas pageants. I resented Sunday-morning screenings of *Hour of Power* instead of cartoons. I wasn't socialised into religion, so in some ways I don't perceive myself as an atheist but simply as 'not religious'. This is my social norm. I was raised by the principles of mateship rather than worship, and perhaps this cultural idealism of egalitarianism fosters the image of Australians as inherently sceptical people.

Spiritualism is multi-belief but not overtly religious, and perhaps this is why it appeals to some Australians. We like the celebrations without the ceremony. We don't like to get up early on Sunday mornings for Church, but we like our Easter holidays. There appear to be pockets of spiritualist communities in Australia, like Bellingen in New South Wales, and Queensland's Sunshine Coast. Everyone knows of the local counterculture township with the dreadlocked hippies, bohemian coffee shops, and village feel. Spiritualism is a lazy, non-committal, secular 'religion' for those not ready to give up the trappings of religion. But it is a break away from religion. For some people, perhaps spiritual beliefs are stepping stones on the path to letting go of religion.

Perhaps we're all a little spiritualist by cultural necessity. Spiritualism is accessible for everyone, and many everyday acts are perceived as 'spiritual'. I'm not averse to burning an aromatherapy candle because I like the scent. I eat tofu because I like the taste. I volunteered with St Vincent de Paul because I wanted to help homeless people. Spiritualism is seen as everyday because it tends to reflect popular culture. It's a lifestyle 'religion'. In a sense, we demonstrate that we are products of our own time and culture when we say 'Oh my God!', speak of 'the Australian spirit', burn an incense stick, shop for organic food, read our stars in the newspaper, self-medicate with vitamin supplements, or try a home remedy. But we shouldn't assign unrelated significance to these acts.

Some see spirituality in every experience. One commentator believes: 'Every action, whether it's cooking for the kids, resolving problems with a partner, cleaning toilets, if done with awareness is a spiritual experience.'[14] But to the sceptic, correlation does not equal causation. And it's all about personal perception. To pattern-seeking minds, a simple thought becomes an epiphany. Emotions become intuition. Ideas become messages from beyond. Truths are found in poetry and philosophy. A hurricane becomes an act of God. A solar eclipse is seen as a bad omen. Bonding with an animal becomes mystical. Surviving an accident triggers religious sentiment. Birth becomes miraculous. Death becomes sacrosanct.

Some find spiritual experiences in society. For these people, coincidences become synchronicity. Luck is mystical, not made. There is magic afoot, and outside influences affect our lives daily. We choose our parents before we're born. Landing the job of our dreams is meant to be. Our friends are kindred spirits. Our partner is our soulmate, the person we were destined to be with, and it was written in the stars. We think this way because we tend to observe the hits and ignore the misses. We recall that chance encounter that led us to meet our best friend, or partner, but we forget the car accident, the unsuccessful relationships, and the lost jobs. Or we put these down to 'bad luck', and construe the failures as 'life lessons' we're meant to have on the path to finding our true selves.

Some find spiritual experiences in nature. We derive immense emotional satisfaction from physical phenomena. We wish on stars and rainbows. A shooting star means good luck. The magnitude of mountain ranges and the expanse of oceans fill us with wonder. Sunsets and night skies inspire romance, wistfulness, and hope. These feelings are powerful, humbling, and moving. They can be so overwhelming they seem to come from beyond; but they come from within.

This is the naturalist connection to the universe of which Carl Sagan spoke,[15] but the sense of awe and majesty is misconstrued as divine revelation. The beauty and complexity of nature is misinterpreted as 'evidence' for a creator, an architect, or a designer. These perspectives can inhibit our true understanding and appreciation of reality. They also reveal our unwarranted sense of spiritual superiority. Similarly, this sense of cosmic vanity leads some to deny evolution.

In these days of fast food and sound bites, what is holy? Holy is what we make holy; this is about meaning. We tend to think our 'spiritual experiences' are unique and deeply meaningful, and they are — to us. They are no doubt profound, but they are human experiences, and individual experiences. Assigning irrelevant importance to these experiences is an inaccurate attempt to understand the objective world. Spiritualist beliefs afford subjective meaning and purpose to our existence.

To talk about our existence, religious and spiritualist beliefs still offer useful conceptual metaphors. For the sceptic, agnostic, and atheist, the real miracles are medical advancements, our relationships are sacred, charity is compassion, reverence is for nature, prayer is hope, faith is confidence, the spirit is personality, the soul is the mind, and answers are found in science.

For many proponents of spiritualism, the answers are never found. Spiritualism is an ongoing quest. This religion-shopping often masks discontent. The seeker could be depressed, or anxious, and feel lost, confused, or unhappy. The selectiveness of beliefs and practices often leads to hypocrisy. The search for truth ends in falsehood. The shamans, clairvoyants, and gurus are false gods. Like The Beatles' audiences with the Maharishi Mahesh Yogi, enlightenment becomes disillusionment. The search for spiritualism never ends.

NOTES

1. J. Randi, *An Encyclopedia of Claims, Frauds, and Hoaxes of the Occult and Supernatural*, St Martin's Griffin, New York, 1997.
2. H. Houdini, *A Magician Among the Spirits*, Arno Press, New York, 1972, p. 5.
3. See for example J. Canfield and M. Hansen, *Chicken Soup for the Soul: 101 stories to open the heart and rekindle the spirit*, Health Communications, Inc., Florida, 1993.
4. See A. Lluch, *Enjoy Life and Be Happy in 30 Seconds: daily steps to enrich your life*, WS Publishing, San Diego, 2009.
5. See K. Trudeau, *Natural Cures 'They' Don't Want You To Know About*, Alliance Publishing, Alabama, 2005.
6. P. Ragnar, 'Magnetic Qi Gong', at www.roaringlionpublishing.com
7. S. Browne, *Phenomenon: everything you need to know about the paranormal*, HighBridge Company, Minneapolis, 2005, p. 251.
8. D. Chopra, *Life After Death: the burden of proof*, Harmony, New York, 2008.

9. See D. Chopra, *The Seven Spiritual Laws of Success: a pocketbook guide to fulfilling your dreams (one hour of wisdom)*, Amber-Allen Publishing, San Rafael, 2007 and W. Dyer, *Excuses Begone!: how to change lifelong, self-defeating thinking habits*, Hay House, Carlsbad, 2009.

10. Dr B. Lipton, 'Uncovering the Biology of Belief', at www.brucelipton.com

11. See W. Wattles, *The Science of Success: the secret to getting what you want*, Sterling, New York, 2007 and W. Wattles, *The Science of Getting Rich: find the secret to the law of attraction*, Wilder Publications, Michigan, 2007.

12. A. McDowell, *Uncommon Knowledge: new science of gravity, light, the origin of life, and the mind of man*, Author House, Bloomington, 2009.

13. Zeek, *The Art of Shen Ku: the ultimate traveller's guide of this planet*, Perigee Trade, New York, 2001.

14. N. Fee, 'Energise Yourself', *The Green Parent*, August/September 2009, p. 20.

15. C. Sagan (ed. A. Druyan), *The Varieties of Scientific Experience: a personal view of the search for God*, Penguin, New York, 2006.

LIFE, DYING, AND DEATH: REFLECTIONS OF A HUMANIST

Rosslyn Ives
President of the Council of Australian Humanist Societies, editor of
Australian Humanist, former president of the Humanist Society of Victoria,
retired secondary-school science teacher

> The ponies run, the girls are young,
> The odds are there to beat.
> You win a while, and then it's done —
> Your little winning streak.
> And summoned now to deal
> With your invincible defeat,
> You live your life as if it's real,
> A thousand kisses deep.
> — *Lyrics to* 'A Thousand Kisses Deep'

THESE LINES BY POET AND SONGWRITER LEONARD COHEN EVOKE THE vibrancy of life while hinting that death is never far away. In our daily lives, we mostly concentrate on living, and attend to dying and death only occasionally. Rightly so, for we are living, and it is life that we truly experience. And it is what we cling to even under appalling conditions. Humans, along with all other living creatures, do their utmost to avoid death. Yet, this universal 'will to live' should not be mistaken for an awareness of death, for the sense of being fully aware of death — our own and that of others — seems peculiar to humans. Recognising our own mortality leads us to give meanings to life and the inevitability of death — meanings we draw primarily from the worldview we hold.

Those of us who use science and other evidence-based knowledge to explain life and give it meaning go by many names: atheist, secularist, rationalist, and, as they will be referred to in this essay, humanist. This growing segment of the population also includes many others who are unaligned with any named 'ism', yet fall under a generally humanist umbrella by rejecting religion and supporting a pragmatic ethical stance towards living. From this position, a range of basic human rights are recognised, and death itself is seen as simply being part of a community's responsibility to the dying and the living. All life ends in death, and therefore forms an integral part of living. So, armed with this worldview, humanists, atheists, and many others with an essentially non-religious outlook seize, as Cohen says, their 'little winning streak' and try to live a good life in the here and now.

Those thinkers whose ideas have contributed to the humanist worldview broadly concur that the features of a good life are personal liberty used responsibly; seeking knowledge; engaging in pleasures that do no harm to others; deriving satisfaction from the arts, physical activity, and personal relationships; and the sense of belonging to a community. These guiding principles, resting on nothing more than goodwill, civil decencies, and social hope, underpin the United Nations Universal Declaration of Human Rights, as adopted by most countries around the world.

The widely endorsed concept of human rights, and our striving towards them, are considered to be an advance in the cultural development of humanity. These human rights form the foundations of the humanist worldview. It is a view that requires us to acknowledge our interdependence and connectedness to the rest of life on Earth, rather than to imagine ourselves as specially created beings beholden to creator gods or spirits in another world. Its values are drawn from the human capacity for empathy, compassion, and sociability, tempered by experience. The humanist worldview lacks dogma and in order to live a good life, those who identify with it live with uncertainty and a willingness to adapt to new situations based upon fresh evidence. This approach to life has been summarised in different ways throughout the ages; for example Socrates (469–399 BCE) suggested that the best life was the examined life — one that was free, informed, and freely chosen.

In the 1880s, the English explorer, soldier, and orientalist Richard Burton, writing in the manner of the humanist Persian poet Omar Khayyám, penned that the good life was to: 'do good for good is good to do! Spurn bribe of heaven and threat of hell!'[1]

In census data both here and in countries such as Canada, the Netherlands, Norway, and the UK, the non-religious are an increasingly significant proportion of society. And with a general decline in active religious involvement, such countries are arguably secular, both socially and politically. Standards of education are high, freedom is the norm, and average life expectancy exceeds the biblical three-score years and ten. It therefore seems that, once the conditions for leading a good life are well satisfied, religions, with their dogmatic restrictions and dubious promises of an afterlife, have less appeal.

The humanist worldview considers all knowledge of human life, whether admirable, bizarre, backed by evidence, or imagined, as essential for understanding the human story in its entirety. For example, one widely held belief that has had profound implications for human attitudes towards death is the idea that a person consists of both physical and non-physical parts, which in philosophical terms is called dualism. The non-material part, commonly called the spirit or soul, is widely believed to survive death. Indeed, it is disconcertingly apparent that when a dead body is compared to a live body its life force or animating spirit has quite obviously vanished. Those both present and past with only a limited understanding of the biology of living things typically explain this by saying that the animating spirit leaves the body upon death. This duality concept has been further reinforced by claims that some people have 'seen' a spirit leaving a body upon death, and also by early researchers who claimed to have recorded a weight loss immediately after death, interpreted to be the spirit leaving the body.[2]

However, to the best of my knowledge, no modern scientific study has been able to replicate either of these claims. Instead, science has determined that living bodies are animated by nothing more than all the complex living processes working within them. And so long as dangers are avoided, food, oxygen, and water supplied, and wastes removed, life continues until age-related deterioration causes death. We also know that when vital life processes are interfered with by disease, excessive fluid loss, oxygen shortage, or the accumulation of toxic compounds (either ingested or produced by the body), dying begins, and death can result.

Even though modern medical treatments can reverse failing processes and restore wellbeing temporarily, eventually we still all die. Life is a complex but singular phenomenon.

The idea of humans consisting of two separate parts is so deeply embedded in human culture and language across all societies that shifting to an alternative paradigm of life as a singular phenomenon is only in its early stages. Therefore, those with a humanist worldview are sharing a world with a greater majority of people who are still deeply attached to the much older notion of duality; a view that was formulated by our ancestors deep in the past.

From archaeology, we have evidence of deliberate ceremonial burials dating back as far as 120,000 years ago. Similarly, we know that beginning about 11,000 years ago, as humanity took the step from hunter–gatherer to farmer, burials and associated religious rituals became more elaborate, as evidenced by structures such as the pyramids of Egypt. Such displays of care for the dead imply an intense regard for the need to prepare ritualistically for an 'afterlife'. Preparation was most evident in relation to leaders and people of high social standing, but carried through to commoners, too, albeit on a smaller scale. All this describes a deep-seated human need to deal with the fact of Earthly death and, in that pre-scientifically literate time, a priesthood arose to codify this into religious rituals. These rituals engaged with people's needs at both an individual and group level.

On the individual level, belief in a life after death is also associated with the widespread idea that other states of being can be experienced and other spirit worlds visited. In numerous studies, anthropologists have shown that many cultures have developed practices which enable their members to deliberately induce mind-altering states in order to facilitate 'out-of-body' experiences. The methods used include ingesting hallucinogenic substances, going without food or sleep, and engaging in rhythmic chanting and dancing. All of these activities can affect the normal functioning of the brain, leading to atypical brain sensations. Despite merely being due to anomalous brain functioning, these experiences have convinced the people having them, and those who are witnesses, that a supposed 'spirit' can leave the body, travel through time, and even survive death. It seems that with the knowledge of our own mortality has come a deep-seated yearning that some part of us continues after death. This has produced an extensive stock of cultural interpretations of our supposedly dual nature. While it is accepted that the body disintegrates, there has long existed the fervent hope, indeed the expectation, that a spirit part goes to an afterlife or is reincarnated.

From studies in both archaeology and history, we have descriptions of a variety of human behaviours surrounding death and dying, with anthropology further revealing ritualistic practices and doctrines. The various brain experiences resulting from these types of activities have been variously studied by psychologists and by those working in the comparatively recent discipline of neuroscience. The research from these areas seems to support a sceptical view of both the soul and life after death, concluding that the self is purely a function of a living brain. It has also shown the brain to be susceptible to belief in supernatural things. One such occurrence widely believed by many in the general population to be an indicator of an afterlife is so-called near-death experiences, where in Western culture the person reports going down a tunnel, seeing bright lights at the end, everything seeming peaceful and calm, and then being drawn back into the chaos of conscious living. *Mortal Minds* (2005) by Dutch anaesthesiologist G. M. Woerlee usefully covers near-death experiences and other paranormal brain related phenomena from a medical-research point of view.[3] Needless to say, despite the anecdotes and the appeal of such experiences, Woerlee demonstrates that a brain under stress combined with oxygen deprivation easily accounts for what patients have experienced.

Despite our strong sense of ourselves as having a mind operating independently of our body, and/or having a body and spirit, the evidence indicates otherwise. Investigations strongly support the contention that when our brain dies, both the mind and the imagined spirit can no longer exist. In other words, the duality concept is an epiphenomenon constructed by our complex brains. As mortal beings, we stride the stage of life but briefly until death; or, as Shakespeare put it, 'each life is rounded with a little sleep' — the sleep that is death. So, in response to these phenomena and the inevitable fact of death, the humanist or atheist approach to life is one of *carpe diem* — seize the day.

Living in a modern, technologically advanced society like Australia means most of us are shielded from the experience of dying and death —

unless our occupation as a nurse, doctor, carer, or undertaker brings us in close contact with death and dying. Few of us, therefore, pass much time in the company of people in the last stages of dying, and if we omit films, television, et cetera, neither do we get to see more than the occasional dead body. Indeed, such is our desire to avoid contact with the death, even the option of 'viewing the body' of a dead loved one is often shunned nowadays.

Being separated and shielded from dying and death was not true for our ancestors. Until a few generations ago, the dying and the dead were very much among the living, as most people died at home, with their bodies laid out by close family members. Family and neighbours would view the body prior to the funeral service, which was often held at home before the body was taken for burial or cremation. It was also a time when most people died before they reached old age. A time when many died of infectious diseases — now prevented through vaccinations and better hygiene, or cured via antibiotics. Deaths from disease and accidents have been substantially curbed, reducing the contact most have with death among friends and family. We now live in a time when death before a person has reached old age is considered as tragic: a failure of modern medicine, poor safety standards, or just bad luck.

Our current Western cultural practice of separating the dead and dying from daily life is the extreme culmination of practices that have developed by all complex societies. It has been described by the UK archaeologist Timothy Taylor, in his book *The Buried Soul: how humans invented death*, as 'visceral insulation'.[4] By this term, he means that the living are shielded from the messy processes of sickness, dying, death, and the disposal of bodies. Specialists in specially designated places now handle these duties. Taylor explores what humans of various cultures think about death, including burial rituals, human sacrifice, and even cannibalism. He describes Western citizens as being 'viscerally insulated' from death and dying, more so than any other peoples past and present.

Confronting our own mortality and that of others is a challenge. So when someone close to us dies, or our own death is imminent, among the heightened feelings are fear, anger, loss, and grief. While cultural customs lead to grief being expressed in different ways, there is no evidence that the anguish and sorrow felt is any less or more because of a person's worldview. Grieving over the dead is universal. And regardless of whether dying is sudden or protracted, we are greatly comforted in our grief by the sympathetic support of family, friends, and community. Rituals and ceremonies that honour the dead and console the bereaved are features of all societies.

In our Western tradition, as practised in Australia, funerals until very recently have been largely shaped by religious worldviews, the dominant one being Christianity. This has given rise to some avowed atheists and humanists, who vehemently reject religion and all they associate with it, to leave instructions that they want no funeral ceremony upon death. If their wishes are strictly adhered to, family and friends are thereby denied the comfort of ritualised, collective mourning. This can prolong the grieving and even cause psychological damage. Ceremonies are valuable, as one of the early appointed civil celebrants, Dally Messenger, argues passionately in his book, *Ceremonies & Celebrations* (1999), and articles such as 'The Power and Purpose of Secular Ceremonies'.[5]

Until about three decades ago, as mentioned above, most funerals in Australia were religious in form. However, since 1974, following the initiation of the civil celebrant program by the then attorney-general, the late Lionel Murphy, a secular alternative has been growing in popularity. Though the main aim of the civil-celebrant program was to provide a legal, secular option for marriage ceremonies, in addition to a registry office, celebrants have been increasingly in demand for funeral ceremonies. This means that instead of families with no connection to any religious organisation seeking the services of a member of the clergy, who in all likelihood didn't know the deceased, they have been able to engage the services of a civil celebrant.

In discussion with the family, the celebrant is able to tailor a ceremony, usually called a celebration of life, with a better match between the worldview of the deceased and her or his family and friends. According to a local funeral director in Melbourne, around 50 per cent of funerals for people from inner suburbs are now conducted by a combination of family and celebrants, with the funeral service personnel acting as coordinators. And in the outer suburbs, celebrant-conducted funerals can be as high as 80 per cent.[6] These essentially secular ceremonies celebrate the life of the deceased person. They eulogise the person's life with love, with humour, and in a way that personalises the ceremony. This humanist outlook strongly asserts that we are mortal and that, though death is the end, each person leaves traces in the memories of the living. Most memories are just of the simple pleasures of shared times with family and friends — celebratory meals, holidays by the beach, music on the verandah, the kindness of strangers — but sometimes a person leaves a more lasting legacy in the form of works of art, buildings, publications, musical compositions, or contributions to community and public life. It is all these memories that family, friends, and the wider community celebrate and also remember.

In Australia, we are fortunate to live in a country with a very high standard of living. Each of us probably expects to survive the many hazards of disease, malnutrition, famines, and other natural disasters. We can expect to live into our eighth decade. But, paradoxically, this has created a growing problem of many people being kept alive, often wracked with the pain and indignity of a terminal or age-related illness, long after their capacity to lead an enjoyable and dignified life has ceased. With a medical profession focused almost obsessively on enhancing and extending life, facilitating an easy death when appropriate and requested is a seriously neglected area.

A combination of the existing laws and a conservative 'do no harm' approach means few doctors are willing to offer an ill person or their intimates the medical means to end life at a place and time of the patient's choosing. Laws framed many years ago, when the culturally dominant Christian views about death and dying determined what was acceptable practice, forbid those who want to exercise the option of voluntary euthanasia from legally doing so. Meanwhile, contemporary opinion is seriously at odds with existing laws. The latest polling, conducted mid-October 2009, shows 85 per cent of people support the option of voluntary euthanasia, with 10 per cent opposed and 5 per cent undecided.[7] Yet Australia's parliamentarians have been most reluctant to legislate on this issue. The standout exception was Marshall Perron who, as chief minister of the Northern Territories, managed to convince the NT parliament to pass the *Rights of the Terminally Ill Act* in 1995. Even though the majority in the NT medical profession were hostile to this Act, it worked well due to the personal bravery of Dr Philip Nitschke, who was prepared to help four terminally ill people to die at their request. Unfortunately, the Act was overturned eight months later by a private member's bill passed in the federal parliament, which has overriding jurisdiction over the Northern Territory.

Since 1996, no Australian parliament has passed any legislation supportive of voluntary euthanasia, though unsuccessful attempts have been made in several state parliaments as well as federally. These include private member's bills proposed to state parliaments of Victoria (2009) and South Australia (2007 and 2009). Those with a humanist worldview strongly support the right of autonomous persons to freely choose the option of voluntary euthanasia. They also strongly advocate the use of advanced-care plans (also known as advanced directives or living wills), in which a person sets down their choices on future medical treatment.

Australian philosopher and ethicist Peter Singer has for many decades written about ethical issues with the aim of promoting the wellbeing of all sentient beings. In *Rethinking Life and Death* (1994) he outlines a set of 'commandments' that summarise a key aspect of the humanist worldview, namely that, as death is the end of life, living well ought to be emphasised.[8]

His first new commandment is to recognise that the worth of human life varies. Here Singer argues that instead of investing resources and time in trying to maintain life for all, just because the medical technology to do so is available, future quality of life for each case needs to be evaluated. Reasonable judgement needs to be made that, in some cases, the future quality of life makes the investment of resources of dubious value. In earlier times, when medical technology was limited, severely deformed babies, terminally ill patients, and others with little prospect of an improved quality of life were kept comfortable and allowed to die. Singer thoroughly examines this option and argues in its favour.

The second of Singer's commandments is to take responsibility for the consequences of your decisions. This new ethical proposal draws attention to the less-than-clear-cut distinction between killing and allowing a patient to die. He argues that there are cases where assisting a person or an animal to die is far more humane and ethical than merely allowing them to die by perhaps withholding food and water. If a person no longer wants to continue living and requests assistance to die, this desire ought to be respected and facilitated.

His third commandment is to respect a person's desire to live or die. This contrasts with the view of 'never taking your own life, and always try to prevent others from taking theirs'. This latter religious injunction against suicide is the cause of great anxiety for both those who have no desire to keep living and their loved ones, who must live on with the opprobrium of suicide being classed as a sin. Undoubtedly, the older religious view contributes to the vehement opposition to legalised voluntary euthanasia from a vocal minority.

In the fourth commandment, Singer raises the need to only have children who are wanted and can be cared for. This forms a long-held humanist attitude that finds expression in the advocacy for family-planning measures that would include abortion.

The fifth commandment is: 'do not discriminate on the basis of species'. Here Singer wants to assert that all sentient beings ought to be able to live lives that enable them to flourish and thrive in the manner of their kind. Singer is particularly concerned that animals used by humans for work, food, companionship, or other purposes ought to be treated well and given the space, food, and other things necessary for them live well.

In his writings, Singer convincingly argues for pragmatic, humanist, ethical guidelines for living and dying. These are focused on quality of life and the right of the individual to flourish as an autonomous person. They are made coherent by a pervading empathy for other living beings, both human and animal. Other contemporary philosophers have also put forward arguments for leading a good life using humanist ethics, based on compassion, reason, and common sense. These include UK humanist philosophers Richard Norman and A. C. Grayling, and American philosopher Richard Rorty, who died in 2007.[9] In what was to be his last interview with reporter Danny Postel, Rorty expressed the opinion that:

'The most important advance that the West has yet made ... is the shift in outlook resulting from its having "cobbled together, in the course of the last 200 years, a specifically secularist moral tradition—one that regards the free consensus of the citizens of a democratic society, rather than the Divine Will, as the source of moral imperatives".'[10]

In this essay, I have argued that several hundred years of science has provided evidence-based knowledge on which to build an ethical approach to leading a good life in the here and now. This is contributing to a shift in the basic ethical framework of Western societies. In this ongoing process, particularly among the life and death issues discussed above, the battle is still being fought between the more enlightened humanist worldview and a small but fervent minority of religious dogmatists.

As the history of social changes over the last few hundred years demonstrates, the humanist worldview of seeking knowledge, freedom of thought, care, and compassion for others, personal autonomy, and responsibility for actions is gaining ground. Being armed with a humanist worldview enables life's brief sojourn to be lived well and, as Cohen poetically puts it, with an intensity of being 'a thousand kisses deep'.

NOTES

1. Cited in R. Dahlitz, 'Do Good for Good is Good to Do. Spurn Bribe of Heaven and Threat of Hell!', *Australian Humanist* 75, Spring 2004, p. 15. He discusses the use of Burton's quote as the masthead of *The Rationalist* monthly magazine (established in 1924), when under the editorship of John Langley.
2. L. Fisher, *Weighing the Soul: the evolution of scientific belief,* Weidenfeld and Nicolson, London, 2004.
3. See G. M. Woerlee, *Mortal Minds: a biology of the soul and the dying experience,* de Tijdstroom, Utrecht, 2003.
4. T. Taylor, *The Buried Soul: how humans invented death,* Fourth Estate, London, 2002.
5. D. Messenger, *Ceremonies & Celebrations,* [4th edition of *Ceremonies for Today*], Lothian, Melbourne, 1999; D. Messenger, 'The Power and Purpose of Secular Ceremonies', *Australian Humanist* 96, Summer 2009, pp. 1–3.
6. Consultant at Le Pines Funeral Service, East Kew, in interview with author. The variability is largely determined by availability of clergy and their connections to the deceased.
7. Report in *Update*, Dying With Dignity Victoria, 148, Spring 2009, p. 1.
8. P. Singer, *Rethinking Life and Death: the collapse of traditional ethics,* Text Publishing, Melbourne, 1994.
9. R. Norman, *On Humanism*, Routledge, London, 2004; A. C. Grayling, *What is Good?: the search for the best way to live,* Phoenix, London, 2003 and *The Choice of Hercules: pleasure, duty and the good life in the 21st century,* Phoenix, London, 2007.
10. D. Postel, 'Obituary of a Boring Atheist,' *New Humanist*, July–August 2007, pp. 38–39.

* POLITICS

PARLIAMENT AND PRAYER

Hon. Ian Hunter
Labor Member of Parliament, Legislative Council, Parliament of South Australia

NOT ALL PARLIAMENTS IN AUSTRALIA HAVE SAID PARLIAMENTARY prayers since their establishment. But the practice gradually became the norm. As I will outline, this practice didn't meet universal approval when first instituted — and it is increasingly being brought into question in modern times.

Why all the fuss? Why should we bother to challenge this archaic practice, which is just like so many other parts of the old, fusty traditions of parliament that are pretty much ignored by most people? Aren't there more important things to be getting on with?

One can easily dismiss the issue as being of little importance, but at the very least there are implications for the legitimacy of parliament as a truly representative body for the community. Society is changing — and has changed dramatically since the first parliaments were established in Australia. Do we really want our parliaments to display a bias towards any one religion by saying a Christian prayer at the commencement of each sitting day? Granted, one minute of each sitting day does not really seem like much. But, like much of our parliamentary system, the action isn't what is of importance — it is about the symbolism.

So, are prayers in parliament relevant any longer in an institution that is the keystone of our modern, diverse, secular democracy? Do prayers in one particular Christian form undermine the secular basis of democracy?

First and foremost, Australia is a secular society. Our parliaments are secular parliaments. While some individual members are guided by their Christian faith, and may seek the spiritual support that praying offers them, Christianity (or any other faith, for that matter) has no place in the proceedings of any Australian parliament. To understand how parliamentary prayers have become part of daily procedures, then, we must look back at the history of Australian parliaments — and at the Westminster system, on which our system is based.

Since European civilisation of Australia, our country has been run as a secular society. We have no state religion, and the founders of the country planned it that way. Section 116 of the Australian Constitution states:

> The Commonwealth shall not make law for establishing any religion, or for imposing any religious observance, or for prohibiting the free exercise of any religion, and no religious test shall be required as a qualification for any office or public trust under the Commonwealth.

Those who wrote our Constitution could not have been clearer — they saw a very definite separation of the church and state, and they supported a multi-sect society, if not at that time a multi-faith one. And while the census of 1901 — the year of our federation — may have shown that 96 per cent of Australians were Christian, the times have changed and society has moved on. The census in 1901 did not even count the Aboriginal people of Australia — unthinkable now.

As for the percentage of Australians who identify as Christian, that figure is continually declining, and religion plays a much less central role in Australian society than it has in the past. It is not even clear what the category 'Christian' means in regard to the census — and, of course, one has to treat census data with caution here — but it probably includes those with no real Christian commitment other than a vague personal notion of inherited belief.

The reality is that most Australians do identify as Christian. But identifying as Christian and actively following Christian practices (like praying) are two very different things. The 2005 Australian Survey of Social Attitudes found that less than 15 per cent of Australians attend religious service once a week or more. But 65 per cent of the population attend not more than once a year (almost 36 per cent say they 'never' attend religious service).

So, while many people may fill in 'Anglican' or 'Catholic', or one of the other Christian denominations on the census form, that cross on the statistics form doesn't translate into religious adherence in their own lives. It is hard to imagine, then, that most Australians feel the need for their elected representatives to say a prayer before they get down to the business of running the country.

Parliaments are steeped in tradition, from the colours of the chamber to the way that we address each other to the attired donned by the staff. And following from that traditionalism, prayers in parliament continue with very little real debate about their relevance to Australian society, and very little reflection of contemporary Australian views.

The first Australian parliament was opened on 9 May 1901 by His Royal Highness the Duke of Cornwall and York, in the Exhibition Building, Melbourne. At the opening, Lord Hopetoun, the governor-general, read a number of prayers, including the Lord's Prayer and a prayer of petition similar to those still recited in Australia's parliaments.

In this, the Australian Commonwealth parliament was mirroring the Westminster tradition. The tradition of daily prayer in the English parliament is thought to have begun in about 1558, becoming common practice by about 1567.

Until the 1580s, the prayers took no fixed form. It is generally believed that the present form of prayers recited in the Houses of Westminster date from the reign of Charles II (1660–1685). It was also under Charles II that the Clarendon Code was developed, a series of laws designed to reinforce the prominence of the Church of England. And so, as firmly based on Westminster as the Australian parliament was, it was almost inevitable that this aspect of the daily routine would be incorporated into the fledgling Australian parliamentary system.

As part of developing standing orders for the houses, the issue of daily prayer was referred to each house's Standing Orders Committee for consideration. As standing orders are resolutions for the houses, and not laws, the issue of prayers in parliament in no way contravened Section 116 of the Australian Constitution.

In recent times, some debate has occurred — in Australia, but also a little in England — about the relevance of prayers in modern parliaments. In early 2009, Conservative MP for South-West Bedfordshire Andrew Selous introduced a debate on Christianity in public life into the English parliament. While the bulk of the speeches focused on the importance and good works of Christianity in English society, John Mason, then MP for Glasgow East, did speak about the ongoing relevance of prayers in parliament. He said:

Since arriving at Westminster, I have been interested in the vestiges of Christianity around the place. For example, there is Prayers at the start of each sitting. Is that a good thing? I have mixed feeling about it ... Some attend only to book their seat for whatever business comes next, and I fear that the prayers themselves give a dry and dusty view of Christianity.[1]

Despite voicing such concerns, Mason went on to tell the house that, on the opening of his new office, he decided 'on the spur of the moment to have a prayer'. And so it seems destined that, for the foreseeable future at least, the tradition of Westminster's parliamentary prayers shall continue. In a debate such as the one that was held, to have only one person raise the quietest voice of dissent shows the level of acceptance for the practice in the Mother Parliament.

In Australia, a more serious and sustained debate about the relevance of prayers in parliament has surfaced in recent years. The first salvo in this debate in recent times was fired by the then leader of the Australian Democrats, Lyn Allison, who moved for the abolition of parliamentary prayers in 2006. The motion was defeated without debate, with the Australian Labor Party and the Coalition opposing it.

The issue once again arose in 2008, when Harry Jenkins, the Speaker of the House of Assembly, called for public debate on the relevance of prayers in parliament (while maintaining his own neutrality on the issue). Mirroring Independent MP Rob Oakeshott's sentiments, from Oakeshott's maiden speech, the Speaker questioned whether daily acknowledgement to the traditional owners of the land might be more appropriate. However, both major parties completely rejected the notion of removing parliamentary prayers from the daily routine, with the respective leaders of the parties pointing to Australian heritage as the reason for doing so.

Debate of the issue followed, with church groups (naturally) coming out to support the continuation of the practice, while others vigorously opposed it. The Australian Federation of Islamic Councils' president Ikebal Patel voiced his support of the continuation of the practice, but expressed the opinion that the prayer should be non-denominational and should acknowledge the spiritual connection of Australia's Aboriginal people with the land.

The Australian press were, to a large degree, opposed to such a change in parliamentary practice, and used their pages to advocate the continuation of the status quo. The *Sydney Morning Herald*'s editorial stated:

> We think the prayers strike the right balance of recognition of higher purpose to the political struggles without forcing any particular version of belief down anyone's throat. Those of atheist or agnostic persuasion can stay silent, or at least give humanistic support to its message if they like.[2]

But plenty of other commentators came out in support of the abolition of prayers in parliament (or, at least, serious and constructive debate as compared to the off-handed dismissal that some offered). Leslie Cannold, a columnist for the *Sun-Herald*, asked, 'If parliament began each day with an ode to the political supremacy of white men, would anyone cite "tradition" as a good reason to preserve it?'[3]

In the *Sunday Canberra Times*, Graham Downie took issue with the tokenistic spirit of the prayer as it is received in parliamentary prayers, and noted — as I have, many times — that the prayer seems to have no bearing on the behaviour of parliamentarians, particularly during question time.[4]

The issue soon faded from the public consciousness, and prayers seem to be firmly entrenched in the Australian federal parliament for the time being. Similar debates have occasionally arisen in most state parliaments around Australia. The most substantial debate about the practice has existed in New South Wales. In 1996, Liberal MLC the Hon. Dr Brian Pezzutti, then in opposition, asked the Hon. Michael Egan (then leader of the government in the Legislative Council) whether the Australian Labor Party would consider removing the prayer from the start of the day's business. Egan informed the chamber that whilst he personally had some issue with the prayer, no consideration would be given to removing it.

In October 2001, then Greens MLC Lee Rhiannon moved to remove parliamentary prayer from the daily routine of the New South Wales upper house, replacing it with a time of quiet, personal reflection for members. The ALP, Liberals, and Nationals all indicated that they would not support such a motion and, following debate, the Rhiannon motion was defeated, five votes to 31. Prayers currently continue in both chambers of the New South Wales parliament.

Victorian parliamentary prayers have been subject to very little debate. In 1994, when debating a bill, Labor MLC Brian Mier commented that the reference to Christianity in the chamber was outdated. It appears, though, that his comments did not prompt any further debate on the subject, and it does not appear to have been raised since.

As of the commencement of the 53rd Queensland parliament, on 21 April 2009, there was no requirement for a daily parliamentary prayer in Queensland's Standing Orders. A prayer was read by the governor at the official opening of parliament, but not every day thereafter. This reversed a tradition of the Queensland parliament that had been in place since 1860.

In 2007, the *Advertiser*, the South Australian weekday newspaper, reported that I had been reading during parliamentary prayers. I am an atheist, and it is my common practice to use the time given to prayers to catch up on some reading, or to prepare upcoming speeches or questions, but on this occasion, for some reason, it was deemed newsworthy and reported by Nick Henderson. There followed a heated debate on the pages of South Australia's newsapers, with many writing very passionate letters (either in support of me, or expressing their dismay in me) that were published in, primarily, the *Advertiser*.

This was not the first time that prayers in parliament had been a matter of contention in recent history in South Australia. In the 1980s, the Hon. Anne Levy, in her role as president of the Legislative Council, expressed concern that, as a non-believer, she was required to read the prayer, and wished to delegate the responsibility to the clerk of the Legislative Council. However, such a move — which would have required a suspension of standing orders — was not passed by an absolute majority of the council.

In May 2003, Liberal member for Unley David Pisoni was criticised by Labor member for West Torrens Tom Koutsantonis for refusing to remove his hands from his pockets during parliamentary prayers. Pisoni has regularly voiced his opposition to the ongoing practice of prayers in parliament, stating, 'we are a multicultural society ... Government and Parliament should be separate from religion because Parliament should reflect society'.[5] However, no real move has ever been made in South Australia to remove the practice of parliamentary prayers. But this does not mean that there has always been support for the practice: on the contrary, the introduction of prayers into the South Australian parliamentary sitting day took more than 50 years, and much vigorous debate.

The first bicameral parliament was held in South Australia in 1857. Parliamentary prayers were introduced into the House of Assembly in 1918, and the Legislative Council in 1919. In the intervening years, members of the parliament debated the pros and cons of parliamentary prayer.

In 1886, Robert Caldwell (member for the Yorke Peninsula) moved a motion calling for parliamentary prayers to be included in the standing orders. The motion, which was ultimately unsuccessful, was opposed for a number of reasons: Rowland Rees (member for Onkaparinga) contested the notion, believing that to 'introduce the element of worship as suggested, and you will see history repeat itself by such worship becoming a mere matter of form and indifference, and finally being availed by the very few'.[6]

The issue arose once again in the aftermath of World War I. In August 1918, Robert Nichols, member for Stanley, moved a motion once again calling for the introduction of parliamentary prayers in the House of Assembly. Among those who opposed their introduction was John Gunn, member for Adelaide, who reflected that in federal parliament prayer 'is read glibly by somebody. Nobody takes particular notice of it'.[7] Member for Burra Burra Henry Buxton argued that the inclusion of parliamentary prayers would lead to hypocrisy among members who would pray and then be at each other's throats shortly thereafter in the cut-and-thrust of parliamentary debate. However, such opposition was overridden on this occasion, and parliamentary prayers were introduced in the House of Assembly on 5 November 1918.

The following day, a motion was introduced into the Legislative Council, calling for the proceedings of the upper house to be opened with a daily prayer. Other members generally agreed, and parliamentary prayers were introduced into the Legislative Council on 10 July 1919.

Some attention has been given to the practice in the Tasmanian parliament, where parliamentary prayers became a daily occurrence from 1930. A proposal to change the prayer was made in 1989 by Greens member of the House of Assembly, the Reverend Lance Armstrong. The motion, which Armstrong proposed because he felt that the behaviour of members in the chamber was generally the antithesis of Christian behaviour, and thus devalued the sentiment, was never moved to debate.

In 2003, further attention was given to the use of parliamentary prayer in Tasmania, with suggestions that the Christian content should be removed and replaced with something better befitting the times (an acknowledgement of the Aboriginal connection with the land was the preferred option). There was much public outcry on the issue, and then premier Jim Bacon reaffirmed Tasmania's commitment to parliamentary prayer.

Prayers have been said to open both chambers of the West Australian parliament since their inception. To date, no debate has occurred about the ongoing relevance of the practice, as far as I am aware. Similarly, the Northern Territory parliament, which only has one chamber, begins each day with a prayer, copied directly from the House of Representatives' practice. No effort has been made to remove parliamentary prayers in the Northern Territory.

In 1995, the Australian Capital Territory took the unusual move of voting to remove parliamentary prayers from their daily routine. Time is now given where members, in silence, can either pray or reflect on their duties as elected representatives of the people of the ACT.

The debate about the relevance of parliamentary prayers is not about getting rid of religion by stealth; it is about reflecting the reality of contemporary Australian society. The reality is that those who identify as Christian in our society, while still a majority, is steadily declining, as are the participation rates of organised religion. I would assume that there are many people in our community who identify as Christian, too, but who would be bemused by the idea of starting their professional day with a group prayer with their fellow workers.

Australian society has moved on since parliamentary prayers were introduced into the various chambers around our nation. It's time that the practices of our parliaments did, too.

We do not sit in parliament representing only our own personal beliefs — we are the elected representatives of the people. And as we sit in the various houses of parliament, we are representing a diverse community: a community made up of Christians, of course, but also of believers of other faiths and non-believers. And, as with all duties we perform in our roles as parliamentarians, we do not represent only our personal views but also the views of the constituency that has granted us the right to sit there. So, why enshrine in a parliament a practice that divides the community, rather than uniting it?

I would argue that, if a moment for reflection was deemed necessary, it might be more beneficial for members to take the opportunity to consider our own inner dialogue, whether we believe that to be motivated by some form of higher being or by our own reasoned morality, for a minute before we enter the chamber.

Or, in the alternative, perhaps the speaker could offer some form of meditation on our role as legislators that is not couched in the archaic form of religious belief, but which instead reflects on our duties as representatives of the people. But, really, I think that we have enough time to give thought to our actions and our roles as parliamentarians in our day-to-day life — there is no need to waste parliament's valuable time on it.

NOTES

1. Hansard, HC Deb, 11 March 2009, c113WH.
2. Editorial, 'Deliver Us From Diversions', *Sydney Morning Herald*, 28 October 2008, p. 10.
3. L. Cannold, 'Church and State Should be Separate', *Sun-Herald*, 2 November 2008, at www.cannold.com/media/2008-11-02-church-and-state-should-be-separate
4. G. Downie, 'The Use of Prayers in Parliament Alienates and Excludes', *Sunday Canberra Times*, 2 November 2008, p. 24.
5. H. Gout, ' "Archaic" Parliament', *Independent Weekly*, 31 October 2008, at www.independent weekly.com.au/news/local/news/general/archaic-parliament/1348778.aspx
6. R. Rees, South Australian Parliamentary Debates, 28 July 1886, p. 535.
7. J. Gunn, South Australian Parliamentary Debates, 28 August 1918, p. 122.

EVER WONDERED WHY GOD IS A BLOKE?[1]

Lyn Allison
Former senator for Victoria

THERE IS NOT A LOT OF DETAIL AROUND ABOUT WHAT GOD IS EXCEPT THAT he made men to look just like him — in his own image. I always thought he and Jesus would look like any other English chap, but with a beard and wearing a sheet. African Christians no doubt imagine him dark-skinned.

The Bible tells us he is capricious, cruel, vengeful, and filled with hatred for those who don't worship him, for blacks, Jews, gays, and women.

And in monotheism, you can't shop around for a nicer personality.

If the Ancient Greeks weren't keen on Zeus, who was in charge of the weather, they could go for his daughter Artemis, the Virgin goddess of hunting, the wilderness, and childbirth, or her handsome twin brother, Apollo, god of music, healing, poetry, and archery, associated with light, truth, and the sun. Hestia was another virgin, but keen on cooking, home, and hearth. Hera, queen of Heaven and goddess of marriage and childbirth, was beautiful, wore a crown, and held a lotus-tipped staff.

They procreated with one another, and with humans, creating hundreds of demigods and deities with every imaginable portfolio. Plays and poetry were written about their interactions. They were lots of fun.

As a child, I was told how totally good and loving and caring the Christian god was — which is exactly what is said today to five-year-olds in our secular state schools who are unlucky enough to have a chaplain or religious tuition. They probably won't be told that women must not have authority over men, and that they must be silent because, unlike the animal world, Adam was formed first, then Eve from one of his ribs.

In the twenty-first century, even school children would be at least puzzled by both propositions; however, the churches have subtle ways of getting the idea across. 'Shine' is a program devised by Hillsong Church, and is being used by chaplains in state schools. It targets girls with low self-esteem, giving them advice on being polite, personal grooming, and deportment. The message is that they need to conform and be pretty.

At Sunday school, we were steered away from the more unpalatable passages in the Bible, like the one in which Eve was punished severely for her and Adam's sin in eating fruit from the tree of knowledge when it was forbidden by God. Religion obviously valued ignorance as a virtue for women — as do the Taliban today, and the boards of corporations populated only by men.

Adam was exonerated because Eve had led him astray — a plea successfully used by men charged with rape until quite recently.

Eve's sorrow would be greatly multiplied in childbearing, which was taken by theologians to mean, variously, that women should expect great pain in childbirth and endure it without complaint. So women braced themselves, and the prophesy became self-fulfilling. Others thought they should scream out loud, because this would please God, and in the nineteenth century, when pain killers were available, it was declared sinful for birthing women to use them.

The Catholics largely took the curse to mean that sex in marriage was a necessary evil, and should only be used for the purpose of procreation. It follows that there is no need for contraception. Thanks to this marvellous doctrine — mostly ignored by those with money and education — 250 million couples in poor countries have no access to condoms or anything else to limit the number of kids they bear.

The women of East Timor, on our doorstep, have on average eight children whom they can neither feed or educate adequately. Apparently this is what God wants.

It also follows that priests, who have no fathering role, will not need sex and can be trusted not to sexually abuse children in their care.

The Bible is contemptuous of women's bodies and natural functions. Leviticus says:

A woman who becomes pregnant and gives birth to a son will be ceremonially unclean for seven days, just as she is unclean during her monthly period ... Then the woman must wait thirty-three days to be purified from her bleeding. She must not touch anything sacred or go to the sanctuary until the days of her purification are over. If she gives birth to a daughter, for two weeks the woman will be unclean, as during her period. Then she must wait sixty-six days to be purified from her bleeding.[2]

The Bible uses words like 'whore' to describe women who offend against the double standard that applies to sexual behaviour, and women can be put to death for being unfaithful or even for being raped. Honour killings still happen in some countries.

Girls who are sexually autonomous today run the risk of being labelled sluts, too. There's a long history in Western culture of punishing women for sex outside marriage or for shunning conventional roles of obedient wife and mother. Femme fatales in film noir of the 1940s and 1950s typically seduced strong men, and the plot was resolved by their usually violent murder. Others were repatriated, their power over men neutralised and social order restored. At that time women needed some persuading to give up the independence and wage-earning power they discovered after being drafted into wartime work.

Powerful women continued to meet their demise for being sexually active outside marriage in many James Bond and Alfred Hitchcock films in the 1960s and 1970s. More recent Australian films, including award-winning *Lantana* (2001) and *Moulin Rouge!* (2001), polished off their sexy women, too.

Thanks to cameras on mobile phones, women may find photographs of their naked bodies being emailed to men unknown to them. Footballers get away with abusing and denigrating young women because of their importance on the field.

According to the Bible, women may not divorce their husbands, but husbands can dissolve a marriage and take the children and the assets. The Gospel according to Matthew says men will be made immortal for forsaking — that is, leaving — their wife and children for Jesus' sake.

It took a very long time for most civilised countries to treat women more fairly in family matters, and gains won by women in family law are often lost, as was the case in Australia when the Howard Government introduced so-called shared parenting. This arrangement was sold as fairer on dads, encouraging them to be more involved in the lives of their children; however, requiring Family Court judges to look first for an equal time arrangement left women financially worse off and, according to a government review, turned out to be not always in the interests of children.

St John the Apostle 14:4 tells us men who do not allow themselves to be defiled by having sex with women will be saved as a special offering (first fruits) to God and Jesus. The Bible is, of course, full of such dangerous nonsense, all written by self-appointed men of God who were certainly ignorant by today's standards, and probably representative of a very patriarchal, tribal, violent, and intolerant society.

We don't need to cite all the anti-women parts of the Bible, or to cover the 2000 years of persecution, witch-burning, and general denigration of women by the Abrahamic religions. But I find it puzzling that twenty-first century adherents to the word of this god they believe in can so easily ignore this history, particularly women. There is, of course, a large population of theologians who devise complex arguments and language to confuse and explain away that which is absurd and should outrage women today.

Population censuses on the question of religion are grossly misleading because people are encouraged to identify with a religion whether or not they hold religious beliefs; however, it is the case that 34 per cent of Australian women describe themselves as deeply religious, whereas the proportion of deeply religious men is just 16 per cent. This difference is greatest in those over 60 so, over time, gender may be less of a factor.

I prefer to leave religion to the religious, but with fewer than 10 per cent of the population going to church, religion still has great power and influence over women's lives. Indeed, it is arguable that this influence has grown since the 1960s. Consider this speech by John F. Kennedy, made 50 years ago, when he was president of the United States:

> I believe in an America where the separation of church and state is absolute, where no Catholic prelate would tell the president (should he be Catholic) how to act, and no Protestant minister would tell his parishioners for whom to vote, where no church or church school is granted any public funds or political preference, and where no man

is denied public office merely because his religion differs from the president who might appoint him or the people who might elect him.[3]

We will all die waiting for such a spirited defence of the separation of church and state from our current political leaders. Prime Minister Gillard's welcome admission that she had no faith in a god was quickly followed by several announcements leaving no doubt that the close relationship between church and state would continue to be nurtured.

John Howard co-opted God for his own political advantage, insisting that Australian values all stemmed from our Christian heritage, and endorsing ratbag churches like Ministries of Fire and the Exclusive Brethren. He did not say that sending Australian troops in to attack Iraq was encouraged by God, but God-fearing George W. Bush must have told him this was where his own riding instructions came from. So it was with great relief that Barack Obama mentioned people of 'no belief' in his inauguration speech. Thank you, President Obama! The very fact that saying this was such a big deal shows how 'politically correct' — and I hate the term — we have become when it comes to pandering to religious sensibilities.

The debate concerning women and the Church tends to be limited to the ordination of women, which of course has its roots in the biblical insistence that women remain silent in church. Yet, a century ago, prominent women openly challenged the authenticity of the Bible as the word of God, arguing that the subjection and degradation of women throughout was entirely invented by its male authors and that God's intention was for gender equality. With a team of fellow American feminists, Elizabeth Cady Stanton set about writing *The Women's Bible* (1895), which would provide a feminist critique. It said in the introduction:

> The bible teaches that women brought sin and death into the world, that she precipitated the fall of the race, that she was arraigned before the judgment seat of Heaven, tried, condemned and sentenced.
>
> Marriage for her was to be a condition of bondage, maternity a period of suffering and anguish, and in silence and subjection, she was to play the role of a dependent on man's bounty for all her material wants, and for all the information she might desire ... I know of no other book that so fully teaches the subjection and degradation of women.[4]

She was, however, a believer, as was most of the population in nineteenth-century America, and she set about writing a bible for women. She said:

> When women understand that governments and religions are human inventions; that bibles, prayer-books, catechisms, and encyclical letters are all emanations from the brain of man, they will no longer be oppressed by the injunctions that come to them with the divine authority of 'thus saith the Lord'.[5]

I like to think that, if Elizabeth Cady Stanton was alive today, she would have given up on God as well as the male construct that claims to be his word.

Religion may be irrelevant to most Australians, but its legacy lives on, and until we challenge out loud the moral authority that the Church insists it has, women will never be considered fully human.

I'll finish with a quote from Simone de Beauvoir:

> Man enjoys the great advantage of having a god endorse the code he writes; and since man exercises a sovereign authority over women it is especially fortunate that this authority has been vested in him by the Supreme Being. For the Jews, Mohammedans and Christians among others, man is master by divine right; the fear of God will therefore repress any impulse towards revolt in the downtrodden female.[6]

It's little wonder God is a bloke.

NOTES

1. This essay was delivered as a speech at the 2010 Global Atheist Convention in Melbourne on 13 March 2010.
2. Leviticus 12: 1–8.
3. J. F. Kennedy, 'Address to Southern Baptist Leaders', text at http://usa.usembassy.de/etexts/democrac/66.htm
4. E. C. Stanton, *The Woman's Bible* (vol. I), 1895, p. 4.
5. ibid.
6. S. de Beauvoir, *The Second Sex*, Vintage, 1989.

POLITICS AND THE EXCLUSIVE BRETHREN

Michael Bachelard
Sunday Age journalist, author of *Behind the Exclusive Brethren* and *The Great Land Grab*

7 AUGUST 2007, AND JOHN HOWARD WAS THREE MONTHS AWAY FROM THE end of his 11-year reign as prime minister. It was clear by then to everyone except the most one-eyed Liberal supporter that his power was slipping away. Last desperate measures — the Northern Territory Aboriginal intervention, the Mersey Hospital takeover, a massive advertising spend to try to redeem WorkChoices — were reaping no political benefit, and the bad polls kept coming.

Even so, on that Tuesday afternoon, a busy sitting day of federal parliament, the prime minister found time to meet his old mates from the Exclusive Brethren.

Four of them came that day. The world leader, the 'Man of God' of this tiny and extreme sect, Bruce Hales; his brother, Stephen Hales; and the Brethren's chief parliamentary lobbyist, Warwick John. The fourth man was Mark Mackenzie, then under police investigation for questionable disclosures surrounding $370,000 of pro-Howard electoral funding during the previous election campaign.

The meeting had not been prearranged. Warwick John had apparently bumped into Howard in Parliament House that afternoon and proposed they get together. When the PM agreed, John summoned from Sydney the sect's leader, Bruce Hales, a furniture salesman, known to his flock as 'BDH' or 'Mr Bruce' or the 'Elect Vessel'.[1]

Hales, 'knowing the opportunities to meet Mr Howard these days were very scarce', boarded his private jet with two cohorts and his security guard, checked in to Parliament House, and went straight to Howard's office.[2] It's worth remembering who Howard opened the door to that day. The Exclusive Brethren do not vote. They comprise only 15,000 members in Australia, and 40,000 worldwide, but they believe devoutly that they are the 'saints', favoured people in God's eyes. They maintain their 'position' with a strict policy of separation from the 'evil' of society generally — their leader has instructed them to 'get a hatred, an utter hatred of the world'.[3] They deny contact between members who have quit the Church and those who remain faithful, prompting the traumatic and well-documented splitting of hundreds of families in the past five decades. Women are second-class citizens who cannot speak in church or work independently of their husbands' businesses, and who must wear headscarves in public. Sources of external information — television and radio — are banned, and internet is strictly for business only. Their members are not permitted to go to university lest their eyes are open to worldly influences. In other words, the Exclusive Brethren shares all the basic features of a cult.

Neither party to the discussion between Howard and the Brethren that day has revealed what they talked about, though the Brethren insist it was 'nothing critical', only 'economic matters in general'.[4] They also prayed for Howard.

But it's probably no coincidence that, not long after that meeting, during the federal election campaign, money was being offered in the political equivalent of a brown paper bag, to a Liberal Party electoral operative at the state level. The operative told me, on condition of anonymity, that he had been approached in the lobby of a city building by a small group of Exclusive Brethren men. They wanted to know if he would accept donations from individual members in amounts of less than $10,500. (Howard had recently changed the electoral law to mean that any such donation would not have to be publicly declared.) In theory, millions of dollars could have changed hands in cheques of $10,499 each, and we, the Australian public, would be none the wiser. The operative, to his credit, turned down the offer: 'In my view, if you accept this money, you're arguably accepting some of their opinions,' he told me. 'We're in the business of ideas and so are the Exclusive Brethren. I regard many of the

[Liberal] Party's views and those of the Exclusive Brethren as inconsistent. What the Party stands for should not be confused in the mind of the electorate by the acceptance of donations from fringe groups.'

It's very likely that in some states, however, the financial offer was accepted. The offer of campaign funds to the Liberals fits with a pattern of Exclusive Brethren behaviour that started at the 2004 Australian federal election, where hundreds of thousands of dollars were spent by them on pro-Howard, anti-Greens advertising. It spread around the world, where they poured money into political advertising for George Bush; then for the campaign against legalising gay marriage in Canada; then to New Zealand, where the National Party outsourced their most extreme advertising slogans to the Brethren in the attempt to overthrow the Labour government. In the event, the strategy, which was hatched in secrecy, failed. When it was revealed publicly in the week before polling day, Nationals leader Don Brash lost his cleanskin reputation and, a few days later, the election.[5]

By 2006, in the Tasmanian state election, the Brethren had become so bold that they drove trucks sporting anti-Greens advertising slogans through the main streets of Hobart, wearing fright masks.[6]

Masking was a feature of each of these campaigns — the Brethren's role was hidden, sometimes in quite sophisticated ways, using shelf companies and other business arrangements registered to abandoned addresses.[7] They used interstate identities and people's middle names to authorise advertisements, hiding the real source of the money. As one of the Brethren's American lobbyists put it, this group preferred to 'fly beneath the radar'.[8]

The connections between politics and religion are, in Australia, often hidden behind such masks. Neither constitutionally nor culturally do we maintain a strict separation of church and state. Yet, ironically, unlike the United States, which does maintain such a separation, religion has traditionally not played a large public role in political life. Protestations of faith are not a necessary precondition for high office in Australia, though some (notably Kevin Rudd) have chosen to make them.

Behind the scenes, though, it's a different story, and it's behind the scenes that the Exclusive Brethren and groups like them work most effectively. This is a problem because, when lobbying and the exchange of funds and favours happen in secret, what is offered, what is accepted, and how much it costs has the potential to corrupt the political system.

What's little known is that members of the Exclusive Brethren, a sect which lies at the extreme end of the spectrum of religious doctrinaires, have become experts at the political game over a surprisingly long period. They have been successfully courting politicians in Australia since the 1940s, pressing their special interests and winning laws that favoured them and them alone. Their most constant and most successful argument has been that their particular religious beliefs demanded special treatment, without which they could not fully exercise their constitutional freedom to practise their faith.[9] It's a seductive argument for politicians and, history suggests, one that's very difficult to resist.

It all began in the 1940s, when the Exclusive Brethren leader of the day, American John Taylor, suddenly issued an edict to his flock that, in separating themselves from the world, the Brethren should refuse to join any 'worldly' society or association. The particular targets of this edict were trade unions and professional societies (such as chambers of commerce).

In most places around the world, Exclusive Brethren make a living by running small- and medium-sized businesses in the light industrial and manufacturing industries. On the whole, they do so very profitably. In Australia in the 1940s, the workplace conditions for Brethren businesses were set by industrial awards negotiated centrally. At that time, their employees were virtually required by legislation to be members of unions. So, faced with a sudden change in the dictates of their 'conscience', the Australian Brethren sought out politicians to argue that they needed a special exemption: a conscientious objector's clause just for them.

Queensland Labor premier Ned Hanlon was the first to buy the argument. In 1948, he inserted just such a clause into the state's industrial relations legislation, and allowed this tiny group to object, on grounds of religious freedom, to being members of a union. The Brethren lobbyists visited politicians on the subject all over the country, relentlessly making the argument, citing the precedent. Eventually, it flowed to every state jurisdiction except Victoria and, by 1956, to the Commonwealth legislation.

The lobbying continued, of course, on the application of such laws. But then, in 1996, something happened that would change the Brethren association with politics in Australia fundamentally: John Howard became prime minister.

The senior Brethren men in Sydney had been visiting and lobbying Howard, their local member, offering moral support and prayer, since he was elected to the seat of Bennelong in the 1970s. As one former member told me, 'He was seen as the ideal candidate for prime ministership long before he was anywhere near that position'.[10]

Here was a politician who was Christian, pro-small-business, and socially conservative on questions of the family and the rights of women and gay people. He was even an old boy of Bruce Hales' school, Canterbury Boys' High School.

Importantly, Howard was as anti-union as they were. His 1996 industrial relations legislation should have rendered their special exemption obsolete, because it outlawed compulsory unionism everywhere in favour of a guarantee of freedom of association. But, at the last minute, under persistent lobbying from the Brethren, minister Peter Reith reinstated their conscientious-objector clause to the draft that was under negotiation with the Australian Democrats.

But with their good friend John Howard in The Lodge, this was still not enough, and they sought more. In 2001, by flying under the radar, by meeting and persuading their fellow Christians and men of conscience in Parliament House, they succeeded, winning a new clause that allowed them to prevent a union official from even visiting their workplace to talk to employees, as long as their employees agreed. This was a significant step up. But in 2006, with another Christian, Kevin Andrews, as minister for workplace relations, they had another victory. The WorkChoices Act authorised Brethren employers to ban unions visiting their workplaces, for whatever reason, whether or not their employees agreed.

It's an exemption that makes no sense — the Brethren employees themselves had been banned since the 1940s from joining a union, so the law only affected the non-Brethren staff, of which Bruce Hales tells us there are about 4000 nationwide. Surely these staff members should be allowed to join a union. If they had a grievance — about workplace safety, discrimination, bullying, anything — they were precluded from seeking union help. Labor and the Greens finally abolished the exemption, over the opposition of the Liberal and National parties, in its Fair Work Act in early 2009.

Industrial relations was but one example of the lobbying of the Exclusive Brethren in federal politics. By the final year of the Howard Government in 2007, they had six men authorised, with parliamentary passes, as lobbyists. These passes are reserved for individuals spending 30 days or more per year in Parliament House. The Brethren obtained them using forms that did not mention their affiliation — they simply applied as a 'Christian lobby' — but the applicants were all endorsed as being of good character by Christian Liberal or National Party MPs, including the front rank of Howard ministers — Alexander Downer, Brendan Nelson, Tony Abbott, and Eric Abetz. It's unlikely any group other than the Exclusive Brethren, with as few as 15,000 members in Australia, could muster the lobbying clout of six people treading the halls of federal parliament.

They visited politicians and wrote to them on subjects ranging from abortion and euthanasia to Medicare, building regulations, and the family law. They met John Howard numerous times, writing letters that supported the Iraq War, and even suggested how he might dig himself out of electoral difficulties by instituting a big water project.[11]

But in all their lobbying, there was a remarkable tendency to focus on issues of 'conscience', which also delivered a tangible financial benefit to Brethren members. Fortunately, such attempts were not always successful. They once tried to have the vehicles of their own elders rendered tax exempt, basing their argument on the fact that the priests of other religions enjoy such a tax exemption. But their request was rejected when it was discovered that they believed an organised priesthood was a sin against the Holy Spirit. They also tried, unsuccessfully, to argue that they should be exempt from paying electronic tolls on the Melbourne CityLink expressway, on the ground that radio waves are an instrument of the 'man of sin'. (Car-radio antennas were, at one stage, referred to as 'sin sticks'.)[12]

It is these people that various Liberal MPs have endorsed as genuine Christians with a conscience; people whom Peter Costello said it would be a crime to refuse to meet.

More sinisterly, the Brethren have tried on numerous occasions to influence the Family Court to give special recognition to their belief that when a member leaves, or is excommunicated from, the church, he or she should be cut off entirely from any other member of their family who stays faithful. Children are particularly fiercely fought for by the Brethren, using, if necessary, a large legal fighting fund to buy the best lawyers. There are numerous preconditions before a religion can be considered a cult, but erecting such barriers between members of families is a big one, and it's one of the defining characteristics of the Exclusive Brethren.

But without doubt their greatest triumph as lobbyists has been in setting up a school system almost entirely funded by either tax-free donations from their businesses or by Commonwealth money. The lobbying over schooling has been undertaken with both state and federal governments, and involves the transfer of tens of millions of taxpayer dollars every year to the sect.

It started in New South Wales in the early 1990s in two different ways. The first was when a (Christian) minister, Virginia Chadwick, was prevailed upon to approve the registration of an Exclusive Brethren school in an old house in the north-western Sydney suburb of Meadowbank, just over the back fence from the then Man of God's home. The second policy win for the Brethren elders was to gain from the same New South Wales government special permission to teach students in country areas by correspondence, at taxpayer expense, even if they lived next door to a state school. The motive in both cases was to get Brethren children out of the public school classroom.[13]

Letters sent to Don Hayward, the Liberal education spokesman in another state, Victoria, at around the same time, show exactly why they wanted this and how they went about getting it.[14]

In summary, their submissions to Hayward argued that state school teachers had 'abandoned moral principles' in favour of teaching evolution and 'sex and AIDS education'. There were televisions and computers in the classroom, they complained. But most particularly, the Brethren opposed the 'defiling' literature on the English syllabus, full as it was of 'fornication, adultery and sodomy ... blasphemy, violence, disregard for authority, filthy language'.

They also could not tolerate the 'increasing and sometimes extreme emphasis on "independent" and "free and lateral" thinking' — open discussions which threatened their strict control over the minds of their members. This, they said, could emerge at any time and in any classroom. Equality, they complained, was based on 'the lowest moral denominators', including that homosexuality 'is openly propounded as being "normal"'.

They provided pages of testimonials from Brethren students about the alleged transgressions that they had been forced to endure at the hands of teachers — transgressions that perpetrated 'serious violations of a child's right to moral integrity'.[15]

Rather than throwing these special pleadings in the bin, Hayward, when he became education minister in 1992, began work on delivering the Brethren's wishes. In 1993, their Year 10, 11, and 12 students were out of the classroom and learning through the state-funded correspondence school (on highly beneficial financial terms), and the following year every Brethren child from kindergarten onwards was allowed to opt out of mainstream schooling.

But soon the elders began to complain in similar terms of problems with the correspondence courses. One complaint involved a teacher at a face-to-face teaching session wearing a skirt that was immodestly short, imperilling the morals of the Brethren boys in attendance. From the schools' perspective, the arrogance and aggressiveness of the Brethren students and their parents was also making the situation unhappy. By 2000 in New South Wales, the new Labor Government had lost patience. The department told the Brethren that their special access to correspondence education was ending.

The Brethren's response was to seek help from their best political friend, John Howard. In May 2000, they wrote to the prime minister, seeking special federal funding, arguing it would be a severe strain on their resources to teach all their correspondence students through their own school at Meadowbank. But Howard went one better. In 2001, he introduced a school funding system so generous to private and religious schools in general, and so particularly generous to the Exclusive Brethren, that they could afford to build and staff their very own schools in any country town they chose to.

After losing office, Howard boasted about these private education policies, confirming that religious organisations had been at the centre of his social-policy firmament:

A conservative edifice must always have at its centre the role of the family and ... faith-based organisations in maintaining and strengthening social infrastructure ... The major growth sector amongst independent schools has been in the low-fee independent Christian category. This is a direct result of more liberal funding arrangements initiated by my government. It is hard not to see this growth as other than a collective search by parents for a more values-based education experience for their children.[16]

'Values', in the case of the Exclusive Brethren, means keeping students out of the clutches of the worldly education system and all its evils. The worst aspect of this system is that it removes the ability of Brethren children to ever socialise with children who live outside their own high walls.

'Soon these kids won't even know what "normal" people are like, and it will be even easier to indoctrinate kids with how sinful outsiders are,' says a former Brethren member, 'Janie':

> This really worries me because I know how much I owe the distance–ed teachers I had in high school — they might have been a long way away, but they were the only people I could have real conversations with. They saw potential in me and encouraged me to follow my heart. These kids are being taught by teachers who have signed a contract not to do this.[17]

Janie left the Brethren because she was not prepared to live a life of subservience, childbearing, and ignorance. Her teachers in the state school system were the ones who opened her eyes to this. Her experience is precisely the reason the Brethren hierarchy want to build and maintain their own bastions of education.

'It was set up to deliver the young people from the world,' said Bruce Hales to his flock. 'So they can face up to the world, and find their way effectively through it, without coming under the power of it ... to deliver them from an area of defilement and contamination.'[18]

In this project, the Exclusive Brethren have been mightily assisted by the Australian taxpayer. This was begun and accelerated during the regime of John Howard, and continued unabated under Kevin Rudd and Julia Gillard. Gillard also agreed to keep the existing funding system in place until 2013. Funding for Exclusive Brethren schools was $13.9 million in 2009, with an in-built escalator which will make it about $17.2 million by 2012. All this pays for somewhere between 2000 and 3000 students nationwide. In addition, the Brethren have been full beneficiaries of the

Building the Education Revolution funds, despite Mr Rudd's comments before the 2007 election that they were a cult that breaks up families.

Further, through a complex formula of family trusts and private businesses, the Brethren business people are able, unlike parents of ordinary private school children, to avoid paying any tax on the vast proportion of the school fees they pay.

It is little wonder that Hales promotes the continuance of all political lobbying, right up until the Rapture: 'I don't think we should ever let up making representation to government while we're here.'[19]

Every time they visit or write to a politician to ask for some policy carve-out, the Exclusive Brethren couch their entreaties in the language of religious conscience — the true freedom to practise their religion. It's an argument that's had great success over the years, mainly with conservative MPs. But even Kevin Rudd, after describing them as an 'extremist cult' in the 2007 election campaign, subsequently declined the suggestion that he investigate their activities, saying: 'an inquiry could unreasonably interfere with the capacity of members of the Exclusive Brethren to practise their faith freely and openly'.[20] (The Brethren were delighted, Daniel Hales boasting in a subsequent interview that 'Labor has done well representing the conscience of Brethren members, in fact better than the conservatives'.)[21]

To those interested in these arguments about religious freedom, the Brethren have, conveniently, spelled out their views in a submission to the Australian Human Rights Commission's Inquiry into Freedom of Religion and Belief. Their submission, by three senior elders including the Man of God's brother, Daniel Hales, is a hard-to-follow but unwittingly hilarious document. It tries to tread the fine line between deploring 'religious extremists' (Muslims, we assume, though they are never mentioned by name), while seeking to entrench even further the right of hard-line Christians like themselves to act as they see fit and discriminate against whom they like:

> Most conservative Christian groups ask that their members be excused from inclusion in anything that they consider would violate their principles or conscience, and this situation does not threaten the continuance of Australian society.
>
> However certain intolerant non-Christian religious elements insist

on society changing to suit them rather than seeking exemptions. Allowance or provision for their approach will result in the destruction of the Australian society.[22]

Their thesis is that Christianity is the 'solid foundation ... of Australian society', and that 'the emergence of a multifaith Australia will lead to problems unless the voice of Christianity is dominant and decisive'. Doing this will mean that all laws must make provision for 'genuine conscience', otherwise you do not have freedom of religion.

'There is currently not adequate protection of the conscientious right to discriminate in particular contexts,' they write.

They argue Christians should be able, unfettered, to practise separation from people they disagree with (and presumably have courts help them enforce it). Their conscience dictates the need to preach in the street, to build churches despite the views of local councils, to apply a religious dress code to their adherents 'unless they are a clear and obvious threat to security or social order', and to 'exclude a person from employment because of their sexuality'. Conscience clauses should also allow them to opt out of technology, particularly the internet, in schools. And they criticise the media, saying, 'freedom to express our religion is certainly hindered by current media practises'.

An aversion to scrutiny, keeping tight control on their members' sources of external information, the imposition of a dress code, and the threat of punishment, including separation and financial damage, against those seeking to leave a church, are all classic features of a cult, not a religion.

The example of the Exclusive Brethren shows a number of things about politics in Australia. It shows the sheer power a religious lobby group can gain over politicians by playing the 'conscience' card. It also shows that our thinking on the subject of religion is dangerously woolly, and our laws therefore inadequate. The founding fathers saw it as important to discourage the persecution of genuine religions. But cults, religiously founded or otherwise, are different. People trapped in a cult are not free to question its doctrine or its leader, no matter how bizarre or dangerous, without taking enormous personal risks. People are not free to leave cults. Cults gain unhealthy influence over them, their families, and their finances, and they leave big scars.

The feeling of security and safety, the feeling of belonging, the feeling of exclusivity and enlightenment are powerful when you are inside a cult. One woman I interviewed had been brought up in the Open Brethren and, to her cost, left it. Then she took up with another group, Revival Centres International, and felt immediately at home in its suffocating environs. Within that group, her pastor convinced her and her husband to 'invest' hundreds of thousands of dollars with him, on the basis that he could be trusted as a man of God. Her eventual disillusionment with him prompted her to leave the church, but the damage was enormous. The feeling of being excluded, cast out, was compounded by the financial and psychological effects of being owed money. The church, typically, stood by him, not her and her family, who were branded as troublemakers and outcasts.

And yet, three years after all these events, there was still a voice, deep in this woman's head, mouthing the cult 'line' that she was somehow unworthy and at fault, using its own special language. That voice had an explanation for everything, a riposte to every criticism. Whatever it is that appeals to people about religious or spiritual communities is used ruthlessly by the people who run cults to insert this voice into people, and it continues to speak up and torture them with guilt, often long after they have left the church.

There are stories of elderly former members of the Exclusive Brethren, kicked out during one of the many purges in the 1960s or 1980s, who are still living lives of miserable isolation, convinced that they have sinned and that, if they show appropriate repentance, they might still be restored to the 'right position'. People die alone in this condition. Or, sometimes, are visited in their final illness by Exclusive Brethren 'priests' — elders who restore them to favour for long enough to gain benefit from their estate.

In his book *Cults, Terror, and Mind Control* (2009), cult counsellor Raphael Aron points out that terrorist groups use similar techniques to control their suicide bombers as cults use to convince their members that they are close to God.[23] In each case the psychological effects are the same, even if the Exclusive Brethren have never threatened a bomb attack.

Aron points out that, in 1998, an Australian government committee recommended that 'significant emotional harm' inflicted by religious groups or other cults should be classified as a criminal offence. That recommendation, part of an investigation into the harmonisation of the criminal codes across all states, acknowledged that the coercion, control, and fear instilled by organisations such as the Exclusive Brethren had real and harmful effects on people, and that this should be punishable under the criminal law.

But before any such worthwhile law can be passed, it's clear that we need to get better at recognising the damage done by rogue religions. Politicians and judges need to be educated about the features of cults and the symptoms of the damage that they cause, which the victims are often too indoctrinated to recognise or complain about.

One thing we, as taxpayers, should never do is allow our money to be paid by governments to cults to fund them to further entrench their separateness — as successive governments have done with their funding for Exclusive Brethren schools. Their example shows that a sufficiently motivated and well-organised group, no matter how offensive, can appeal to sympathetic politicians and use the 'religious freedom' argument to obtain exemptions, enforced by the law of Australia, which entrench the iron-fisted control they hold over their members. This offends against basic notions of human rights.

Perhaps we should impose this law on religious groups: they should not be free to claim tax exemptions or school funding unless their members are free to ask critical questions, or to quit the church with their families, finances, and emotional health intact. That would cast a new light on woolly notions about 'religious freedom'.

NOTES

1. The information in the preceeding paragraphs is taken from M. Bachelard, *Behind the Exclusive Brethren*, Scribe, Melbourne, 2008.
2. Letter from Warwick John to *Four Corners* presenter Quentin McDermott, 12 October 2007.
3. B. D. Hales, *White Book* 161, Bible and Gospel Trust, 18 March 2006, p. 11. (White books are transcripts of Exclusive Brethren 'ministry'. Through its publishing arm, the Bible and Gospel Trust, the Brethren assert strict and exclusive copyright over this material.)
4. Letter from Warwick John to Quentin McDermott, op. cit.
5. The information in this paragraph can also be found in D. Marr, 'Where Art Thou, Brethren?', *Sydney Morning Herald*, 20 January 2007, at www.smh.com.au/news/national. where-art-thou-brethren/2007/01/19/1169095977274.htm
6. See 'The Brethren Express', *Four Courners*, broadcast 15 October 2007, transcript at www. abc.net.au/4corners/content/2007/s2060198.htm

7. See *Behind the Exclusive Brethren*.

8. L. Morgan, '"Beneath the Radar" Group Behind Late Pro-GOP Ads', *St Petersburg Times*, 2 November 2004, at www.sptimes.com/2004/11/02/State/_Beneath_the_radar__g.shtml

9. For further discussion, see *Behind the Exclusive Brethren*.

10. Bob Hales, interview with the author, 27 February 2008.

11. For further discussion, see *Behind the Exclusive Brethren*.

12. ibid.

13. ibid.

14. Letters from Brethren elders Euan Chirnside, Norman Mauger, Alistair Shemilt, and Philip Grace, in 'Submission to Mr. Don Hayward M.P. Shadow Minister for Education', 1992.

15. For further discussion, see *Behind the Exclusive Brethren*.

16. J. Howard, Irving Kristol lecture to the American Enterprise Institute, March 2008, text at www.aei.org/speech/27613

17. Interview with the author, 14 October 2006.

18. B. D. Hales, 'Notes of Meetings, Berwick, Australia', *White Book* 51, Bible and Gospel Trust, 26 July 2003.

19. All quotes from the Exclusive Brethren are taken from its White Books. Most ministry quotes can be viewed at www.peebs.net.

20. Press release from Kevin Rudd's office to the author, 6 May 2008.

21. Cited in 'Brethren are Kevin 07 Fans After All', *WA Today*, 25 September 2008, at www.watoday.com.au/national/brethren-are-kevin-07-fans-after-all-20080925-4o24.html

22. D. Hales, J. Myhill, and D. Stewart, 'Submission to the Australian Human Rights Commission on Freedom of Religion and Belief in the 21st Century', at www.hreoc.gov.au/frb/submissions/Sub1057.Hales_Myhil_and_Stewart.doc

23. R. Aron, *Cults, Terror, and Mind Control*, Bay Tree Publishers, 2009.

ATHEISTS FOR FREEDOM OF SPEECH

Dr Russell Blackford
Co-editor of *50 Voices of Disbelief*, Conjoint Lecturer in the School of Humanities and
Social Science at the University of Newcastle

RELIGIOUS TEACHINGS PROMISE US A DEEPER UNDERSTANDING OF REALITY, more meaningful lives, morally superior conduct, and such imaginary benefits as rightness with a Supreme Being, liberation from earthly attachments, or a blissful form of personal immortality. One way or another, they offer spiritual salvation, or something very like it. If any of religion's teachings are rationally warranted, it would be good to know which ones. At the same time, however, religious teachings can be onerous in their demands: if they can't deliver on what they promise, it would be well to know that. I take it, then, that there can be no defensible objection to the rational scrutiny of religious teachings. Even if reason can take us only so far, it would be good to explore just how far.

That said, it might appear that the rational scrutiny of religion is not an urgent task — at least not if the scrutiny is conducted in public, and especially not in a modern, and apparently secular, liberal democracy such as Australia. Isn't Australian religiosity rather unobtrusive and undemanding? So why, God's advocates might ask, is there any need to engage in strong, publicly prominent criticism of religious teachings, the organisations that promote them, or the leaders of those organisations? Perhaps rational critiques of religion should be available somewhere — maybe in peer-reviewed philosophy journals — but no great effort should be made to debunk religion in popular books, magazine or newspaper articles, media appearances, and so on.

I disagree. All too often, religious organisations and their representatives seek to control how we plan and run our lives, including how we die. At various times, the religious have opposed a vast range of activities and innovations: anaesthesia, abortion, contraceptive technologies, stem-cell and therapeutic cloning research, physician-assisted suicide, the teaching of well-corroborated scientific findings, such as those of evolutionary biology, and a wide range of essentially harmless sexual conduct involving consenting adults. Even in Australia, churches and sects frequently lobby for laws that restrict our freedoms.

Public scrutiny and criticism of religion's truth-claims and moral authority would, indeed, be less urgent if the various churches and sects unequivocally agreed to a wall of separation between themselves and the state. Unfortunately, however, they often have good reasons (by their own lights) to oppose strict secularism. Some churches and sects do not distinguish sharply between guidance on individual salvation and the exercise of political power. They may be sceptical about the independence of secular goals from religious ones, or about the distinction between personal goals and those of the state. Some religious groups do not accept the reality of continuing social pluralism. Instead, they look to a time when their (allegedly) righteous views will prevail. They may be sceptical about the danger that liberal-minded people see when adherents of competing worldviews jostle to impose them by means of political power.

As in other Western democracies, religious organisations in Australia are not always politically liberal or even moderate. On the contrary, recent years have seen the increasing influence of very large Pentecostal organisations, such as Hillsong and Catch the Fire Ministries, which pursue a political agenda little different from that of the Christian Right in America. Conservative Catholics, such as Cardinal George Pell, actively seek to influence political affairs. Even the Anglican Church, supposedly the most moderate of Christian denominations, does not necessarily take progressive or tolerant stances on such issues as sexuality or the role of women in the family (and society as a whole).

Indeed, the most powerful Anglican diocese, that of Sydney, has moved in an increasingly conservative social and theological direction, especially since Peter Jensen took over as Archbishop of Sydney in 2001, with his younger brother, Phillip Jensen, becoming the Dean of St Andrew's

Cathedral in 2002. The stage was set at the beginning of Peter Jensen's tenure as archbishop, when he announced in 2001 that the Church would carry out a grand project, 'the Mission', to get 10 per cent of Sydney's notoriously ungodly population worshipping in 'bible-believing' churches within a decade.[1] By contemporary standards, the Jensen brothers are hardline, conservative evangelicals who cling to the authority of the Bible, read at face value wherever possible.

In recent years, we have seen considerable activism from Australia's religious lobbies, and successive governments have blatantly pandered to Christian moral concerns. In 1997, for example, the Howard government overturned the Northern Territory's decision to legalise and regulate voluntary euthanasia. Potentially valuable medical research involving early human embryos (tiny blobs of mindless and insentient protoplasm) is drastically restricted by the *Prohibition of Human Cloning for Reproductive Purposes Act 2002 (Cth)*, largely to placate various religious lobbies, with their benighted ideas of morality. Many other examples could be given.

When religion claims authority in the political sphere, it is unsurprising — and totally justifiable — that atheists and sceptics question the source of this authority. If religious organisations or their leaders claim to speak on behalf of a god, it is fair to ask whether the god concerned really makes the claims that are communicated on its behalf. Does this god even exist? Where is the evidence? And even if this being does exist, why, exactly, should its wishes be translated into socially accepted moral norms, let alone laws enforced by the state's coercive power? When these questions are asked publicly, even with a degree of aggression, that's an entirely healthy thing.

Atheists and sceptics should, no doubt, defend secularism: the idea that the state ought to pursue essentially secular goals (peace and security, the alleviation of poverty and misery, social coordination, economic productivity and efficiency, the education and welfare of children, and so on) without being influenced by distinctively religious teachings. But if we are realistic, we will understand that the idea of secularism does not enjoy unequivocal support from religious organisations or their adherents, and it has little traction in societies where the authority of religion is taken for granted. Advocating secularism and directly challenging the epistemic-cum-moral authority of religion should not be viewed as two alternative strategies for atheists and sceptics who wish to resist the influence of religion. Rather, these strategies are mutually supportive and ought to be pursued in tandem.

In short, there is plenty of reason to challenge religions and contest their doctrinal claims, not just as an academic exercise, but as a matter of real urgency.

If atheists and sceptics wish to challenge religion in the sphere of public debate, they require the freedom to do so. This gives us a special reason to be free-speech advocates, but freedom of speech and expression (henceforth, I will usually refer simply to 'free speech') merits forthright advocacy in any event. Arguably, this is the most important of all political freedoms in a modern liberal-democratic society — yet it has become unfashionable and vulnerable to attack.

Indeed, the Labor government of Kevin Rudd proposed new laws that would give it potentially sweeping control of information available to Australians via the internet. In December 2009, Senator Stephen Conroy, the minister for broadband, communications, and the digital economy, announced plans for mandatory internet filtering, with the misleading title: 'Measures to improve safety of the internet for families'.

As I write, the fate of this initiative is doubtful. Following Julia Gillard's ascendancy to the Labor leadership, concessions were made in the face of popular opinion and the scheme was deferred, pending review. Subsequently, the Coalition parties indicated that they would not vote for such an internet filter. The proposal may be effectively dead for now, but it is disturbing that it ever got so far. We should expect renewed attempts at internet censorship — and we must be prepared to fight them. If a similar initiative were ever adopted, it would assist in the suppression of whatever categories of speech might elicit moral panic from time to time ... into the indefinite future.

Perhaps it could be argued that free speech should be exercised within the constraints of civility, as in an academic seminar. However, the idea normally includes freedom for robust, sometimes even offensive, kinds of expression that would be strongly inhibited, if not actually forbidden, in such a formal setting. There is a public interest in permitting debate that is not so restrictive of the parties involved, or so likely to exclude many parties who don't meet the stereotype of middle-class, perhaps middle-aged, academics. Free speech allows people to express themselves on subjects that arouse passion, emotions, and competing loyalties.

We need not be absolutists about free speech to recognise its great social importance. Any exceptions to it should be identified specifically, defined narrowly, and distinguished as special cases. One legitimate exception was pointed out by John Stuart Mill. Imagine that a demagogue is addressing an angry mob outside the house of a corn dealer, inciting the mob to lynch the corn dealer, on the basis that 'corn dealers are starvers of the poor'. Mill would allow for a law against that, essentially because of the close proximity of the speech and the harm. The immediate danger to the corn dealer cannot be averted in less restrictive ways. But Mill would not have accepted censoring the same claim that 'corn dealers are starvers of the poor' if it appeared in a newspaper (or by implication in a book, or a film).[2]

In particular circumstances, values such as individual reputation, or individual or public safety, might sometimes justify exceptions to freedom of speech, but the exceptions must not be allowed to gobble up the rule.

Unfortunately, Australian law has increasingly overreached in censoring free speech, especially when issues of social identity and multicultural harmony are raised, as with racial and religious vilification. As Laurence Maher has written in this context, 'there is a new mood of censorship abroad and the right to dissent — in essence, the right of the individual to be different — is under sustained and, to some extent, successful attack'.[3]

It is especially unfortunate that race and religion are frequently conflated, when they are not at all the same thing. A body of religious doctrine consists of ideas, which are always fair targets for attack in a liberal democracy. Different religions are in a struggle of ideas against each other, and against those of atheists and religious sceptics; this struggle should be permitted with minimal intervention by the state. Moreover, religious doctrines influence the social and political attitudes of their adherents in ways that merit comment (favourable or otherwise), and many religious organisations exert vast power and influence. It is in the public interest that this be subject to monitoring and criticism. By contrast, nothing like this applies to the category of 'race'.

Nonetheless, Australian experience with racial-vilification legislation displays two tendencies that apply equally to religious vilification laws.

First, it appears that a tribunal given the power to suppress or punish certain kinds of speech will tend to ensure that the power is actually used. The most important Australian case in this area, *John Fairfax Publications Pty Ltd v. Kazak*, is a textbook example.

Kazak involved a forcefully worded opinion in *The Financial Review* that was held to have breached a provision of the *Anti-Discrimination Act 1977 (NSW)* forbidding communications to the public inciting 'hatred, serious contempt or ridicule' of a person or group of persons on the ground of their race. The article contained about 250 words of robust, opinionated criticism of 'the Palestinians' for turning against the US when Iraq was bombed in 1998. Towards the end, there was a most unfortunate statement that 'it would appear that the Palestinians remain vicious thugs who show no serious willingness to comply with agreements'. In context, however, the article was clearly attacking the Palestinian leadership, specifically Yasser Arafat, rather than 'the poor of Gaza', whom Arafat was condemned for supposedly neglecting in favour of 'his military and bureaucratic elite'.

Although this piece was intemperate, it is difficult to imagine that *The Financial Review*'s business-oriented readership interpreted it as a message that Palestinians are legitimate targets for racial hate. Yet, when the case was heard at first instance, the tribunal rejected the argument that the article was directed at the leadership or administration of the Palestinian people rather than Palestinians as such.[4]

Fortunately, the outcome was reversed on appeal to the New South Wales Administrative Decisions Tribunals Appeal Panel.[5] The Appeal Panel found that the tribunal had erred on this precise matter of fact, as well as on issues of law. Yet, the original decision in *Kazak* received little public criticism. On the contrary, writing in the *UTS Law Review*, journalist Marcus O'Donnell claimed 'the decision is in fact a carefully argued and balanced one'.[6] A media release issued by the Press Council did express 'grave concern' about the decision, worrying that such an approach from tribunals could 'stifle debate on contentious issues'. The release concluded with what O'Donnell's article glibly dismisses as a 'hyperbolic warning': the (not-so-hyperbolic) warning that 'totalitarian governments come to power on the back of organisations that do not permit unfashionable or politically incorrect opinion to be heard'.[7]

Notwithstanding O'Connell's apologetics, this decision showed the lengths to which tribunals charged with administration of vilification laws can go in order to suppress perfectly legitimate speech on matters of public interest. Not one word in O'Donnell's discussion acknowledges even the possibility that the impugned article was merely a strong denunciation of the Palestinian leadership. O'Donnell's contribution provides a fine example of the second tendency that should cause concern: the tendency for much elite opinion, for example that of many politicians, academics, and lawyers, and even journalists, to deprecate the importance of free speech, treating it as an outdated relic of the (much-maligned) Enlightenment era. According to this way of thinking, free speech must yield to contemporary anxieties about the sensibilities and harmonious interactions of various racial, religious, and cultural groups.

Thus, it becomes possible to heap praise on the supposed balance and sophistication of egregiously bad decisions, such as the first-instance decision in *Kazak*. Admittedly, the ill-founded claims made in the case were ultimately resisted, on appeal, but it took a respondent with the immense resources of a major media corporation to fight for an outcome that gave due regard to free-speech values. Obviously, there are few litigants with such resources and sufficient tenacity.

What about religious vilification, in particular? The most salient experience to date is from Victoria, where the provisions of the Racial and Religious Tolerance Act 2001 (Vic.) have been tested by litigation involving the Islamic Council of Victoria and Catch the Fire Ministries. Three Muslim converts attended a Catch the Fire Ministries seminar in March 2002, recorded the presentations of two Assembly of God Ministers, and took written notes. These notes and recordings were subsequently relied upon as evidence in lengthy and expensive proceedings before the Victorian Civil and Administrative Tribunal (VCAT).

Sitting as a VCAT member, Justice Higgins handed down a decision in December 2004;[8] he made orders (including an order for an apology) in June 2005.[9] He upheld the claim that the two pastors had engaged in religious vilification. In their presentations, which were essentially about how to 'witness' to Muslims and convert them to Christianity, the pastors had supposedly vilified Muslims by putting a one-sided and false account of Islam, as well as making allegations that Muslims are demons. The case was subsequently appealed to the Victorian Court of Appeal, which found, in December 2006, that Justice Higgins had made mistakes of both fact (including his finding that the pastors said Muslims are demons) and law.[10] The case was sent back to VCAT, to be heard again by a different tribunal member. Ultimately, it was settled in mediation in June 2007.

The Court of Appeal was required, in particular, to interpret Section 8 of the Act, which stated that: 'A person must not, on the ground of the religious belief or activity of another person or class of persons, engage in conduct that incites hatred against, serious contempt for, or revulsion or severe ridicule of, that other person or class of persons'. Also relevant to the proceedings was the correct construction of a defence provided in Section 11, which exempts conduct 'engaged in reasonably and in good faith' for various purposes.

The judges of the Court of Appeal handed down three separate judgements, leaving a number of issues open for future cases, particularly the issue of how clear a distinction can be made between hatred of a religion as opposed to hatred of its adherents. However, it is fair to portray the gist of the judgement, on which there was considerable agreement among the three judges, as follows: the issue raised by Section 8 is whether the natural and ordinary effect of a speaker's conduct, taken as a whole, on an ordinary person in its actual audience would be to create hatred (or serious contempt, or revulsion, or severe ridicule) for the people with the religious beliefs, on the ground of those religious beliefs.

While this is complex, it is clearer than the convoluted drafting of the section itself, and to that extent is useful. As for Section 11, 'good faith' can be taken as meaning 'honestly and conscientiously for the purpose', while criticism of religion will be considered reasonable as long as it is not so ill-informed, misconceived, ignorant, or hurtful as to be beyond the bounds of toleration in a multicultural society.

Note that the test under the Victorian Act is not whether the sensibilities of the religious have been upset by the speech, nor is it anything as strong as inciting the people hearing the speech to violent or unlawful acts. Rather, the provisions work as follows:

Assume that the speech comes from person A. The test is whether people B, in the audience hearing the speech, are thereby likely to be aroused to feeling hatred, serious contempt, et cetera, for a person or a class of people C, based on the latter's religious beliefs. For example, think of a newspaper cartoon (by person A, a cartoonist), addressed to the public at large (audience B), mocking the local Catholic bishop (C) if he supports the Vatican's policy on contraception. This is ridicule, and it may incite further ridicule (but how severe is 'severe' ridicule?).

The findings of the Court of Appeal give some much-needed clarity to the Act. They impose a relatively strict test for the prohibition in Section 8, and provide a relatively broad interpretation of the defence in Section 11. One lesson from this case is that a well-resourced and determined defendant can probably resist most claims of religious vilification, one way or another, unless its actions have been truly shocking. Accordingly, we should feel concern rather than panic. Nonetheless, the course of the litigation is troubling overall.

First, not all respondents are as well-resourced or determined as Catch the Fire Ministries proved to be. Such legislation remains intimidating: it must tend to chill legitimate, though robust, criticism of religion, particular religions, or religious organisations, and their leaders and adherents. Second, it is apparent that tribunal members and judges will tend to take different attitudes to such legislation and to the importance of freedom of speech. Some will find ways to apply the legislation expansively, and dangerous precedents will result. At the same time, third, it is difficult to draft legislation of this kind, making the results all the more unpredictable. Again, this may deter perfectly legitimate speech. Fourth, some specific issues have been left in a state of uncertainty, including the significance of the distinction between criticising a religion and criticising its adherents.

More fundamentally, it is not entirely predictable what speech will make hearers more inclined to feel hatred or revulsion or some level of contempt for third parties, or more inclined to treat those parties as (to some extent or other) simply ridiculous. 'Hate' and 'revulsion' are very strong words, but what about a certain degree of contempt or a certain sense of the absurdity of a doctrine or practice? Our continued right to criticise or satirise religious doctrines, organisations, and leaders, may be left hanging on the willingness of courts and tribunals to place much weight on the two words 'serious' and 'severe'. A tribunal (especially at first instance) could easily find that some legitimate speech tends to incite, say, 'severe' ridicule of a group.

For example, might a journalistic investigation of Scientology bring many readers to feel contempt for Scientologists as a group? What about severe contempt? What about a legitimate article on paedophilia within the Catholic Church — could this lead, perhaps unfairly, to serious contempt for Catholic priests as a group? How can we satirise doctrines that seem ridiculous (such as the Catholic Church's doctrine on birth control) without exposing individuals who advocate such doctrines to severe ridicule? Indeed, is severe ridicule necessarily inappropriate in all cases? Laurence Maher wisely observes, discussing a provision in Tasmania's Anti-Discrimination Act 1998:

> Throughout recorded history some religious ideas, beliefs, affiliations and activities have, understandably, produced hatred towards, contempt for and/or ridicule of those ideas, beliefs, affiliations and activities. Moreover, we are all free to denounce the very concept of religion. The individual adherents of religious ideas (or entire groups of adherents) may or may not be the intended or accidental targets of anti-religious speech. At a minimum, it seems contrary to principle that persons who embrace religious beliefs, affiliations and activities which are regarded by others as (severely?) ridiculous should be shielded from such ridicule.[11]

As far as religious doctrines go, it is not acceptable if beliefs of any sort are protected from opposition, criticism, or satire. Generally speaking, the citizens of a liberal democracy may believe whatever supernatural nonsense they like, and their right to do so should be respected. But this does not entail that other citizens ought to give religious beliefs any credence, deference, or esteem. Nor are they required to give any special esteem to individuals who are credulous or superstitious (as opposed to respecting the individuals' political and legal rights).

Anti-vilification laws are meant to supersede the Enlightenment concern with individual freedom. They supposedly work against the demonisation and scapegoating of vulnerable minorities: they are meant to support inclusion and social harmony, to heal division in the community. However, it is doubtful whether they have this effect in contemporary Australian circumstances, particularly where the laws concerned cover religion. Even if it were appropriate to pursue social harmony by such oppressive means as bans on speech — something which I strenuously deny — laws that provide judicial or quasi-judicial forums for redress from 'religious vilification' tend to create further division in the community, rather than to heal it. In the Catch the Fire Ministries case, the law was used to try to suppress the views of one group (Pentecostal Christians), and it has undoubtedly lowered the general public's estimation of Muslims, who are widely seen as opposing liberal values. Such laws, which are meant to address subtle, pervasive harms, are likely to achieve the exact opposite of what is intended.

There is plenty more cause for concern when we consider free speech at the international level. Article 20 of the International Covenant on Civil and Political Rights (the ICCPR) contains a provision requiring that:

> Any advocacy of national, racial or religious hatred that constitutes incitement to discrimination, hostility or violence shall be prohibited by law.[12]

This document, which is supposed to protect individual rights and liberties, requires that signatory nations criminalise any speech that can be classified as 'religious hatred', but does no more than incite 'hostility' to a religion or to its practitioners. Potentially, this is a very dangerous provision. If interpreted too loosely, it could have far-reaching and draconian consequences.

Any denunciation of an organisation or a body of ideas is likely to incite at least some hostility. Accordingly, the only thing that prevents the books of so-called 'New Atheists' — the likes of Richard Dawkins, Christopher Hitchens, or Michel Onfray — from being caught by laws based faithfully on Article 20 of the ICCPR is that their critiques of religion do not amount to 'advocacy of ... religious hatred'. Of course they don't; in historical context, the phrase surely does not refer to legitimate criticisms of organisations, leaders, and belief systems. However, there is a tendency in recent times for religious apologists to blur the distinction between harsh criticism and expressions of hatred.

Thus, Alister McGrath comments sneeringly on Dawkins: 'Dawkins preaches to his god-hating choirs, who are clearly expected to relish his rhetorical salvoes, and raise their hands in adulation'.[13] And in a recent article in *Christianity Today*, Alvin Plantinga provides a more worrying example:

As everyone knows, there has been a recent spate of books attacking Christian belief and religion in general. Some of these books are little more than screeds, long on vituperation but short on reasoning, long on name-calling but short on competence, long on righteous indignation but short on good sense; for the most part they are driven by hatred rather than logic.[14]

Hatred of God, even if such a being existed, would presumably not fall foul of laws enacted in compliance with Article 20 of the ICCPR. But many such accusations of hatred, such as Plantinga's, do not specify hatred of a supernatural (or imaginary) being. Although I don't claim that it should be illegal, Plantinga's kind of language is grossly irresponsible. It is only one step away from characterising your opponents as motivated by hatred to calling for their speech to be suppressed and for stigmatising them as enemies of the social order. Allegations of hatred should not be made so lightly, or without compelling evidence.

Meanwhile, the Organisation of the Islamic Conference — the Muslim nations in the UN — continues to campaign for international recognition of a concept of 'defamation of religion'. Though the boundaries of the concept are nebulous, it is far broader than any concept of religious vilification recognised in Australia. It would cover much speech and expression that, for example, satirises religious figures or criticises the harmful effects of religion — or particular religions. The majority of nations in the UN have accepted this dangerous idea whenever resolutions condemning 'defamation of religion' have gone to a vote of the General Assembly or the Human Rights Council. This not only offers the high moral ground to dictatorships and theocracies, it also strengthens the arms of local adversaries of free speech — in Australia and elsewhere.

Atheists and religious sceptics have good and urgent reasons to challenge the authority of religious organisations and leaders to pronounce on matters of ultimate truth and correct morality. None of these organisations can speak for a superior being, such as a god, with a claim to our obedience or deference. The emperor has no clothes, and we ought to say so. In particular, religious leaders are not moral leaders, much as they might pretend to be. Their non-existent credentials ought to be exposed. This will require persistent, cool argument, but also moments of outright denunciation or unashamed mockery of religion's most absurd actions and truth-claims. In particular, we should not flinch from expressing the view that no religion has any rational warrant, and that many churches and sects promote cruelty, misery, ignorance, and human-rights abuses.

This is not a popular viewpoint, especially at a time when many politicians, lawyers, academics, and journalists are in a mood for state censorship (all, of course, in the interest of social harmony). But that makes the need to express it all the more urgent. What's more, it gives atheists and sceptics an additional reason to become free-speech advocates — additional, that is, to the intrinsic merits attaching to freedom of speech and expression. We should, right now, demand the repeal of existing laws that restrict our freedom to oppose, criticise, or satirise religion in general, or any specific religion, or religious traditions and organisations, or their practices, their associated cultures, and their leaders and adherents. We should strongly oppose any new or strengthened provisions that restrict such an important freedom. Generally, we should stand proudly for free speech.

Vigilance, and perhaps political struggle, will be required. Let's get on with it.

NOTES

All legal decisions or judgements, law-review articles, and statutes mentioned in this article are easily accessible via the Australasian Legal Information Institute (AustLII) website: www.austlii.edu.au

1. M. Porter, *The New Puritans: the rise of fundamentalism in the Anglican Church*, Melbourne University Press, Carlton, 2006, p. 9.
2. J. S. Mill, *On Liberty*, Penguin, London, 1974, p. 119.
3. L. W. Maher, 'Free Speech and its Postmodern Adversaries,' *Murdoch University Electronic Journal of Law* 8(2), June 2001, paragraph 2.
4. *John Fairfax Publications Limited v. Kazak* (2000), New South Wales Administrative Decisions Tribunal, at www.austlii.edu.au/au/cases/nsw/NSWADT/2000/77.html. Paragraph 7 of the report contains the full article from *The Financial Review*.
5. *John Fairfax Publications Pty Ltd v. Kazak* (EOD), (2002), New South Wales Administrative Decisions Tribunal 35, at www.austlii.edu.au/au/cases/nsw/NSWADTAP/2002/35.html
6. M. O'Donnell, 'Hate Speech, Freedom, Rights and Political Cultures: an analysis of anti-vilification law in the context of traditional freedom of speech values and an emerging international standard of human rights', *UTS Law Review* 5, 2003, pp. 23–47, 41.

7. ibid. Apart from the Press Council's media release, the most trenchant criticism was probably in my own article, 'Free Speech and Hate Speech', *Quadrant* 373, January–February 2001, pp. 10–17, 13–15.

8. *Islamic Council of Victoria v. Catch the Fire Ministries Inc.* (Final), (2004), Victorian Civil and Administrative Tribunal 2510.

9. *Islamic Council of Victoria v. Catch the Fire Ministries Inc.* (Anti Discrimination — Remedy) (2005), Victorian Civil and Administrative Tribunal 1159.

10. *Catch the Fire Ministries Inc. & Ors v. Islamic Council of Victoria Inc.* (2006), Supreme Court of Victoria 284, 14 December 2006, at www.austlii.edu.au/au/cases/vic/VSCA/2006/284.html

11. 'Free Speech and its Postmodern Adversaries', p. 46.

12. Article 20 of the International Covenant on Civil and Political Rights, issued by the Office of the United Nations High Commissioner for Human Rights, at www2.ohchr.org/english/law/ccpr.htm

13. A. McGrath and J. C. McGrath, *The Dawkins Delusion?: atheist fundamentalism and denial of the divine*, SPCK Publishing, London 2007, p. x.

14. A. Plantinga, 'Evolution vs Naturalism: Why they are like oil and water', *Christianity Today*, 1 July 2008, at www.christianitytoday.com/bc/2008/julaug/11.37.html. Plantinga's substantive argument is that biological evolution alone could not have produced creatures (like us, supposedly) with reliable cognitive faculties. But it is not true that our cognitive faculties are terribly reliable — as is well known, they mislead us and require correction in many circumstances. This is more plausibly explained as an outcome of evolution than as the act of a god. Nor is it at all apparent that evolution alone could not have produced beings with cognitive faculties as reliable as ours actually are.

THE ROLE OF SECULARISM IN PROTECTING RELIGION

Dr John Wilkins
Author, blogger, Assistant Professor of Philosophy at Bond University

IT IS A WIDELY HELD BELIEF THAT MODERN SOCIETY IS SECULAR, AND that this is contrary to the interests and values of religion. In the United States, Christian pulpits and outlets repeat the claim that theirs is a 'Christian country' whose morals and values reflect their Christian origins, and that secularism is responsible for the decline of those morals and values. A similar claim has been in made in Australia by Cardinal George Pell, who stated that without Christian moral foundations Australia is tending towards a moral relativism and 'might is right' philosophy. More recently, the Cardinal has attacked human rights as restricting 'religious freedom'.[1]

At the other corner of the ring are the heavyweight atheists who deny this, and assert that modern society is founded on Enlightenment principles and that religion is mere superstition that is ineluctably going to fade away in the face of evidence, reason, and science. Richard Dawkins, in a series shown in the United Kingdom and intended to magnify the glory of Charles Darwin, asserted that Darwin is responsible for atheism being respectable and widespread in Western society — exactly the thing that the Christian (and to a lesser extent, Jewish and Islamic, and even Hindu) critics of secularism fear. And it is ironic, as Darwin himself never wanted his views to play that role.

Is there a third option? I think so, and I want to make that case here. The third option is that secularism is a means of protecting religion.

It prevents, in other words, a religion from being supplanted by coercion by any ideology or set of values and beliefs whatsoever. It is the only way, in a society of plural beliefs, that a religion can contribute to a social discourse democratically. And, in the course of doing this, it means that atheists, agnostics, and members of other religions are equally protected and empowered. The end result is that a society is freed to evolve naturally, as it were, and to find whatever mixture or equilibrium of religious and non-religious values may serve to maintain that society in a state of health.

So here I am going to make out several lines of thought. The first is that secularism is defined unfairly by those in a position of religious influence as that which is contrary to their own goals and their desires to control others, under the guise of it being an attack upon 'religious freedom'. Another is that secularism is needed to avoid the sorts of inflammatory religious conflicts that the history of Europe, the Indian subcontinent, and other regions, shows is inevitable whenever religions are permitted to attempt to control people — the current conflicts in central Asia are only the latest in a series of these conflicts. A third line of thought is that secularism is the way religious societies developed in order to adapt rapidly to economic and technological changes. Finally, I will argue that democracy itself is only possible when secular society is the constant aim of social policy.

Secularism is not so much an attack upon the religious believers and institutions of modern society as it is a defence of religious freedoms. I will defend secularism as a way to ensure that no religion is able to take over the social policy in a way that is detrimental to other religions. Catholics cannot be repressed or coerced by Protestants, nor Muslims and Hindus by Christians, and so forth, in a properly secular society. The cost, from the perspective of the religious believer, is that they must forgo control of the social agenda themselves, and they must tolerate the non-religious as much as they themselves are tolerated. They should do this because it is in their own interests to do this, such 'costs' notwithstanding.

SECULARISM AND ITS ORIGINS

The term 'secular' is both ancient and contemporary. In Latin it means 'ages', and the phrase in the Latin mass *in secula seculorum* means 'forever and ever'. Secular authority came to be the term used for authority not of the Church, but rather of the age. In the middle ages, there was a continuing conflict between secular authority — the Holy Roman Empire (which was 'neither Holy, nor Roman, nor an empire' as Voltaire said), following the Carolingian dynasty in the mid-eighth to late-ninth centuries — and the hierarchy of the Church, which played out in various ways. One of my late-medieval heroes, the emperor Frederick II of Hohenstaufen, even managed to get himself excommunicated twice for not obeying the pope: first, for saying that the emperor was not beholden to the papacy (which was itself also a 'temporal' power), and the second time because he negotiated a peaceful coexistence with the Muslims in Jerusalem, instead of slaughtering them as a good Christian king should have done.[2]

The Reformation introduced a further conflict between temporal and celestial authority: now, instead of there being one church to which all principalities and kingdoms were asked to submit, many churches and rites sprang up throughout Europe. This was not the first time distinct religious traditions challenged the authority of the Church, of course — the Albigensian massacre by the Catholics in southern France in the thirteenth century was only the latest imposition of a religious orthodoxy by political and military means, in a tradition that goes back to Constantine. But now the fabric of European society was being rent by the transition from a monopoly of one religion to a market place of many. Sweden, Holland, Switzerland and, most famously, England and Scotland, all took advantage of this to set up state religions that imposed an orthodoxy different to the hegemony of Catholicism. In response, Spain, France, and the Italian states imposed Catholic orthodoxy by the state's instruments of law and military power.

In the face of this, theologians had to define the extent and limitations of both the church and the state, and the Lutheran solution — the so-called 'Two Kingdoms' doctrine in which each authority had its own divinely circumscribed scope that the other should not tread upon — was the one that came to be employed in Protestant states. It was eventually also adopted by all but the most uniform Catholic states, which in turn depended upon the absolute nature of the monarchies in those states. And of course in uniformly Catholic states, the Church assigned the privileges of the prince anyway, as it had done in Catholic societies since the medieval conflict between church and emperor.

We shall consider the various religious wars later. For now, let us merely note that a de facto secularism is in place well before the Enlightenment. However, it is a very limited secularism — one only has the 'right' as a monarch to choose one's religion (and that of one's country, under the principal *cuius regio, euius religio*). Individual citizens have no such right. Each state still has an imposed orthodoxy, but starting out with the notion that the Church controls all aspects of society this is a major step towards secularism, merely by admitting the possibility of an authority not under the control of religion.

The Enlightenment's role in secularism is well known, and I won't repeat it here, but let us note that the Enlightenment leaders, people like Voltaire and Kant, did not suppose religion would be eliminated, merely that its superstitious elements would be. Reason would triumph, and religion would be rational for the first time. However, at this time, anti-clericalism also began to develop into full-blown atheism, with Jean Meslier the first post-Christian atheist in the early-eighteenth century, and Baron d'Holbach the first public atheist in the late-eighteenth century.

In the nineteenth century, secularism was increasingly anti-religion. Mind, this is a period in which Catholics in Catholic countries could take Jewish children from their families legally if someone, like a nanny, baptised them in secret. And if you were of the wrong religion, you might never get a government position in practically every country in Europe and the UK. You might not even be permitted to earn a living. Freethinking arose at this time as a general movement among intellectuals.

Also at this time, there arose a view of cultural evolution. It was, not surprisingly, for the time progressive. According to the view of society promoted by August Comte, known as 'positivism' and adopted widely throughout the nineteenth century, cultures start out with magical thinking, then move to theological, and then, of course, become scientific. So secularism was tied into the idea that if religion was not enforced, it would eventually die away from sheer historical necessity. This positivist view of history found its way into the Marxist dialectic of history, and underpinned, among others, Hegel's and Toynbee's view that history would undergo predetermined stages, and a kind of irreligious eschatology (the doctrine of the 'last days').

SECULARISM AS A SOLUTION TO RELIGIOUS CONFLICTS

When the United States was being founded, it had a particular problem of competing churches seeking to become the 'state church' of the 13 colonies. In the subsequent debate over the role of religions, it was decided that no church could seek to impose its doctrines on any citizen or organ of government. In fact, the government was prohibited, under the doctrine of what is now called the 'wall of separation', from instituting or legislating in favour of any religion or church. This is the first constitutional secularism, and it is designed to prevent adherents of any church or religion from being treated as second-class citizens.

Unfortunately, the intellectual inspiration for this, John Locke, in his 'Letter Concerning Toleration', explicitly exempted atheists and unbelievers from official toleration on the grounds that they couldn't be trusted to keep their word when they swore an oath. This is particularly ironic, given that a good many of the post-Mennonite churches, such as the Amish, the Shakers, and so on, refused to make an oath on theological grounds.[3]

Of course, such intentions as the largely deist founding fathers had were often honoured in the breach. Catholics were excluded from government in many states, and Jews from all kinds of occupations and stations in society, right up until the beginning of World War II. After the Holocaust, leading American Catholics like Fulton Sheen attempted to integrate Catholicism into American society, and even to influence that society to adopt previously 'Catholic positions' like being anti-abortion. Despite this, secular toleration developed for different religions, although often the marginal religions like Islam, Sikhism, Hinduism, and of course Judaism are regarded as somehow anti-American by a substantial proportion of the American population.

In Australia, secularism was imported from Europe into the burgeoning socialist movement, and was played out in the context of government-provided education.[4] The churches immediately attacked, but all states began to offer secular education, and eventually a provision prohibiting the favouring in federal-government policy of one religion over another found its way into the Australian constitution, in line with similar ideas overseas.[5] In recent years, however, particularly under conservative governments and parliamentary majorities, but also under the present Labor government, funding by the Commonwealth of religious schools has increased out of proportion to their representation in the student population. This appears to be due to the personal disposition of recent party leaders towards various religions.

Returning to history, though, let us consider the Thirty Years' War. This was a war held largely on German-speaking territories, which included the Lutheran Swedes, Catholic German principalities and France, Protestant Holland, and Catholic Spain, and so on. I'd like to quote what Wikipedia says about this long-running religious conflict, a series of small and large wars that waged across Europe between Catholic and Protestant states:

> So great was the devastation brought about by the war that estimates put the reduction of population in the German states at about 15% to 30%. Some regions were affected much more than others. For example, the Württemberg lost three-quarters of its population during the war. In the territory of Brandenburg, the losses had amounted to half, while in some areas an estimated two-thirds of the population died. The male population of the German states was reduced by almost half. The population of the Czech lands declined by a third due to war, disease, famine and the expulsion of Protestant Czechs. Much of the destruction of civilian lives and property was caused by the cruelty and greed of mercenary soldiers, many of whom were rich commanders and poor soldiers. Villages were especially easy prey to the marauding armies. Those that survived, like the small village of Drais near Mainz would take almost a hundred years to recover. The Swedish armies alone may have destroyed up to 2,000 castles, 18,000 villages and 1,500 towns in Germany, one-third of all German towns.[6]

That is what a religious war looks like. We have seen religious wars with similar attrition rates more recently in the Middle East, Northern Africa, central Asia, and southern Asia. Likewise, the English Civil War, which was founded on the religious rejection of a Catholic king by parliament, was fresh in the minds of those who drew up the American Constitution: Locke himself had been involved, as had Hobbes (although Hobbes says he ran away from it, writing in his autobiography, 'Fear and I were born twins'.[7] He was in exile in Paris during the Civil War until 1651).

In the 1960s, religious opinions began to diversify among the bourgeoisie, incorporating increasingly distinct Eastern-religious traditions, manufactured sects, and so on. The liberal orthodoxy was to include all these, and even atheists and agnostics, into normalised American and other Western societies, including in Australia, which allowed a census option of 'no religion' beginning in 1971. This liberalism lasted all of three or four years.

In the 1970s in the US, conservative evangelicals and conservative Catholics started a movement to try to 'take back' the political discourse of their country. This had already happened in the UK and Europe after Vatican I, in the 1870s and afterwards. Fearing that they had no voice in political circles and forums, the conservative religious undertook a deliberate strategy to gain one. I can recall sitting in these discussions as a young Australian evangelical 'intellectual' in Melbourne in the mid-1970s, as we planned how to 'witness' to the 'secular humanist' world. Secularism, humanism, and atheism were all regarded as identical, evil, and the cause of all social ills.

The eventual outcome of these strategies was the 'Focus on the Family' movement in the US, the 'Silent Majority', the 'Moral Majority', and similar organisations, many of them explicitly religious, a few supposedly not — but actually they all were. Republicans in the US courted these movements in order to shore up their overall support, and this is when Catholics and Protestant conservatives took up arms together on matters like abortion.

These movements make out that secularism is an attack upon their right to exist and to enforce moral standards. They are partly right: as secularism has been sold, it was presumed that if we can establish a secular state religion will ultimately wither away and die, leaving us in John Lennon's state of imagination. I think this is fundamentally mistaken. Religion is an inevitable aspect of human society, and in the foreseeable future it will not wither away.

This is a rather unusual challenge to the secularist presumptions of the past, so I had better give my reasons for it. No society has been free of religion, and in fact even in those supposedly atheist regimes of the Soviet Union and China, while religious observance may have fallen, when the Soviet Union collapsed, the majority of Russians were still Orthodox after 70 years. Most Chinese are even now religious in one form or another. This is evidence that religion is very hard to displace. There is census data that states like Australia have become less religious, but the majority remain self-described believers, even if formal observance has dropped. But the fundamental reason for thinking that religion is, if not inevitable, highly likely in any urban society, is that religion is an outgrowth of our species-typical psychologies, and so unless displaced by something that requires the depth of commitment of religion, it will be the dominant expression of those psychologies.

The assumption that religion would die was based on the positivism of August Comte, who held that societies and ideas go through a series of developmental stages, just as an organism does, and so 'each of our leading conceptions — each branch of our knowledge — passes successively through three different theoretical conditions: the Theological, or fictitious; the Metaphysical, or abstract; and the Scientific, or positive'.[8] Many secularists hold something like this — as we free our society from religious strictures, we remove the brakes holding religion in place, and so we will move through the remaining stages.

This is a mistake for many reasons. First of all, as I said, religion will not fade away. I believe, although I am not religious myself, that religion is a standard response of human beings to urbanised and agrarian society, and so long as we live in such societies religion will persist. That is an argument that will be presented later.

Second, history does not inevitably move from simple to sophisticated, from theological to scientific. In some cases it has, but that is no guarantee that it always will. There are major religious revivals in many countries right now, including two of the secularist pin-ups, Turkey and India. If we want to support and justify secularism, we had better do it on more realistic grounds than that.

Third, in societies that are largely religious, like the United States, we cannot establish secularism if that means opposing religion. Well, we could, but only if we are prepared to act in a high-handed and undemocratic manner, and use force, and we know how well that turns out in the long term. If we want secularism to flourish, we had better take the religious along with us. It must be seen to be in their own interests. And, it turns out, it is.

SECULARISM AS THE GOAL OF DEMOCRATIC PLURALISTIC SOCIETIES

The ethicist John Rawls, in a famous and influential text on legal philosophy, proposed a formal test of just laws, called 'the original position'.[9] The idea here is that a rational agent in a position of setting up a legal framework that served their own interests would choose a just law only if they were effectively unaware of their social and financial position in society. In other words, they must draw a 'veil of ignorance' over themselves before choosing a law. Rawls wrote that in this case:

> no one knows his place in society, his class position or social status, nor does anyone know his fortune in the distribution of natural assets and abilities, his intelligence, strength, and the like. I shall even assume that the parties do not know their conceptions of the good or their special psychological propensities. The principles of justice are chosen behind a veil of ignorance.[10]

In short, the veil of ignorance ensures that decisions are made only on general principles. The law has long had a similar rule, that laws must apply to everyone, and not merely to named subgroups or individuals (there should not be a law that applies only to Catholics or Jews, for example). In the United States, this goes under the label of 'equal protection': a law may not be uniquely applicable to any single individual or group (the 14th Amendment). Australia, and the common law system from which it sprang, has a legal principle that laws must not name individuals or particular groups, and must apply equally to all, which is roughly the same view. How you get such equality from a rational perspective is what Rawls is trying to explain through the veil of ignorance.

One justification for the veil is that you really do not know what your position is going to be down the track — that is, you, or your progeny, as the 'interest bearers' of legal protection, may end up among the homeless down the track even if now you are among the wealthy and powerful. Your choice of law is based on a test of fairness: if you did end up there (or your progeny did, about whom you presumably care as much as you do for yourself), you'd want the law to protect you from arbitrary arrest, loss of privileges, onerous tasks or duties, and the like.

Notice that I have added in here one's progeny. Usually, the interest bearers in these discussions are the individuals making the choice of law — I am adding those for whom the individual may care. My rational decision ought to be about protecting all those in whose welfare I have an interest. This is rather different to the standard view, but I justify it on the basis that we are human beings, and we do in fact care about our kin, and our group. To deny this when considering what human beings should evaluate is to make a serious biological error. We are not robots, nor are we ants.

So, to my argument. Consider a reasonable, indeed a rational, agent who is a member of a religion. I will not consider the question of whether it is rational to be in a religion in the first place, and presume that it is possible, indeed that it occurs, that people in religions may be rational in assessing their interests. All we are interested in is this question: what social institutions should a rational believer support to serve their interests as believers? First, we must consider what their interests are:

* They presumably want freedom to worship and believe the tenets of their faith. This includes the practising of rituals, such as dress and modes of speech. The laws they would support must not abrogate this.
* They presumably wish to contribute to the public discourse about moral standards and policies of government, like any member of the democracy. This includes being able to take office in secular roles of government and social institutions. In short, they will want at least the same freedoms of speech and participation as any other member of society.
* They want protection by the law and state from exploitation and so forth, in virtue of their religion. In other words, being Jewish is not enough to prohibit someone from farming, as it was in the Middle Ages.

So they will choose laws that do these things. But it is a human failing to desire laws that are exceptional on your own behalf. Accordingly, Catholics will want laws that prohibit abortion, and Jews will want laws that prohibit working on the Sabbath, and so on. It is interesting to note the difference between the two religious communities' responses here, at least in Australia. The Jewish laws are laws enjoined solely upon Jews. But the Catholic laws are proposed, historically, for the whole community.

Suppose a Catholic were in the majority religion in Australia. Catholic laws of this kind could be passed with impunity. Abortion could be criminalised, as it is in Ireland. I want to offer a Rawlsian argument for why a rational Catholic ought to oppose this.

Under the veil of ignorance, the Catholic ought to choose no laws that give any religion exceptional treatment in society, for they cannot predict whether or not they are going to be in the majority in some future, or even present, era. If they give exceptionalism a run, because when they are in the majority they can impose Catholic virtues through the law, then if the Protestants, Muslims, or communists get control of the democratic apparatus in the future, they have been given a licence for themselves to be oppressed through the same laws.

In the future, the majority of believers may be Muslim. Catholics now should want a constitution that prevents Muslims from imposing Sharia law when that occurs, if it does.

Similar principles apply, for example, when a government considers breaking a convention for short-term gain — if they do it, then their opposition may claim equal justification in a later administration. Of course all kinds of internal justifications can be given — 'we are the one true church' — but that has no force outside the community, so if there is the slightest chance that your community will not be in power in future, and in a democratic society there ought to be, you should rationally choose not to impose religious values through the law. That is, you should protect your religion through secularism.

What can be done when people are unable to see things other than in absolute terms, and so decide that their religion, being True, is entitled to do anything it can to bring about the Proper Society? All I can say is that we should all stand against such absolutism, with arms if necessary, to protect freedoms, ours and others', and the Open Society. No principle or reasoning can prevent this.

All of this relies on there being only rational actors in the consideration of how to set up society and the law. Of course, there are not. There are those who think that God will come down in the End Times next week and smite all the unbelievers. Millenarian views like this come and go, and are, I suspect, correlated with social rates of change – the greater the society is changing, especially if it is modernising, the more millenarianism is about. Much religious opposition in society is, I think, opposition to modernism itself, not the specific aspects. For example, opposition to abortion is more about having some control over who may mate with whom and how in a permissive society, than it is about the theological issues, which were not operative before the thirteenth century so far as I know, and prior to the nineteenth was often not a crime. There are always those who think it only right that they control society, because they are God's agents, or at least the agents of Providence or History.

CONCLUSION

I said I would argue for four things. Let me sum these up. The misunderstanding of secularism by those who think society is a humanistic-atheist conspiracy against them is in part the fault of secularists. We need to abandon the view that secularism equates to a loss of religion.

By adopting a secularistic social order, we protect against such events as the Thirty Years' War or the Troubles in Ireland. By all means, let religions compete; but they must do so civilly. If the Catholics are worried about Protestant hegemony as it played out in the past, so too the Protestants ought to worry about Catholic and other hegemonies in the future. Secularism protects us all from crusades, internecine wars, and general strife between faiths. As a consequence, it also protects non-believers — agnostics and atheists — and the uninstitutionalised religious. But that is not its primary aim, despite the historical origins of secularism.

And that historical origin is itself due to the ways in which conflicts between religions developed out of the Middle Ages. Of course, there are within-religion disputes, and between-religion disputes. The present battle between Islamism and Western society is not so much, from the Islamic perspective, about a clash of civilisations as a clash of religions. They see secularism as the loss of religion. It would help enormously if they were to see secular Western society as protecting religions.

Of course, some think their religion must form all of society. Islamists hold that Islam must form a global *Umma*, or motherland. But Islamism is fed by the discontent of those Muslims who fear their religion is being sidelined or discriminated against. We must get the message across that they are protected, even if they cannot have total control.

And when that non-rational desire for total control is encountered and is resistant to argument, then and only then do we enforce the standards of secular society.

NOTES

1. G. Pell, 'Might is right', speech to the National Press Club, 21 September 2005, Canberra, text at www.ad2000.com.au/articles/2005/nov2005p3_2097.html. Cardinal Pell's comment on religious freedom in 'George Pell and Human Rights: ideology dressed up as social justice', *Anglicans in Melbourne and Geelong*, at www.melbourne.anglican.com.au/main.php?pg=news&news_id=22704&s=151

2. D. Abulafia, *Frederick II: a medieval emperor*, Allen Lane/Penguin, London, 1988; P. Andrewes, *Frederick II of Hohenstaufen*, Oxford University Press, London, 1970.

3 Relying upon the scriptural text, 'But let your communication be, Yea, yea; Nay, nay: for whatsoever is more than these cometh of evil', Matthew 5:37. Some also think this justifies the use of binary code in computers...

4. A. Barcan, *A History of Australian Education*, Oxford University Press, Australia and New Zealand, 1980; B. Bessant, 'Free, Compulsory, and Secular Education: The 1872 Education Act', *Paedagogica Historica* 24 (1), 1984, pp. 5-25.

5. W. Phillips, *The Protestant Churchmen's Campaign Against Secularism in Australia in the Late Nineteenth Century*, Uniting Church Historical Society, Moorabbin, 1983; I. R. Wilkinson et al., *A History of State Aid to Non-Government Schools in Australia*, Educational Transformations, Canberra, 2006.

6. See 'Thirty Years' War', at http://en.wikipedia.org/wiki/Thirty_Years%27_War

7. T. Hobbes, 'Part I: human nature', 'Part II: de corpore politico', *The Elements of Law, Natural and Politic* (ed. J. C. A. Gaskin), Oxford University Press, New York, p. 254.

8. A. Comte, *The Postive Philosophy of Auguste Comte* vol. 1 (trans. H. Martineau), John Chapman, London, p. 1.

9. J. Rawls and E. Kelly, *Justice as Fairness: a restatement*. Harvard University Press, Massachusetts, 2001.

10. J. Rawls, *A Theory of Justice*, Belknap Press, Massachusetts, 1971.

WHY A BOOK ON ATHEIST THOUGHT IN AUSTRALIA?

Warren Bonett
Bookshop owner, artist, blogger

AT TIMES, THE DEBATE BETWEEN THE DEFENDERS OF FAITH AND ATHEISTS seems like an immensely tedious game of ideological tennis, where the game never progresses past the 140 mph serve and missed return — both sides having heated arguments with the umpire about the ball being out. Atheists generally acknowledge that it's a game they're extremely unlikely to win. They have to admit this: the evidence for the tenacity of religious and superstitious belief is simply too strong and widespread. In my experience, however, most Australians, including the atheists, barely acknowledge any religious influence on society at all, let alone a negative one. For them, religion appears to be confined to church-group cake stalls and helping Grandma out when Grandpa dies. So why put together an Australian book of atheism? Why should Australia, a secular nation, be singled out for consideration here?

While I generally hate questions being answered with questions, I am compelled to ask, in response, how can a country that pays $150 million plus to have a Catholic World Youth Day, and that places faith-based groups in charge of social services, also regard itself as being secular? There is no separation of church and state here, religion is embedded in our political system. It's not my argument that religion needs to be banned from every mind, but that it shouldn't have an automatic and largely unquestioned place in the public forum.

Most peculiarly, the resurgence of publicly declared political religiosity

327

runs counter to the decline of religious observance in Australia. This in and of itself is problematic, although there seems to be no shortage of religious defenders (some of whom, like Ian Plimer, are atheist) to claim political territory for religion, as if by right.[1] Take this quote by Paul Kelly, editor-at-large of *The Australian*:

> The frustration of the secularists was vented on this page last week when Melbourne writer Pamela Bone said it was 'now too dangerous for religion to be given the special status it has always had'. She appealed to the media to cover religion with a new aggression in the cause of a less religious and more secularist world. This would be a serious mistake, provoking a religious backlash based upon rejection and alienation.[2]

A serious mistake to criticise religion because the religious would respond with what sounds like aggression? Remarkable logic. All the more so given that in the same article Kelly acknowledges that, despite the decreasing religious observance of the population of Australia, religion is more present than ever in its politics. It's also noteworthy that he characterises as aggressive Pamela Bone's statement, which read as follows:

> It is time to get rid of the taboo that says religious beliefs have to be quarantined from **criticism**. It is time to hold **some** religious beliefs up to ridicule.[3] *[my emphasis]*

Public criticism of religious ideas is frequently branded by people like Kelly or theologian Tom Frame, as aggressive, strident, and intolerant, as if such absurd name-calling is an answer to the questions being raised. They commit a number of logical fallacies by equating any criticism with 'militant secularism' and the headlong pursuit of 'Social Darwinism'.[4]

In response to this I'd like you now to imagine a religious militant, and how they might express themselves, and a so-called militant atheist. Would it be generalising or discriminatory to suggest the former is probably pictured wielding a gun and the latter is Richard Dawkins with a bit of colour in his cheeks? Are they really equatable?

When an atheist refers to fundamentalist and militant religionists, they're speaking of people who believe the world is 10,000 years old or younger and who solve religious differences with bombs and guns. I would also argue that, if a person wishes to propose an argument on the basis of revelation, rather than evidence that can be genuinely shared and evaluated, they would also be using fundamentalist though not militant processes. Why? Because revelation, as a divinely inspired, internal experience cannot, by definition, be open to any external evaluation, which is at the heart of any atheist argument.

All ideas should be up for critical evaluation and, yes, even ridicule. What possible reason could there be for them not to be? Apologists like Kelly and Frame are of the idea that, without religion, society would somehow disintegrate due to secularism's lack of values and moral ambivalence and that, because of this, religion must have a place in the political sphere. In the spirit of critical evaluation, atheists and other secularists merely ask for the evidence that this extraordinary claim is made upon.

The biblically derived idea that society would suffer terribly without the moral underpinnings that religions provides found, perhaps, its most determined political proponent of recent years in former prime minister Kevin Rudd, who stated that it's only strongly held religious convictions, leveraged on a public stage, that prevent 'rampant secularism' from pushing society into a very dark place.[5] Religious conviction, so described, is the friend of family, health, and morals; so, by default, secularism is the antithesis to these things. This false dichotomy is the foundation upon which such rhetoric is built. In actuality, secularism arrives at its positions on these issues using reason and evidence in a manner that is entirely open to public scrutiny. Religion, on the other hand, is restricted to a doctrine that may have only limited or tangential things to say about the matter at hand — which, strangely, doesn't restrict the absolute nature of conviction displayed. For instance, Christians frequently display complete opposition to such things as homosexuality and abortion, despite the scriptures at the heart of their doctrine devoting only a few lines, at best, to these subjects. These few words result in a fog of righteous moralising, buttressed by the unspoken rule: you can't criticise ideas if they are religious beliefs.

Not only does this taboo afford them such protection, it buys access privileges: in discussions on morality, ethics, and healthcare; in our tax and education systems; in our foreign policy and human rights reviews; in fact, in virtually every facet of life.[6] But what is it that actually gives churches and believers these extraordinary rights? What special skills does a religious leader provide in any of these matters? How does familiarity with a single book automatically bestow upon an individual such a broad range of excellence and expertise in matters as diverse as stem-cell research, climate change, and the psychological care of troubled teenagers? Even someone who had memorised the entire multivolume *Encyclopaedia Britannica* wouldn't have this position by right. Few, it seems, have really thought much about this.

Is it this automatic access for the religious to core components of our society that led a number of governments in Australia to tacitly support religion by bringing chaplains into schools?[7] Or why the federal government awarded health contracts to Catholic healthcare providers in order to slow down or stop access to abortions?[8] In my experience, most religious defenders think that such acquiesence to religion is just an American phenomenon — 'it wouldn't happen here'. For me, these two examples alone are reason enough for removing religious influence over public policy matters, but there's a long line of people more than happy to argue the point. Then prime minister of Australia, John Howard, illustrated this with his government's entire approach, which he summarised in a speech he gave to the American Enterprise Institute in Washington, DC, in 2008. His thrust was that traditional Christian family values stand at the core of everything he feels matters in the world. He spoke about having sought to place religious bodies in positions where they could help make this happen during his term:

> The former government in Australia gave faith-based groups direct involvement in policy making and execution, adding to their traditional roles of relieving distress and providing spiritual support.[9]

This speech, which celebrated the transfer of some of the Howard government's social responsibilities to Christian groups, also rejoiced in the 33 per cent of education services being largely managed by government-subsidised Christian schools. Other religions are also supported in their schooling preferences, ensuring that the increasingly under-funded state schools become the only place subsequent generations can learn to live in a multicultural society.[10] As with many faith-based, politically conservative initiatives, such issues are usually fought down the centre of left- and right-wing politics, although this changed under Rudd's Christian Socialist-inspired ideology, and continue to dominate the agenda under Julia Gillard's leadership.

Given that it took less than 24 hours for the religious commentators to hit the headlines after prime minister Gillard announced her atheism in July 2010, it's probably no surprise she decided to play nice with the Christian vote. Surely no one could doubt the influence of religion on both sides of politics after Gillard announced the $222 million extension to the National School Chaplaincy Program and $1.5 million to help celebrate the canonisation of Mary MacKillop.[11] Paradoxically, before these measures were announced, commentators and pollsters assured us that the general public didn't care about Gillard's lack of belief, and yet off she went to meet with the Australian Christian Lobby.[12] Perhaps it was a case of compensating for a possible downside to her electability during a tight election race that she decided to spend more than either Howard or Rudd on these Christian enterprises.

Now it could be a trick of memory, and an expression of confirmation bias while researching this essay, but it seems to me that until the turn of the century that the conflict between atheists and religious defenders was mostly dead and buried, or at least confined to Monty Python movies and quiet, respectful discussions behind closed doors in universities. The religious generally accepted that some of their beliefs were at least a little bit silly, and atheists mostly believed religion was a harmless cultural fossil that would inevitably be worn away by the winds of modernity. So what changed? Some middle-class, well-educated men flew planes filled with people into buildings — also full of people. They were Islamic, and members of a militant Islamic terrorist group, but perhaps it is more important to note that people and planes had become the new ammunition in a war that most Westerners didn't even know was going on. A war of ideas. Some view these opposing ideas as being Western imperialism versus everybody else; others as Christianity vs Islam; and still others as secularism versus theocracy. Wherever you choose to draw the line is where the battle is to be waged.

Flying planes into buildings highlighted and exacerbated the notion of 'them' and 'us', and the difference between 'their' values and 'ours', and we were reminded again and again thereafter that our values are good traditional Christian values. Because 'we' value what is good, 'they' must by default value what is bad. This type of reasoning is not merely reserved for wartime, it is given a very loose leash during election times as well. The following inflammatory words were from a group set up to *educate* Christians on how 'Christian' a party's policies, and therefore their values, were:

> With the balance of power in the Senate, anytime the government wants to put through legislation, the Greens will get the final say before it can be passed.
>
> For Christians and for anyone believing in Christian values this should be a cause for grave concern.
>
> The Greens are ideologically anti-Christian with a specific anti-Christian agenda … We have an opportunity to make our collective Christian voices heard, before our values and our rights as a Christian people are eroded away.[13]

This indulges in something I call the 'endangered species' fallacy — where the majority by population and power claim underdog status. The appropriation of the wartime language of threats made to our way of life by a well-defined 'them', seems to be a common method of propagating the message of the importance of Christian values. The result is a virtual stampede by politicians claiming solid Christian heritage. Even Julia Gillard, as an atheist, referred to her church-shaped values:

> [M]y values were formed in a strong family, in a family that went to church, and I've brought those values with me.[14]

Her careful language is of the type one would find in a court of law, with the person in the dock speaking as someone well coached to not incriminate themselves. That her values were formed in a strong family and that the family went to church are unrelated non-causal items. The implication, however, is clear: 'my values are that of a good church-going family', who in turn have taken their values from the Bible. But is it really a good source of value-based guidance?

Any values based upon religious texts penned long ago are only tenuously relevant and, as a result, require external ideas to help make them fit the problem to which they're being applied. 'Good, traditional Christian' values say nothing about the pre-existing ethical framework in people's minds that enable them to navigate scriptural dogma of a truly contradictory nature. What, for instance, makes people regard 'love thy neighbour' and 'don't eat shellfish' in a different way? Why is 'making images with a likeness of things in heaven and on earth' entirely ignored, but 'a man lying with a man' is not? Obviously, there's another set of values at work here in these decisions. This begs a whole host of questions: If you take out half the ethical laws contained in the Bible, does it still remain Christian? If they are God's laws, who decides that some don't count? If you obey a cherry-picked version, are you more a follower of the cherry picker than the original? And if it is okay to pick and choose, then let's make this process transparent and open to rigorous analysis, without appeals to 'God's laws', which clearly have already been heavily edited.

Few parents today would follow through if their child broke the fifth commandment by stoning them to death, even though it is a recommended course of action in the Bible (by the way, where's the commandment for parents respecting the rights of their child?). Nor would they murder their neighbours for worshipping another deity. At some point in history, maintaining these positions simply became untenable and was dropped. Other modern-day freedoms were harder won, such as religious freedom itself — the right to not be persecuted for your private beliefs; or freedom of speech; or the transparency of democratic governance.[15] It is because these freedoms were so hard-won and others took so long to nurture that, in order to prevent them from being lost to a rising wave of literalist and anti-science soldiers on the mental landscape, atheists have been compelled to respond (I suspect most of them really would rather be having a nice cup of tea).

Within Australia, however, it isn't the biblical literalists who are the biggest problem. It's the more moderate followers, such as former prime minister Kevin Rudd, who have used their religious compass to navigate political, social, and scientific terrain. Take this statement by Rudd, quoting the American evangelical reverend Jim Wallis in *The Monthly* in 2006:

> God is not partisan: God is not a Republican or a Democrat. When either party tries to politicise God, or co-opt religious communities for their political agendas, they make a terrible mistake. The best contribution of religion is precisely not to be ideologically predictable nor loyally partisan. Both parties, and the nation, **must let the prophetic voice of religion be heard. Faith must be free to challenge both right and left from a consistent moral ground.**[16] *[My emphasis]*

The first part of this sounds fine — don't politicise God in a partisan way — but then it all falls apart when we hear that the prophetic voice of religion *must* be heard by *both* parties — seems a bit like loading the spiritual dice, and a little less moderate than keeping religion a private matter. The answer for the then prime minister wasn't less personal religious ideology in the political sphere, but more. In the same article, he states that modernity, science, and secularism have run rampant and undermined the Christian influence on life, which may now even be on its way to a minority position again. It is a little rich to claim this 'endangered species' status for Christianity when various institutions under its banner have at least one building in virtually every single town in the nation. For example, in my hometown of Pomona, in Queensland, with a population of a little over 1000, there are four churches or outreach centres.

The idea that Christianity and all it stands for is under threat is a common tactic of evangelists and apologists in attempting to provide themselves with the aura of the oppressed, which is absurd, as historically the biggest oppressors of Christians have been other Christians.

The under-threat position was the basis upon which Rudd stated with confidence that Christianity has key insights and moral precepts that require us to give it a voice in social and political arenas — as if it had earned this by right somehow:

> the Gospel is as much concerned with the decisions I make about my own life as it is with the way I act in society. It is therefore also

concerned with how in turn I should act, and react, in relation to the state's power ... A Christian perspective on contemporary policy debates may not prevail. It must nonetheless be argued. And once heard, it must be weighed, together with other arguments from different philosophical traditions, in a fully contestable secular polity. A Christian perspective, informed by a social gospel or Christian socialist tradition, should not be rejected contemptuously by secular politicians as if these views are an unwelcome intrusion into the political sphere. **If the churches are barred from participating in the great debates about the values that ultimately underpin our society, our economy and our polity, then we have reached a very strange place indeed.**[17] *[my emphasis]*

Would it really be so strange to require Bronze and Iron Age moralists to bring to the table something other than attenuated ancient ideology supported by severely compromised data when debating matters of fact or ethics? Does any outdated and surpassed system of knowledge require a place by right at any modern table of discussion?

Historically, the pressure that mounted to separate church and state arose when arguments were weighed together with other philosophies, and religious desire for political power was found wanting — even by the religious. In fact, it was in order to escape persecution from other Christians that the notion of separating church from state entered into the American constitution, and later the Australian one, in the first place. Does each post-Enlightenment generation need to defend this aspect of social governance? Perhaps the anachronistic nature of this becomes more obvious when you consider that the religious philosophy being brought to bear on modern-day affairs was written for a world without guided nuclear missiles, corrective eye surgery, or knowledge of genetics, and around six billion less people.

At its most basic level, Bronze or even Iron Age beliefs and morals are simply not up to the job of managing twenty-first century populations and problems. Just as an ancient health practitioner wouldn't belong in a modern hospital, or a Viking warrior on the Iraqi fields of battle, nor would the simplistic moralising of prophetic goatherds have relevance when discussing contemporary ethical issues. It is time to confine to history and philosophy books the ideas of people for whom papyrus was a state-of-the-art communication device and exorcism the best in mental-health care.

It's not slurring the good names of those long-dead men to recognise the extreme limitations of their understanding. The fact that these people and their ideas were of their time should not be a problematic statement. Unfortunately, institutions arose to enshrine in stone and law this folk wisdom as if it could never be bettered.

These institutions have fought to defend certain ideas against any threat. This defensiveness has led to some quite remarkable lethargy in responding to change in society, particularly with regard to racism, slavery, the rights of women, conjugal rape, the Earth's movement through space, and even the printing of the Bible itself — which the Catholic Church opposed for fear of loss of power if they were no longer to be the sole conduit of scriptural truth.[18]

Some of the big religious institutions have finally addressed these issues, but getting them to do so does feel a little bit like pushing a legless elephant uphill. Perhaps this slow response to change in society has been part of the reason why more adaptable, personal, and almost pagan spiritualism surged back into community life, and support at the church pew declined, as evidenced in this 2005 *Age* article:

> there is a gap between the number of people in Australia who say they believe in God (about 70 per cent) and those who attend church at least once a month (about 20 per cent according to the National Church Life Survey). The last survey, a five-year census of churches in Australia, was released in February 2004. It found attendances declining among the Lutheran, Presbyterian, Salvation Army and Anglican churches, with the biggest decline among Catholics (13 per cent) and Uniting Church worshippers (11 per cent).[19]

The non-churchgoing 'soft' believers are often left out of discussions of atheism because they've generally not been organised into institutions or any other group with political power. Whether they have a personal relationship with Jesus, unrecognisable to any Christian doctrine, or are more partial to spirit guides and balding Eastern gurus, many are best characterised as pseudoscientific deists of the New Age variety. They wield the postmodern phrase 'that's not my reality' as if it means something. If an average follower of religion is a cherry picker of various barbarous fairy tales, a New Ager is the ultimate spiritual pick'n'mixer, with a penchant for self-help guides, 'other ways of knowing', and ancient healing remedies.

In a 2009 *Sydney Morning Herald* article, David Marr reported on a 2009 Nielsen survey which found that about 68 per cent of Australians identify themselves as believers in a god, and the majority of these call themselves Christians — and this is in a report that purports to show good news for atheists:

> Belief is shrinking and disbelief is growing. But slowly. Like the Greens, atheism is always about to break through but never does. Those sceptics who believe time will, of its own accord, wipe Christianity out in this country are fooling themselves. The more religious Baby Boomers are heading for the grave — confident, by the way, in life after death — but Christians keep rolling off the production lines. Sceptics can take this comfort: they now make up the biggest denomination, followed by Catholics and then Anglicans.[20]

Unfortunately, non-belief in a god, at about 30 per cent, is slightly behind belief in UFOs, at 34 per cent, and astrology, at 41 per cent. But, thankfully, we're ahead of belief in witches, at 22 per cent. It seems that society has passed from the Information Age into the 'I'm-Influenced By-Crap-Television-Age'.

Despite this apparent waning of institutional religious adherence, we seem to be currently experiencing a resurgence in the involvement of religious belief in public life. Not just the public life that gives religion tax and legal privileges, but that which enables celebrities of one sort or another to have a national voice merely as a result of their religious beliefs.

The Australian Tax Office describes the religious as having 'belief in a supernatural being, thing or principle and acceptance of canons of conduct that give effect to that belief'.[21] The latter is of greatest importance to the atheists' argument because if the belief didn't result in systematic and organised behaviour (such as tax avoidance, and exorcisms) in the real world, there would be few motivated to argue against it. As it is, religious institutions are actively involved not only in lobbying policy makers, but also in the process of government itself.

Leaders of different religious groups are highly visible on the Australian political and social landscape. Cardinal George Pell warned Catholic members of parliament that there would be consequences if they voted on a bill that would scrap the ban on stem-cell research.[22] Reverend Fred Nile is the longest-serving member of the New South Wales Parliament, and has tabled motions and bills such as the Close Abortion Clinics Bill and the Gay Mardi Gras Prohibition Motion. He has also stated that same-sex marriage is 'an abomination, immoral, unnatural, abnormal and blasphemous against God's Creative Purposes'.[23] And Danny Nalliah, president of the Assemblies of God (now the Australian Christian Churches) and ex-candidate for the Family First Party, commented that the Victorian bushfires of 2009 were punishment from God for the state decriminalising abortion:

> That His conditional protection has been removed from the nation of Australia, in particular Victoria, for approving the slaughter of innocent children in the womb.[24]

Perhaps more alarming are supposedly secular politicians, such as the then federal minister of education Dr Brendan Nelson (who is Catholic), saying:

> As far as I'm concerned, students can be taught and should be taught the basic science in terms of the evolution of man, but if schools also want to present students with intelligent design, I don't have any difficulty with that. It's about choice, reasonable choice.[25]

No, Dr Nelson, evolution is about science. Real science. It's possible that Nelson didn't know at the time that intelligent design (ID) had been famously constructed by the Discovery Institute, a conservative American non-profit public-policy think tank, as a marketing 'wedge' strategy to bring creationism into schools.[26] Perhaps if the doctor did, he wouldn't have made such an appalling anti-science statement. Hopefully he and others will now be better informed about the changing wedge strategy as it morphs in the US from the increasingly useless terminology of ID and into 'Academic Freedom'.

No doubt, it won't matter how the strategy changes, though: at some point, religious powerbrokers merely decide to make something happen because in their own peculiar interpretation of the Christian doctrine it seems to be a good idea. Perhaps that was what then prime minister John Howard was thinking when he created the $145 million Chaplains in Schools program, which his successor, Kevin Rudd, then extended with a further $42.8 million, followed by the astounding Gillard addition of $222 million.[27] The chaplains don't, of course, teach — they're not qualified.[28] In fact, they're not qualified to do anything, really; and if, according to the constitution, they are not permitted to promote their religion, what exactly are they there for? They've apparently been hired to help with troubled students — *in a non-counselling role*. The primary quality these chaplains possess is that they are practicing members of a church. It seems that our federal government values our troubled youth so much that they wish them to be guided by unqualified groups and individuals with a religious agenda.

> As a report on the program reveals, many chaplains are unclear about their role. A majority admits they do deal with student mental health and depression issues, student alcohol and drug use, physical/emotional abuse and neglect, and suicide and self-harming behaviours. What most don't do is refer to appropriate professionals when out of their depth.
>
> This is not an argument against religion in schools, though one can clearly be made. Rather it is an argument about wrong choices made for bad reasons that are putting our most vulnerable schoolchildren at risk. In a world of scarce resources, money spent on chaplains is money that could have brought-wait for it-around 5000 qualified counselors into our schools ... So what did our children do to deserve our negligence? Nothing. It's just that Labor needs to pick up an additional 1% of the religious vote in Queensland.[29]

Of course, all this won't get much scrutiny from the Opposition, with ex-seminarian Tony Abbott in the leadership seat. He has stated quite clearly that teaching of the Christian Bible should be a central aspect of a modern education, so he's unlikely to have any problem with chaplains who, as bad as they may be, aren't central to educational services. Hiding behind a desire for children to have a good understanding of history and geography, Abbott says:

I think everyone should have some familiarity with the great texts that are at the core of our civilisation ... That includes, most importantly, the Bible. **I think it would be impossible to have a good general education without at least some serious familiarity with the Bible and with the teachings of Christianity.** That doesn't mean that people have to be believers.[30] *[My emphasis]*

Abbott and I clearly have different definitions of 'impossible'. Walking on water — now that's impossible. Surely, if you wanted people to have profound knowledge about the core of our civilisation, you might want to start with the best and latest work from political science, sociology, and anthropology? As Newton famously said, 'If I have seen a little further it is by standing on the shoulders of Giants'. What came before, if useful, has been incorporated into more robust systems of thought and practice. A modern-day astronomer need not study Ptolemaic cosmology to help him understand the skies.

I can see some value in learning about a wide range of religious belief systems and their effects on society both historically and currently, but singling out the Bible for preferential status doesn't seem warranted. If an understanding of the philosophy underpinning modern society was the aim, then surely *On Liberty* (1859) by John Stuart Mill or *The Rights of Man* (1791) by Thomas Paine would be among the leading contenders for inclusion in the syllabus.

The only community groups given the right to respond to Abbott's statements in the article in which his words appeared were other religious groups who, understandably, were a little defensive. Why is it that the opinions of a group larger than any other single denomination, non-believers, so rarely make it into such pieces? While researching this essay, I spoke with a number of journalists from various Australian newspapers. One told me that the papers will censor some articles critical of religion in order to avoid dealing with the intensity and duration of the complaints by religious officials. If this is true and widespread, the broader quest to protect free speech has taken a quiet turn for the worse.

So we have newspapers under pressure to be uncritical of religious ideas; leaders of government who foist their religion onto the children of the entire country; influential religious figures given prominent media coverage for outrageous statements; religious communities pushing prejudicial health, education, and sexuality bills in parliament — and all this in a society with a supposedly waning interest in God. Perhaps this is what religion does when its back is against the wall. You can almost hear the whoosh of the pendulum of history swinging back into its supernatural state after spending a short time in the real world.

In the US, the party that most embodies the separation of church and state at the heart of their constitution, the Democrats, has been compelled by the American religious resurgence to bring its spiritual credentials to the fore, claiming territory once the preserve of the Republicans. And so we return again to Kevin Rudd, who rode the same wave:

> I think it's time that those people who have a view of faith from the other side of politics actually spoke out and dealt with this challenge, and I've therefore got a responsibility and others of faith within our political tradition have got a responsibility to start speaking out, and that's what we're trying to do.[31]

To put it another way: I don't like the way you push your view of God into politics, so I'm going to push my idea of God. Or, in order to combat right-wing Christian conservatism, we need left-wing Christian conservatism. Am I missing something here?

If Rudd's reactionary statement seemed like a childish response to a disagreement about some ancient, vague writings, consider the impact of one of the speeches that put his opposition counterpart, Abbott, on the map:

> Now the last thing that anyone would want to do is to criminalise people who are party to abortion. Still, abortion is a stain on our national character that can and should be reduced. We can and should do something about it. I respectfully put it to church leaders that if, on a per capita basis, Catholics devoted as much moral energy to these 100,000 extinguished lives as we do to the far smaller number of children in detention, if senior Catholics were as morally indignant about the unambiguous moral tragedy of abortion as we are about the less clear-cut question of immigration detention, then there would be change.

If, as a society, we put as much interest in discouraging premature sexual activity as we do in discouraging drink-driving or cigarette-smoking; if, as a society, we re-established adoption as an alternative to abortion or sole parenthood; if, as a society, we cherished and celebrated motherhood as much as we cherish and celebrate success in the workplace, there would be far fewer abortions and we would be a happier and better society.[32]

So stains on national character, war, smoking, immigration detention, sex, drink-driving, and the 'unambiguous moral tragedy of abortion' are comparable moral minefields that the Christians have unequivocally found the best way to navigate? And they found the tools to do this in a work penned in the Bronze and Iron ages by scribes of a couple of warring Middle-Eastern tribes who, as luck would have it, stumbled across an ethical and moral system of conduct more profound than anything that came before or after? Literalists or not, this is the effective creed that politicians like Rudd and Abbott nail themselves, and the rest of us (including their successors), to.

Under questioning, I have no doubt both politicians would retreat to a more metaphorical, and even poetic, interpretation of their bible of moral guidance. So how does this metaphor-reliant, modern view of religious, truth-bearing documents result in such certain answers about the how, what, why, and when of everything including what I do with my penis, or what one of my friends does with a bunch of nonsentient cells in one of her internal organs?

Could any literary critic provide such 'to-die-for' certainty about Homer's 'Iliad' or Sophocles' 'Oedipus Rex'? Perhaps they could, but as a society we probably wouldn't afford them special dispensation as a result; in fact, we may even suggest that they are barred from discussion groups on the subject because they have no capacity to admit error when they submit their arguments based on the circular reasoning: that 'they're true because they are based upon truth'.

Ironically, the retreat from literalism makes the fight against such arguments more difficult, because it's been replaced by internal, personal relationships with higher truth. Tactically, it's a brilliant move — even if it is an unconscious one. The thought equivalent of the terror cell. Less a gentleman's battle of armies on the fields at dawn than person-to-person combat with anyone, anywhere, anytime. And don't forget, each of these minds is protected by an 'I'm offended' force-field.

Here's where we find attacks on free speech in the name of freedom of religion, where the idea that 'everyone is entitled to an opinion' prevents critical evaluation of said opinions, where the universality of the Golden Rule becomes the reason to accept all Christian doctrine, and intolerance becomes a byword for any criticism of anybody's views, especially if supernatural causality figures highly in them. Because the legitimacy of these ideas is now found inside the believer's head, the ideas become almost invulnerable, which is not very promising if things need to change.

The best ideas on any map of thought are those that reflect reality well and enable humanity to do better — socially, culturally, and ethically — than the generations preceding it. Now it's quite likely that religious ideas in our distant past enabled strong cohesive groups to form and survive by enabling useful co-operation in the battle for limited resources. However, it stands to reason that systems of conduct that work in small groups may have problems scaling up to cities, nations, and ultimately the whole planet. And then there are the cultural mechanisms that operate between groups. On a small scale, problems are localised and contained; in the twenty-first century, they can be global in a matter of minutes.

While there's relatively little threat of violence in Australia, many religious groups are attempting to marginalise the beliefs and practices of others through various influences over policy-making — of which I've mentioned only a fraction. I haven't detailed the extraordinary tax breaks received by religious groups (perhaps our recent financial crisis could have been quickly solved by removing them), nor have I mentioned their disastrous treatment of Australian Aboriginals, or how widespread the teaching of creationism is in Australian schools. There is such an abundance of religious influence on our political and social structures that it would take a number of volumes to list them.

So consider this book volume one. Australian atheists have decided that morality, ethics, and rights need better, more informed advocates. They have looked critically at these self-appointed institutional moral guardians, and found them wanting. Like many generations before us, we too are prepared to fight for more transparent democratic processes, freedom of speech, human rights, healthcare without doctrine and, crucially, the right to criticise bad ideas. Bad ideas underpinned by belief in things for which there is no evidence, just the dead weight of lukewarm traditions, threatening our ever-burgeoning population's ability to learn, adapt, and change.

NOTES

1. Plimer has appeared on ABC's religious program *Compass* as an atheist, and on an *Intelligence Squared* debate as a defender of religion.
2. P. Kelly, 'A New Kind of True Believer', *The Australian*, 23 August 2006, at www.theaustralian. com.au/news/opinion/a-new-kind-of-true-believer/story-e6frg74x-1111112162391
3. P. Bone, 'Faith Full of Folly', *The Australian*, 18 August 2006, sourced at www.theaustralian. com.au/story/0,20867,20126665-7583,00.html [page no longer available]
4. T. Frame, 'The New Crusade?: militant secularism, strident atheism and social harmony', Australian National University Public Lecture series, flyer at www.anu.edu.au/hrc/ freilich/event_flyers/2008/Screen%200809016%20Frame.pdf. It is also worth noting Frame's article 'Questions Darwinism Cannot Answer', *Brisbane Times*, 9 February 2009, in which he states: 'A dedicated Darwinian would welcome imperialism, genocide, mass deportation, ethnic cleansing, eugenics, euthanasia, forced sterilisations and infanticide'. See www.brisbanetimes.com.au/news/opinion/questions-darwinism-cannot-answer/2009/02/08/1234027847281.html
5. K. Rudd, 'Faith in Politics', *The Monthly*, October 2006, at www.themonthly.com.au/ monthly-essays-kevin-rudd-faith-politics—300
6. J. Perkins and F. Gomez, 'Taxes and Subsidies: the cost of "advancing religion"', *Australian Humanist* 93, Autumn 2009, pp. 6–8. Consider, for instance, that the Jesuit priest Father Frank Brennan was offered the position of Chair of the National Human Rights Consultation Committee, when his views on a range of issues (such as abortion and euthanasia) stem directly from Catholic Church edicts, not from a transparent and evidence-based line of reasoning, as should be the case in a democracy.
7. More information at www.highcourtchallenge.com.
8. 'Doorstop Interview, Pregnancy Support Counselling, Manly Electorate Office, Tuesday 2 January 2007', *Department of Health and Ageing*, at www.health.gov.au/ internet/ministers/publishing.nsf/Content/health-mediarel-yr2007-ta-abb020107. htm?OpenDocument&yr=2007&mth=1
9. 'John Howard's Irving Kristol Lecture', *The Australian*, 6 March 2008, at www.theaustralian. com.au/politics/opinion/john-howards-irving-kristol-lecture/story-e6frgd0x-1111115727675
10. Although adaptation to multiculturalism is being undermined here, too, with the federally supported National Schools Chaplaincy Program.
11. B. Zwartz, 'Gillard Bid to Win Back Christians,' *The Age*, 6 August 2010, at www.theage. com.au/federal-election/gillard-bid-to-win-back-christians-20100805-11krh.html; S. Stephens, 'The Prime Minister Puts Her Faith in Chaplaincy', ABC, 10 August 2010, at www.abc.net.au/news/stories/2010/08/10/2978352.htm
12. 'Pollster Gary Morgan, of Roy Morgan Research, says the PM's atheism hasn't been an issue', cited in J. Elder, 'Will Atheism Spell Trouble for Gillard?,' *The Age*, 18 July 2010 at www.theage.com.au/federal-election/will-atheism-spell-trouble-for-gillard-20100717-10ff0.html

13. OneVote.com.au, at http://onevote.com.au. OneVote describes themselves as: 'OneVote. com.au is an independent, non party specific web site set up by concerned Christians who want nothing more than to keep Christian values in every part of our lives including government, schools and our community.'

14. 'The Prime Minister Puts Her Faith in Chaplaincy'.

15. There is a useful introduction to these ideas at http://en.wikipedia.org/wiki/ Transparent_government

16. 'Faith in Politics'.

17. ibid.

18. The Catholic Church famously took 400 years to admit that Galileo was right: the Earth wasn't the centre of the solar system; the Sun revolved around it, not the other way around.

19. 'A Decline in the Community of Believers', Editorial, *The Age* 27 March 2005, at www.theage.com. au/news/Editorial/A-decline-in-the-community-of-believers/2005/03/26/1111692674302.html

20. D. Marr, 'Our Faith Today', *Sydney Morning Herald*, 19 December 2009, at www.smh.com.au/ national/our-faith-today-20091218-l5w6.html

21. 'Is Your Organisation a Charity?: income tax guide for non-profit organisations', Australian Tax Office, at www.ato.gov.au/nonprofit/content.asp?doc=/Content/34267.htm&page=22

22. 'Cardinal's Threat Over Cloning Bill Under Scrutiny', *The Australian*, at www.theaustralian. com.au/news/nation/pell-comments-to-be-probed-by-nsw-parliament/story-e6frg6nf-1111113757237

23. *News Bulletin*, The Australian Federation of Festival of Light Community Standards Organisations, February 1994, p. 4.

24. R. Fenely, 'Abortion to Blame for Fires: pastor', *Brisbane Times*, 10 February 2009, at www.brisbanetimes.com.au/articles/2009/02/10/1234028017844.html

25. D. Wroe, '"Intelligent Design" an Option: Nelson', *The Age,* 11 August 2005, at www.theage. com.au/articles/2005/08/10/1123353386917.html

26. 'The Wedge', Center for the Renewal of Science and Culture, available for download at www.antievolution.org/features/wedge.pdf. Last accessed 30 March 2010.

27. 'The Prime Minister Puts Her Faith in Chaplaincy'.

28. There's a variety of references here well worth reading, including: M. Metherell, 'Catholics and Carr Wary of School Chaplains Plan', 30 October 2006, at www.smh.com.au/news/ national/catholics-and-carr-wary-of-school-chaplains-plan/2006/10/29/1162056867079. html; C. Overington, 'School Chaplains "Worked Miracles" ', *The Australian*, 6 December 2008, at www.theaustralian.com.au/news/nation/school-chaplains-worked-miracles/ story-e6frg6nf-1111118239078

29. L. Cannold, 'Why Are We Robbing our Littlies to Preach Paul?' *The Sydney Morning Herald*, 16 August 2010, atwww.smh.com.au/opinion/society-and-culture/why-are-we-robbing-our-littlies-to-preach-paul-20100816-125xp.html

30. A. Langmaid, 'All Kids Must Read the Bible, Federal Opposition Leader Tony Abbott Says', *Herald-Sun*, 18 December 2009, at www.heraldsun.com.au/news/national/all-kids-must-read-the-bible-federal-opposition-leader-tony-abbott-says/story-e6frf7l6-1225811885777

31. K. Rudd, *Compass*, ABC TV, aired 8 May 2005.

32. Abbott was at this time the healthcare minister for John Howard, who awarded the Catholic Church's health and welfare arm, Centacare, a $51 million pregnancy counselling contract 'aimed at reducing the number of abortions in Australia'. See http://parlinfo. aph.gov.au:80/parlInfo/download/media/pressrel/1LFE6/upload_binary/1lfe65.pdf;fileTy pe%3Dapplication%2Fpdf. It is worth noting that the 100,000 figure quoted by Abbott is overestimated by over 15,000. See www.lawreform.vic.gov.au/wps/wcm/connect/2022d58 0404a0cac9718fff5f2791d4a/VLRC_Abortion_Report.pdf?MOD=AJPERES.

* PHILOSOPHY

GOOD WITHOUT GOD

Dr Robin Craig
Scientist, philosopher, writer for Australian Mensa, co-founder and managing
director of biotechnology company Genesearch and director of IT company
Thoughtware Australia

SOME TIME AGO, AT A DINNER I ATTENDED, AN INTELLIGENT WOMAN SAID
that, while she did not believe in God, she still sent her children to a
Christian school. When I asked her why, she said that religion is needed to
teach children morality.

The belief that morality requires belief in God is widespread, often
asserted by religious apologists, but, as the example above illustrates, it is
a view also held by many atheists and agnostics. In a sense, it comprises a
'practical' argument for theism: the argument that without God, or at least
belief in God, society would descend into ruins and slaughter. As well as
being an argument for the value of religion, it is also a motive of religious
attacks on diverse secular achievements, from the separation of church
and state to the theory of evolution.

On the face of it, it is a strange claim. Attempts to ground morality in
reason are as old as philosophy itself; for example, it was a major concern
of Socrates, Plato, and Aristotle, among others.[1] So, how did religion come
to be equated with ethics?

An obvious answer is that secular philosophy might have started with
attempts to reach a rational definition of the good life, but it has failed,
and more, it has conceded the case. A key observation, first made in 1740
by David Hume, is that an ought cannot be derived from an is: that is,
knowledge of reality does not have any logical implication for how reality
ought to be, if indeed anything 'ought' to be anything other than what

349

it is.[2] Of course, that includes how people ought to act, which is the subject of ethics. This is called the 'is–ought problem'.

From that starting point, philosophy can only fork into two roads, both well travelled in the centuries since Hume: retreat into faith or acceptance of relative and subjective morality. That is, we can take it as proof of either the inadequacy of reason or the unreality of ethics. The latter might try to ground morality in individual or collective whim, but both are equally subjective — and the end of that road is Sartre's 'If God is dead, everything is permitted', and the nihilist creed that nothing has meaning, purpose, value, or morality. Such conclusions, of course, are the very fuel that feeds the religious fire. Yet, wherever it might lead us, the power of the is–ought problem cannot be ignored, and can be illustrated by applying it to some examples of modern, secular ethical philosophies.

NOMA

Eminent evolutionist Stephen Jay Gould famously put forward 'Non-overlapping Magisteria' (NOMA) as an olive branch between science and religion: the view that science and religion cannot comment on each other's areas of authority.[3] It attempts to free science from religiously motivated suspicion and attack by removing the fear that science undermines religion. However, it does so by ceding the moral high ground to religion, in accepting the claims of religious apologists that religion is not only a source of morality but has the authority to pronounce on such matters. Thus, it is a perfect example of accepting the is–ought dichotomy by removing moral concerns from secular thought and handing them to religious faith.

It is true that science is not directly concerned with moral questions: it is concerned with questions of fact that can be answered by experiments. However, science is an arm of rational, secular thought, a product of the Enlightenment and the power of reason. That science cannot properly answer questions of ethics does not mean that the rational philosophy upon which it is grounded, and of which it is a part, cannot. Further more, even if rational philosophy could not answer questions of morality, that does not mean that religion can. For reason to give up the fight to such an extent that it does not merely say, 'I cannot answer this question', but goes on to add: 'and thus I acknowledge the authority of unreason to answer it', is something that should be viewed with horror by all who recognise the value of reason and the heritage of the Enlightenment. It is to leave to reason the realm of solving practical problems, while handing the questions of what problems to solve and how to live the lives it serves, to the negation of reason.

A THEORY OF JUSTICE

In the 1970s, John Rawls published *A Theory of Justice*, a widely read book of political and ethical theory, which argued that the just, moral way to distribute goods in society is to maximise the position of the least well off.[4] Rawls' argument was that, if people were to choose what system to be born into, in advance of any knowledge about the details of that system, their parents' position, or their own talents, then that is what their self-interest would lead them to choose. This, then, provides a fundamental conception of justice: fair to all because it is removed from self-serving prejudice. It is, after all, far easier to support the divine right of aristocrats to rule when you are one yourself, than it is if you have a 99 per cent chance of being born one of the peasants they live off. Consequently, what might otherwise be conflicting aims of liberty, self-interest, and social justice all converge.

This theory sidesteps the is–ought problem by attempting to derive the ought from an abstract principle of justice.

One could argue against Rawls on many grounds, especially his assertion of what people would and should choose. But its deeper, fatal flaw is that, if there is no ought in an is — how can there be an ought in what the theory itself confesses is not? If the real world cannot lead us to morality, how can a hypothetical state that never did or could exist do it, instead? Effectively, its solution to the is–ought dichotomy is to ignore the is entirely and replace it with a fantasy. But that just removes the resulting ethics even further from reality, therefore divorcing them from truth.

THE ETHICS OF PAIN

Another respected secular thinker is Peter Singer, who derives rights from the utilitarian principle of minimising suffering. Thus, in *Animal Liberation* (1975), he argued that animals have rights based on their ability to feel pain.[5]

This attempt is an improvement over Rawls', in at least trying to derive ethical principles from the real rather than the imaginary. Again, one could argue against it on various grounds. For example, we are told that, because we are morally equivalent to animals, we have to be concerned about the fate of animals though they don't have to care about each other at all. Thus, the argument relies on us having something animals do not have; while using that fact to negate itself. And if the relief of pain is the basis of morality, this theory is nowhere near good enough. Why is it not our moral duty to wipe all carnivores from the face of the — Earth, indeed, to wipe out all species whose members are incapable of treating their own and other kinds with moral kindness? What people do to animals is trivial in comparison to what they do to each other.

But also again, there are deeper flaws inherent in the very attempt to derive ethics in this way: the theory falls at the hurdle of the is–ought problem. Yes, animals feel pain, but why should that imply moral precepts? If I have empathy for animals — misguided or not — well, that may affect how I behave towards them. But it is no grounds for an ethical theory. What, in the fact that animals can suffer, means I should do anything about it — especially anything more than the animals themselves do about it?

That last point is a key. How things are in reality cannot tell us how things should be. So how can the way animals do not respond to the fact of pain guide us better? Yes, animals feel pain and attempt to avoid it (that is what pain is for), but they couldn't care less about each other's pain. If you have ever seen a cat play with a mouse, killer whales playing ping-pong with a seal, or the total unconcern of animals in a drought for the fate of their fellows, you will see what animals themselves think of Singer's theory. Thus, as with Rawls' theory, it is an attempt to ground ethics, not in what actually happens in reality, but in what specifically does not. And therein lies its most fundamental flaw.

The only link between is and ought in this theory is a feeling of pity. But this does not give us an objective link: it simply attempts to raise personal pity to the status of an ethical absolute, to make personal feelings the basis of moral commandments, and to marshal enough similar pity in others to impose itself on the rest of humanity. But if feelings are the basis of our morality, then we have nothing but the illusion of objectivity, and no grounds for rational discussion with those who feel differently.

EVOLUTIONARY ETHICS

At the other end of the spectrum from Gould are secular thinkers who explicitly address a scientific basis of ethics. A good example of this trend is Michael Shermer's *The Science of Good and Evil* (2004), which attempts to understand morality in terms of our evolutionary past.[6]

In particular, Shermer argues that good (cooperation, altruism, helping family and neighbours) and evil (xenophobia, war, murder, rape, and pillage) are two behavioural sides of the same nature. We owe both to ape ancestors who lived in small groups and who, in order to survive, had to both help and compete with each other within those groups, while resisting the depredations of enemies that included other groups of the same species. Drawing from a wide field of evolutionary thought, Shermer argues that altruism and selfishness, kindness and cruelty, and honesty and dishonesty, are behavioural tendencies inherited from our prehuman past.

As a tool for learning the detailed facts of reality, science is unsurpassed. Unfortunately, increasing the depth and detail of our understanding of what 'is' does not give us any better link to what ought to be. And so, even if we agree with all his assumptions, Shermer's thesis, like the others, does not survive Hume's is–ought problem. For example, why are some aspects of our ancestors' mode of life good and others evil? Surely they are equally good or evil — if those terms even apply. A mere evolutionary explanation is no tool for moral evaluations, let alone ethical prescriptions.

The most cursory view of history illustrates the problem. The ancient Greeks, and even more so the Romans after them saw no contradiction between instituting a civilised way of life within their own communities, while simultaneously engaging in conquest, looting, and enslavement abroad. Look at any society of the past and the same pattern emerges: Shermer's 'good and evil' are visible in every culture, and those cultures accept both as not only the norm but as virtuous, too. That is, it is virtuous to be good to your friends — and equally virtuous to give your enemies no quarter. These were people like us, yet they saw no conflict between loving their families, on the one hand, and casual brutality to outsiders, on the other.

It is worth pointing out that this is not some flaw peculiar to secular morality. Religious morality is no better: 'Go and attack the Amalekites and completely destroy everything they have. Don't leave a thing; kill all the men, women, children and babies; the cattle, sheep, camels and donkeys', ordered God in 1 Samuel 15:3 — just one example of many similar cases. And while Jesus may have preached a gentler, kinder morality, the history of his church shows how easy it is for religion to preach kindness while it is living under the sword, and then how easily it reverts to type when it holds that sword.

TOWARDS A SOLUTION

Let us grant, for a moment, the proposition that there is truly no morality outside of religion. That would imply that, in reality, there is no reason to live a life of honesty or justice, and every reason to live by theft, murder, rape, and pillage.

Most people, if faced with such a conclusion, would understandably cry that they cannot live that way, that it is a prescription for disaster.

They would be right. To see why, consider that people cannot exist by browsing off trees in an untouched environment. Everything we require, at least for lives beyond the quality and quantity of that of monkeys, requires production over a span of time: from the growing of food to the building of houses, to the invention of aeroplanes and television. There is no escaping this fundamental. Even criminals, who choose to live by theft and violence, are dependent on it: without people who produce, they would have no victims to plunder in order to feed themselves.

So if human life is to exist with any quality worth living, people must live together in such away that production is rewarded and depredation defended against. It is no accident that so much of morality is concerned with just that: people need morality to live. But now we have reached a conundrum. Our survey of secular ethics has shown the deep power of the is–ought problem to derail diverse attempts to derive a rational morality. And on the face of it, it is true: no amount of description can imply ethical prescription: what is simply is, immune to value judgements. Yet we have identified a crucial requirement for morality in human life. Are we then forced to agree with theists that in order to live we need morality, but that reason leaves us powerless to achieve it?

LIVING PROOF

What might sound like secular ethics' final surrender names its own solution. There is, in fact, a link between what is and what ought to be, and that link is the conditional nature of life.

Life has three relevant, intertwined qualities.

First, it is fragile. A fundamental law of existence is the law of entropy: left to themselves, all systems become more disordered with time. But life is characterised by maintaining and increasing order. And it is no simple task to achieve it. Living things are built on enormously complex and delicate interacting systems, from the organic macromolecule that make up your cells to the organ systems that make up your body, all acting together to extract energy from the environment and apply that energy in a directed fashion to build, maintain, and multiply those very systems. Any failure in those systems, whether from malfunction, loss of resources, or attack from without, and the organism dies. The atoms it was made of continues, but its life ceases to exist.

Second, life is self-directed action. What living things have to do to survive is done by those living things themselves, for that very purpose. The very and sole reason those complex, delicate systems exist is to continue that existence. Thus, for all life's fragility, it is tenacious. Every living cell in your body is, in a real sense, nearly four billion years old: each can be traced through an unbroken chain of living cells back to the first life to appear on Earth.

Third, each type of living thing has its own requirements to stay alive, set by that organism's nature. Thus, an amoeba, a plant, a cow, a dog, and a human being all have quite different needs — those needs are set by their natures, and their natures are geared to meeting those needs.

Thus there is a simple, logical link between is and ought: if you want to live, then you have to act as the reality of your nature demands.

This is, of course, dependent on wanting to live. Fortunately, reality is again on our side. Every living thing 'wants' to live, even if the 'want' is simply biochemical programming, as in bacteria: otherwise, you would not be the end product of those four billion years of continuous life. In other words, it is the nature of life to seek its own continued existence (including via reproduction, as all individual organisms must die).

Plants and animals have no choice in this. They cannot decide to act against their own lives; they just do what they do, according to the dictates of their nature. People are in a different category, because we think. The proof is, of all the creatures on Earth, it is only you and your fellows who worry about these questions, who can read and understand this book you are reading; it is only human beings who care about morality and 'the meaning of life', because all other animals have neither awareness nor choice about those things. The ability to think and to choose your values by thinking about them is the basis of free will, so you are not forced to choose to live. However, there is, quite literally, every reason to want to live. Reality is all there is. There is nothing outside of it, no values, no happiness, no hope, nothing but the zero of non-existence. On the scales of the decision between life and death, there is all that exists on one side, and absolutely nothing on the other.

That does not mean it is never rational to want to die. The 'all that exists' may be unbearable, so the zero of nothingness is preferable. But then your choice is to die. Every second you choose to delay that death is your choice to live and therefore to bind yourself to the principle of life: 'if you want to live, then you must act accordingly'. The residue of Hume's is–ought problem remains: nothing in reality forces you to choose life, and nothing in reality forces you, having chosen life, to act as that life truly requires. These are matters of choice — if they weren't, if you were as automatically rational as a plant is automatic in seeking the sun, then there would be no need for morality, which presupposes choice between alternative actions. But you must choose something, and you must do something, and you can escape neither the necessity of choice nor the consequences of acting wrongly.

FOUNDATION

The is–ought problem is a powerful wrecking ball for demolishing the foundations of any theory that ignores it. But the principle of life has even greater power: by solving the is–ought problem, it gives us the foundation upon which we can build an objective, secular theory of ethics.

Those ethics comprise the answer to the question: what are the fundamental requirements of human life? That is an objective question, as objective as any science, because, like the principle of life itself, it depends entirely on reality: on the nature of human beings, on our particular method of survival.

We are not concerned here with the autonomic functions of our bodies. They just happen, and ethics is concerned with what we ought to do; that is, with chosen actions. And the fundamental voluntary requirement of human life is thinking. Everything that we have above the population density and quality of life of apes in an untamed wilderness is the product of the thinking mind. Everything from stone tools to agriculture, to metallurgy, all the way to science, aeroplanes, electronics, and modern medicine, is the result of someone applying their reason to determine the facts of reality and to adapt those facts to the end of improving their lives.

Therefore, there are two things that reality requires if we are to survive: we must think, and we must be able to apply and enjoy the results of our thought. If we do not think, we must at least live off the thinking of others, or die. And as the purpose of thinking is to create the values that support our lives, we must be able to use them for our benefit.

The power of reason is illustrated by how far we have come in the last 100,000 years, the last 5000, the last 100. But what is it about reason that gives it its power? The sole power of reason is to make our thinking consistent with reality: reason is how we discover truth, how we identify in our own minds what is or is not out there in reality. This might seem fragile, but it is enough, as life is conditional on acting in accordance with the demands of reality.

This gives us a clue to the more detailed meaning of what it means to live by reason: it is to choose to live, as far as you are able, consistently with the nature of reality. Reality then determines the fundamental values we need to pursue and the virtues that requires. Ayn Rand, who first articulated the principle of life (at least explicitly, fully, and consistently), defined values as that which we act to gain and/or keep, and virtues as the actions required to achieve them. In that context, she wrote:

My morality, the morality of reason, is contained in a single axiom: existence exists — and in a single choice: to live. The rest proceeds from these. To live, man must hold three things as the supreme and ruling values of his life: Reason — Purpose — Self-esteem. Reason, as his only tool of knowledge — Purpose, as his choice of the happiness which that tool must proceed to achieve — Self-esteem, as his inviolate certainty that his mind is competent to think and his person is worthy of happiness, which means: is worth of living. These three values imply and require all of man's virtues, and all his virtues pertain to the relation of existence and consciousness: rationality, independence, integrity, honesty, justice, productiveness, pride.[7]

A full explanation of why such virtues are 'implied and required' is beyond the scope of this essay and should be pursued in the works of Rand and the Objectivist philosophers who followed her.[8] But the basic principles can be summarised easily. If reason is our tool of survival, then rationality, the choice to actually use and live by reason to the fullest extent you can, is necessarily your highest virtue. Independence is the recognition that it is your reason, your mind, and your efforts on which your life fundamentally depends — as it is your brain in your head that is your tool of survival and your actions whose purpose it is to direct. Integrity is acting consistently with your own beliefs, the content of your own mind: for, if you disconnect your reason from your actions, then you separate reason from its purpose, and act against the truth you have identified. Honesty is keeping your actions consistent with your words, and without it reality and other people's reason become your enemies and a perpetual threat to your goals — a game you cannot win. Justice is treating people as, in fact, they deserve, just as you must treat all things in accordance with their nature. Productiveness is the application of reason to creating the requirements of your life, which is the purpose of reason and why it is a value. Pride is the recognition that your life is, and should be, your highest value, but that value must be earned and defended.

By the nature of life, which is self-directed action for its own continuance, it is your own life that is your fundamental value. You do not exist for the sake of other people — and they do not exist for the sake of you. Certainly you can, and should, help other people whose lives and happiness are a value to you. But a life of reason does not demand the sacrifice of some for the unearned benefit of others, for there is no reason you can point to in reality, for why someone can rightly demand such a sacrifice or their victims should agree to it. This ethics could be called rational self-interest, except that the first word is redundant: the only way to achieve one's interests, in reality, is by a life of rationality.

The identification of our fundamental requirement for life — the free use of our thinking mind — implies our rights, which are the inalienable conditions we can and should, morally demand of anyone who wishes to deal with us. Consequently, the only moral interactions between people are voluntary: the use of physical force is anathema to reason. Thus, the basic principle of politics demanded by this morality is individual rights — meaning every person must be allowed to live according to their own reason, with other people banned from forcing them to do otherwise. Certainly, people can choose to do otherwise — that is what criminals do. But then they are acting not for life but for death (not only yours but, in the long run, their own), and you have every right to resist.

RELIGION AND MORALITY

Thus, contrary to claims of a religious monopoly on ethics, we can develop an objective, secular ethics. These ethics are not based on minimising suffering or escaping pain, nor are they grounded in the social psychology of prehuman ancestors: their basis is life, its purpose is happiness, and they are defined by what makes us uniquely human — our thinking mind.

And if there is an objective basis for ethics, then there is an objective basis for evaluating religious ethics — and it does poorly. The fundamental quality of religion is that it is based on faith, meaning belief without, indeed in spite of, evidence and proof (once it is based on evidence from the world of perception, it is independent of any religious origin). Then, even if specific religious tenets have some basis in reason and the requirements for life, the very act of making them religious commandments removes them from the realm of the reasonable. For example, if it is good for you to take a day of rest every week, then you can accept that idea and apply it within the overall goals of your life. But make it a religious commandment, and it changes from a good idea to a tool of death: 'Anyone who does any work on [the Sabbath] day is to be put to death. Do not even light a fire in your homes' (Exodus 35:2–3).

As that example illustrates, faith's inherent quality of being beyond reason means there is no arguing with its precepts or its conclusions. If the scriptures you believe in say, 'thou shalt not eat pork or lobster', then you can't, however much modern science and hygiene might trump any rationale there may have been for such prohibitions thousands of years ago. And where faith cannot convince, yet it names dissent as evil, its only recourse is to physical force. So it is neither coincidence nor anomaly that, whenever religion achieves secular power, force is what it applies. Thus, a religion that starts with 'blessed are the meek' ends up burning Giordano Bruno at the stake for making scientific hypotheses that harmed nobody and threatened nothing except the irrational prejudices of the faithful.

But that is not the worst of it. Reason sets life, values, and happiness as your proper goals, with rationality as your highest virtue and the right to think and act independently, free from physical force, as your inalienable right. Yet religion demands sacrifice in this life in order to focus on an unseen afterlife — faith in the unseen and incomprehensible as its justification, and obedience backed by threats of eternal damnation as its end. If there is a God behind religion, we would have to judge Him not as the highest good in the universe, but as the sworn enemy of mankind.

Theists would claim that men have no right to judge God — an argument God himself is credited with when justifying his appalling treatment of Job (Job 38–41). But do we really have any choice about it? Socrates once asked, 'Is what is holy holy because the gods approve it, or do they approve it because it is holy?' Following that line of argument leads us to the conclusion:

Either goodness cannot be explained simply by reference to what the gods want, or else it is an empty tautology to say that the gods are good — in which case the praise of the gods would simply be a matter of power-worship. As Leibniz put it ... Those who believe that God has established good and evil by an arbitrary decree ... deprive God of the designation good: for what cause could one have to praise him for what he does, if in doing something quite different he would have done equally well?[9]

Thus theistic ethics, far from being the only possible source of morality, contradict objective morality in practice and are reduced to abject power worship in principle. Hence, the supposed source of absolute morality gives us no objective means to judge between the man whose faith leads him to defend the innocent and the man whose faith tells him it is a neat idea to fly passenger planes into skyscrapers. Both believe God told him so and, if feelings, faith, and sacrifice are our benchmark, who is the greater believer?

Of course, we are not actually judging God. God is not here. What we are judging are the claims of men who say they speak for God, or perhaps our own personal feelings about God. And we have a perfect right, indeed responsibility, to judge the truth of those. If someone says that you dare not question God, it is his own words or feelings he is trying to hide from the judgement of reason.

Therefore, far from needing religion to give us morality, the answer to the is–ought problem not only shows us a morality whose end is life and whose tool is reason, but it also turns the argument on its head. It actually gives us a powerful moral argument against theism — not so much against the concept of God, but against the particular beliefs in God that men claim as true. If a religion teaches us a morality that is at odds with the objective morality of life, then that religion is anti-life, and therefore wrong — factually, and morally.

NOTES

1. W. Windelband, *A History of Philosophy*, Paper Tiger, New Jersey, 2001, pp. 72–87, 116–154.
2. Book III, Part I, Section I in D. Hume, *A Treatise of Human Nature*, Penguin Classics, London, 1985.
3. S. J. Gould, 'Nonoverlapping Magisteria', *Natural History* 106, March 1997, pp. 16–22.
4. J. Rawls, *A Theory of Justice*, Harvard University Press, Massachusetts, 1999.
5. P. Singer, *Animal Liberation*, Random House, New York, 1975.
6. M. Shermer, *The Science of Good and Evil: why people cheat, gossip, care, share, and follow the golden rule*, Times Books, New York, 2004.
7. A. Rand, *Atlas Shrugged*, Signet, New York, 1992, p. 944.
8. A. Rand, *The Virtue of Selfishness*, Signet, New York, 1964; L. Peikoff, *Objectivism: the philosophy of Ayn Rand*, Penguin, London, 1991; A. Bernstein, *The Capitalist Manifesto*, University Press of America, Maryland, 2005; T. Smith. *Ayn Rand's Normative Ethics: the virtuous egoist*, Cambridge University Press, 2006.
9. A. Gottlieb, 'Socrates', in *The Great Philosophers* (ed. R. Monk & F. Raphael), 2000, pp. 28–29.

ATHEISM AS A SPIRITUAL PATH

Ian Robinson
Philosopher, educator, editor, author, President of the
Rationalist Society of Australia

PEOPLE COMMIT THEMSELVES TO RELIGION FOR ALL KINDS OF REASONS: some because they were born into it; some because they came under the influence of a charismatic teacher; some because they felt lost in the world, and religion seemed to offer a solid foundation, or they felt frightened, and religion seemed to offer comfort; some because they simply wanted to feel they belonged. And there are some who come to religion as a result of genuinely embarking on a spiritual quest, seeking a spiritual path.

While honouring that intention, I believe that, in stopping at religion, such people have not gone far enough on the journey. Anyone embarking seriously and rigorously on a spiritual quest, setting off diligently along a spiritual path, if they are tenaciously honest about it, must arrive sooner or later at atheism.

'Following a spiritual path', or 'embarking on a spiritual quest', are of course metaphors for devoting a significant part of your life to seeking answers to what are called, also metaphorically, 'the big questions', for example: Why are we here? Why is there something rather than nothing? What is the meaning of life, the universe, and everything? Is there a unity behind the multitudinous variety of the universe? Can we connect to a greater reality, and honour the awe and reverence we feel, as we contemplate the universe and human existence?

If we are going to take these questions seriously, and not merely use them as props to shore up our pre-existing beliefs and prejudices, we

364 THE AUSTRALIAN BOOK OF ATHEISM

must embark on this journey without any preconceptions as to what the answer might be. And in particular we must not assume that the answer necessarily entails the existence of two spheres or levels of being — the so-called material and the so-called spiritual. The question of whether this is, or is not, the case is precisely at the heart of the spiritual quest; it cannot be a presupposition on which the quest is based. If the spiritual quest is the quest for the essence of 'life, the universe, and everything', then it must be an open question as to what this essence involves, and we cannot assume the existence of a separate spiritual realm from the start.

In other words, belief in a god is not a prerequisite for asking the big questions, but merely one aspect of a possible partial answer. In fact, some have held that adherence to a religion, far from facilitating the spiritual quest, precludes or truncates it, because answers to the above questions are already given within most religious frameworks, and raising such 'difficult' questions rigorously within the religious context can often lead to persecution, or even death.

By contrast, many if not most atheists came to their belief in atheism precisely because they confronted these questions in a rigorous manner. They came to their assertion of atheism at the end of, rather than at the start of, a spiritual journey, a quest for the truth about life and the universe.

Our starting point in this quest must be affirming the existence of the material world, the world of common sense. All of us rely on it every minute of the day, and it is affirmed by, and implicit in, most of our actions, from the use of technology and medicine to enhance our lives to the ingesting of food and the breathing of air to stay alive.

However, many people claim we cannot seek the answers to our 'big questions' in this material world. They point to the existence of another level of reality, a spiritual realm, as the only place where the answers to the 'big questions' may be found. The idea that there is such a realm is at the heart of most religions, so we need to seriously explore this possibility.

The first thing to notice is that, in proposing the possibility of a spiritual realm over and above the physical, we are already moving away from our original idea of finding an explanatory unity, a single underlying mode of being. We are saying there is not just one thing, the universe, but there are two things, the universe and the spiritual realm, so the hope of finding a unity, a oneness, is abandoned.

The second thing to notice is that there is no support for the existence of such a realm from common sense or from science. Every effort to find convincing scientific evidence for any supernatural forces or entities has failed; every initially promising experience of the spiritual realm has been found on closer, more rigorous examination to be illusory. I do not have space to argue for this here, but see for example Andrew Neher's *Paranormal and Transcendental Experience: a psychological examination* (1990).[1]

Thirdly, whatever our professed beliefs may be, we live most aspects of our lives as if there were no spiritual realm. When an engineer is designing a bridge, she takes account of gravitational forces, but she doesn't allow for the impact of spiritual forces. When an architect is designing a church or a mosque, she relies entirely on physical structures to carry the weight of the roof; she doesn't factor in a proportion of the load to be borne by God. When an accountant is doing a balance sheet, she doesn't have a column for transcendental income, pennies from heaven.

I think it is very clear that if we base our conclusions solely on science and common sense, which are our normal sources of knowledge, then we would have to accept that there is no such thing as a spiritual realm.

However, for many religious people this argument is just not good enough. For them, if science cannot reveal God then so much the worse for science. They claim to find a spiritual reality through other channels: the medium of religious experiences, inner inspirations, and intuitions. They are certain that the spiritual realm exists because they claim direct experience of it, and they adhere with great strength to this belief.

But for the person rigorously pursuing a spiritual path and assiduously seeking the truth, personal experience cannot, in itself, and in the absence of other evidence, be a reliable guide to the truth. They will be aware of the long history of such claims being shown to be false and the many ways in which our biases, our preconceptions, our expectations, and our wishes and desires can distort our perceptions.

In the first place, the rigorous seeker will know that, as the great Indian philosopher Sarvepalli Radhakrishnan pointed out in his influential book *An Idealist View of Life* (1932), there is really no such thing as a direct inner experience, of a spiritual or of any other non-subjective reality: 'Ideas which seem to come to us with compelling force, without any mediate intellectual process of which we are aware' are all 'unconsciously interpreted' and 'determined by hereditary and culture'.[2] Thus, Hindus don't have visions of the Virgin Mary, and Christians don't have visions of the Buddha.

Moreover, he or she will know that the degree of certainty some people feel about their perceptions is no guarantee of veracity. Psychological research has demonstrated that there is no correlation between the amount of certainty a person feels about their account of their experiences and the objective accuracy of that account.

Thirdly, since every person's account of their inner experience of the spiritual is different, how will a spiritual seeker know which ones to accept? For example, if I have highly intense and protracted mystical experiences during which I feel that I am in touch with the essence of everything that exists, and I tell you that, on the basis of my experience, there is no spiritual realm, no God, while someone else has an equally intense mystical experience in which Krishna or the Virgin Mary appears to them in resplendent glory, and they are equally adamant that there is a spiritual realm, there is no way anyone can tell, on the basis of our accounts alone, which of us is right. The delusional experiences of psychotics, which we know to be false, seem just as real to them as the spiritual vision does to the believer.

Experience alone cannot, for the rigorous seeker of truth, be a warrant for veracity. If we have no way of choosing between such experiences, we have no valid reason to choose any one of them. For this reason, human beings have developed an extensive intellectual apparatus for subjecting our fallible experiences to various tests of veracity. Although there is no ultimate and comprehensive set of such rules or procedures, there are many sets of principles, such as the rules of logic, principles of reasoning, like Ockham's razor, and the methodology of scientific investigation, which, applied appropriately, tend to ensure that beliefs based on our experiences are true enough.

Of course, we need to exercise judgement about how far in any instance it is appropriate to apply such standards. With trivial or non-controversial claims, we would tend to be more accepting. But with issues of cosmic significance, such as a person claiming to experience a being called God who created and continues to maintain the universe, and requires our worship, we would expect that person to have very considerable non-subjective evidence that supported the claimed experience.

In the end, the seeker for truth is driven towards science-fiction writer Philip K. Dick's dictum: 'Reality is that which, when you stop believing in it, doesn't go away'.[3] The salient fact is that when you stop believing in the spiritual realm and in God, they do go away, so we can safely conclude they are not real.

Religious believers can all see this clearly enough with respect to supernatural beliefs that are different to their own. In this sense, they are all atheists except about one last god, the one they believe in. But if you are serious about the spiritual path, you need to let go of this last delusion and become an atheist.

The history of the human species is a history of relinquishing such spiritual or supernatural delusions. Early humans believed they could see a plethora of supernatural beings everywhere. Every feature of the landscape, every animal, even every bush and stone had a spirit in it. With the rise of the early civilisations, we became more sophisticated, and pared our deities down to a manageable group in the sky, such as the Greek Pantheon. This, in turn, was eventually whittled down to the idea of the 'One God' of monotheism. Finally, in the wake of the Enlightenment, the rigorous seekers began to see there was no sign of God or the spiritual anywhere, and they became atheists.

In this case, ontogeny does seem to recapitulate phylogeny. The trajectory of most people's spiritual development has been this same journey from the many to the one, and finally to none. In childhood we have many 'gods' — in the Christian West, not just God the Father and Jesus and possibly the Virgin Mary, but also Santa Claus, the Easter Bunny, the Tooth Fairy, and our own private invisible friend. As we mature, we gradually divest ourselves of most of them until we are left with the Trinity or with Allah. Finally, some of us, if we follow this typical trend, will become atheists.

This idea of letting go as a feature of the spiritual path was put forward over 2000 years ago by the ancient Chinese philosopher, Lao Tsu, in the *Dao De Ching*, or *The Book of the Way and its Virtue*:

In the pursuit of learning, every day something is added on.
In the pursuit of the Way, every day something is left behind.[4]

For those on the spiritual path, seeking a spiritual Way, one of the things that must finally be left behind is the idea of God.

So we're thrown back on the material world for the answers to the 'big questions' that sent us out on the spiritual quest in the first place. How does it fare? I can do no more than sketch possible answers here.

Is there a unity behind the multitudinous variety of the universe? Yes. If we discard the dualism inherent in religion and other claims for the supernatural, then there is ultimately only the physical universe, which one day human beings hope to explain with a discrete number of laws and maybe even a TOE (or Theory of Everything). But probably not in our lifetime.

Why are we here? We are here because of a remarkable series of coincidences that led from the initial 'Big Bang' to the expansion of the universe, the formation of the planet Earth, the emergence of life, the evolution of the human species, and the long sequence of fortunate matings by our ancestors that led to each individual's eventual birth and maturity. The chances of us not being here are astronomical, but then the universe is astronomically big, so that improves the odds considerably. Some people believe this means that we couldn't be here without God's help. But this is to confuse probability with ontology. Someone once worked out that if you spent $50 a week on lotto tickets you should win on average once every one hundred and fifty years. But the thing is, that once could just as easily be the first time as the 7,800th time, so to win with your first ticket is not in conflict with the laws of probability. So our existence is in no way an argument for the existence of God, but certainly makes a case for awe and wonder at the universe.

What is the meaning of life [the universe and everything]? In order to answer this question we first need to consider what the idea of life [or the universe] having a meaning involves. Life — the phenomenon, not the word — doesn't have meaning in the linguistic sense that a word, for example 'cup', has meaning (meaning that is given to the sounds represented by the three letter combination c—u—p by users of the English language). When we ask, 'What is the meaning of life?', we are not asking for this dictionary kind of meaning. I think what we are doing is asking such questions as, 'What is the purpose of life?' or 'What is the significance of life?' or 'What is the value of life?'. We can ask the same sorts of questions of our cup. It certainly has a purpose — to hold liquids of various kinds and to be a vehicle for conveying them to the mouth for drinking. It has value — both monetary value (especially if it is Royal Doulton, for example), and practical value as a container for fluids. It may be significant, especially if it is the Premiership Cup or the cup your grandfather gave you when you turned ten.

However, all these forms of 'meaning' are imposed on the cup from the outside, by the human beings that use it. Human beings typically give such 'meaning' to most of the things around them. The question is, who or what can give such 'meaning' to human life? The religious answer is that the meaning comes from outside us, as with the cup, and that the meaning of our lives is given to us by God or some other 'spiritual' presence. However, as we have established that there is no sound evidence that such a separate spiritual reality exists, we must give our own lives meaning: we must decide the purpose or purposes of our lives, we must decide to place a value on our own life and those of others, we must decide that we and other human beings are significant. It seems to me that the atheist answer, that human beings give meaning to their own lives, is far more satisfying than the religious answer, that the meaning of our lives is imposed from the outside by a deity. The latter seems to put us in the same passive position as the cup, the meaning of which is only given by those who use it.

Why is there something rather than nothing? Because, as Nobel Prize-winning physicist Frank Wilczek tells us, 'nothing' is an unstable state, and thus, the transition nothing-to-something is quite a natural one, not requiring any external agent. Something, rather than nothing, is what we should expect, and our expectations are not disappointed.

Can we connect to a greater reality and honour the awe and reverence we feel as we contemplate the universe and human existence? The best way I could find of describing my own 'mystical' experience referred to earlier was that I fell in love with the universe. So it was with a sense of recognition that many years later I encountered in the late Bobby Solomon's stimulating book *Spirituality for the Skeptic* (2006) his characterisation of what he calls 'naturalised spirituality': 'the thoughtful love of life'.[5] According to Solomon, spirituality both requires thought and thoughtfulness, but also 'has everything to do with passion and the passions of life'. And it is not just a conclusion, a bare set of philosophic truths. 'How we think and feel about ourselves has an impact on who we actually are,' says Solomon. 'Spirituality must also be understood in terms of the transformations of the self.' Connecting to a greater reality and honouring the awe and reverence we feel as we contemplate the universe and human existence is what the thoughtful love of life entails.

Thus atheism can provide cogent answers to all the 'big questions' that generated the spiritual quest. Of course it cannot do some of the other things that draw people to religion. Atheism cannot provide comfort — it tells us 'we are incidental, accidental. Far from being the raison d'être of the universe, we appeared through sheer happenstance, and we could vanish in the same way. This is not a comforting viewpoint ...' [6] Atheism cannot offer the afterlife as a hedge against the fear of death. Although most of the atheists I know are friendly enough people, atheism cannot enfold you in the adrenaline rush of belonging that you find in singing 'Jesus loves me, this I know' with others at a charismatic church gathering. However, if you are genuinely following a spiritual path, you will seek the truth no matter how it makes you feel. In the words of Ayaan Hirsi Ali:

> The only position that leaves me with no cognitive dissonance is atheism. It is not a creed. Death is certain, replacing both the siren-song of Paradise and the dread of Hell. Life on this earth, with all its mystery and beauty and pain, is then to be lived far more intensely: we stumble and get up, we are sad, confident, insecure, feel loneliness and joy and love. There is nothing more; but I want nothing more. [7]

I invite anyone reading this who is truly seeking spiritual enlightenment, and has not already done so, to abandon the last of their illusions and become an atheist.

NOTES

1. A. Neher, *Paranormal and Transcendental Experience: a psychological examination*, Dover, 1990.
2. S. Radhakrishnan, *An Idealist View of Life*, George Allen and Unwin Limited, London, 1932, p. 98.
3. P. K. Dick, 'How to Build a Universe That Doesn't Fall Apart Two Days Later', 1978, text available at http://deoxy.org/pkd_how2build.htm

4. Lao Tsu, *Dao De Ching*, Chapter 48, author's translation.
5. R. C. Solomon, *Spirituality for the Skeptic: the thoughtful love of life,* Oxford University Press, 2002.
6. J. Horgan: 'Buddhist Retreat: why I gave up on finding my religion', *Slate,* at http://slate.msn.com/id/2078486
7. A. Hirsi Ali. 'How (and Why) I Became an Infidel' in Christopher Hitchens (ed.) *The Portable Atheist,* Da Capo Press, 2007, pp. 477–80.

ATHEISM AND THE MEANING OF LIFE

Professor Peter Woolcock
Adjunct Senior Research Fellow in the Division of Education, Arts, and
Social Sciences at the University of South Australia

A STORY TOLD ABOUT THE FAMOUS ATHEIST PHILOSOPHER BERTRAND
Russell is an appropriate place to begin. 'Only the other evening,' a London
taxi driver is reported to have said, 'I picked up Bertrand Russell, and
I said to him, "Well, Lord Russell, what's it all about?" And, do you know,
he couldn't tell me.'[1]

A conclusion we might be inclined to draw from this story is that, if
an atheist of Bertrand Russell's philosophical acumen cannot answer this
question, then atheism doesn't have much to offer anyone who wants to
know the meaning of life. Maybe we would be better off looking for an
answer in theism, that is, in one of the many systems that assert the
existence of a god or gods. I intend to show that this optimism about
theism's capacity to do better than atheism is unwarranted. Showing this
will take us some time, which may well explain why Bertrand Russell
declined to launch into the enterprise during a short taxi trip.

Just before we do this, however, it will be useful to say briefly what I will
mean by the term 'atheism'. The Collins Dictionary defines it as 'rejection
of belief in God or gods'. This, of course, is perfectly correct. However, one
can reject belief in God or gods for all kinds of reasons, for example, that
it is inconvenient, or uncomfortable, or dangerous, or because one can't be
bothered thinking it through. None of these are the kind of atheism I have
in mind. My concern will be with atheism as the rejection of belief in God
or gods on the basis of evidence and argument. It is a position arrived at

on the basis of reasoning aimed at arriving at truth. The kinds of reasons that lead one to reject as untrue all claims that God or gods exist are also likely to lead one to reject the existence of any form of the supernatural, such as the Buddhist notion of karma and most versions of life after death. I shall stretch the notion of atheism, therefore, to include rejection of any form of the supernatural.

MEANING AS PURPOSE

What is it, then, that worries people about the meaning of life in a godless world? One concern is that unless there is a god, there is no purpose behind the existence of the universe and, in particular, no purpose behind human life. The feeling appears to be that their own lives have a purpose only if human life can be shown to have a purpose. Is this so?

Some religious people believe that God created humans as part of a plan he has for the universe as a whole, his plan being such as to give each of us a special role to play. These people find the meaning of their lives lies in uncovering precisely what God wants them to do and then putting this into effect. This kind of view can be found within Christianity, Judaism, and Islam. Even the caste system of Hinduism has a supernatural underpinning, although it doesn't appear to be tied to any particular god.

People who hold this kind of view are faced with a number of challenges. The first challenge, of course, is to satisfy themselves that the God (or supernatural power) that they believe in really does exist. If he doesn't, then clearly he cannot supply their lives with the meaning they expect. The second challenge is to satisfy themselves that they have arrived at the correct account of what role he wants them to play in his plan. This seems to imply that he has chosen to bless them, rather than the rest of us, with privileged insight into his intentions. If they are wrong about this, they will be mistaken about what meaning their life actually holds.

But even if these two challenges are met, there is still a third one. Why take upon oneself a meaning for one's life formulated by someone else, even if that someone else is God? After all, there have been many cases in human history of leaders of nations formulating a meaning for the lives of their citizens — the glory of the French nation in the case of Napoleon, the dominance of the German peoples in the case of Hitler, the triumph of communism in the case of Lenin. Each of these led to the deaths of millions of people and to untold suffering. Just because their leaders had such a role in mind for them was surely not a sufficient reason for those citizens to endorse that role. These citizens had to decide for themselves whether or not they agreed the plan containing that role, whether their compliance with the plan should be willing or whether they would have to be coerced. Likewise, just because God has a role for us to perform we do not thereby lose our freedom to decide whether or not to adopt that role. As the atheist philosopher Jean-Paul Sartre reminded us, insofar as we are rational human agents we are all 'condemned to be free'.[2] We cannot escape the responsibility for our voluntary choices by saying that this is what someone else wanted us to do. In the end, if we willingly adopt that role, we do so because we believe that it is a good thing to do.

The theist may reply that, by definition, the God they believe in is all-powerful, all-knowing and all-good. If God has developed a purpose for the universe in which humans have a role, then the actions required to fulfil that role have to be morally good ones. An all-good God would not have given our lives a bad or evil meaning. This reply, however, is of no help to the theist because the onus is on them to show that the God portrayed in their scriptures is really all good. The mere fact that their scriptures say he is all good is hardly sufficient proof, especially given the kinds of things that various scriptures have told us God has commanded.

Consider, for example, these cases from various scriptures: the Hebrew God orders Abraham to sacrifice his son Isaac (Genesis 22); the Hebrew God delivers the cities of Makkedah, Libnah, Lachish, Eglon, Hebron, and Debir to Joshua, who puts all the inhabitants to the sword (Joshua 10:28–39); some youths call the prophet Elisha 'baldhead' and 42 of them are mauled to death by two bears when Elisha calls down a curse on them in the name of the Hebrew God (2 Kings 2:23–25); Jesus causes the death of 2000 pigs just to drive an evil spirit out of one man (Mark 5:13); the Christian God causes a man to be born blind so that, after the man has presumably endured 20 or more years of blindness, Jesus might display God at work with a miracle cure (John 9:3); the Christian God causes Lazarus to sicken and die so Jesus may display the glory of God by resurrecting him four days later (John 11:4); and Allah requires his followers not to take prisoners of war until the land has been thoroughly subdued (Surah 2:194). By any modern standards of morality, these are all morally wrong. Only with verbal gymnastics and embarrassment can a theist say that death by bear is an appropriate punishment for calling a bald man 'baldie'.

If theists choose to see their lives as having the meaning they believe such a God has given it, then they are morally required to take responsibility for this choice. The blame cannot be anchored anywhere else. They cannot defend themselves by saying it is God, not them, who has given life this meaning, any more than atheists can blame someone else for the meaning they choose to give their lives. Theism has no advantage over atheism in this respect.

MEANING AS VALUE

On one interpretation of the Christian story, God's purpose in creating humanity was to bring into existence creatures capable of appreciating his act of grace in creating them. Humans have value because they can express their appreciation through worship, and through obedience to God's idea of what is good for them. If there were such a purpose, then in Jean-Paul Sartre's words, our essence as human beings would have preceded our existence.[3] We would be a kind of artefact, made to a blueprint in God's mind.

Atheism, however, rejects the view that there is any such thing as a supernatural creator of the universe, and so it rejects the idea that human life is there to serve a plan or purpose. The function or purpose our lives serve is something we have to determine for ourselves. Even if someone wants us to perform some role in a grand plan, it only becomes the purpose or meaning of our lives if we decide to endorse it. Who we are and what our lives add up to or mean is not something settled in advance of our choices. To repeat Sartre, 'our existence precedes our essence'.[4]

DOES IT MAKE SENSE TO BE MORAL?

One kind of life that many people think is especially meaningful — that has a special value — is a life lived in a morally honourable way, a life in which we try to do what is right and good and avoid what is evil and despicable, even if this comes at the expense of our own advantage or self-interest. Does a life with this kind of meaning only make sense if there is a God? If there is no God then is it the case, as Dostoyevsky explored in his novel *The Brothers Karamazov* (1880), that all is permitted?

Dostoyevsky's suggestion is a misleading one. What is really at issue is not what is permitted, but what is punished. If there is an all-powerful and all-knowing God, then punishment is guaranteed for those who disobey him. If there is no such God, then there are no behaviours that are guaranteed to be punished. The worry, then, is that if there is no guaranteed punishment or reward, doesn't this make it meaningless to endure the restrictions and discomforts imposed by living a morally good life? Isn't the moral life only a meaningful one if, in the long run, justice prevails — that is, the good eventually are rewarded and wrong-doers are eventually punished? God is seen as the one guaranteeing that this happens because he has given each of us an eternal soul and, being all-knowing, all-powerful, and all-good, is in a position to ensure that everyone gets their just deserts.

Appeal to a God is not an essential part of this idea. A supernatural but non-theistic account of what makes the moral life meaningful can be derived from the Buddhist notion of karma, which holds that the universe is constructed in such a way that reincarnation appropriately rewards and punishes us, even though there is no God to oversee this distribution of desert.

It may seem, then, that theists or believers in a supernatural power such as karma have the advantage over atheists, in that they can feel assured that the sacrifices they make to live moral lives are not rendered meaningless by the triumph of the wicked. Their moral resolve need not be undermined by the fact that evil people often seem to lead happy lives and may escape all retribution for their crimes in this life. They can feel confident that, even if they endure torture, humiliation, degradation, or death in the cause of acting rightly, it is not in vain.

The problem with this view appears to be that it shows a lack of commitment to the moral life. It seems to imply that being a morally honourable person is not something that a rational person would value for its own sake. This, however, is to confuse rationality itself with a particular narrow application of rationality. In its most general sense, rationality is just the feature that people possess when they choose a course of action on the basis that it is the best means they know for achieving the goal under consideration. The goal does not need to be a selfish, self-interested one. What may matter most to a person is that everyone be treated as if they were of equal value or worth. If so, it would then be rational of such a person to avoid taking advantage of someone else, even if he or she could get away with it. People who think that only selfish or self-interested actions are rational reveal themselves to value only their own self-interest. This suggests that, if they do act in a moral manner in this life, it is only because they are afraid of what will happens to them in the afterlife, not because they actually place any value on behaving morally for its own sake.

Richard Dawkins makes this point well in *The God Delusion* (2007). In response to the question, 'If there is no God, why be good?', Dawkins writes:

> Posed like that, the question sounds positively ignoble. When a religious person puts it to me in this way (and many of them do), my immediate temptation is to issue the following challenge: 'Do you really mean to tell me the only reason you try to be good is to gain God's approval and reward, or to avoid his disapproval and punishment? That's not morality, that's just sucking up, apple-polishing, looking over your shoulder at the great surveillance camera in the sky, or the still small wiretap inside your head, monitoring your every move, even your every base thought.'
> ... Michael Shermer, in *The Science of Good and Evil*, calls it a debate-stopper. If you agree that, in the absence of God, you would 'commit robbery, rape, and murder' you reveal yourself as an immoral person, and we would be well-advised to steer a wide course around you. If, on the other hand, you admit that you would continue to be a good person even when not under divine surveillance, you have fatally undermined your claim that God is necessary for us to be good.[5]

So we can reasonably say that God provides believers with additional reasons for doing the right thing. However, if God were your only reason for acting morally, then shame on you. You cannot be considered a truly moral person at all, but merely a selfish or self-interested one who has been frightened into behaving morally by belief in God and an afterlife. As H. L. Mencken says, 'People say we need religion when what they really mean is we need police'.[6] If you were a truly moral person, you would be just as committed to acting morally in the absence of God and the afterlife. Truly moral people conceive of themselves as a certain kind — the kind of person who would find benefitting themselves unfairly at another's expense to be contrary to what they admire or care about. They would refuse to act in such a way even if there were no afterlife. The English philosopher Philippa Foot expresses the point nicely. She says:

> It is perfectly true that if a man is just it follows that he will be prepared, in the event of very evil circumstances, even to face death rather than act unjustly — for instance, in getting an innocent man convicted of a crime of which he has been accused. For him it turns out that his justice brings disaster on him, and yet like anyone else he has good reason to be a just and not an unjust man. He could not have it both ways and while possessing the virtue of justice hold himself ready to be unjust should any great advantage accrue. The man who has the virtue of justice is not ready to do certain things, and if he is too easily tempted we shall say that he was ready after all.[7]

MEANING AS SIGNIFICANCE

Is the worry about atheism, perhaps, that it renders human life insignificant in a way that theism doesn't? The idea here is that the universe is enormously vast. Humans are a small part of the life on a minor planet in a solar system that rotates around one of the 1,000,000,000,000,000,000,000+ stars in the universe. If there is a God whose purposes require a universe made on such a grand scale but also require our existence, then human life has significance. We can see ourselves as essential, not as some merely accidental outcome of impersonal and uncaring physical forces. Without such a God, we have no significance at all.

According to this theistic story, the universe does not have significance in itself but gains its significance from its relationship to God's purposeful consciousness. God himself, presumably, is not important solely because of his relationship to some other such consciousness. A distinction, then, can be drawn between two kinds of significance or meaning that a thing can have. If it is a purpose-having consciousness, then it can have what I will call 'an internal significance', one it derives from its own purposes. By this reasoning, something that is not a purposeful consciousness can only have external significance. But, just as God has internal significance with respect to himself, so humans, given the power of freewill, can have internal significance with respect to themselves. The significance they gain from their role in God's plans is not the only kind of significance they can have.

Now, for the theist, the universe as a whole gains external significance from its relationship to God, but even the most megalomaniacal human does not have external purposes that involve the whole universe. Nonetheless, those parts of the universe that do connect with human purposes, or with the desires of any other sentient beings, are invested with external significance. Rather than being rendered insignificant by the minuscule place we occupy in the universe, we and other sentient beings give significance to those parts of the universe that are involved in our purposes.

So, from the perspective of the atheist, the universe itself does not possess any internal significance. It does not have any purpose for itself, nor is it able to invest other things with significance — or, for that matter, with insignificance. The universe is not a gigantic sentient being. It holds no opinions on what is or is not important. Even if it did, these would still be external to our purposes and would not show that our purposes were insignificant in themselves.

MEANING AS MAKING A DIFFERENCE

Another possible concern about atheism is that, if correct, then in time the world will be as if we had never existed. Whereas if there is a God, then even if humans disappear we will continue to live in His memory, if not in heaven. The Russian novelist Leo Tolstoy expressed this kind of anxiety in *A Confession* (1933):

> Today or tomorrow sickness and death will come (they had come already) to those I love or to me; nothing will remain but stench and worms. Sooner or later my affairs, whatever they may be, will be forgotten, and shall not exist. Then why go on making any effort?[8]

In this passage, Tolstoy seems to think the fact that he will eventually cease to exist justifies his no longer acting in the present. Suppose, however, that as he was writing this passage his wife spilt burning oil on herself. If he acts immediately he can put the fire out, save her life, and prevent her from suffering horrendous pain and injuries. Of what possible relevance to his acting immediately is the fact that he will one day be dead and forgotten? Is he seriously suggesting that a universe in which his wife suffers excruciating agony is not a worse universe than one in which the fire is promptly extinguished, that it makes no difference which kind of universe is brought into existence by his actions? Such a view just seems plainly mistaken and totally unwarranted by the reasons offered for it.

The underlying idea could be that the end outcome for either universe will be the same — the big crunch, or the heat death of the universe — so if we were to assess each universe in terms of how things eventually turn out, it would make no difference which universe we opted for. The end result would be the same. But why place this value on the end result? We have no interest in the end result. We will not be there, and it plays no part in our plans and projects. What happens along the way to the end result, however, can make a big difference to us. As Bertrand Russell puts it:

> I believe that when I die I shall rot, and nothing of my ego will survive. I am not young, and I love life. But I should scorn to shiver with terror at the thought of annihilation. Happiness is nonetheless true happiness because it must come to an end, nor do thought and love lose their value because they are not everlasting.[9]

Consider, for example, a scenario in which we learn, with absolute certainty, that human life will come to an abrupt end in 50 years time. Does everything we could do in that 50 years thereby become meaningless? Does the fact that we will all cease to exist in half a century warrant mass suicide now? Would someone who had the power to destroy us all immediately be doing a morally good thing if they did so? Admittedly, the thought that we will just vanish at a future moment will place a dampener on much of what we do but, if we can put this aside, there would still be much of value to be found in the time left — the enjoyment of friends and family, the appreciation of beautiful things, the pleasures of food and wine, delight in the happiness of others, humour and laughter, the joy of love, the rewards of challenge and discovery.

AN ATHEIST MEANING FOR LIFE

What advice then, if any, does atheism have to offer on the meaning of life? As we have seen, atheism is the denial that there are any gods or other supernatural forces so, by logical extension, then there is no supernatural source of external meaning for human life. The importance of this conclusion should not be underestimated: it means that the supposed warrant for many of the codes of conduct that were thought to give meaning to life has been removed. Ways of life based on those codes will have to find some other justification, a justification cast in purely naturalistic terms. This may well be easier said than done. Why, for example, would you continue to avoid planting your field with two kinds of grain, or continue to avoid wearing clothes woven of two kinds of material (Leviticus 19:19) if the only justification for doing so were the cryptic instructions of a God in whom you had ceased to believe?

Can atheism transcend its negative role of telling us what the meaning of life is not and give us some positive advice on what it actually is? It seems so. For example, if the supernatural does not exist — including whatever supernatural underpinning is thought to support life after death — then each of us only has one life. There are no second chances. Atheism 'concentrates the mind', to paraphrase Dr Johnson. If there is only one life for each of us, then the concern with having a meaningful life may well be the concern that this unique chance is not wasted, that you do not end your life failing to give it the meaning you intended. Whether or not you end up wasting your life, from the perspective of its internal meaning, will depend on whether or not you managed to engage with or further the things that mattered to you. What these are will depend on what kind of person you are — on your talents, your interests, your values, and your likes and dislikes, as well as on the opportunities available to you.

Atheism, as such, gives no direction as to what things should matter to you; it leaves this entirely up to you. However, it may well be the case that humans have evolved in such a way that they are more likely to find satisfaction from certain kinds of lives. Australian philosopher Peter Singer, for example, thinks that we need to be committed to a cause 'larger than the self, if we are to find genuine self-esteem'.[10] He notes that there are many causes in which the individual is less important than the group — ranging from sports clubs to businesses to religious and political membership — but it is living an ethical life that gives the firmest foundation for a sense that your life has substance and worth. In *How Are We to Live* (1993), he writes:

> The more we reflect on our commitment to a football club, a corporation, or any sectional interest, the less point we are likely to see in it. In contrast, no amount of reflection will show a commitment to an ethical life to be trivial or pointless.[11]

Although what Singer says here seems to be true, it does not follow from atheism as such. Atheism does not direct you to live the moral life or the immoral life; as we saw earlier, either of these can count as 'rational lives'. This leaves it open that even people we may regard as immoral can be said to have had meaningful lives if they come to the end of their time having engaged with or furthered the things that mattered to them. These may be 'bad' meanings, but they are meanings nonetheless.[12]

While it is important, then, that people lead meaningful lives, we must respect the meanings they attach to those lives, as each person is an autonomous rational agent. Even if some of us feel our lives would have a fuller sense of meaning if we had the power to unfairly privilege ourselves over others, this is not a meaning to which we are morally entitled. A richer meaning for one's own life does not justify using other people, in the words of the Enlightenment philosopher Immanuel Kant, as mere means to our ends, as if the meaning we attach to our lives deserve special treatment just because it is ours. Likewise, respect for the equal dignity of autonomous agents requires us not to force our own conception of the meaning of their lives on other people. It may even be the case that attempts to force a sense of meaning on other lives will create an antagonistic scenario that impinges on everyone's ability to create meaning.

Important as it is that people lead meaningful lives, it is unlikely that they will have an equal chance to do so unless we all work together to create the conditions to make this possible. Contributing your fair share towards this outcome would undoubtedly add meaning to your life, even if there isn't a God.

NOTES

1. J. Baggini, *What's It All About?*, Granta Books, London, 2004.

2. J. P. Sartre, 'Existentialism is a Humanism', in W. Kaufmann, *Existentialism from Dostoyevsky to Sartre*, Meridian Books, New York, 1956, p. 295.

3. ibid., pp. 289–90.

4. ibid.

5. R. Dawkins, *The God Delusion*, Houghton Mifflin Company, New York, 2006, pp. 226–27.

6. H.L. Mencken, cited in R. Dawkins, ibid., pp. 228–9.

7. P. Foot, *Virtues and Vices*, Basil Blackwell, Oxford, 1978, pp. 129–30.

8. L. Tolstoy quoted in R. Perret, *Death and Immortality*, Martinus Nijhoff, Dordrecht, 1987, p. 68.

9. B. Russell, 'What I Believe', in Joan Konner, *The Atheist's Bible*, Hardie Grant, Prahan, 2007, p. 133.

10. P. Singer, *How Are We to Live?*, Text Publishing Company, Melbourne, 1993, p. 216.

11. ibid, p. 218.

12. *What's It All About?*, pp. 175–78.

RELIGION AND VIOLENCE

Dr Tamas Pataki
Author of *Against Religion*, Honorary Senior Fellow in the Department of Philosophy,
Anthropology and Social Inquiry at the University of Melbourne

AT LEAST FROM THE EARLIEST TIMES ACCESSIBLE TO HISTORICAL STUDY, religion has had an intimate association with violence. All religions are concerned with mastering violation and death. The human animal is frangible; violence terrifies, scars, and destroys. Religion is charged with protecting us against the violence of the world and sacralising the violence we direct against it. Gods once demanded sacrifices, not so long ago human sacrifices, to vouchsafe their protection of humans, especially in times of war and other extremity. They are less demanding today, though petition, prayer, propitiation, self-abasement, and self-sacrifice still form part of the essential repertoire of the serious votary.

In a major work published in 2007, Charles Taylor averred that although violence has been bound up with religion, the numinous endorsement of violence — in war, ritual, sacrifice — has progressively receded, and we have moved 'towards a point where, in some religions, violence has no place at all in the sanctified life'.[1] There is obviously some truth in this, but the current surge of violence from fundamentalist religious and religio-nationalist movements across the Abrahamic spectrum and among some Hindu and Buddhist sects exposes its limitations. And when we consider the still-widespread religious endorsement of capital punishment, and corporal punishment of children; the abnormal association between childhood sexual abuse and religious orders; and the persistent teaching of ferocious religious texts, it is natural to wonder whether religious violence is a phenomenon in recession or the manifestation of a necessary connection. This essay explores the latter possibility.

FORMS OF RELIGIOUS VIOLENCE

The relations between religion and violence are various and complex, and an exhaustive inventory cannot be offered here. However, some typical relations may be mentioned. To begin with, we should certainly concede that there are instances in which religion functions as a cloak for violence and even wars that have territorial or economic motives. The history of religion in Great Britain provides ample examples of these motives. Sometimes religion is a cloak for psychopathic behaviour. Religious leaders such as Shoko Asahara of the Aum Supreme Truth; possibly Yigal Amir, who murdered Israeli prime minister Yitzhak Rabin; and perhaps most members of the Christian Identity movement fall into the pathological class. For various reasons, religions attract and sometimes manage to accommodate and repair people suffering mental disturbances.

In these cases religion does not function as a cause of violence, but there are many other instances where it clearly does. Religious ideology, practices, and institutions have been responsible for initiating or precipitating violence; religious distinctions and concepts have facilitated and amplified violence; religious doctrines or rulings have been used to legitimate or justify violence. These are, in a broad sense, causal relations, though of different kinds. No one casting their eye over the contemporary scene can fail to identify many instances of one kind or another. Let us discuss are a few examples.

Donald Capps has argued that religion is 'inherently disposed toward the abuse of children' because it provides theological legitimation for the punishment of children and promotes ideas and beliefs that are 'inherently tormenting to children'.[2] The idea that a child enters the world with a sinful will that has to be broken with beatings is part and parcel of Biblical literalism. The religious household where corporal punishment is seen as Biblically endorsed, even if not going so far as stoning the rebellious child, delivers pernicious consequences. The religiously cultivated child who is beaten is more likely to believe in a personal, punitive, and uncaring God. For the child, an impending beating may loom as a catastrophe — as the end of the world — and his prayers for protection from God will go unanswered. It has often been noticed that Protestant Christians who advocate harsh physical punishment are often intensely apocalyptic.

Capps also argues that religious ideas may be as abusive as physical punishment. The doctrine of hell and eternal punishment, the hard attitudes towards natural sexual feeling, the breaches between friends occasioned by religious differences and segregation, can cause great torment to a child. Often there is perversity in it. Richard Dawkins cites the case of Pastor Robert's hellhouses, which contain terrifying representations of infernal punishments designed to deter twelve-year-olds from sin.[3] One is reminded of Nietzsche's saying that all religions are systems of cruelty.

The sexual abuse of children by clergy has been much in the news. This sexual abuse is of course not restricted to religious orders but is unusually common among them. At least one class of cases, that of abusing Catholic priests, has been studied intensively. Psychoanalyst Mary Gail Frawley-O'Dea argues that both the Church doctrine and organisation, especially the teaching and practices in the training institutions, are causally implicated in the character malformations that are likely to lead to such abuse.[4] She discusses, among many others, the following aetiological factors. The Church is a hierarchical and authoritarian institution that organises relationships through dominance and submission. The aspirant who wants to get ahead knows he has to submit to his father-bishop and mother-Church. That structure of dominance encourages sadomasochistic modes of relating and, of course, attracts people with such needs. It is likely to stimulate rage and cruelty in one direction, combined with submissive, inhibited attitudes in another. These attitudes, reinforced by Church teaching valorising suffering, may lead to the victimisation of powerless young individuals, and indifference to their suffering. The institutions are also infantilising in recreating structures of dependency: the priest's feeling of powerlessness in relation to the seemingly omnipotent parental representatives may be countered by a reversal in which the child abuse is an unconscious attempt to identify with omnipotence while projecting his own powerlessness onto the victim.

Although indoctrination with violent religious teaching is not, as we shall see, a sufficient condition for violence, such doctrine is frequently used to try to justify or legitimate it. Violent Islamic jihad is justified by appeal to the Koran, and the violence of Israeli settlement in Palestinian land is justified by Biblical covenant. Terrorists such as Osama bin Laden always pointedly claim to be acting on God's word. Yigal Amir found justification in rabbinical teachings. As Malise Ruthven noted, religious 'fundamentalism releases the violence contained in the text'.[5]

Religion also amplifies nationalist rhetoric and conflict by giving it a cosmic, absolutist dimension.

> Where religious language is invoked, as in Ireland or Israel-Palestine, the play of interests is transcendentalized, subsumed, as it were, into a much grander, Manichaean contest, between polarized opposites of absolute good versus evil ... [T]he religious 'fundamentalism' in Israel-Palestine, Chechnya, Kashmir, Sri Lanka, and many other of the world's most troubled regions is best understood as an intensification or deepening of nationalism by way of religion's mobilizing potential.[6]

This 'absolutisation' is inherent in the grandiose conceptions of religion and in the generation of religious group psychology. But also, as Ruthven notes, 'people respond positively to political messages couched in language associated with religion, because religion is thought of as "good".'[7]

Many commentators argue that religious fundamentalists see themselves as besieged by secular modernity; they feel that their very existence or way of life is under threat and turn to violence to defend themselves. There is something in this, though in a secular society ensuring freedom of worship, the survival of the religious groups is clearly not the issue. The real threat is not to their survival, but to the primacy and dominance of their religion, on which their self-esteem often precariously depends. Influential Islamist theorists such as Sayyid Mawdudi and Sayyid Qutb, who insisted on a world dispensation dominated by Islam, were really insisting that everyone must recognise the primacy of their religion — and hence them — in line with a fundamental narcissistic need. Religious and cultural differences can become intolerable to people who require the world to mirror them, and have to be eliminated, by violence if necessary. If the world wants to destroy Islam, as many contemporary Islamists believe, that just shows all the more how important they are.

ERRORS OF THE APOLOGISTS

Religious apologists confronted with examples such as these respond in a number of different ways. Many concede that religion causes violence but, in a *tu quoque* (you too!), retort that secular ideologies and movements have been more violent. Thus an Australian theologian, Tom Frame, has recently written of 'the face of Russian atheism, which had led to the brutal extermination of those who opposed Soviet hegemony, and German apostasy, which had prompted the Holocaust...'.[8] Similarly, Karen Armstrong:

> Born of modern scientific racism, the Holocaust ... showed that a secularist ideology could be just as lethal as any religious crusade ... The Holocaust was also a reminder of the dangers that can accrue from the death of God in human consciousness ... The symbol of God had marked the limit of human potential and, in the conservative period, had imposed a constraint upon what men and women could do ... But the Holocaust and the Gulag show what can happen when people cast off all such restraint or make the nation or polity the supreme value.[9]

It is plain that even if these historical claims were true — even if the allegedly atheist dispensations have been more bloody than religious ones — this constitutes no defence of religion. The charge against religion is that it causes violence, not that it is the only cause: the apologists' observations do nothing to disarm that charge.

But in any case, the historical claims are reckless. The assertion that the Holocaust was 'born of modern scientific racism' is an egregious distortion. The inherent assumption that scientific racism is simply a piece of secular ideology is in itself peculiar, since racialist speculations and doctrines have their roots in ancient thought, especially Biblical (recall the sons of Noah), Cabbalistic, and other occult doctrines about innate human differences.[10] It is true that conceptions of racial hierarchy reached a climax in the primitive anthropology of the Enlightenment and in nineteenth-century biological and philological thought, and were later embraced by the Nazis and accepted by most educated people in the first half of the twentieth century. But though these conceptions — including distorted conceptions of Darwinian evolution — were used in justifying pseudo-racial distinctions, their causal influence was miniscule compared to the socioeconomic conditions, popular racism, and ethnic hatreds (which long antedated scientific racism's misconceived typologies) that led to the Holocaust. Theoretical conceptions can be misused, just as a butter knife can be used for murder. But, as Hannah Arendt famously said, 'There is an abyss between the men of brilliant but facile conceptions and men of brutal deeds and active bestiality'.[11]

The claim that the Soviet and Nazi exterminations were caused by Russian atheism and German apostasy is even more extraordinary. Even if it were true that the atheism of the Soviet leadership and the weird cult of a few Nazi leaders spread beyond the elites to the peasantry, middle classes, and armed forces who were the agents and accomplices of extermination, the apologists would have to show that it was by virtue of their atheism that these regimes perpetrated their enormities. In establishing a causal relation between two objects or events, it is necessary to specify the properties of the causal entity that are causally efficacious. When a stone breaks a window, the causally efficacious properties of the stone are likely to include its mass and velocity, and to exclude its colour and odour. Some Nazis were atheists, as well as being martinets, art lovers, brutal racists, and so on. It is incumbent on apologists such as Frame and Armstrong to demonstrate that it was by virtue specifically of their atheism that Nazis committed their atrocities and, indeed, that the Nazi state was principally impelled by atheism. No author I am acquainted with has come remotely close to demonstrating that.[12]

It is also worth recalling that atheism is not the same as hatred of religion: neither entails the other. In the Russian case, Bolshevik contempt for the institutions of the Orthodox church and for religion in general played a role in the persecution of religious institutions and orders, but to generalise that fact to atheist responsibility for the wholesale exterminations and gulags is an historical absurdity; the claim that German apostasy was responsible for the Holocaust is a still greater absurdity. Armstrong's assertion that in the past God had 'imposed a constraint upon what men and women could do' seems to show at best a Sunday-school reading of history.

Charles Taylor also accepts that religion is implicated in violence, but then, in another version of the *tu quoque*, tries to palliate the charge by asserting the universality of the psychological mechanisms underlying violence. He refers specifically to the numinous violence of pre-Axial days (gods of war, ritual human sacrifice) and to the theologically inspired terrorism of our times. But sacred violence, he says, has been moderated in post-Axial times, and its manifestations today are driven by much the same motives and facilitated by the same mechanisms as those of secular violence, 'the terrible violence powered by atheistic and/or anti-Christian ideologies, like Marxist–Leninism and Nazism'.[13]

Taylor thinks that the critical mechanism is scapegoating. When our fundamental sense of order, superiority, goodness, or purity are threatened, the evil or chaos we sense within us is projected onto scapegoats, who are then attacked and eliminated. Sacred killing thus 'offers a form of purification'. 'Moreover, since God is the source of purity, in so fighting, we identify with him, we are on his side'. In this way violence ascends to a higher plane, it is 'in the service of the Higher' (the Wrath of God) and becomes 'all the more implacable, ruthless and thorough'.

That conceded, Taylor proceeds to neutralise the case against religion by assimilation: the projective and scapegoating mechanism in the service of purification 'recurs in ideological-political forms which are resolutely lay, even atheist'. But this argument is flawed. In the first place, Taylor narrows his attention to just one mechanism — scapegoating — which could hardly answer for all the forms of religious or secular violence. Second, and oddly comporting with his apologetical intent, he does recognise distinct religious motives and the distinctive cast that religion gives violence. Thus, he notes the identification with God, acting in 'service of the Higher', the need for purification, superiority, and order, but then proceeds to ignore these features, as if they characterised non-religious violence as well. Obviously, all of them do not.

A different apologetical response is represented in William James. He affirms that, despite appearances, religion does not cause violence:

The baiting of Jews, the hunting of the Albigenses and Waldenses, the stoning of the Quakers and ducking of Methodists, the murdering of Mormons and massacring of Armenians, express rather that aboriginal neophobia, the pugnacity of which we all share the vestiges, and the inborn hatred of the alien and of eccentric and non-conformist men as aliens, than they express the positive piety of the various perpetrators. Piety is the mask, the inner force is tribal instinct... At most we may blame piety for not availing to check our natural passions, and sometimes for supplying them with hypocritical motives.[14]

James accepts that piety may be a permissive cause in failing to restrain murderous tribal instinct — a failure, one might think, that goes to the heart of religion. But the efficacious motive is tribal instinct or innate hatred of the alien and new: religion is just the mask. James does not say why tribal instinct should naturally issue in violence; presumably violence is the extremity of an exclusionary hatred of the alien, which he seems to consider innate. Nor is it entirely clear what is meant by 'mask': is religion a pretext, an exploited marker of group identity, an innocent bystander confounded with the causes of things?

There are, of course, many conflicts in which religious, nationalist, ethnic, xenophobic, and other enmities are compounded. And religion is sometimes merely the mask for other motives. But it would take much more than a handful of questionable examples to show that religious ideology or group identity is never causally involved in motivating violence. There certainly seem to be clear cases — indeed some of James' own examples on reasonable interpretations are such cases — where religion is just such a cause. James seems not to see that because he thinks of religion in such radically individualistic terms — the feelings and acts 'of individual men in their solitude'. It does not to occur to him that the 'mask of piety', religion, may itself create or shape an exclusionary tribal identity with all the 'inborn hatred of the alien' and pugnacity attached.[15]

But perhaps if only we examined closely enough all the cases that appear to be instances of religious violence — wars of religion, pogroms, bonfires of heretics, and so on — we would discover that the real motives were actually non-religious ones. That is extremely unlikely, although possible, and the possibility subsists and will feed apologetical ingenuity as long as we continue to consider the connection between religion and violence as merely contingent. But what if it could be demonstrated that (most) religion is intrinsically violent? I believe that such a necessary connection exists and will shortly outline the argument for it. First, however, let us consider some sins of the atheists that point in the same direction.

ERRORS OF THE ATHEISTS

In his book *God is not Great* (2007), Christopher Hitchens sweeps through the history of religious iniquity and concludes that religion is 'violent, irrational, intolerant, allied to racism and tribalism and bigotry, invested in ignorance and hostile to free inquiry, contemptuous of women and coercive toward children'.[16] Despite the views of James and the like-minded, there is no dearth of evidence causally linking religion to violence, and Hitchens is not frugal with his reprehensions: Islamists, Protestant fundamentalists, Sri Lankan Buddhists, Japanese Buddhists in the years leading up to the World War II, male circumcisers, female mutilators, and many others operating under religious inspiration get a drubbing. Hitchens' accounts of Catholic Church complicity — at least at lower levels — with the Rwandan genocide, and with fascism and Nazism — at the highest levels — are particularly disturbing. His indictment of the Church for having only ever excommunicated one Nazi leader, Goebbels (for marrying a Protestant) astonishes.

However, embarrassing religion with its history and bad eggs can yield only limited results. Hitchens' intention is to show that religion is intrinsically evil, but the most his mode of argument can show is that it is contingently so. Religious apologists would quickly concede the bad eggs and tragic lapses, but urge that these are aberrations, misuses of religion, religion used as pretext, and so on. And the apologists would have a point. Hitchens' inductive argument accumulates incriminating associations between religion and its vicious consequences, but does not show what it is about religion that necessarily generates these consequences.

Hitchens does not see this clearly because he has a simple, but false and misleading, understanding of the nature of religion — one he shares with many other atheists. They believe that people's religious attitudes and beliefs are products of religious educations based on crude and violent foundational texts: so, for example, monotheistic fundamentalists subordinate women and abominate homosexuals because they have imbibed sections of the Bible or the Koran which state that women are inferior and homosexuals are to be abominated. Exodus states that 'Thou shalt not suffer a witch to live', and this was 'the warrant for the Christian torture and burning of women who did not conform'. And so on.

This understanding explains why these critics expend so much energy exposing the inconsistencies and moral horrors of the foundational texts. But it does not explain why so many people, even today, readily embrace these savage old texts. Why do people permit themselves to be seduced by them, even to extremities of violence? Hitchens offers only commonplaces for religious conviction: a 'religious impulse — the need to worship', human credulousness, and, rather casually, fear: there would be no churches 'if humanity had not been afraid of the weather, the dark, the plague, the eclipse, and all manner of other things now easily explicable'. Absent here is any serious sense of connection between religion and fundamental motives to it — human dependency, fear of abandonment, self-respect, and group identity. The multiplicity of the profound needs that motivate religion, and the ways in which those needs can turn angry and violent, pass unnoticed.

Richard Dawkins is another who believes that religion is violent basically for doctrinal reasons, but he offers a more detailed accounting. He notes several causal factors: religion provides markers of group differences that can be exploited in conflict; it facilitates terrorist violence because of 'the easy and beguiling promise that death is not the end'; its doctrines legitimate violence. But the main thing is indoctrination into the condition of blind faith. Thus the suicide bombers are motivated:

> by what they perceive to be righteousness, faithfully pursuing what their religion tells them. They are not psychotic; they are religious idealists who, by their own lights, are rational. They perceive their acts to be good, not because of some warped personal idiosyncrasy, and not because they have been possessed by Satan, but because they have been brought up, from the cradle, to have total and unquestioning faith.[17]

Similarly, Paul Hill, who murdered an abortionist, is alleged not to be a psychopath but one whose mind had been 'captured by poisonous religious nonsense'.

The limitations of this approach become evident as soon as the key concepts are probed. What is it to have one's mind captured by poisonous religious nonsense or to be indoctrinated into unquestioning faith? What kind of conditions are they? Why are the views of the religiously indoctrinated immune to rational considerations and held so tenaciously? Can one be indoctrinated in the truths of physics or history and hold them with unquestioning faith? Why not? And why are some people susceptible to the violent aspects of religion and not the pacific elements that are also present in most religions?

The fundamental weakness in Dawkins' account is that its conception of indoctrination, of being inducted into unquestioning faith, is limited to learning doctrine — maybe a lot of doctrine, maybe by rote every day. But no matter how inculcation of doctrine is intensified at this level, it won't yield that quality that resists rational considerations and revision. Moreover, it does not explain why some of the religious choose violence and others do not. Evidently, only a small percentage of those exposed to these religious educations graduate into the school of mayhem and murder.

The impulse to religious violence is not to be found solely or principally in the content of religious doctrine, or in its schooling. Various factors are involved, but the most important of these, I will suggest, are the processes by which religious doctrine, practices, and institutions are able to satisfy symbolically or substitutively certain unconscious wishes or needs, partly formed under the impress of religion, and imbricated with early internalised interpersonal or 'object-relationships'.[18] That is how religious doctrines and teaching can 'capture the mind' and be held with 'unquestioning faith'. The next section briefly outlines the way in which those psychological processes can create an intrinsic causal connection between religion and violence.[19]

AN INTRINSIC CONNECTION

There are many different motives to religious belief: pressures to conform to traditional norms, the security conferred by group belonging, the belief that religion underwrites virtue, and so on. Among these are motives that arise from specific character needs. For example, people with strong narcissistic needs, such as feeling superior to others, having to deny envy, or achieving a kind of inflated identity through membership of an exalted group, may find their needs satisfied, or at least attenuated, in religious affiliations. Beliefs such as that one is a member of the Elect favoured by an omnipotent god, that one walks in the path of righteousness, that one is saved while others are not, are obviously narcissistically gratifying.

Religion can also satisfy many hysterical, obsessional, and other character needs, for example in its Manichaean conceptions separating the pure from the impure, and in its rigid rituals. But let us focus on the narcissistic needs.[20]

The idea of being a 'chosen people' with a special mission is a conception quite widespread among religious groups, Buddhist, Jewish, Islamic and Christian alike, and not just among fundamentalist ones. At an unconscious level their beliefs often (symbolically) satisfy the need to feel omnipotent or to maintain the unconscious relation with idealised parents on which their self-esteem and security are fundamentally predicated. How do these needs arise and how do religions satisfy them?

From early in infancy — we do not need to be too specific here — the infant wants to feel secure, to be free of hunger and discomfort, and he wants his objects (at first, mother) to be all-good and provident. He wants to live in the circle of an omnibenevolent world. Parental solicitude is never perfect and the world is not omnibenevolent, but the infant has available various means of regulating his feelings and environment. By splitting off (withdrawing attention from) bad aspects of his experience and projecting it in wish-fulfilling 'omnipotent' phantasy — think here of the transiently veridical dream and daydream — into his objects, or by internalising in phantasy good aspects of his objects, the infant can, as it were, alter the dispensation of pleasure and pain, of good and bad, in his experiential world.[21] The regulation of good states of the self, of primitive self-esteem or narcissistic wellbeing, which at first depends largely on feeling loved by others and later on the capacity to value and love oneself, becomes a primary aim.

Another important mode of regulating self-esteem is idealisation. Children invariably try to sustain the belief that parents are loving, omnipotent, and omniscient, especially if they feel insecure and persecuted and when, inevitably, parents disappoint. Figures who are needed for protection, security, and love may be idealised by having their 'bad' aspects split off so as to prevent contamination of their desired goodness. The child may then bask in the idealised parents' radiance or, by identifying with them, augment his own sense of omnipotence. Sometimes the child will internalise the split-off bad parts in order to keep the object pure, and this leads to self-hatred and self-abasement. Under the impress of omnipotence, the child's overriding need to retain proximity to mother and monitor her whereabouts may develop into an exceptionally urgent need for omniscience. It is remarkable, is it not, that omnipotence, omniscience, and benevolence are the key perfections attributed to God.

The above processes are more or less normal and transitional but in some circumstances they can lead to the creation of unconscious grandiose, god-like conceptions of the self that dominate the entire personality. If, for example, conceptions of God or other powerful supernatural beings are introduced vividly to the child, then the attitudes appropriate in interpersonal contexts may be transferred to the divine figures who then partly substitute for, and become fused with, the parental figures. And the child may then attempt to establish a relationship in phantasy with the supernatural figures and bask in their radiance, much as he will try later with pop stars or sporting heroes.

Or he may surrender part of his conscious self-love but restore it in some measure by unconsciously identifying with God — a condition not at all rare. In that way he can achieve a superficial humility, while unconsciously extending his narcissism in loving God (since he is identified with God) and in God's love for him. This strategy may be invoked especially where narcissism is forcefully extinguished with threats or punishment. Children raised in a cold or crushing atmosphere — as we saw it is often part of religious upbringing to crush the child's natural narcissism (egoism or 'will') — are more likely to depend on supernatural or other substitute imaginary figures to contain their narcissism. Their self-esteem will be precarious, and sustainable only through unremitting effort — prayer, sacrifice, self-abasement — to stay in emotional proximity to a remote and silent God.

Finally, a later, critical strategy for achieving narcissistic wellbeing is to idealise the religious group to which one belongs and then to identify with it: that way the virtues conferred on the group can be claimed for oneself. Identifying with an idealised racial or religious group — even a football club or rock band — is a common way of elevating self-esteem. The logic is simple: if the group you belong to is special, you are special. This strategy also has the advantage of appropriating (in phantasy) the group's achievements and thus diminishing envy. It also enhances one's power, and the scope for exercising it, in the groups' ability to 'throw its weight around', an expression of narcissistic assertiveness.

Well, how does this slender tale connect with religious violence? The outlines may perhaps be emerging. The inescapable need to preserve security, identity, and self-esteem is accommodated, shaped, and stimulated by religious conceptions and internalisations. The narcissism surrendered in infancy may be retrieved by establishing a 'special relationship to God', or through identification with images of God (or other supernatural figures) and, later, idealised religious groups. Since in most instances narcissism is not painlessly relinquished, those images will be coloured by the projections of a hurt, angry, and deprived child. In homes where parents are particularly domineering or aggressive, the images of God may take on those characteristics, and the child may identify with God as a controlling, angry aggressor, or live in fear of one. Religion thus becomes a repository for relinquished narcissism, especially of a more or less distorted and pathological character.

The aggression and violence intrinsically associated with unmodified infantile and pathological narcissistic needs is expressed through religion in many ways. Becoming a member of the Elect is a gratifying exclusionary process: being special means being one of the Few, not the Many. Consigning non-believers to hell, or converting them, is also gratifying. Proselytising is a doubly rewarding act: consciously, there is the pleasing knowledge of bestowing a grace upon another; unconsciously, there is the pleasure of stripping converts of their former identity and aggressively incorporating them into your group. Compelling others to think and act as you do not only confirms your faith and eliminates challenges to it, but also nourishes grandiose self-conceptions by testifying to your power.

It is often noted that before the advent of monotheism, religious intolerance and persecution were hardly known. The bullying associated with Abrahamic religions is a result partly of the aggression inherent in group narcissism, and partly defensive. In the latter case, it is often a reaction to the instability of the identifications underlying religious faith and the inevitable ingress of reality. Religious people often fear, privately, that religion, or much of it, is a house of cards. Faith, as Mark Twain's schoolboy said, is believing what you know ain't so. Many salient episodes in the social history of religion comprise more or less violent attempts by the faithful to shore up their faith against other faiths, heretics, and self-doubt. Religious communities are often support groups for self-deception. Those who do not share the faith threaten it, and must be segregated, converted, exiled, or eliminated.

Even small differences become major threats to those who require the world to mirror them narcissistically. The idea that people should be killed for holding errant religious beliefs deemed threatening to the faithful seems to be an entirely Abrahamic conception. But deviations other than heretical ones are also felt to be intolerable. In a Christian dispensation of almost 2000 years, it is only in the last 200 years that atheism, blasphemy, homosexuality, and witchery — infractions under religious sanctions — have not been cruelly punished. There are still places under religious influence where some of these transgressions are punished, and it is evident that there are many religious folk elsewhere who believe that they should be.

The distorted narcissistic needs we have touched on here certainly can find non-religious expressions, and as noted earlier there are many other character needs playing important roles in religious experience that we have left aside. But even these brief considerations indicate why there seems to be an intrinsic connection between violence and religious psychology, especially at the fundamentalist end of the spectrum. Certainly, ordinary activities and non-religious group identities can serve as vehicles for the satisfaction of thwarted and distorted narcissistic needs, for example, membership of a supposedly superior race or football club. But it does not follow that all ideologies or groups are equally amenable to becoming instruments of narcissistic violence. Religions are particularly fitted because their key ideological conceptions — commerce with an omnipotent supreme being, membership of an Elect, moral certainty, and incorrigible knowledge — both feed and create the lopsided narcissism that needs to assert itself.

NOTES

1. C. Taylor, *A Secular Age*, Harvard, Cambridge, 2007, p. 689.
2. Capps, *The Child's Song*, John Knox Press, Louisville, 1995, p. xi. (Capps is Professor of Pastoral Theology at Princeton Theological Seminary.)
3. R. Dawkins, *The God Delusion*, Houghton Mifflin Company, Boston, 2006, p. 320.
4. M. G. Frawley-O'Dea, *Perversion of Power: Sexual Abuse in the Catholic Church*, Vanderbilt University Press, 2007.
5. M. Ruthven, *Fundamentalism*, Oxford University Press, 2005, p. 190.

6. ibid., pp. 167–68.

7. ibid., p. 168. The role of religious conceptions and group psychology in amplifying conflict are discussed in more detail in my *Against Religion,* Scribe, Melbourne, 2007.

8. T. Frame, 'Godless Nation No Longer Beggars Belief', *Australian Literary Review*, August 2009, 17.

9. K. Armstrong, *The Battle for God*, Random House, New York, 2001, p. 201. Another repeat offender is Alistair McGrath. See for example *The Twilight of Atheism*, Random House, London, 2004, 232ff.

10. For a brief discussion of these issues see the 'Introduction' in Michael Levine and Tamas Pataki (eds.), *Racism in Mind,* Cornell University Press, Ithaca and London, 2004, pp. 2–7.

11. H. Arendt, *The Origins of Totalitarianism*, Harcourt Brace, San Diego, 1976, p. 183.

12. It is time that the canard that Nazism was a form of atheism was put to rest. Most members of the Nazi party, including Hitler, remained professing Christians. Moreover, Nazi ideology was anything but atheistic. An authority sympathetic to religion writes: 'The rise of National Socialism in Germany earlier in the 1930s and 1940s while not explicitly religious, carried overtones of millenarian Christianlty. Heinrich Himmler and other formulators of nazi ideology relied on a mixture of quasi-religious images and ideas, including symbols associated with the Knights Templar; nature worship from the German Volk movement of the 1920s; the notions of Aryan superiority from, among others, the Theosophists; and a fascination with the occult from a particular strand of German Catholic mysticism. To the degree that the nazi movement was religious, then, one could consider the second world war as a war of (or from the Allies point of view, against) Nazi religion'. See Mark Juergensmeyer, *Global Rebellion*, University of California Press, Berkeley, 2008, p. 168.

13. Taylor, 2007, p. 687. Successive quotations ibid.

14. W. James, *The Varieties of Religious Experience*, Fontana, London, 1971, p. 331.

15. There is the one about the Irishman stopped by paramilitaries: 'Are you Catholic or Protestant?' 'I'm an atheist', he replies. 'But are you a Catholic or a Protestant atheist?'

16. C. Hitchens, *God is Not Great: how religion poisons everything*, Allen and Unwin, Crows Nest, 2007, p. 56. Successive quotations ibid.

17. *The God Delusion*, p. 304.

18. The forces of social compliance investigated by social psychologists are especially important factors I do not discuss here.

19. A more detailed discussion is *Against Religion*, where some references for the following discussion may be found.

20. The *locus classicus* for narcissism is Sigmund Freud's 'On Narcissism: An Introduction'. Very useful are: Otto Kernberg, *Borderline Conditions and Pathological Narcissism*, Jason Aronson, New Jersey, 1975; and Elsa F. Ronningstam (ed), *Disorders of Narcissism*, Jason Aronson, New Jersey, 1998.

21. It is important that internalisation of this sort is not just learning (except in the broadest sense); certainly not a matter of learning doctrine: self-experience is fundamentally modified.

* RELIGION AND THE BRAIN

THE NEUROBIOLOGY OF RELIGIOUS EXPERIENCE

Dr Adam Hamlin
Research Fellow in The Queensland Brain Institute at the University of Queensland

WHY HAS SCIENCE FAILED TO BANISH BELIEF IN THE SUPERNATURAL? Scientists from the Enlightenment period predicted that as we came to understand the truth about nature, this would banish the need for belief in the supernatural to explain the natural world. We would welcome in an age of reason. Considering that some 200 years have since past and we now have extremely compelling scientific evidence on the creation of the universe, the forces of nature, and the evolution of life, why do people continue to believe in supernatural powers as a valid explanation, even in the face of overwhelming evidence to the contrary? Why has science failed so spectacularly in this endeavour?

One of the sciences attempting to understand this discrepancy is neuroscience. Is irrationality and therefore belief in the supernatural a functional consequence of brain organisation? A recent Nielsen poll has shown that 68 per cent of Australians believe in God or a universal spirit of some form.[1]

Religious belief is uniquely human, with no equivalent animal experience, and is found across all cultures, from antiquity to the present. The basis of religious belief has been hotly debated by numerous and diverse disciplines such as anthropology, cosmology, genetics, philosophy, and psychology. Contemporary theories, such as 'theory of mind' and 'social cognition', consider belief in the supernatural as a complex brain-based phenomenon that emerged in our ancestors, along with the development of complex cognitive processes that presumably arose when specific regions of the brain, such as the prefrontal and temporal cortices, expanded.

Before we embark on the neurological basis of religious belief, we must firstly understand what the brain is and its basic function, a tall order given the complexity of the human brain. It is only through modern technological advances in human-brain imaging that we are beginning to identify the regions of the brain that are responsible for belief in the supernatural. One thing that has become clear is that there is no 'God spot', as was so widely reported by the media after Dr Ramachandran's symposium presentation for the Society for Neuroscience, where he discussed his group's findings that patients who suffer from temporal lobe epileptic seizures experience intense religious or spiritual encounters during these seizures.[2] The emergence of religious belief requires complex and integrated neural networks.

THE HUMAN BRAIN

The story begins some 550 million years ago, when the first brain appeared on Earth in an ancient ancestor of the modern insect, the arthropod. Over the next 550 million years, the brain would evolve into the most complex phenomenon in the known universe.

The human brain is a remarkable organ — it weighs only three pounds and is about the size of a medium cauliflower, and yet its functional capacity and complexity is truly astounding. It is functionally divided into four main regions: spinal cord/brain stem, cerebellum, forebrain, and cerebrum. All except the cerebellum are primitive parts of the brain that we are largely unaware of, as they exist in the unconscious realm. That's not to say that they are not interesting in their own right, or do not have a huge influence on our conscious experience.

The spinal cord contains billions of axons that carry information from higher centres in the brain out to the body, and from the body back to the brain. This poses a problem for researchers working on spinal cord injury every day — getting neurons to grow and cross the damaged region is one thing, getting them to wire up correctly is another. The spinal cord can also act independently from the rest of the brain to control walking and reflexes. The brain stem is what keeps us alive, controlling our respiration, cardiovascular system, and other organs. When this system fails, we are pronounced brain dead. The cerebellum (meaning 'small brain') smoothes out all of our motor actions and controls those well-learned motor patterns that we don't have to think about, such as riding a bike, driving, or playing the piano, so our conscious brains can concentrate on other tasks. You often find that becoming aware or conscious of these tasks while performing them can actually be detrimental to their performance. The forebrain is buried deep inside the brain. Its primary function is to control our basic drives, such as food and sex, as well as regulating the physiological responses of emotions.

The cerebrum, or cortex — and in particular an area of the cortex called the neocortex — was the most recent part of the brain to evolve, and is what really separates us from other species. The ratio of neocortex to total brain volume in humans is approximately 4:1; this is about 50 per cent larger than the maximum value for any other primate species.[3] None of these other primate brains have spiritual experiences. That's not to say that many of the same emotions don't flood their cortex, but it is the interpretation that we give to these emotional signals that separates us from other primate species. The neocortex controls the body's conscious experiences and voluntary movements. It allows us to feel, think, and create, and to store and retrieve memories. Combined, these generate the human experience.

The neocortex is divided into four lobes which each perform different functions: frontal, parietal, temporal, and occipital. The occipital lobe is right at the back of the brain and contains the visual cortex; this is where a very disjointed, tiny, upside-down visual image received by your retina is turned into the visual world you recognise. Even without your visual cortex, you are still able to move around and interpret emotional signals from facial expression, processes that occur deep within your unconscious mind. The parietal lobe contains the sensory-motor cortex, which controls all conscious movement and gives us spatial awareness of our bodies. The temporal lobe is of primary importance to our auditory processing, speech generation, and generation of long-term memory. The frontal lobe contains areas devoted to abilities that are enhanced in humans or unique to our species, such as complex language processing, social and emotional processing, memory, planning, problem solving, and imagination. It is the latter two

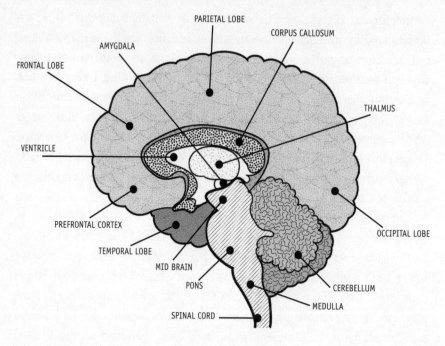

PARIETAL LOBE

CORPUS CALLOSUM

AMYGDALA

FRONTAL LOBE

THALMUS

VENTRICLE

PREFRONTAL CORTEX

OCCIPITAL LOBE

TEMPORAL LOBE

MID BRAIN

PONS

CEREBELLUM

MEDULLA

SPINAL CORD

structures that research has shown to be critical in formulating belief in the supernatural.

The real work of your brain goes on at the level of individual cells. An adult human brain contains about 100 billion nerve cells, or neurons, with branches that connect at more than 100 trillion points. Signals travelling through the neuron forest form the basis of memories, thoughts, and feelings, as well as controlling unconscious functions vital for life. Neurons are incredibly complex cells. The soma, or cell body, contains the nucleus and all the usual machinery of a cell, such as mitochondria and endoplasmic reticulum, and is where protein synthesis occurs. Branching off from the soma is the dendritic tree, where the neuron receives input from between 1000 to 100,000 other neurons. To communicate with other neurons they send out a single branch called an axon, which is covered by another type of brain cell called an oligodendrocyte that insulates the axon and assists in fast, smooth communication. The axon will undergo extensive branching, sending information to more than 1000 other neurons. Some of these axons are incredibly long, travelling all the way from your spinal cord right down to your big toe. Furthermore, inside every neuron there are more molecules than there are stars in the galaxy.

Neurons are not in physical contact with each other; there is a tiny space (approximately one micron wide) between them called a synapse. They communicate using specialised chemicals called neurotransmitters that bind onto receptors on the postsynaptic neuron. It's a bit like a key and lock system that opens hundreds of thousands of little doors. When the key opens a door, it allows charged chemicals to flow into and out of the cell along the electrical and chemical gradient, causing an electrical impulse. This all happens at a phenomenal speed. This process is best described in Bill Bryson's 2003 book, *A Short History of Nearly Everything*:

> If you could visit a cell, you wouldn't like it. Blown up to a scale at which atoms were about the size of peas, a cell itself would be a sphere roughly half a mile across, and supported by a complex framework of girders called the cytoskeleton. Within it, millions upon millions of objects — some the size of basketballs, others the size of cars — would whiz about like bullets. There wouldn't be a place you could stand without being pummeled and ripped thousands of times every second from every direction.[4]

The synapse is incredibly malleable, and it is the key to learning and memory. In addition to electrical impulses, neurotransmitters also induce a cascade of intracellular chemical events inside the neuron, which transmit information to the nucleus. These messages reach the DNA that lies inside every living cell. The DNA uses the information to construct new proteins from the extraordinary number of different molecules floating around inside the cell, strengthening the synaptic connection between the two neurons. It does this by building more keys, locks, and doors, so that the next time less effort will be required for the two neurons to communicate. If this information is perceived as important to our survival, there is a second wave of intracellular biochemical signalling and information processing. It occurs during sleep, and consolidates this information and stores it as a memory. This means that every time we learn something, there are physical changes occurring inside our brains. Let's try a really simple example to demonstrate just how phenomenal the brain is:

I want you to wiggle the big toe on your right foot.

If you choose to perform this simple task, it would have appeared to happen almost simultaneously with you reading the instruction. So what did the brain have to do to process this information and turn it into a motor function? The contrast shapes on the page arrived at your retina at the speed of light. The retina, via six layers of neuronal communication, sent a chemical signal to the primary visual cortex (via a massive relay station called the thalamus) from which this information was then sent to secondary and tertiary cortical areas, where the visual signal was interpreted as language. No small accomplishment, considering how much training our brain needs to be able to interpret symbols on a page as a form of communication.

The information then underwent further interpretation, where it was perceived as an instruction to perform a motor task and sent to the motor cortex. There it sent an instruction, via at least three separate synapses and smoothed out by several more, to release a chemical at the neuromuscular junction, which would contract and relax separate muscles to perform the task. After a tiny delay, this information then reached your consciousness. If this information is perceived as something that may need to be learned, then there is another whole level of complexity.

As you can see in this brief overview of the intricacy and complexity of the human brain, neuroscience has a great challenge ahead if it is going to understand the fundamental basis of irrationality and belief in the supernatural. However, one thing is certain: this basis for belief is a fundamental component of our psyche, and therefore a consequence of our neurobiology. If we start by understanding what the cortex is doing, we can begin to understand where and how belief in the supernatural manifests.

So what is the neocortex doing? It is trying to understand the world we live in so as to best increase the chances of our species surviving. As a consequence of this we form bonds with fellow humans, reduce the fear and stress in our lives, become motivated by rewarding stimuli, and make associations between our actions and their outcomes. These four primary functions inevitably lead to both a belief in the supernatural and resistance to rational thought.

THE SOCIAL MIND

A large portion of our neocortex is dedicated to social cognition. Our social mind resides in a complex network of cortical structures, including the anterior medial prefrontal cortex, the temporopolar region, and the temporo-parietal junction.[5] These structures also emerged in non-human social mammals such as dolphins, orcas, wolves, wild dogs, horses, hyenas, lions, and elephants — all demonstrate many of the sophisticated traits of complex social behaviour, such as working together, forming alliances, and understanding others.[6] These regions continued to expand in the human brain. Today, we are totally driven by this area of the brain — just look at how popular gossip magazines are.

To be at one with the group is an extremely powerful desire. Throughout human history, those who did not follow the group consensus were ostracised from the group, inevitably and dramatically reducing their chances of becoming an ancestor. Therefore, it became a genetically desirable trait to agree with the group. Belonging to a religious group fulfils this same need. It is a natural desire and one that does only manifest in religion — even atheist and sceptics attempt to form relationships with like-minded individuals.

FEAR

One of the consequences of having such a large prefrontal cortex is our ability to both see into the remote future and put ourselves in someone else's shoes. With this comes the knowledge of our own mortality. This insight generates an incredible amount of fear and stress in our lives that, if it were not controlled, could become detrimental to day-to-day functioning. A large part of our brain is dedicated to processing fearful emotions, some of which are buried deep inside the forebrain and temporal cortex in a brain region called the amygdala, whose primary role is to evoke physiological responses to fearful stimuli. The amygdala is intimately linked with prefrontal cortical areas involved in planning, cognition, decision-making, and moderating social behaviour. Therefore, psychological stressors, such as dealing with the unpredictability of life and the inevitability of our own deaths, have very powerful emotional and physiological outcomes that, if they get out of control, can lead to anxiety disorders.

A strategy humans have used to overcome these fears is to 'surrender' to what is perceived to be a benevolent higher power. Belief in this higher power plays two roles in reducing fear. Firstly, it makes the chaos and unpredictability of life seem somehow part of a larger plan and gives us a sense there is some purpose and meaning to it all. Secondly, it allows us to believe that there is some part of our consciousness that cheats death and continues to exist in some form. These two beliefs have the capacity to reduce the amount of stress in our lives considerably. Remember that the brain is obsessed with being able to predict the future, so when unexpected incidents occur, it can interpret these events and provide them with disproportionate emotional significance.

There are inevitably consequences in not believing in a higher power, and in accepting that the current evidence shows that we are just a conglomeration of molecules that have come together very briefly in some insignificant part of our vast universe. As mind-boggling and incredible as this evidence is, it seems to suggest that life is chaotic, without predetermined meaning, and that our conscious experiences are mortal.

Recent studies by Michael Inzlicht's research team found that religious people, or even people who simply believe in the existence of God, showed significantly less brain activity in the anterior cingulate cortex (ACC) in relation to their own errors (or mismatches between event and response) compared to non-believers. Furthermore, the stronger their religious zeal and the more they believed in God, the less their ACC fired in response to their own errors.[7]

The ACC is a region of prefrontal cortex that is involved in modifying our behaviour by signalling when attention and control are needed, predominantly as a result of an anxiety-producing event, such as making a mistake. This data suggests that believing in a supernatural power may actually be beneficial in reducing the stress caused by making errors. This small insight into the brain's responses to potentially negative stimuli implies that people who believe in a supernatural power have less overall stress in their lives.

In contrast, some religions have utilised this innate fear system as a form of social control, indoctrinating people into believing that if they don't follow the laws of the religion they will be eternally condemned to a life of damnation. Research shows that fear of God's anger is associated with smaller cortical volume in two regions of the cortex — Brodmann's Area (BA) 7 (somatosensory association cortex) and 11 (orbitofrontal area) — and in another part of the brain, the left precuneus. These regions are involved in cognitive empathy and in controlling excessive emotional responses to negative stimuli.[8] Therefore, people with smaller BA 7 and 11 may be more susceptible to fearing the wrath of God because of their compromised regulation of modulating fearful emotional responses.

ASSOCIATIONS

If there is one region of our neocortex that has expanded considerably compared to other species, it's the associative cortices. This region is involved in high-level processing of information, and forming memories of actions and their outcomes. It's what makes any species successful. Being able to associate action with outcome is essential to a species' survival.

In order to survive, we need to make associations between our manipulation of the environment and the outcome of these actions. Sometimes these associations are rational and based in fact. Sometimes they are not — for example, we danced and it rained or, in contemporary society, we were wearing our blue undies and our football team won. It is this very process that contributes to irrational superstitious beliefs. The association between a positive emotion and a religious experience can be just as powerful as a rational association, and very difficult to dismiss. What the brain is trying to do in these circumstances is predict the future (if I perform this behaviour, this positive emotion will happen).

Religious experiences have been shown to be generated in the temporal cortex — often thought of as the 'God spot'. Patients with temporal lobe epilepsy (TLE), which causes an increase in activity in the temporal lobe, often report having strong religious experiences.[9] These experiences can be so powerful that some individuals refuse to be medicated or undergo surgery to correct the problem.

To illustrate this with an anecdote, a 49-year-old man, who was raised in a conservative Jewish home but became a non-believer in adulthood, underwent surgery to remove a tumour from his left temporal lobe. After this, he started having strong religious experiences that culminated in visions of the Virgin Mary — which was ironic considering that he was brought up with a different set of beliefs. After consultation with his neurologist, it was confirmed that he had developed TLE.

Cognitive neuroscientist and university professor Michael Persinger has attempted to recreate such experiences using weak magnetic-field stimulation of the temporal lobe. Persinger's chapter in the book *Neurotheology* (2003) reports that stimulation of the left temporal lobe can lead to powerful sensations of being at one with a supernatural being.[10] It has even been suggested that many historical religious leaders may have suffered from TLE.

In order for these associations to consolidate, there exists in the human brain an intricate and poorly understood learning and memory system, able to merge a plethora of stimuli with a temporal occurrence — apparently regardless of whether they are real or not. It is still not fully understood how memories are stored or how they are retrieved. We are only just beginning to uncover the neurological basis for learning and memory and whether or not it requires synaptic plasticity to occur. Synaptic plasticity is the basis of all learning and memory, and requires a cascade of intracellular events that physically strengthens the efficiency to which neurons communicate.

This is a far from perfect system and is not to be trusted to provide us with rational factual information.

REWARD

If believing in a supernatural power achieves the objectives of reducing fear and forming strong social bonds and powerful associations between religious experience and positive emotions, it will be rewarding and will continue to be sought. Rewards are powerful motivators that arise from deep inside our forebrain. A large part of forebrain is dedicated to seeking out that which gives us positive emotion. This system is predominantly focused on desires that help the survival of the species, such as food and sex, but can be hijacked by any behaviour that has perceived positive valence, whether that be appetitive or the removal of a negative outcome. A rewarding experience causes the brain to release a number of neurotransmitters, such as dopamine, noradrenalin, and endogenous opioid peptides, which flood the brain to give us a positive feeling. These neurotransmitters also cause a cascade of intracellular events leading to learning and memory, and the formation of associations between the stimuli (in this case, belief in the supernatural) and the positive emotional outcome. Therefore, they will continue to be sought, which is why people find it so difficult to give up their beliefs even in the face of overwhelming evidence to the contrary.

RELIGIOUS EXPERIENCE FOR THE NON-BELIEVER

We all have some experiences, religious ones included, that we perceive to 'have happened'. Even though they may not be within the realms of reason or fact, they are experiences created by the nervous system, so therefore in a sense they are real.

One recent study has suggested that prenatal and pubertal-adolescent androgen levels may dictate our propensity to become believers in supernatural powers, indicating that the tendency to believe in the supernatural may be predetermined before birth.[11] So how do atheists, as non-believers in a supernatural being, get to experience the benefits of religion without believing in the supernatural? We can form social networks with like-minded individuals, which we are doing and which is an inevitable consequence of being human. This also has the benefit of reducing the amount of fear and anxiety in our lives, making us more psychologically stable and increasing our chances of becoming ancestors.

Psychedelic drugs have been used across cultures throughout history to evoke religious experiences during religious ceremonies. They have also been used under experimental conditions to evoke religious experiences in participants. Psychedelic drugs alter our brain chemistry, opening our brains up to different perceptions. The main neurotransmitter system that is stimulated by these drugs is the serotonergic system. The temporal lobe is an area that receives a substantial input from serotonin neurons, which is consistent with what we know of the sites of action of psychedelic drugs. Research into compounds that stimulate the release of serotonin, such as lysergic acid diethylamide (LSD), psilocybin, dimethyltryptamine (DMT), and mescaline, has consistently shown that these compounds have the capacity to evoke religious experiences.[12] As shown by Persinger and colleagues, a similar effect can be achieved by magnetically stimulating the temporal lobe.

Meditation is another method that can be employed to experience inner peace without believing in the supernatural. Research into the effects of meditation on brain activity have shown a quietening of the parietal lobe, a region that also aids with navigation and spatial orientation during meditation.[13] It has been speculated that this lowered activity during meditation underlies the perceived dissolution of physical boundaries and the feeling of being at one with the universe. Increased activity in the prefrontal cortex has also been reported during meditation.[14] The prefrontal areas are critically involved in attention and planning, and the recruitment of the cortex during meditation may reflect the fact that such contemplation often requires intense focus on a thought or object.

Based on this evidence, I see belief in the supernatural as a natural consequence of the evolution of the human brain's quest to understand the environment so as to increase the chances of the species surviving. I also think that it is also possible to satisfy these desires without believing in a supernatural force.

NOTES

1. See J. Maley, 'We Believe in Miracles, and UFOs', *Sydney Morning Herald*, 19 December 2009, at www.smh.com.au/national/we-believe-in-miracles-and-ufos-20091218-l5p8.html
2. V. S. Ramachandran, W. S. Hirstein, K. C. Armel, E. Tecoma and V. Iragui, 'The neural basis of religious experience', *Society for Neuroscience Abstracts,* 1997, p. 1316.
3. H. Stephan, H. Frahm and G. Baron, 'New and revised data on volumes of brain structures in insectivores and primates', *Folia Primatol*, Basel 35, 1981, pp. 1–29.
4. B. Bryson, *A Short History of Nearly Everything,* Black Swan, 2004, p. 457.
5. H.L. Gallagher and C. D. Frith, 'Functional imaging of "theory of mind"', *Trends in Cognitive Sciences* 7, 2003, pp. 77–83.
6. N. Emery, 'The Evolution of Social Cognition', in A. Easton and N. J. Emery (eds.), *Cognitive Neuroscience of Social Behaviour,* Psychology Press, Hove, 2005.
7. M. Inzlicht, I. McGregor, J. B. Hirsh and K. Nash, 'Neural Markers of Religious Conviction', *Psychological Science* 20, 2009, pp. 385–92.
8. D. Kapogiannis, A. K. Barbey, M. Su, F. Krueger and J. Grafman, 'Neuroanatomical Variability of Religiosity', *PLoS One,* 4:e7180, 2009.
9. V. S. Ramachandran et al., p. 1316; O. Devinsky and G. Lai, 'Spirituality and Religion in Epilepsy', *Epilepsy and Behavior* 12, 2008, pp. 636–43.
10. M. A. Persinger, 'Experimental Simulation of the God Experience: implications for religious beliefs and the future of the human species', in R. Joseph (ed.), *Neurotheology: Brain, Science, Spirituality, Religious Experience*, University Press, San Jose, 2002, pp. 267–84.

11. M. Voracek, 'Who Wants to Believe? Associations between digit ratio (2D:4D) and paranormal and superstitious beliefs', *Personality and Individual Differences* 47, 2009, pp. 105–109.

12. R. J. Strassman, 'Human psychopharmacology of N,N-dimethyltryptamine', *Behavioural Brain Research* 73, 1996, pp. 121–24; N. Goodman, 'The Serotonergic System and Mysticism: could LSD and the nondrug-induced mystical experience share common neural mechanisms?', *Journal of Psychoactive Drugs* 34, 2002, pp. 263–72; R. R. Griffiths, W. A. Richards, U. McCann and R. Jesse, 'Psilocybin Can Occasion Mystical-type Experiences Having Substantial and Sustained Personal Meaning and Spiritual Significance', *Psychopharmacology (Berl)* 187, 2006, pp. 268–283; discussion pp. 284–92.

13. A. Newberg, A. Alavi, M. Baime, M. Pourdehnad, J. Santanna and E. d'Aquili, 'The Measurement of Regional Cerebral Blood Flow During the Complex Cognitive Task of Meditation: a preliminary SPECT study', *Psychiatry Research* 106, 2001, pp. 113–22.

14. ibid; J. A. Brefczynski-Lewis, A. Lutz, H. S. Schaefer, D. B. Levinson and R. J. Davidson, 'Neural Correlates of Attentional Expertise in Long-term Meditation Practitioners', *Proceedings of the National Academy of Sciences of the United States of America*, 104, 2007, pp. 11,483–88.

NEUROSCIENCE, RELIGIOUS EXPERIENCE, AND SENSORY DECEPTION

Dr Rosemary Lyndall Wemm
Clinical neuro-psychology specialist

THE HUMAN BRAIN IS AN EXTRAORDINARY INSTRUMENT FOR DECODING and storing sensory information. Yet, wonderful as it is, it is an imperfect processor that does some things very badly. Even when it performs well, it is subject to many errors of perception, memory, and function.

Some of the brain's biggest strengths are also its greatest weaknesses. For instance, it finds patterns and structure in perceptual data, which is extremely useful when decoding unambiguous information with real-world consequences, but it can be problematic when the patterns are not really there or are imposed onto ambiguous data. The brain's reflex to attach emotion and meaning to data is necessary for selective attention and for the storage of memories for later retrieval, but it can become dysfunctional when intense experiences and memories become intransigent but delusional beliefs. The brain compensates for missing and imperfect data below the level of awareness. When these things are not there, not possible, masked, or not happening, our brain adds them, imposes them, invents them, or distorts them. We cannot normally detect the blind spot in our vision or the holes and biases in other aspects of our perception, memory, and thinking. This makes the brain a very unreliable witness and assessor of reality, which is all too frequently at odds with tangible and measurable evidence.

None of these brain limitations and dysfunctions are controversial, and all are supported by considerable evidence. Two areas of human endeavour specifically attempt to compensate for the brain's limitations: the sciences and the legal system both impose mechanisms for screening out these inherent and inevitable failings of human perception, thinking, and memory. Experimental psychology applies psychometrics and scientific methodology, and the justice system applies rules of evidence, which give a low rating to unsubstantiated human testimony. On the other hand, religious belief systems do not. These systems typically reverse the hierarchy by demanding that the most reliable forms of evidence be dismissed if they are inconsistent with evidence obtained from the most unreliable sources: subjective human experience, emotion, interpretation, and semantic restructuring.

Although resistance to scientific investigation of religion is still extremely strong in many regions — especially those associated with repressive cultural systems and low standards of scientific education — research into the full range of religious and spiritual beliefs and experiences has grown. Along with scientific discoveries and investigations that discredit or raise serious questions about the truth of many religious doctrines, there is now a considerable body of information about how religious beliefs are obtained and maintained, even in the face of overwhelming contradictory evidence.

The previous essay by Dr Adam Hamlin has provided an overview of the field, and this essay will narrow the focus to look at the association between powerful religious and spiritual experiences and permanent or temporary dysfunction of particular regions of the brain. This is an important area because many still regard tales of people experiencing strong feelings of the divine that 'defy natural explanation' as profound and accurate representations of real events.

We'll focus on a couple of specific areas of the brain and their associated disorders in order to explore natural explanations for experiences that continue to grip some members of the community. These powerful experiences have traditionally been explained as divine revelation or connection with gods, spirits, or vital truths, but the neurosciences are increasingly able to explain such events within the prosaic and far less exotic scope of ordinary and specifically dysfunctional brain activity.

BASIC BRAIN ANATOMY

Contrary to public mythology, we make use of all the sections of our brains at various points during a typical day. In brains that are functioning normally, only those sections that are relevant to the current task predominate. More is not better: when working on similar material, an expert will utilise fewer sections of their brain than a novice. A person whose whole brain is firing strongly all at once is having a grand mal epileptic seizure. Shorter seizures result in damage or death of neurons; a prolonged seizure is a life-threatening emergency.

Higher-order functions are processed in the cerebral hemispheres. For the majority of people, the left hemisphere is language dominant and the right hemisphere is visuo-spatial dominant. It is the right hemisphere that is responsible for comparing new sensations with old input and determining whether there is any difference. People with a compromised right hemisphere are often spectacularly unaware that they have cognitive, motor, or memory deficits, although this may be very clear to other observers. Intriguingly, should the person recover the use of the 'checking function' of the right hemisphere, they will maintain that they were always aware of deficits that they firmly denied during the time they were deficient. They have permanently lost the ability to compare their previously compromised state with either the far remote past or the present. Remember this point, as it has important implications for material that is to follow.

The cerebrum is divided into two sections by a central fissure. The back half of the cerebrum deals with the processing and storage of incoming information, while the front half acts on that information and on external stimuli. The motor strip (controlling muscle action) is located immediately in front of the central fissure and the sensory strip (processing tactile information) is located immediately behind it. The back part of the brain processes visual information. The front tip of the brain is the master controller and deals with planning, organising, and the monitoring and regulation of behaviour. Damage to this area results in anti-social behaviour and personality change. This has implications for the notion of wilful 'sin'.

The parietal lobes of the brain are located behind the central fissure and include the sensory strip. They are involved in the processing of sensory and tactile information, including balance and spatial positioning.

The side regions of each cerebral hemisphere are called the temporal lobes. They are concerned with auditory sensation and perception, auditory and visuospatial input, organisation and categorisation of verbal material, and language comprehension. The amygdala, located in the lower portion of these lobes, is involved in emotion. Positive emotions are a function of the left side, while negative emotions are a function of the right, a fact that has implications for the doctrine of joy as a function of religious commitment. The amygdala has a pivotal role in converting immediate memories to long-term storage. It determines which experiences are important enough to store based on their emotional significance. Emotion is thus intimately involved in the processing of long-term memories.

The hippocampus is an internal structure of the temporal lobes that shifts short-term memories to long-term storage. And deep inside the hemispheres and on top or the brain stem is an evolutionarily primitive circuit known as the limbic system. This consists of a ring of structures that are well connected to one another and to the temporal lobes. They are involved in the control of emotion, emotional response, hormonal secretions, mood, motivation, sexual feelings, parenting instincts, bonding, and the sensation of pain and pleasure. They are also involved in the processing of material for long-term memory storage and in the emotional interpretation given to freshly experienced and recalled events.

The two hemispheres of the brain do most of their communicating via a thick bundle of fibres called the corpus callosum. If this bundle is severed or fails to develop, the person has two separate brains with two distinct personalities in their head. Since complex language is confined to one hemisphere, they must communicate by visual or tactile means. The presence of multiple discrete personalities and styles of processing presents serious challenges for the concept of a unitary 'soul', and for the doctrine of the post-death judgement of one's actions and verbal beliefs.

RELIGIOUS ECSTASY AND THE TEMPORAL LOBES

Advances in the understanding of how the brain is organised and how it works frequently come from observation of its output when damaged or malfunctioning. A particularly fruitful area of examination has been seizure activity. Seizures range from focal (affecting a specific area) through partial (affecting a region or neighbourhood) to general (spilling over into the rest of the brain). While general seizures are relatively easy to identify — because they involve the motor strip and result in tonic-clonic muscle spasms — partial and focal seizures are easy to miss or mistake for something else. Yet it is the study of these more limited phenomena that has resulted in the greatest advances in knowledge.

The electrical peculiarities of the temporal lobes make them especially vulnerable to focal seizure activity. Temporal lobe epilepsy (TLE) can result in simple 'absences' that are commonly mistaken for laziness, rudeness, or failure to pay attention; or they can result in complex repetitive behaviours, paranoia, aggressive rages, and increased sexual activity.

A lesser known feature of TLE is the propensity of victims to have intense religious, ecstatic, and 'spiritual' experiences.[1] These experiences cannot be differentiated from reality by those living through them and continue to seem profoundly real to the perceiver even after the seizure has ended. While the phenomenon is often a mixed bag of the blissful and the terrifying, people typically minimise the negative aspects and promote the positive ones. Patients with TLE can be reluctant to take medication or submit to surgery if they are persuaded that the treatment could remove their ability to experience these ecstatic events.

The earthly underpinnings of these phenomena are apparent when we recognise that the symptoms of these spiritual experiences share physical and neurological characteristics that are indicative of TLE activity, while the interpretations placed upon them are clearly a product of each person's individual life experience and personality. While the unusual profundity of the experience frequently leads victims to an unshakeable belief that they have been in contact with the divine, it is telling that the experience is almost always confined to gods and supernatural phenomena that are specific to their culture and background. There is no persuasive record of anyone encountering a supernatural entity about which they have no prior knowledge, and no one has ever reported encountering a divinity that is unknown to them but known to people in other places or times. The obvious conclusion is that the phenomena stems from an idiosyncratic mix of imagination, immediate environment, and the information and images stored by the person's temporal lobes.

The intensity of seizure activity burns new pathways and emotional associations in the brain, and these are prone to be reactivated not only during subsequent seizures, but during the intervals between them. This is known as the 'kindling effect' and is similar to the 'flashback' phenomena that can result from use or abuse of hallucinogenic drugs.

The temporo-limbic system is responsible for determining the importance, relevance, and meaning of religious experiences as part of the memory-storage processes. The left temporal cortex processes and stores religious archetypes — figures and symbols that have religious significance. The subcortical areas provide emotional meaning. The kindling process can strengthen the electrical pathways between religious information, sensory experience, and emotional context. For these patients, ideas and sensations become profoundly significant.

Those who have had a religious experience as part of a seizure usually display intense religious behaviour between seizures. This behaviour may include serial conversions to a variety of religions as well as bizarre attributions of personal divinity. In fact, TLE is so frequently associated with hyper-religiosity that this phenomenon has become part of the signs that helps to identify the disorder.[2]

Persinger and Makarec found significant positive correlations between measures of complex partial seizure and measures of paranormal phenomena.[3] EEG readings of subjects who were not in the process of having a seizure revealed that the number of epileptic spikes in the temporal lobes was directly related to measures of religious belief, mystical experiences, and the sense of an other-worldly presence, while spikes seen in other areas of the brain were not correlated. Church attendance was unrelated to either measure, suggesting that religious training has less influence on spiritual experience than biological make-up.

Persinger describes three physiologic characteristics of the temporal lobe that could give rise to spontaneous spiritual experience. First, the deep structures of the temporal lobe (the amygdala and the hippocampus) are electrically unstable. This, following significant stimulation (seizures) leads to the kindling effect, giving rise to transient microseizures that are not necessarily related to current sensory input. Second, areas of the temporal lobes are prone to vascular abnormalities, known to be a primary cause of hallucinatory experiences. Third, cell membranes in the area are prone to different types and amounts of merging or fusion, resulting in significant problems for the normal cell functions of the affected region.

This is a predisposing factor for TLE.

The brains of TLE patients who suffer from religious psychopathology have been shown to have asymmetrical hippocampi, the right side being relatively smaller than the left.[4] This might mean that the left hippocampus is less inhibited than normal, and that the cognitive and emotional sensations of the left hemisphere are not being properly filtered by the right hemisphere during the storage process. This is one explanation for why TLE patients are so convinced that their spiritual and religious experiences are real, rather than delusional.

OTHER CAUSES OF FERVENT RELIGIOUS EXPERIENCES

Religious delusional syndromes are also a feature of some forms of psychosis, notably manic and schizophrenic conditions. Surprisingly, there have been relatively few neurological studies of the phenomena in this group. A recent study that attempted to address this investigatory gap used a PET scan to investigate neurological activity in a single subject with a schizotypical religious delusional syndrome. PET scanning uses intravenously injected radioactive dyes to measure the blood flow to various parts of the brain during highly specific activities or time periods. Active areas use more blood than quiescent ones. The authors of this case study found that while the patient was reporting a religious delusion, blood flow to the occipital lobe (involved in vision) was depressed, while blood flow to the left temporal lobe was elevated. While the patient may have been convinced that he was seeing his god, the neurological findings imply that any visions the patient experienced came from his memory and unchecked imagination, not from reality.

Hallucinations, illusions, and unusually intense emotional experiences are known to be the result of a number of conditions that affect the normal functioning of the body and brain. While the effects of mind-altering chemicals are common knowledge among the citizens of modern industrialised societies, there are many other factors that are not so commonly recognised as conducive to such experiences. This includes, but is not confined to, prolonged hunger, thirst, fatigue, pain, sleeplessness, sensory deprivation, pulsing light, intense sound, loud music, chanting, dancing, stomping, clapping, rhythmic movement, shock, emotional exhilaration, life-threatening danger, oxygen deprivation, and CO2 poisoning. Many of these methods of inducing altered states of consciousness are included in the arsenal of those who aim to torture or brainwash people. They are also used by therapists, mentalists, salespeople and evangelists who wish to heighten a person's suggestibility, and by religious leaders who wish to induce ecstasy, glossolalia ('speaking in tongues'), fainting attacks, and the belief that one is possessed by or filled with a supernatural being.

IMPLICATIONS FOR THE TRUTH VALUE OF ANCIENT VISIONS

It should now be clear that it is prudent to question the validity of the strong religious convictions expressed by people with neurological conditions that interfere with reality checking, memory, emotion, and visual integrity. This raises questions of the legitimacy of the religious visions and fantastical events reported in various holy books: bushes which burn but are not consumed, wrestling matches with a supernatural being, divine commands to murder one's child, visions of angels and the backside of Yahweh, stones inscribed by an invisible hand, temptations spoken by the devil, and so on. The accuracy and reliability of the written accounts of ancient aural tradition is likely to be low, and the subjects cannot be tested by modern neuro-scientific investigation. However, there is good reason to suspect that some, if not all, of these stories are pre-scientific accounts of events arising from compromised brains.

Some have speculated that Old Testament prophets may have ingested the ancient equivalent of magic mushrooms, while others have suggested that they suffered from some form of recurrent psychosis. Old Testament prophets and New Testament figures were reported to spend a lot of time on their own atop mountains and in the wilderness, probably without attending to bodily needs essential for physical and mental health. They returned with all kinds of fantastic and unverifiable stories of visions and auditory hallucinations containing events and characters consistent with the prevailing cultural and religious beliefs of their community.

The conversion of Saul of Tarsus to St Paul of the Gentiles was effected on the road to Damascus, when Saul/Paul saw a bright light followed by a speaking vision of Jesus, the man whose followers he was persecuting. He then fell down on the ground and lost his sight for several days. The account is highly suggestive of a TLE-related seizure. The temporary blindness is consistent with head trauma from the concomitant fall, or a constricted blood supply to the visual cortex or the subcortical visual pathway during the seizure. While there is some disagreement in the biblical record over whether accompanying members of the entourage saw a bright light during these events (easily explainable as a retrograde memory distortion among those who believed they did) it is agreed that they did not see the detailed vision of Jesus, hear the voice that went with it, fall down, or become visually impaired. The general consensus suggests that the event existed entirely within Paul's subjective experience.

In spite of Paul's unshakeable belief that he had been vouchsafed a personal communication from the risen Jesus, this did not appear to include knowledge of this preacher's ministry, words, or activities while alive. Paul's preserved writings describe a metaphysical relationship with a Christ who existed in another realm.

Paul was so convinced that his Damascus experience provided him with a personal insight into the mind and mission of the risen Christ that it overrode any compunction he might have had about correcting the opinions of others who were familiar with the earthly life and ministry of Jesus. Paul argued with Peter, brother of Jesus, that Jewish observances such as circumcision should not be required of Gentile converts because they were unnecessary for salvation under the new covenant. If this was the message of the historical Jesus, it is difficult to reconcile with the words and messages of Jesus recorded by the gospel writers several decades later. The Jesus depicted in the gospels was not interested in preaching to the Gentiles, whom he dismissed as 'dogs'. *That* Jesus claimed that he had come to fulfil Jewish law, not to overturn or remove it. Theologians, of course, find ways to spin these into an inventive compatibility. As any psychologist would tell you, the mind is very good at finding ways to reduce the distress of cognitive dissonance.

While there is no doubt that Paul found the Damascus experience so compelling that he became obsessed by it, he is reported to have been equally zealous in his persecution of the followers of Jesus prior to this event. As has been noted, serial religious conversions and obsessions are a common feature of the TLE personality. In other words, Paul's experience of the risen Christ has the hallmarks of being produced by a neurologically impaired brain.

'GOD SPOTS' IN THE BRAIN

In 1997, Dr Vilayanur Ramachandran and his research team at the University of San Diego published a study that compared epileptics who were known to have profoundly religious experiences with two groups of neuro-typical people: one group of people who were deeply religious and another group who were not.[5] Subjects were asked to listen to a mixture of religious, sexual, and neutral statements while the intensity of their emotional reaction was measured by the galvanic skin response, a method that measures the electrical resistance of the skin. Both the TLE and the religious group reacted strongly to statements of a religious nature. Curiously, the TLE group under-reacted to other statements, especially those of a sexual nature.

On the basis of this study and the known connection between TLE and hyper-religiosity, Ramachandran speculated that there might be specific machinery in the temporal lobe concerned with religion, machinery that may have evolved in order to impose order and stability on society. He dubbed this circuit 'the god module', a description that he had cause to regret.[6]

American journalists loved it. The 'god module' was quickly converted to the 'god spot' and splashed around in the media as a scientific justification for America's hyperreligious mindset. The popular media failed to note that Ramachandran was expressing an opinion about the implications of his research, and not a falsifiable scientific theory.

Steve Connor, the science correspondent for the *Los Angeles Times*, suggested that atheists might have different neural circuitry to religious people.[7] The context of the conjecture implied that atheists were, in consequence, less likely to engage in co-operative social behaviour. There are a number of problems with this conjecture.

First, the evidence does not support the idea that atheists are less social or cooperative compared to people who are deeply religious. While there is evidence that religious people hold more conventional values and tend to be more conformist, secular groups have higher measures of social health than religious groups.[8]

Second, the idea that atheists are genetically unable to experience the divine is inconsistent with the idea of a loving supernatural being who rewards or punishes people on the basis of their capacity to experience him.

Third, the idea ignores the existence of the growing number of people who now openly acknowledge that they de-converted from religion because it failed to stand up under scrutiny and critical analysis. Many of these were heavily committed to their religion, including those who were missionaries, evangelists, and members of the clergy, and claim to have had intense experiences of what they believed at the time to be divine. It would have to be explained why such people have had a change of brain circuitry.

Robert Lee Holtz, also writing for the *Los Angeles Times*, reported more honestly that the scientists who conducted the study were unclear about why such a 'module' existed.[9] According to Holtz, the Ramachandran team suggested that one possibility might be that the module developed to encourage tribal loyalty, to reinforce kinship ties, or to stabilise a closely knit clan. A critical analysis of this expressed possibility would have to include the observation that religious beliefs are supportive of intra-group stability, but work against extra-group relations. The anti-social consequences are hatred, bigotry, aggression, and intolerance towards 'out-groups' that do not share the same beliefs, and repression, censure, and even torture of members of the 'in-group' who do not toe the line set by the religious leaders. In other words, it is a primitive society's recipe for barbarism and thuggery disguised as honourable behaviour.

NEURO-TYPICALS AND RELIGION

While people with known neuropathology and psychopathology experience intense states of altered consciousness with an ecstatic affect and a decreased sense of self, similar states are reported, and even deliberately induced, by people who appear to be relatively neurologically normal. The means of achieving these states vary. Their significance is, once again, interpreted according to the background and expectations of the subject.

A question that remained unanswered at the end of last century was how to interpret such religious and mystical experiences, when they are reported by people whose personality and cognitive integrity do not appear to be globally affected. Are they experiencing something that has a basis in metaphysical reality, or does the neuro-scientific evidence provide a secular explanation?

Continuing with the temporal-lobe hypothesis of the origins of religion, Michael Persinger and his assistants developed and tested a device that has become known as the 'god helmet'.[10] This cap stimulated the temporal lobes and adjacent parietal cortex with pulsed magnetic fields.

The helmeted subject was blindfolded and seated in a quiet room for 60-minute sessions. According to Persinger, most reported experiencing religious, spiritual, or mystical experiences involving the sensation of a shadowy alien presence or the sensation of profound bliss. The affected subjects translated these sensations in terms of their religious and cultural backgrounds, terming it God, Buddha, oneness with the universe, or a benevolent or sinister presence. No two experiences were identical. Other researchers have reported that stimulation of cortical areas in the temporo-parietal junction results in disturbed other–self boundaries, such as out-of-body experiences, a sense that the self has been cloned and exists in two places at once, or the sensation that another being is present or shadowing one's actions.[11]

Granqvist and colleagues were unable to replicate Persinger's findings, and concluded that the results were due to subject suggestibility.[12] David Wulff of Wheaton College in Massachusetts noted that those most likely to report mystical sensations tend to be open to new experiences in general and tend towards fantasy.[13]

BEYOND THE TEMPORAL LOBES

Research by later authors (Newberg, D'Aquili, Beauregard, Kapogiannis, Grafman, Davidson, and others) used computerised scanning methods to investigate the areas of the brain involved when non-clinical populations experienced ecstatic and mystical events. The investigations concentrated on events that were self-induced (such as Buddhist meditation and Carmelite contemplative prayer) rather than induced by others (such as charismatic preachers, evangelists, and researchers) or acquired by accident or ill health.[14] Several sections of the brain were found to be highly active, including the pre-frontal lobes, the left temporal lobe, the limbic system, and subcortical nuclei involved in strong irrational emotions.

Contrary to the earlier theories, the pivotal connecting feature was not hyper-stimulation of the temporal lobes, but inhibition of the right anterior superior section of the parietal lobe. This area helps to differentiate the 'self' from the outside world. When it does not function properly, the sense of self is disturbed, resulting in feelings of union with the universe or connection with a supernatural being. Involvement of the left temporal lobe is a secondary process that strives to make sense of the experience.

Without the usual mental breaking system, the left temporal lobe becomes overactive. This hyper-stimulates subcortical areas of the limbic system, which are involved in the development of strong, prolonged, and irrational emotional states such as maternal and romantic love, and in the child–parent bonding process.[15] These irrational emotions are hardwired into the brain because they have strong survival value for the human species. In other words, the ability to experience 'god' is not naturally wired into the brain; instead, the brain, which believes itself to be in ecstatic communion with the supernatural, is hooked into neural circuitry that developed for more primitive reasons.

Johnson and Glass confirmed the primary role of the malfunctioning right anterior superior parietal area.[16] They reported that the development of a new or deepening interest in religion following brain injury was significantly correlated with damage to the right parietal lobe, weakly related to the integrity of the left temporal lobe, and not correlated at all with the functioning of the frontal lobes. The researchers concluded that the prefrontal cortex was activated during meditation and contemplative prayer because of its role in orchestrating and achieving the temporary shutdown of the right parietal lobe. Newberg and Iversen provide a detailed theory of the neuro-mechanics of this process in neuro-typical subjects.[17]

In other words, religious and mystical experiences appear to arise as the result of the temporary or permanent impairment of a specific area in the right cerebral hemisphere, which is then interpreted by a section of the left hemisphere in the absence of the usual mental reality checks. While such experiences appear to be very vivid and profoundly real, this is an illusion resulting from a poorly functioning brain.

Religions invariably treat human testimony based on subjective sensory experience and personal conviction as the most reliable way of discovering spiritual truths. Personal belief in the absence of objective evidence, or faith, is held in the highest esteem. Many go so far as to assert that objective evidence that contradicts such testimony should be demonised, discounted, or reinterpreted to fit the subjective accounts. The lynchpin of experimental psychology is that human sensory experience is an extremely poor measure of reality.

SENSORY ILLUSIONS AND DISTORTIONS

Neuroscientists are familiar with a range of perceptual illusions, delusions, and distortions that the brain generates in order to compensate for missing data, or to make sense of unfamiliar sensual situations or impaired neural processing. These phenomena occur in all of the major senses as well as the higher functions associated with reasoning and intent. While some are associated with brain malfunction, others occur because of the limitations of the normally functioning brain.

The Capgras Delusion is a disorder in which a person believes that someone they know well has been replaced by an impostor who looks just like them. It occurs in patients diagnosed with schizophrenia and in people suffering from brain injuries, tumours, and dementias. Ramachandran argues that it results from the right temporal–parietal facial recognition cortex becoming disconnected from the limbic areas involved in providing meaning and emotional arousal in response to what is seen.

Hemi-neglect syndromes are a common consequence of right-hemisphere stroke. Even when it can be demonstrated that the patient can see or sense objects in both right and left fields, the person behaves as if the objects in one field are not there. Patients with visual hemi-field neglect will draw half a house, half a clock, or a flower with petals on only one side. Such patients have difficulty reading because they only fully attend to the right half of a page, the right half of a word, and the right half of a letter. They are generally convinced that the problem lies with their spectacle prescription and are unmoved by medical explanations of their condition. This is one of many examples where the left brain, unable to identity a deficit in the absence of a functioning, cross-checking right hemisphere, comes up with a subjectively plausible, but objectively faulty interpretation.

The Anton-Babinski syndrome occurs in people whose primary visual cortex is destroyed. Although they are blind, they insist that they can see. It becomes clear to observers that this is not the case when the victim bumps into objects, tries to walk though walls, and describes people in the room in terms that are clearly at variance with how they appear in reality. The patient is unconvinced by conflicting evidence, which is dismissed with imaginative rationalisations such as 'it is too dark in here'.

Korsakov syndrome occurs when part of the memory-processing system is destroyed due to specific vitamin B deficiencies, usually as the result of alcohol abuse or prolonged vomiting. Victims have only a three-minute memory window for information obtained after the onset of the disorder. When challenged to recall information in the preceding minutes, the person will fabricate material that they find subjectively plausible. Such patients exhibit symptoms of anosagnosia (lack of awareness of defect) and confabulation (the involuntary and unconscious production of imaginary scenarios which fill in cognitive or sensory 'holes').

Perceptual illusions and delusions also occur in people with normally functioning brains. Some illusions are induced by a third party. The Pinocchio Effect is an artificially induced perception that one's nose is several feet long. In Virtual Mayhem, the actions of the experimenter persuade a subject that his hand is rising up through a table and becoming part of it.[18] When the experimenter grasps a hammer and pounds that part of the table, the subject recoils in horror. False memory syndrome, the conviction that something which did not actually occur happened, can be artificially induced by a third party or may be self-induced by someone with a conscious or subconscious interest in the outcome.

Other illusions occur with little or no intervention by another party. Phantom Limb syndrome involves the sensation that an amputated limb is still attached to the body and can be moved like those that actually exist. Optic blind spot anasognosia, or lack of awareness of the visual hole in each eye, is a continuous and permanent condition for every human. The brain not only ignores these holes, but fills them in with amorphous material that bears a vague resemblance to the surrounding visual input. Humans cannot locate these visual holes without experimental props.

The imperfections of the human visual system result in a myriad of optical illusions. Straight lines appear bent, static images appear to move, equal lines appear to be of unequal length, two-dimensional images appear to have depth, objects appear to roll up hill, and so on.

The point is that all these sensory mistakes and misrecognitions seem very real to those who experience them. The error may be obvious to observers who can perceive material that the person with the compromised or manipulated brain cannot. In other cases, the subjective experience is at variance with objective measurement or confirmation. The illusionary nature of a sensation is not so obvious in cases where the reference material cannot be touched, measured, or objectively observed by others. Such is the case for religious visions, auditory hallucinations, and sensations of an alien presence, of blissful feelings and a conviction of being in receipt of a valuable 'truth'.

In many cases it is impossible to convince the subject that what they sense is illusionary. One author lamented that:

> If you really want to believe in a spiritual reality, no amount of demonstrations of material-world, neuro-physiological, genetic, or cosmological facts, however probable and compelling, will ever swamp such a belief.[19]

CONCLUSION

The intact and normally functioning brain has an enormous and innately compelling capacity to distort, ignore, avoid, and embroider reality in favour of ideas that are familiar, comfortable, and emotionally attractive. In fact, the brain is hardwired to experience strong emotions with little or no basis in reality. This makes it a poor instrument for determining the validity of unsupported real-world phenomena.

Unusually intense religious experiences are associated with abnormal neurological states and a range of other disconnections from reality. Those who have not had these experiences are nevertheless willing to follow leaders who have uncritically.

It should now be clear that the brain is not hardwired to sense a particular god or supernatural entity. The only consistency is that those who claim to have spiritual or mystical revelations interpret them in terms of the prevailing context and the culture and knowledge to which they have been previously exposed.

All of this seems to indicate that there are better ways of knowing our world and our place in it than relying on the say-so of individuals who to have claim powerful knowledge based upon revelatory experiences. Religion appears to have codified the ramblings of people who, by today's standards, would be at the head of the queue to receive neurological or mental-health treatment. That religion continues to do this in the face of the industrial-strength scientific explanations simply reinforces the fundamental irrationality of our species.

It is time to move forward to an age that can celebrate lofty emotions without contaminating them with supernatural tags.

NOTES

1. D. M. Bear and P. Fedio, 'Quantitative Analysis of Interictal Behavior in Temporal Lobe Epilepsy', *Archives of Neurology* 34 (8), August 1977, pp. 454–67.
2. V.S. Ramachandran, W.S. Hirstein, K.C. Armel, F. Tecoma and V. Iragui, 'The Neural Basis of Religious Experience', *Proceedings of the Annual Conference of the Society of Neuroscience* 23, 1997, abstract 519.1.
3. K. Makarec and M.A. Persinger, 'Temporal Lobe Signs: electroencephalographic validity and enhanced scores in special populations', *Perceptual and Motor Skills*, 60 (3), June 1985, pp. 831–42; K. Makarec and M.A. Persinger, 'Geophysical Variables and Behavior: XLII. negative correlation between accuracy of card-guessing and geomagnetic activity: a case study', *Perceptual and Motor Skills*, 65, 1987, pp. 105–106.
4. J. Wuerfel, E.S. Krishnamoorthy, R.J. Brown, L. Lemieux, M. Koepp, L. Tebartz van Elst and M.R. Trimble, 'Religiosity is Associated with Hippocampal but not Amygdala Volumes in Patients with Refractory Epilepsy', *Journal of Neurology, Neurosurgery, and Psychiatry,* 75 (4), April 2004, pp. 640–2.
5. 'The Neural Basis of Religious Experience'.
6. 'God and the Temporal Lobes of the Brain'. A talk given by V.S. Ramachandran as part of the program *Human Selves and Transcendental Experiences: a dialogue of science and religion,* presented at U.C. San Diego, 31 January 1998. Reviewed by N. Hall, 16 February 1998, at http://cas.bellarmine.edu/tietjen/images/new_page_2.htm
7. S. Connor, '"God Spot" is Found in Brain', *Los Angeles Times*, 29 October 1997, at http://cas.bellarmine.edu/tietjen/images/new_page_2.htm
8. G. S. Paul, 'Cross-National Correlations of Quantifiable Societal Health with Popular Religiosity and Secularism in the Prosperous Democracies,' *Journal of Religion and Society* 7, 2005, at http://moses.creighton.edu/JRS/2005/2005-11.html; F. K. Zimmerman, 'Religion: a conservative social force', *Journal of Abnormal and Social Psychology*, 1934, vol. 28 (4), pp. 473–47.
9. R. L. Holtz, 'Brain Region May be Linked to Religion', *Los Angeles Times,* 29 October 1997, p. 12.
10. L.S. St-Pierre and M.A. Persinger, 'Experimental Facilitation of the Sensed Presence is Predicted by the Specific Patterns of the Applied Magnetic Fields, Not by Suggestibility: re-analyses of 19 experiments', *The International Journal of Neuroscience,* 116 (9), September 2006, pp. 1079–96.
11. O. Blanke, S. Ortigue, T. Landis, and M. Seeck, 'Stimulating Illusory Own-Body Perceptions', *Nature* 419, 2002, pp. 269–70; O. Blanke and G. Thut, (ed. G. Della Sala), 'Inducing Out of Body Experiences', *Tall Tales*, Oxford University Press, 2006.
12. P. Granqvist, M. Fredrikson, P. Unge, A. Hagenfeldt, S. Valind, D. Larhammar, M. Larsson, 'Sensed Presence and Mystical Experiences are Predicted by Suggestibility, not by the Application of Transcranial Weak Complex Magnetic Fields', *Neuroscience Letters* 379, 29 April 2005, pp. 1–6.
13. S. Begley, 'Religion And The Brain', *Newsweek*, 7 May 2001.

14. M. Beauregard and V. Paquette, 'Neural Correlates of a Mystical Experience in Carmelite Nuns', *Neuroscience Letters* 405, 2006, pp. 186–190; E. d'Aquili and A. Newberg, 'Religious and Mystical States: a neuropsychological model,' *Zygon: Journal of Religion and Science* 28, 1993, pp. 177–200.
15. H. E. Fisher, A. Aron, and L. L. Brown, 'Romantic Love: a mammalian brain system for mate choice', *Philosophical Transactions of the Royal Society B* 361, (1476), 29 December 2006, pp. 2173–86.
16. B. Johnstone and B. Glass, 'Support for a Neuropsychological Model of Spirituality in Persons with Traumatic Brain Injury,' *Zygon: Journal of Religion and Science*, 43, December 2008, pp. 861–74.
17. A. B. Newberg and J. Iversen, 'The Neural Basis of the Complex Mental Task of Meditation: neurotransmitter and neurochemical considerations', *Medical Hypotheses,* 61 (2), 2003, pp. 282–91.
18. V.S. Ramachandran, speech given in San Diego, text at http://cas.bellarmine.edu/tietjen/images/new_page_2.htm.
19. N. Hall, 'A Review of "God and the Temporal Lobes of the Brain" ', 16 February 1998, at http://cas.bellarmine.edu/tietjen/images/new_page_2.htm

APPENDIX: THE COST OF ADVANCING RELIGION

THE FOLLOWING INFORMATION SUMMARISES THE FINDINGS OF JOHN L. Perkins and Frank Gomez. It has become the standard reference for media when estimating the magnitude of religious subsidy in Australia.

COST OF RELIGIOUS EXEMPTIONS AND SUBSIDIES TO TAXPAYERS

	AMOUNT (in billions)
Income tax lost	15.1
Capital gains tax lost	6.5
Income lost to state and federal governments	1.6
Grants to religious schools (from the Commonwealth)	5.6
Grants to religious schools (from states)	1.8
Other grants	0.5
TOTAL	31.1

The total, exceeding $31 billion, is based on 2006 data. It is necessarily somewhat speculative. It may be discounted for bona fide charitable works and for expenditures that may otherwise be required. However, it does not include items such as FBT and GST, where we are unable to source data on the value of concessions. The figure gives some idea of the magnitude of the cost of 'advancing religion' in Australia.

Activities that are genuinely charitable should be eligible for tax concessions. The annual grants and benefits of billions of dollars to religious organisations in Australia go far beyond this. The reason for this is that in Australian law, anything deemed to 'advance religion' is considered charitable. The origin of this anomaly dates from the common law of medieval England. Such is the ability of organised religion to evade rational scrutiny.

Due to a lack of information, it is difficult to obtain accurate estimates of the cost of these tax exemptions and subsidies. Religious organisations are not required to file tax returns. Federally, concessions apply to income tax, fringe benefits tax, and the goods and services tax. State government exemptions cover land tax, payroll tax, stamp duties, and car registration fees. Local governments provide exemptions from municipal rates. The figures in the above table are estimations by collating figures from various sources.

For further details, see the submissions by the Secular Party to the federal government's Review of Australia's Future Tax System, and more recently to the Senate Inquiry into a Public Benefit Test for religious exemptions at http://tinyurl.com/29yacem. See also the article by John L. Perkins and Frank Gomez in *Australian Humanist* 93, Autumn 2009, pp. 6–8.

FURTHER INFORMATION

GROUPS & ORGANISATIONS

Melbourne Atheists (The Atheist Society)
www.theatheist.net

Sydney Atheists
www.sydneyatheists.org

Brisbane Atheists
www.meetup.com/brisbaneatheists

Sunshine Coast Atheists
www.sunshinecoastatheists.com

Perth Atheists
www.meetup.com/perthatheists

The Adelaide Atheists Meetup Group
www.meetup.com/adelaideatheists

The Canberra Atheists Meetup Group
www.meetup.com/atheists-596

Atheist Foundation of Australia
www.atheistfoundation.org.au

Reason Australia
www.reasonaustralia.org.au

Freethought University Alliance
www.freethoughtalliance.org.au

Rationalist Society of Australia
www.rationalist.com.au

The Secular Party of Australia
www.secular.org.au

Australian Secular Lobby
www.australiansecularlobby.com

Australian Skeptics (Sydney-based)
www.skeptics.com.au

Queensland Skeptics
www.qldskeptics.com

Sunshine Coast Skeptics Society
http://embiggenbooks.com/skeptics-society

Perth Skeptics
www.meetup.com/perth-skeptics

South Australian Skeptics
www.skepticssa.org.au

Skeptics in Tasmania
www.skepticstas.org.au

Victorian Skeptics
www.vicskeptics.wordpress.com

Canberra Skeptics
www.finch.customer.netspace.net.au/skeptics

Young Australian Skeptics
www.youngausskeptics.com

Council of Australian Humanist Societies
www.humanist.org.au

Humanist Society of New South Wales
www.hsnsw.asn.au

Humanist Society of Victoria
www.victorianhumanist.com

Humanist Society of Western Australia
www.humanistwa.org.au

Humanist Society of Queensland
www.hsq.org.au

Humanist Society of South Australia
www.users.on.net/~rmc/hsofsa.htm

World Truth Day (group set up to protest the publicly subsidised World Youth Day)
www.worldtruthday.org

No to Pope Coalition
www.notopope.com

FURTHER AUSTRALIAN-AUTHORED ATHEIST READING

Adams vs God: the rematch
by Phillip Adams, Melbourne University Press, Melbourne, 2007.

50 Voices of Disbelief: why we are atheists
Edited by Russell Blackford and Udo Shutlink, Wiley–Blackwell, Chichester, 2009.

From Faith to Reason
by Brian Baker, Vivid Publishing, Fremantle, 2009.

Religion: the greatest confidence trick in history
by Dennis Morris, Lulu.com, Morrisville, 2007.

Against Religion
by Tamas Pataki, Scribe, Melbourne, 2007.

Atheism and Theism (2nd revised edition)
by J. J. C. Smart and John Haldane, Blackwell Publishers, Oxford, 2002.

The Purple Economy
by Max Wallace, Australian National Secular Association, Sydney, 2007.

Realising Secularism: Australia and New Zealand
by Max Wallace, Rationalist Society of Australia, Melbourne, 2010.

Unintelligent Design: why God isn't as smart as she thinks she is
by Robyn Williams, Allen & Unwin, Sydney, 2006.

ACKNOWLEDGEMENTS

FIRST THINGS FIRST. I'M NOT A PUBLISHED WRITER. I DON'T HAVE A PhD. I'm not somebody that people pay to listen to. I'm just another bloke on the street. One who thinks that belief in God is increasingly problematic to Australian society. Over time, this thought grew in my mind. I had to do something — write to the papers, call the prime minister, produce a book … that was it — a book! I could do books; I designed them, after all. How hard could it be to pull one together from scratch?

So I started making calls and sending emails to potential contributors. To my astonishment, the replies were almost unanimously positive. Therefore, every single writer contained herein deserves a special thanks for making this happen, as do those who, for one reason or another, didn't make it into the final collection. They are all connected by their recognition of the importance of the issues they've written about and of the general failure for these ideas to command much currency in the political and social landscape of the 'lucky country'.

My next thanks go to my partner, Kirsty Bruce, and our magnificent daughter Monty, for all the reasons you can think of and many more besides. Kirsty has read through every word, and Monty has drooled on them. The next container-load of gratitude goes to Chrys Stevenson, Karen Stollznow, and especially Jodi Matthews for their invaluable help in the editing process. All of these women have a far better command of proofing and editing than me. It's a very tricky thing to be commenting on the work of writers who are clearly smarter than me, so it helped to have a cohort of other intelligent people to draw upon. Any weakness in this volume in this regard, however, is entirely mine, as I had the final say.

I'd also like to express my deep gratitude to Henry Rosenbloom, Nicola Redhouse, and Julia Carlomagno at Scribe for their expertise and encouraging support, and for saying 'yes'. Anthologies like this make publishers nervous because of the potential for the quality and consistency to change from one essay to the next. It would be so easy for something like this to fizzle into a self-publishing sinkhole — something I was prepared for but am extremely grateful did not have to happen.

The tireless online supporters who also deserve recognition are Luke the Atheist, MsNaughty, and Sean the Blogonaut, each of whom has done an enormous amount to help me both get over the line and promote the book to their readers.

There are some groups that are also in my thanking sights: the Australian Chapter of the Atheist Nexus, the newly formed Reason Australia, the Atheist Foundation of Australia, the sceptics societies in each state, the Rationalist Society, the various state humanist groups, the Brisbane and Sunshine Coast Atheist Meetup groups, and the Australian Secular Lobby.

And so I come at last to my biggest and most profound thanks. This person helped at that most difficult of stages, the beginning. She was there to discuss the papers and to help me establish a meaningful structure. She was always available to bounce ideas off, and became a one-person promotion machine when the finish line approached. Yes, I have thanked you before, but it needed one more for good measure. Chrys Stevenson, you are truly a force of nature.